# Colonial Families of the Eastern Shore of Maryland

## Volume 16

Henry C. Peden, Jr.
and
F. Edward Wright

HERITAGE BOOKS
2018

**HERITAGE BOOKS**
*AN IMPRINT OF HERITAGE BOOKS, INC.*

**Books, CDs, and more—Worldwide**

For our listing of thousands of titles see our website
at
www.HeritageBooks.com

Published 2018 by
HERITAGE BOOKS, INC.
Publishing Division
5810 Ruatan Street
Berwyn Heights, Md. 20740



International Standard Book Number
Paperbound: 978-1-68034-747-0

## CONTENTS

## INTRODUCTION

THE COUNTIES

Kent County is first mentioned in the records in 1642. At that time the Governor and Council appointed Commissioners for the Isle and County of Kent.[1] On 16 May 1631 King Charles I granted a license to William Clayborne to trade along the shores of the Chesapeake, and the same year Clayborne established a trading post on Kent Island. The Marylanders who came in 1634 claimed authority over Kent Island, and after many legal disputes with Clayborne, Lord Baltimore appealed to the Committee of Trade and Plantations, and in 1638 they issued a report in favor of Lord Baltimore.[2] As early as 1638 Kent Isle had sent two delegates to the General Assembly: Nicholas Brown and Christopher Thomas.[3] Baltimore County was carved out of Kent County in 1659.[4]

Cecil County, extending from the mouth of the Susquehanna and down the eastern side of the Bay to Swan Point and from there to Hell Point, and so up Chester River, to its head, was established on 6 June 1674. The area included not only a portion of Baltimore County but nearly all of what is now Kent County. In fact it contained Yarmouth town, where at times the Kent County Court had been held. This apparent error by the Governor was rectified by a supplemental proclamation on 19 June 1674, "... upon further consideration hereof it is thought most necessary that so much of the Easterne side as was formerly added to Kent County doe still remaine and belong to the said County as afore notwithstanding ..." The final description of the boundary between Cecil and Kent counties was settled with the act passed by the General Assembly of 1706 which stated, "From and after the 1st of May 1707, Kent county shall begin at the south point of Eastern neck, and from thence up Chesapeake bay to Sassafras river, and up said river to the south end of the long Horse bridge lying over the head of the said river, and from thence with a line drawn east by south, to the exterior bounds of this province." The eastern boundary and northern boundary were contested by the Calverts and Penns until resolved by Mason and Dixon.[5]

Talbot County was erected around 1661. The boundaries at that time were vague. It would appear that the northwestern boundary passed along the eastern Shore of the Front Wye River northward to the head of Harris Mill Branch and thence down Tanyard Branch and possibly up Langford's Bay toward Wharton Creek on the Bay shore. To the west of this line was Kent County; on the east was Talbot County. What became the first and second districts of Kent County may possibly have been an unsettled portion of Talbot in 1667, but it seems more probable that Talbot County did not exercise jurisdiction on the north side of the Chester River. On the 4th of June, 1671, it was ordered that for the future the northeast side of Chester, as far as the bounds of Talbot County were formerly on that side, shall now be added to Kent County.

An Act of 19 April 1706 stated that after 1 May 1706, Kent County would be bounded by a line drawn from the south point of Eastern Neck, up the Bay to Sassafras river, up the said river to the south end of Long Horse Bridge, thence by a line drawn by east and by south to the exterior bounds of the Province and with the exterior bounds [south?] to the line of Queen Anne's County, and with said County down Chester River to Eastern Neck.[6] This same Act provided for the erection of Queen Anne's County.[7]

Somerset County, Maryland, was created in 1666 with the Atlantic Ocean and Chesapeake Bay as its eastern and western boundaries and its northern boundary which today lies well inside Sussex County ... the Nanticoke River. Dispute over the location of Delaware's southern boundary began in 1680 when William Penn received his charter. It continued until 1732 when both parties signed an agreement that the line would lie at 39 degrees, 43 minutes, 19 seconds and be surveyed to continue to the midpoint of the peninsula, then turn north to a point 15 miles south of Philadelphia. Unfortunately for Lord Baltimore, his decision to agree to this compromise was based on an inaccurate map which showed 39 degrees, 43 minutes, 19 seconds as lying at Cape Henlopen. In fact, Cape Henlopen lay 25 miles further north, and Lord Baltimore had inadvertently signed away present day Little Creek Hundred and parts of Broad Creek, Dagsborough and Baltimore Hundreds that had never been claimed by Penn. Realizing his mistake too late, Lord Baltimore fought the agreement in the courts for the next twenty years. When Worcester County was formed in 1742 from the eastern and southern sections of Somerset, he set the northern boundary of Worcester at Broad Creek Bridge, at the site of present-day Laurel, Delaware. From 1763 through 1768 Charles Mason and Jeremiah Dixon conducted the final survey of the so-called Mason-Dixon Line and finally, in January 1769, the new line was officially accepted.

The first evidence of the formation of Dorchester County was the writ issued on 16 Feb 1669, ordering elections to be held in the counties. The bounds of the county on the north and west extended up and along the Choptank River to the territory of New Sweden (later Pennsylvania, and still later Delaware). The eastern line was to run with the Delaware Bay, and River back to the fortieth degree, thus containing a large portion of Delaware called Sussex County. With the new line surveyed by Mason and Dixon, Dorchester County lost Northwest Fork Hundred to Sussex County. Thus families such as the Cannons were originally situated in Dorchester County and when the boundary was finally settled, found their members almost entirely in Sussex County Delaware.

Caroline County was formed in 1773 from portions of Dorchester east of the Choptank and Queen Anne's County west of the Choptank.

THE RECORDS

A variety of sources was used in putting together this series and they are described below.

Land Records were combed looking for statements that provided clues to marriages, descents of property, and places of origin. Sometimes rather complicated family relationships are unraveled on the pages of land records. Sales of land of significant acreage for a small amount of money (usually 5 shillings) suggest that the land was a gift.

There is a large array of land records to consider. Primary genealogical interests in the land records center on the land patents, certificates of survey, deeds, mortgages, leases, rent rolls, and debt books. In the early years of the settlement of the province of Maryland land was granted to persons who transported themselves into the colony and transported others, including members of their own family, either from Europe or from other colonies such as Virginia. This headright system was terminated in 1780 and thereafter land patents were purchased.

Aided by the practice of naming each tract one is able to trace ownership even when the tract was expanded, divided or combined with other parcels - and sometimes even renamed. One of the problems which can be solved by following land ownership is the identification and separation of two or more individuals of the same name. For a description of the records and the process of using them for genealogical purposes, see Donna Valley Russell's article, "By Their Deeds Ye Shall Know Them," *Maryland Genealogical Society Bulletin*, Vol. 31, No. 1:38.

We tend to overlook the possibility that land not mentioned in a will descended to the oldest son during the colonial period in Maryland, and in Delaware the ownership of land was considered to be made up of equal shares with the oldest son destined to receive 2 shares when there was no will or the will failed to specify disposition of the land. At some later time a reference may be found in the deed books to the manner by which the land had been disposed through inheritance.

We have limited our use of land records, citing only a few transactions needed to show relationships, or other genealogical evidence. The researcher interested in a thorough picture of the buying and selling of an ancestor must refer to the complete coverage given in published abstracts or examine the originals (a good idea in any case).

Criminal Proceedings were found to be full of information. Even so-called respectable families sometimes found themselves facing charges of assault, bastardy, trespass, theft, and other violations of the law.

Probate Records, including wills, inventories, administration accounts, and balances of final distributions of estates, are one of the staple resources of genealogical research. The death of an individual prompted the probate of a will if one existed. The estate might be inventoried if it were determined that it was a significant value. A very high percentage of wills were written by males leaving the widow as the executrix (or the administratrix if he died intestate). In the inventory or the succeeding document, that administration account, often reveals the fact that she has remarried and often gives the name of her new husband. The names of children not revealed in the will may appear in the administration accounts and balance books.

Depositions, sworn testimony by witnesses, called deponents, are found in a variety of places. Land records, land commissions, ejectment papers are just a few of the sources for these items, which usually give the name of the deponent and his or her age, and often contain references to other family members. Ejectment Papers referred to cases involving landlords and tenants and ownership of land. The documents in these cases often contain much helpful family history.

Bonds and Indentures were other types of records, frequently over-looked, that were checked. A bond is a promise, backed by a financial consider-ation to perform a certain action. Trustees would post a bond that they would pay the minor children of a decedent their fair share of their father's estate when the child reached majority. Grantors would post a bond that they would convey certain property. Executors and administrators posted bond they would well and truly perform their duties in settling an estate.

Indentures are written agreements and may apply to conveyances of land, but may also be a form of contract between two persons involving matters other than real estate.

With the exception of Somerset County few tax records have survived for the colonial period. Somerset County had an extraordinary run of tax lists from 1722 through 1759. Lists have survived for 30 of the 38 years, although some are in poor condition. Nowhere else in Maryland have such a string of yearly lists survived during the Colonial period. All males and black females, aged 16 or older were taxable, except for certain persons such as the infirm. Those disabled by illness or injury or old age could be exempt at the discretion of the county justices. The first name appearing in an entry was the head of household, for whom the tax would be levied. Much can be derived from these lists. Here are some of the clues that may be revealed:

1. The simultaneous listing of persons living in the locale allows the researcher to discern persons with the same given name.

2. The appearance of the name of a white female, first in the household, followed by names of persons who were in earlier lists associated with a male, suggest that the male had died and his widow now is responsible for the taxables.

3. The appearance of the names of white males in the household of a person with a difference surname offers the possibility that the head of household had married the widowed mother and now had her sons as his taxables.

4. The initial appearance of a male suggests that he turned age 16 sometime during the previous twelve months.

5. Persons listed nearby are likely to be relatives or in-laws.

Chattel Records are documents concerning the transfer of movable property, such as cattle, slaves, furniture or farming implements from one person to another. They contained many examples of parents conveying such movable property to their children or grandchildren.

## THE EARLY SETTLERS

The early settlement of the Eastern Shore was chiefly by British subjects. Land records and depositions often provided a clue to the origins of the settlers. However a variety of other ethnic groups were found among the early settlers. A few examples - In Kent County the Ricaud family had ties to England, but may have been of French descent; John Hendrickson and Cornelius Comegys were from the Netherlands; Hans Hanson was of Swedish descent, while John Peter Zenger and Francis Ludolph Bodien were from Germany.

Among the Dutch settlers of the area that became Cecil County was Augustine Herman, one of the most influential men of Maryland, a native of Utrecht, in New Amsterdam. In consideration of the map of the province of Maryland he prepared for the Calverts, he was granted *Bohemia Manor* in 1662, a tract of about 4,000 acres; and *Little Bohemia* or *Bohemia Middle Neck*. Other Hollander settlers of Cecil County included Isaac and Matthias Van Bibber, sons of Jacob Isaacs Van Bibber.

A significant number of Swedes migrated from New Sweden on the Delaware River, into Cecil County. Note for example, the families of John Carr whose wife Petronella was a daughter of Olof Thorsson; Jonas Auren who m. Keady Justice (Gustafsson); the Numbers (Numberson) family; Evertson family; Sefferson (Severson) family; and many others.

For the most part the founders and early settlers of Old Somerset County were people from the Eastern Shore of Virginia, the present counties of Accomack and Northampton. They were encouraged by Lord Baltimore who desired to settle these lands, in hopes of legitimizing the land as a part of the Maryland charter. Many of the immigrants from Virginia were Quakers, desiring to get away from the ill treatment by the Virginia government. Many other Virginians came north to obtain available land at reasonable quit rents. By May 1662, the settlements at Manokin and Annemessex numbered fifty tithable persons. In August 1662 the county of Somerset was founded.

## FAMILY RELATIONSHIPS

Familial terms such as cousin, son in law, etc. had meanings oft times different in the colonial period than in today's usage. Cousin was used to indicate a niece, nephew or cousin as defined today. Son in law or daughter in law usually meant a step-child but not always. The phrase, "Next of kin," appearing in the inventory of an estate had a very broad meaning, which included in-laws. These were persons who had some relationship to the family who were available to sign off on the inventory. Sometimes it is impossible to determine what the relationship was.

Those who have researched a number of families of the Lower Delmarva will find a surprising number of children who are given their mother's maiden name as their first name. This can be especially helpful when the mother's maiden name is otherwise unknown.

## THE SERIES

This is the sixteenth in a series of volumes of family histories pertaining to the colonial families of the Eastern Shore. Members of nearly all the families described in this volume lived in Dorchester County.

Any additional material concerning the families in this volume will be published in subsequent volumes. Comments and suggestions are welcome.

F. Edward Wright
Lewes, Delaware
2003

## End Notes

1. *Maryland Manual: A Guide to Maryland State Government, 1994-1995.* Ed.by Diane P. Frese. Annapolis: Maryland State Archives. 1994.
2. Edward B. Mathews, "The Counties of Maryland: Their Origin, Boundaries, and Election Districts," in *Maryland Geological Survey: Volume VI* (Baltimore: The Johns Hopkins Press, 1906), p. 511.
3. *Biographical Directory of the Maryland Legislature.* Ed. by Edward C. Papenfuse, et al. (New York: The Johns Hopkins University Press, 2 Vols., 1975-1985), I, 16.
4. Mathews, *op. cit.*, p. 512.
5. Mathews, *op. cit.*, p. 512.
6. Mathews, *op. cit.*, p. 514, cites Acts of Maryland 1706: Ch. 3.
7. Mathews, *op. cit.*, p. 534.

## SOURCES AND ABBREVIATIONS

Source of entry is followed by volume and page number. Other sources are indicated with the entry itself.

1693 Swedes: *The 1693 Census of the Swedes on the Delaware*. By Peter Stebbins Craig, Winter Park, FL: SAG Publications, 1993.

AACR: *Anne Arundel County Church Records of the 17th and 18th Centuries*. By F. Edward Wright. Westminster: Family Line Publications, 1989.

AALR: Anne Arundel County Land Records.

ACW: *Wills and Administrations of Accomack County, Virginia 1663-1800*, compiled and edited by Stratton Nottingham.

ARMD: *Archives of Maryland* (published series).

ACCO: Accomac County, VA Court Orders, compiled by McKey.

ASOS: *A Somerset Sampler, 1700-1776* (edited by Pauline Manning Batchelder. Published by Lower Delmarva Genealogical Society, 1994).

BALR: Baltimore County Land Records.

Baltimore Co. Families: *Baltimore County Families, 1659-1759* by Robert W. Barnes. Baltimore: Genealogical Publishing Company, 1988.

BDML: *Biographical Dictionary of the Maryland Legislature*. By Edward C. Papenfuse et al. 2 vols. Baltimore: The Johns Hopkins University Press, 1979, 1985.

BFD: Balances of Final Distributions (abstracted by Moxey and Skinner).

Bio of Eastern Shore: *Portrait and Biographical Record of the Eastern Shore of Maryland*. Chapman Publishing Company, New York, Chicago (1898).

Bio Record: *Biographical Records of Harford and Cecil Counties Maryland*. Originally published by Chapman Publishing Co., 1897. Reprinted by Family Line Publications, with new index by Harford County Genealogical Society, 1989.

BMGS: *Maryland Genealogical Society Bulletin*.

British Roots: *British Roots of Maryland Families*. By Robert W. Barnes. Baltimore: Genealogical Publishing Co.

Brumbaugh II: *Maryland Records: Colonial, Revolutionary, County and Church, from Original Sources*. 2 volumes. Compiled by Gaius M. Brumbaugh. Reprinted by Genealogical Publishing Co., Baltimore, 1967, 1975, 1993.

CANH: Northwest Fork Quakers (Hicksite). Most of the records of the group prior to the split in 1827 remained with this group.

CANW:Northwest Fork Quakers (Orthodox). This group split with the

Northwest Fork Monthly Meeting members who became identified as Hicksite and joined with the Quakers of Motherkiln Monthly Meeting of Delaware under Wilmington Yearly Meeting of Orthodox Quakers.

CANI: Nicholite Records. The Nicholites were followers of Joseph Nichols whose three meeting houses were all located in Caroline Co. and drew members from Caroline, Dorchester, Kent and Sussex counties. Their doctrine was very similar to that of the Quakers.

CALR: Caroline County Land Records as abstracted by R. Bernice Leonard. Self published, series begins in 1999.

CAW: Caroline County Wills.

CDSS: *Colonial Delaware Soldiers and Sailors, 1638-1776*, compiled by Henry C. Peden, Jr. Westminster: Family Line Publications, 1995.

CECH: *Early Anglican Church Records of Cecil County*. By Henry C. Peden, Jr. Westminster: Family Line Publications, 1990.

CELC: Cecil County Land Commissions.

CELR: Cecil County Land Records.

CEMM: Cecil Monthly Meeting (Quakers); Register 1678-1820; Marriages 1698-1784; Special Collections MSA M908.

CESM: Records of St. Mary Anne's Parish (North Elk).

CESS: Records of St. Stephen's Parish (North Sassafras).

CHPALR: Chester County, Pennsylvania, Land Records (abstracted by Bryant).

Clements/Wright: *Maryland Militia in the Revolutionary War* by S. Eugene Clements and F. Edward Wright.

COES: *Citizens of the Eastern Shore of Maryland* (by Wright).

Craig: An article in *The Pennsylvania Genealogical Magazine*, Vol. XL:4 (1998), "1671 Census of the Delaware," by Dr. Peter Stebbins Craig.

DE Bible Rcds: *Delaware Bible Records*. 6 vols. Compiled by Donald O. Virdin and Lu Verne V. Hall. Bowie, MD: Heritage Books, Inc., 1998.

Dill: *Souls in Heaven, Names in Stone Kent County, Delaware Cemetery Records*, copied by Raymond Walter Dill, William Martin Dill and Elizabeth Ann Bostick Dill, self published, 1989.

DODO: Dorchester Parish Records (Dorchester County)

DOGC: Great Choptank Parish Records (Dorchester County)

DOLR: *Land Records of Dorchester County Maryland* (abstracted by McAllister).

ESVR: *Maryland Eastern Shore Vital Records*. Comp. by F. Edward Wright. 5 vols. Westminster: Family Line Publications, 1982-1986.

FDT: Federal Direct Tax List of 1798 for Somerset County.

Heirs and Legatees: Heirs and Legatees of Caroline County Maryland, compiled by Irma Harper. Westminster: Family Line Publications, 1989.

Historic Graves: *Historical Graves of Maryland and The District of Columbia.* By Helen W. Ridgely. Originally published in 1908, reprinted by Family Line Publications, Westminster, MD, 1992.

IKL: Somerset County Land Records, Liber IKL.

Immanuel Regtr.: The register of the Emanuel (or Immanuel) Protestant Episcopal Church of New Castle, established in 1704 and published in *Early Church Records of New Castle County, Delaware*, Volume 1, Family Line Publications, Westminster, MD, 1994. Earlier published in *Early Ecclesiastical Affairs in New Castle, Del. and History of Immanuel Church*, by Thomas Holcomb, 1890.

INAC: Inventories and Accounts (abstracted by Skinner).

Inhabitants of CE Co.: *Inhabitants of Cecil County, Maryland, 1649-1774.* Compiled by Henry C. Peden, Jr. Westminster, MD: Family Line Publications, 1993.

Johnston: *History of Cecil County, Maryland.* By George Johnston. Originally published Elkton, MD, 1881. Reprinted by Clearfield Company, Inc., Baltimore, 1998.

Jones: New Revised History of Dorchester County Maryland by Elias Jones (1966). Originally published in 1902. Corrections made in 1966 by author's daughter, Mary Ruth Jones.

KEAD: Kent County Administration Accounts.

KECH: Kent County Chancery Records.

KECP: Kent County Court Proceedings.

KECR: Kent County Criminal Records.

KECT: Kent Co. Chattel Records.

KEDELR: Kent County, Delaware, Land Records.

KELR: Kent County, Maryland, Land Records.

KESH: Shrewsbury Parish Register, Kent County.

KESP: St. Paul's Parish Register, Kent County.

KEWB: Kent County Will Books.

LCPC: Lewes and Coolspring Presbyterian Church records. (near Lewes, DE).

Lankford: They Lived in Somerset County by Wilmer O. Lankford.

LODB: Land Office Debt Books.

Marshall's Tombstone Records: Nellie M. Marshall, *Tombstone Records of Dorchester County, Maryland, 1678-1964*, published by DO County Historical Society, 1993}

Maryland Deponents: *Maryland Deponents, 1634-1799.* Compiled by Henry C. Peden, Jr. Westminster, MD: Family Line Publications, 1991.

MCHR: Maryland Chancery Court Records.

MacKenzie: George Norbury Mackenzie, ed., *Colonial Families of the United*

*States* (7 volumes, 1907-1920). *Use this source with caution as a many of the statements of this work are undocumented.*

MCW: *Maryland Calendar of Wills* (from Prerogative Court) by Jane Baldwin Cotton (Volumes 1-8 and F. Edward Wright, Volumes 9-16).

MD DAR Directory, 1892: Maryland DAR Directory, 1892-1965 (Published by the Maryland Society, Daughters of the American Revolution in 1966), cited by Henry C. Peden, Jr., in his *Revolutionary Patriots of Cecil County, Maryland.* Westminster, MD: Family Line Publications, 1991.

MD DAR Directory, 1965: Maryland DAR Directory, 1965-1980 (Published by the Maryland Society, Daughters of the American Revolution in 1985), cited by Henry C. Peden, Jr., in his *Revolutionary Patriots of Cecil County, Maryland.* Westminster, MD: Family Line Publications, 1991.

MD Genealogies: *Maryland Genealogies* (2 vols.). Baltimore: Genealogical Publishing Co., 1980. Taken from the *Maryland Historical Magazine.*

MD Marriages: *Maryland Marriages, 1634-1777.* Compiled by Robert Barnes. Baltimore: Genealogical Publishing Co., 1975.

MDAD: Maryland Administration Accounts; originals are at MSA.

MD Militia, War of 1812: Maryland Militia, War of 1812, compiled by F. Edward Wright.

MDTP: Maryland Testamentary Proceedings; originals are at MSA.

MHM: *Maryland Historical Magazine.*

MHS: Maryland Historical Society, Baltimore.

MINV: Maryland Inventories (now abstracted by Vernon L. Skinner, Jr.).

MMDP: More Maryland Deponents, 1719-1799 (by Peden).

Mowbray: Calvin W. Mowbray, *First Dorchester Families*

MPL: Maryland Land Patents. (As published in *The Early Settlers of Maryland,* edited by Gust Skordas,Assistant Archivist State of Maryland, and *A Supplement to The Early Settlers of Maryland,* compiled and introduced by Carson Gibb, Ph.D).

MSA: Maryland State Archives, Annapolis.

MWB: Maryland Will Book.

NCDELR: New Castle County, Delaware, Land Records.

Nelms: Store Accounts of John Nelms of Salisbury, 1758-1787 by John E. Jacob, Jr. Published by Family Line Publications (1990), Westminster, MD

OSES: *Old Somerset on the Eastern Shore* (by Clayton Torrence).

PA Genealogies: *Genealogies of Pennsylvania Families.* Baltimore: Genealogical Publishing Co., 1983. Taken from *The Pennsylvania Magazine of History and Biography.*

PCLR: Provincial Court Land Records; originals are at MSA.

Polk Family and Kinsmen: *Polk Family and Kinsmen*, compiled by William Harrison Polk. Includes discussion by several early researchers.

QAEJ: Queen Anne's County Ejectment Papers.

QAJR: Queen Anne's County Judgement Records.

QALR: Queen Anne's County Land Records (compiled by Leonard).

QALU: St. Luke's Parish Records of Queen Anne's Co.

Records of Jesuit Mission at Cordova. These were published in *Vital Records of the Jesuit Missions of the Eastern Shore 1760-1800.* Based on compilations of Reverend Edward B. Carley. Published by Family Line Publications, 1986.

Ridgely: *Historic Graves of Maryland and the District of Columbia* by Helen W. Ridgely (1908).

RPCA: *Revolutionary Patriots of Caroline County Maryland 1775-1783*, compiled by Henry C. Peden, Jr.

RPCE: *Revolutionary Patriots of Cecil County Maryland*, compiled by Henry C. Peden, Jr.

RPDO: *Revolutionary Patriots of Dorchester County 1775-1783*, compiled by Henry C. Peden, Jr.

RPKQ: *Revolutionary Patriots of Kent and Queen Anne's Counties, Maryland*, compiled by Henry C. Peden, Jr.

RPWS: *Revolutionary Patriots of Worcester and Somerset Counties*, compiled by Henry C. Peden, Jr.

RPTA: Revolutionary Patriots of Talbot County Maryland 1775-1783, compiled by Henry C. Peden, Jr.

RUSSO: Tax Lists of Somerset County 1730-1740. Compiled by J. Elliott Russo.

SOAC: Administration Accounts of Somerset County.

SOMR: Somerset County Marriage Records (licenses).

SCOC: Abstracts of the Proceedings of Sussex County Orphans' Court, Delaware, Libers 1, 2, 3, 4, A (1708-1709 and 1728-1777). Compiled by Vernon L. Skinner, Jr., published by Willow Bend Books, Westminster, MD. (2000).

SOOP: *Somerset County, Maryland Orphans Court Proceedings* series by David V. Heise.

SJ&SG: *St. John's and St. George's Parish Registers, 1696-1851*. Compiled by Henry C. Peden, Jr. Westminster, MD: Family Line Publications, 1987.

SOA: Somerset County Accounts.

SOCO: Records of Coventry Parish, Somerset County.

SOD: Deeds of Somerset County

SOI: Somerset County Inventories, compiled by Rebecca Miller.

SOJR: Somerset Judicial Records, compiled by Rebecca Furniss Miller.

SOJUD: Somerset Judicial Records Vols. 1-4 Frank V. Walczyk, Peters Row, NY.1998

SOLR: *Land Records of Somerset County, Maryland* (compiled by Ruth T. Dryden).

SOSP: Records of Stepney Parish, Somerset County.

SOPS: Records of Somerset Parish, Somerset County.

SORR: Somerset County Rent Rolls

SOTL: Somerset County Tax Lists

SOW: Somerset County Wills

SOWS: Somerset County Will Books (abstracted by Skinner).

SOWD: Somerset County Will Books (abstracted by Dryden).

Sussex Court Records: *Records of the Courts of Sussex County, Delaware 1677-1710*, Craig W. Horle. University of Pennsylvania Press, 1991. SXPR: Sussex County, Delaware Probate Records (abstracted by deValinger).

SUTL: Tax lists of Sussex County, Delaware.

TAEJ: Talbot County Ejectment Papers.

TAGU: Talbot County Guardianships.

TAJU: Talbot County Judgments.

TALC: Talbot County Land Commissions.

TALR: Talbot County Land Records (abstracted by Bernice Leonard).

TAMI: St. Michael's Parish Records, Talbot County.

TAPE: St. Peter's Parish Records (Anglican), Talbot County.

TATH: Third Haven Monthly Meeting..

TP: Prerogative Court, Testamentary Proceedings.

WCOC: *Worcester County Orphans Court Proceedings*. Compiled by David V. Heise.

WCMN: Wyand, Jeffrey A., and Florence L. Wyand. *Colonial Maryland Naturalizations*. Baltimore: Genealogical Publishing Co., 1975.

WED: Worcester County Estate Docket.

Whitelaw: Ralph T. Whitelaw, *Virginia's Eastern Shore. A History of Northampton and Accomack Counties*.

WI Co. Graveyards: John E. Jacob, Jr., *Wicomico County Graveyards*.

WID: Deeds of Wicomico County

WILR: *Land Records of Wicomico County, Maryland 1666-1810* (compiled by Ruth T. Dryden).

Wilson: *Thirty Four Families of Somerset*, by Woodrow T. Wilson. Baltimore: Gateway Press, 1974.

WOD: Deeds of Worcester County.

WOLR: *Land Records of Worcester County, Maryland 1666-1810* (compiled by

Ruth T. Dryden.

WOSM: St. Martin's Episcopal Church Register.

WOW: Worcester County Wills

WOWD: Worcester County Will Books (abstracted by Dryden).

WOWH: Worcester County Will Books (abstracted by Heise).

WOWJ: Worcester County Will Books (abstracted by Jones).

WOWS: Worcester County Will Book MH3 (abstracted by Skinner).

## OTHER ABBREVIATIONS

| | |
|---|---|
| a. | acre(s) |
| AA Co. | Anne Arundel County |
| adj. | adjoining |
| admin. | administrator or administered |
| admx(s). | administratrix (administratices) |
| afsd. | aforesaid |
| b. | born |
| BA Co. | Baltimore County |
| bapt. | baptized |
| battn. | battalion |
| BC | Baltimore City |
| bro(s). | brother(s) |
| bttn. | battalion |
| bur. | buried |
| c. | circa (about) |
| CA Co. | Caroline County |
| CALR | Caroline County land records |
| CE Co. | Cecil County |
| cont. | containing |
| conv. | conveyed |
| CV Co. | Calvert County |
| dau(s). | daughter(s) |
| dec'd. | deceased |
| dep. | deposed |
| dist. | distributed |
| DO Co. | Dorchester County |
| e. | east |
| exec(s). | executor(s) |
| extx(s). | executrix (executrices) |
| FR Co. | Frederick County |
| inv. | inventoried |
| KE Co. | Kent County |
| KI | Kent Island |
| m. | married |
| n. | north |
| (N): | Name unknown. |
| nunc. | nuncupative |
| plant. | plantation |
| prob. | probable |
| QA Co. | Queen Anne's County |
| s. | south or shilling(s) |
| sd. | said |
| SM Co. | St. Mary's County |
| SU Co. | Sussex County, Delaware |
| s.p. | died without issue |
| TA Co. | Talbot County |
| T.P. | Testamentary Proceedings |
| Test: | Testes (meaning witnesses) |
| tob. | tobacco |
| v.p. | during father's lifetime |
| w. | west |
| wit. | witness |

Standard Postal Service State Abbreviations.

## CORRECTIONS, ADDITIONS, AND COMMENTS TO PREVIOUS VOLUMES

**Reference to Vol. 4**

p. 151 (Thanks to Vernon L. Skinner, Jr.):

*Change line to read,*

9. SAMUEL KINIMONT, son of Joseph (5) Kinimont, m. 9 March 1747, Mary Nuttwell. {TA Co. marr. lic.}

The erroneous assumption that Samuel m. a dau. of John King probably stems from a deposition which says, "Samuel Kinimont deposed ... that John Horney cautioned the surveyors about the orchard belonging to his father-in-law John King ..." *Note however that John King, Sr., had 2 daus., Ann who m. 1st John Horney and m. 2nd John Parr; and Elizabeth who m. Solomon Wright. The deposition should be interpreted that John Horney is the son-in-law of John King, not Samuel Kinimont.*

Also add to this entry,

Samuel was father of ELIZABETH (d. 1784); JOSEPH, prob. m. Margaret Downes who m. 1st John Martin, m. 2nd John Sherwood. {TA Co. Distributions JGA:46}

In addition, Samuel Kininmount is probably the father of BENJAMIN. {Cited in the will of John Kininmont as Benjamin, son of Samuel.

**Reference to Vol. 5:**

p. 58:

*Insert as 8th paragraph:*

Eve Holmes, widow, TA Co., d. leaving a will dated 21 Nov 1724, proved 2 Dec 1724. To 4 daus., viz., Sarah Hopkins, Mary Bowdle, Jane Delahay and Cornelia Delahay, dau in law Mary Mullikin, Francis Isgate and kinswoman Sarah Summers, personalty. To 4 children, viz., Thomas Delahay, James Delahay, execs., Sarah Hopkins and Mary Bowdle, residue of estate. Witnessed by John Holt, Mary Benstead, Mary Speck, Joseph Wray. {MWB 18:327}

*Under Thomas Delahay show*

Thomas Delahay was father of SARAH, m. (N) Hopkins; MARY, m. 1st Henry Withgott, m. 2nd 19 Nov 1724, Thomas Bowdle, m. 3rd Edmund Fisher; THOMAS; JAMES; ELIZABETH, JANE; CORNELIA. {See The Bowdle Family, vol. 16 of this series.}

**Reference to Vol. 8:**

p. 163:

*Change to read,*

7. JOHN LAWS, probable son of John (3) Laws, m. Elizabeth Polk, widow of

Ephraim Polk and dau. of Charles Williams. {See The Polk Family, vol. 15 of this series.}

p. 178:
13. WILLIAM LINGO, son of Robertson (8) Lingo, m. Leah Hearne, dau. of (N) Hearne. Leah m. 2nd Thomas Waller, son of Richard and Ann (Cottman) Waller. {See The Waller Family, vol. 15 of this series.}

William Lingo d. by 18 Sep 1772 when Leah Lingo filed the inventory. Signed as next of kin: Smith Lingo, John Lingo. {MINV 113:399} Distribution was made by Leah Lingo on 17 Nov 1773 (equally) to Joshua Lingo and Elijah Lingo. {BFD 6:229}

**Reference to Vol. 10:**
p. 284:
*In the last entry under GEORGE TRUITT, delete possible marriage of Elizabeth Truitt, dau. of George and Alice Truitt, to John Rickards in 1676.* {In 1678 Elizabeth Truitt chose her brother-in-law Robert Davis as her guardian. {McKey:5:96}; in 1681, she was of age and demanded her chattel. {McKey:6:147}

*Change to read,*
2. HENRY TRUITT, son of George (1) Truitt, m. Elizabeth (N). Elizabeth m. 2nd John Barnes.. {McKey:6:147} John Barnes, Accomack Co., d. leaving a will dated 27 April 1714, proved 5 April 1715. To Henry Truite, als Barns, 1 s. Dau. Ann Mills, 1 s. To dau. Mary Nock, 1 s. Son John Barnes residuary legatee and exec. {ACW:51}

p. 287:
*Change to read,*
7. GEORGE TRUITT, carpenter, son of Henry (2) Truitt, m. Priscilla (N). {McKey 11:48}

*Under George's children, add* ELIZABETH. [On 4 May 1708 Henry Trewett presented and acknowledged a deed of gift of cattle that he made to Elizabeth Trewett (dau. of George Trewett, carpenter). {McKey:10:162}

p. 288:
*Change to read,*
8. HENRY TRUITT. b. c1677, son of Henry (3) Truitt, m. Alicia/Elisha (N). Henry d. 1719 in Accomack Co. Alicia m. 2nd John Wilkins. {ACW:61; McKey:14:8, 20, 28, 156; McKey:9:124; McKey:10:162}
Add,

Henry Truitt d. leaving a will dated 26 March 1718, proved 1 Sep

1719. To son Elias Truitt (under 18), plantation where I now live. Daus. Elizabeth, Tabitha, Hannah and Sarah. Wife Elishe, extx. Witnessed by William Nock, Jr., George Bonwell, Samuel Turner. {ACW:61}

Henry Truitt and Alicia (N) were the parents of: ELIAS b. c711, d. 1745. {ACW:146} Elias married Ann Bell (dau. of Joseph Bell), and had one child, b.c 1745, d.s.p. young; ELIZABETH; TABITHA; HANNAH; SARAH.

p. 294:
*Change to read,*
25. HENRY TRUITT, son of Henry (8) Truitt, son of George (7) Truitt, may have ...[Henry appears on the 1724 tax list in the household of George Truitt.]

P. 295:
27.LITTLETON TRUITT. *Move this entire entry to "Unplaced." It has become apparent that there Is no real evidence as to the father of Littleton Truitt. We are currently pursuing the possibility that he was the son of Job (22) Truitt.*

**Reference to Vol. 11:**
p. 89
*Modify entry to read:*
5. LEVIN DUNNOCK, DO Co., b. 21 Dec 1768, son of William (1) Dunnock.

Written on the back of an old deed in possession of Mrs. Wilber G. Meekins near Golden Hill in Meekins Neck is the following: December 1768 - Levin Donnok, son of William Donnok, was born in the year of 1768 December 21st day of. John Donnok weas born in the year of 1772 December 19th Day. {From Nellie Marshall, *Bible Records of DO Co., Maryland 1612 - 1969 and Baptismal and Marriage Records, 1855-1866 Zion United Methodist Church Cambridge, Md.* DO Co. Historical Society, 1971}

*Add entry:*
7. JOHN DUNNOCK, prob. son of Levin (5) Dunnock, b. 19 Dec 1772.

p. 243.
*Add the following information to entry all based on information "from an old Bible belonging to Martin Maloney of the Wright family of Caroline and Dorchester Co., Md.," held by the DO Co. Historical Society.*

20. JAMES WRIGHT, son of Roger (6) and Mary Wright, m. Sarah Wright on 4 April (or 4 March) 1780. *Add the following pertaining to their children:*

ELISHA WRIGHT, b. 9 March 1787, son of James (20) and Sarah Wright.

AARON WRIGHT, b. 13 Feb 1790, son of James (20) and Sarah Wright.

SARAH WRIGHT, b. 10 April 1797, dau. of James (20) and Sarah Wright.

JAMES WRIGHT, b. 12 July 1799, son of James (20) and Sarah Wright, m. 27 Jan 1824, Livisa Willias (b. 5 Nov 1799), dau. of Thomas and Rhoda (Leverton) Willis. Louisa (sic) Wright, wife of James Wright, d. after a severe attack of pulsing of blood on 8th day of her sickness 25 April 1825. Funeral performed by Rev. Bartine Twiford. James Wright, son of James and Sarah, d. 5 June 1884, aged 84 years, 10 mos., 23 days. James Wright and Ann Cannon m. 20 May 1833. Ann Wright, wife of James Wright, d. 3 April 1838.

James and Levica (Livisa) were parents of MARY ELIZABETH, b. 7 Jan 1825; SARAH ANN, b. 15 Dec 1825; ELISHA, b. 23 Aug 1827, d. 1828.

James and Ann Wright were parents of ANN JANE, b. 28 Feb 1838.

HATFIELD WRIGHT, b. 12 Dec 1802.

SARAH ANN WRIGHT, b. 15 Dec 1825, dau. of James and Levisa Wright, m. 27 April 1865, Andrew Callahan (b. 15 Nov 1807, d. 1 June 1870), son of George and Nacy (George) Callahan. Sarah Ann Callahan, wife of Andrew Callahan, d. 23 May 1913 after a few hours illness, age 87 years, 5 mos., 8 days.

p. 247. *The following is based on Nellie Marshall, Bible Records of DO Co., Maryland 1612 - 1969 and Baptismal and Marriage Records, 1855-1866 Zion United Methodist Church Cambridge, Md. DO Co. Historical Society, 1971.*

*Add an entry following the entry 40. CELIA WRIGHT*

40A. KENNERLY WRIGHT, b. 11 Nov 1798, d. 8 Dec 1885, son of Constantine (24) Wright, m. Celia Lewis (N) (b. 25 Sep 1799, d. 13 Nov 1873).

Kennelly and Celia were parents of CHRISTIANA, b. 10 March 1819, d. 4 Feb 1894, m. (N) Andrew; ARAH ANN, b. 9 April 1821, d. 23 April 1891, m. (N) Hutchinson; MARGARET ANN, b. 6 May 1823, d. 18 June 1903, m. (N) Hazzard; HESTER ANN, b. 25 Sep 1824, d. 16 May 1899, m. (N) Corkran; LOVIE, b. 11 Aug 1826, d. 3 March 1903, m. (N) Trice; JABEZ, b. 31 Dec 1827, d. 15 May 1899; CELIA, b. 29 Aug 1829, d. 5 Feb 1897, m. (N) Hurlock; LEWIS, b. 29 Sep 1830; CATHERINE, b. 25 June 1832; MINOS, b. 9 Dec 1834; BETHANY, b. 16 May 1836; BETSEY ANN, b. 17 June 1840; ABRAM R., b. 27 May 1845.

**Reference to Vol. 13:**

p. 231.

*Add the following information based on Bible of William Byus of DO Co., courtesy of Jane Stanley Terrell (Mrs. W. J. Terrell) of Navasota, TX, from the book by Nellie Marshall, Bible Records of DO Co., Maryland 1612 - 1969 and Baptismal and Marriage Records, 1855-1866 Zion United Methodist Church Cambridge, Md. DO Co. Historical Society, 1971.*

18. SARAH TWYFORD, d. 10 Feb 1806, dau. of Bartholomew (12) Twyford, m. 1st 30 Nov 1775, Benjamin Darby (d. 25 Dec 1787).

Sarah and Benjamin Darby were parents of MARY DARBY, b. 27 Feb 1777; THOMAS DARBY, b. 5 Feb 1779; JAMES DARBY, b. 28 April 1782; NANCY DARBY, b. 15 Feb 1785; JOHN DARBY, b. 5 April 1787, d. 1829.

**Reference to Vol. 14:**

*Add the following information based on Bible of William Byus of DO Co., courtesy of Jane Stanley Terrell (Mrs. W. J. Terrell) of Navasota, TX, from the book by Nellie Marshall, Bible Records of DO Co., Maryland 1612 - 1969 and Baptismal and Marriage Records, 1855-1866 Zion United Methodist Church Cambridge, Md. DO Co. Historical Society, 1971.*

p. 5:

2. WILLIAM BYUS, b. c1705, d. Jan 1778, aged 84 years, poss. son of William (1) Byus, m. 1st, 16 Sep 1727, Mary Hicks and m. 2nd 23 Dec 1734, Elizabeth Ennels (d. 12 Feb 1790, aged 84 years).

p. 8:

William and Mary were parents of MARY, b. 19 Dec 1729; JOHN, b.8 Jan 1732.

William and Elizabeth were parents of WILLIAM, b. 3 Jan 1736; JOSEPH, b. 14 Dec 1737; ANN, b. 16 May 1739; LINEY, b. 28 June 1741; LEVEN, b. 26 Jan 1743; JAMES, b. 18 Dec 1744; STANLEY, b. 19 Oct 1747, d. 14 Jan 1796; ELIZABETH, b. 29 Sep 1750.

*Make the following additions based on Bible dated 1856 in possession (June 1956) of Susan E. F. Stevens (Mrs. Hayward Seward) and published in Nellie Marshall, Bible Records of DO Co., Maryland 1612 - 1969 and Baptismal and Marriage Records, 1855-1866 Zion United Methodist Church Cambridge, Md. DO Co. Historical Society, 1971.*

p. 11.

STANLEY was father of JAMES, b. 16 July 1780.

*Add entry,*

JAMES BYUS, son of Stanley (7) Byus.

James was father of ROBERT, b. 24 April 1798; WILLIAM, b. 29 Aug 1800; MARIA, b. 12 Oct 1803; MARY, b. 24 Nov 1805; SARAH, b. 5 Dec 1807.

p. 97.

*Change to read,*

ESTHER (HESTER) LECOMPTE, DO Co. and TA Co., dau. of Anthony (1) Lecompte, m. 1st Henry Fox and m. 2nd William Skinner. *[the father of William, Jr.]*. {See The Thomas Skinner Family, vol. 4 of this series.}

William was father of PHILEMON; ESTHER.

# THE WILLIAM ANDREWS FAMILY

1. Lt. Col. WILLIAM ANDREWS m. Mary (N) who m. 2nd William Smart.

In the admin. of the estate of John Bentley, Northampton Co., VA, 23 Feb 1643/4 there is reference to his extx (unnamed) and the depositions of Mary Andrews (wife of William), of Emma Leigh (aged 36) and of John Leigh (aged 40), referring to the estate. {Marshall:15}

Lt. Col. William Andrews, Gent. of Hungars, Northampton Co., d. leaving a will dated 20 Feb 1654, proved 28 Feb 1655. To my beloved wife Mary Andrews her 1/3 of all my goods and chattells, and the other 2 parts to be equally divided by my children (borne of her body). My wife to enjoy my entire estate during her widowhood. My wife also to enjoy the priviledge of my house and land as described in a deed of gift made to my son John Andrews dated 4 Jan 1653. To my son Robert Andrews the first mare foale. To my dau. Susanna Stringer the next mare foale. To my dau. Susanna 200 a. at Nandue butting upon the land of my son William Andrews. To my two grandchildren Elisheba Andrews and her sister Elizabeth, a yearling heifer apiece. My wife relict and extx. My sons John and Andrew to be at age at 21, and my daus. at 16 or day of marriage. Witnessed by Edmund Mathews, William Andrews Jr. Note William Smarte m. Mary the widow ane extx., and confirmed the dec'd's gifts to his children John, Andrew, Mary and Ann Andrews. William Andrews is the bro. of Samuel Chandler. {Marshall:40}

Mary Smart d. by 19 Feb 1659, formerly the wife of William Smart and of (Lt. Col.) William Andrews. [Note: John Tankred m. Sarah Smart, dau. of William Smart. 1680-1692]. {Marshall:61}

William was father of JOHN; ROBERT; SUSANNA, b. after 1638, m. Stephen Stringer; MARY, b. after 1638; ANN, b. after 1638; WILLIAM, b. after 1634; ANDREW, b. after 1634.

## Second Generation

2. JOHN ANDREWS, son of William (1) Andrews, d. by 28 Jan 1667. Admin. Col. John Stringer on behalf of Andrews Andrews. Approvers: William Westerhouse, Sampson Robins, John ?Haggoman?, William Gaskins. {Marshall:81}

3. ROBERT ANDREWS, son of William (1) Andrews.

Robert Andrews, Gent., d. leaving a will dated 2 Oct 1656, proved 30 March 1657. To wife (unnamed), extx., to inherit all, and at her death this land to go to the two children of my bro. William Andrews, and if either child dies its part to go to my sister Susanna Stringer or to her child when she has one. Tobias

Selve to have his 21 year lease from the date hereof with the ground? over against Tony Johnson's. I wish to be carryed to my father and be buryed by my father and my mother. witnessed by Richard Hamby, Tobius Selve. [Note: The widow's name may have been Rebecca Andrews who signed a marital agreement with Stephen Fisher.] {Marshall:49}

4. SUSANNA ANDREWS, dau. of William (1) Andrews, m. Stephen Stringer.

Stephen Stringer d. by 29 Jan 1655 when the admin. of his estate was granted to Susanna Stringer, widow of the dec'd. (Capt.) Stringer claimed to be his bro. {Marshall:43}

5. WILLIAM ANDREWS of Northampton Co., VA, b. c1632?, son of William (1) Andrews, m. 1st Elizabeth Walker, dau. of Peter Walker, m. 2nd Dorothy Evelin, dau. of Obedience and Grace Robins and widow of Mountijoy Eveling (Evelin). {Marshall:70}

Obedience Robins made an oral will which was proved 30 Dec 1662. Some years since the testator was very sick, his wish was that his estate should be divided by his wife (unnamed) and children. And that his wife, the mother of this deponent [Maj. William Waters], was to have the use of his estate for life and that her younger son Obedience Robins was to have the 900 a. on the s. part of his dividend at the seaboard side, part of which John Daniel now dwells on. Also he desired that this deponent [William Waters] and his bro. in law (Capt.) William Andrews[1] would assist our mother to see his will performed. Witnessed by Maj. William Waters, aged 39 and Capt. William Andrews, aged 30, son in law of the testator. [Notes: Dorothy, the dau. of Col. Obedience Robins m. Mountioy Eveling. Mrs. Grace Robins is the mother of William Waters. Grace Robins is the wife of Lt. Col. Obedience Robins.] {Marshall:70}

Maj. Peter Walker d. by 29 Jan 1655. Admx. Alice Walker, widow. Note: Elizabeth Walker, dau. of Peter Walker, m. William Andrews. Mrs. Alicia Walker m. Mr. John Custis. {Marshall:43}

Major William Andrews, Gent., Northampton Co., d. leaving a will dated 24 July 1673, proved 28 Aug 1673. To my son in law George Evelin when 21 the estate set apart for him at the time I was married to his mother. And as I have made use of some of his animals to prevent the wolves from getting them all, I give him a feather bed, rug and gun. To my son William Andrews, the house and that part of the plantation I now dwell on bounded on the s. and e. by Old Plantation creek and on the west by a small creek called Gilles Creek

---

[1] Here he uses the term bro. in law to mean husband to his sister rather than the general usage of the time to mean step-brother.

issuing out of Old Plantation Creek (dividing this my son William's land from the land hereafter give to my son Obedience Andrews) and on the northeast by Hutchisons Creek (which parts William's land from the land hereafter given to my son John Andrews. To son William my best gun and cuttlesse. To my son Obedience Andrews the house and orchard that was Jonathan Gills and all the land lying on both sides of Gilles Creek to the Bay and northwardly butting upon William Sterling's land, and one gun and my rapier and belt. To my son John Andrews the house and orchard bought of Mrs. Robert Hutchison and the land on that side of the branch where the house stands bounded on the s. and e. by Old Plantation Creek, on the w. by Hutchisons Creek which runs northwesterly (and divides this land from the land before given to my son William), and on the n. by a small creek issuing out of Old Plantation Creek (dividing this land from land formerly belonging to William Jones and by him sold to George Traveller), and then by a line of marked trees from the head of the small creek running northwest into the woods and old field to the head of Hutchisons Creek, containing about 100 a. To my son Robert Andrews 500 a. lying near the upper part of Nanduee Creek called the Forked Neck, a gun and case of pistolls. To my two daus. Grace and Susanna Andrews 300 a. lying near Forked Neck near the head of Nanduee Creek that fell to me by the death of my father (Lt. Col.) William Andrews. If any of my sons die under 18 then the land above given to fall to the survivors. To my dau. Elisheba the now wife of Peter Reverdy one heifer, and I confirm to her the goods already given her. To my grandchild Katherin Reverdy one heifer. To my loving wife Dorothy Andrews 1/3 of the remainder of my estate, and the rest to my six children William, Obedience, John, Robert, Grace and Susanna to be equally divided. Wife extx. Sons of age at 18 and daus. at 16. My bros. in law William Waters and John Robins to oversee. Witnessed by (Lt. Col.) William Waters, Mrs. Agnes Powell. Note: William Andrews, Sr., is bro. in law of Stephen Stringer - 1651-1654. F. 190. {Marshall:87}

George Evelin d. made a verbal will in Feb 1676, proved 30 Dec 1679. To my bro. William Andrews one mare. To my bro. Obedience Andrews one mare. To bro. John Andrews my riding horse. To bro. Robert Andrews a horse. To my sisters Grace and Susanna Andrews one mare when Grace is 16. To Obedience, Edward, and Littleton Robins, the sons of my uncle one heifer a piece. My dear and loving mother Mrs. Dorothy Andrews residuary legatee and extx. My two uncles (Lt. Col.) Waters and John Robins to oversee. Witnessed by Henry Masman, Thomas Viner. {Marshall:110}

Mrs. Dorothy Andrews d. by 29 March 1683 when the admin. of her estate was filed by William Andrews, admin., son of the dec's on behalf of himself and the rest of his bros. and sisters. Securities: Andrew Andrews, Capt.

Nathaniel Walker. Approvers: Thomas Hunt, Richard Whitmarsh, William Sterling, George Clarke. {Marshall:115}

Grace Robins [mother of Dorothy Andrews] d. by 2 March 1682.{Marshall:114}

William was father of WILLIAM; OBEDIENCE; JOHN; ROBERT; GRACE, b. after 1763, m. Thomas Harmanson; SUSANNA; ELISHEBA, m. Peter Reverdy; ELIZABETH (mentioned in her grandfather's will).

6. ANDREW ANDREWS, son of William (1) Andrews, m. Elizabeth (N).

Andrew Andrews d. by 28 May 1688 when the admin. of his estate was granted to Elizabeth Andrews, widow of the dec'd. Securities: Obedience Johnson, Thomas Johnson. Approvers: John Luke, Henry Gascoine, Isaac Hagamond, Adrian Westerhouse. {Marshall:133}

Andrew was father of WILLIAM; ANDREW.

## Third Generation

7. Major WILLIAM ANDREWS, son of William (5) Andrews, m. Comfort, sister of John Haggaman.

John Haggaman d. leaving a will dated 3 May 1688, proved 28 May 1688. To my bro. Isaac Hagaman a gray mare. To my bro. Samuel Tomlinson a ewe and cow calf. To my loving mother Margaret Tomlinson, a brown cow now running in Nevills Neck. To my sister Patience Atkinson 2 sowes. To my sister Comfort, now wife of William Andrews, 2 sowes. To my cozen Margaret Andrews, dau. of my bro. in law William Andrews, one calf. To cozen Nathaniel, son of my said bro. in law, one lamb. To my cozen Rachell, dau. of James Atkinson, one lamb. To my cozens Frances and Elizabeth, both daus. of Joseph Warren, one ewe lamb a piece. To Andrew, son of Andrew Andrews, dec'd., one mare colt. To my respected friend Mrs. Bridget Foxcroft, a pair of silver ear wires. To John Jennings for his tender care and trouble during my sickness, 2 pairs of new shoes. To Mr. John Watts in consideration of his poverty ½ of the £80 he owes me. My loving wife Sarah Hagaman residuary legatee and extx. In case my wife should die without issue my bros. in law Richard Nottingham, Jr. and Joseph Warren to act as trustees. {Marshall:135}

William Andrews immigrated from the Eastern Shore of Virginia. His son ISAAC, b. c1711. {Loose leaves found in Higgins Bible, owned by Mrs. Lester B. Kinnamon}

William Andrews, DO Co., d. by 13 Sep 1717 when the admin. account of his estate was submitted by John Kirke. Payments to Maj. Woolford. {INAC 388:79}

William was father of prob. MARCUS (Marquis); NATHANIEL; DOROTHY, m. (N) Hastings; MARGARET; ISAAC, b. c1711.

8. JOHN ANDREWS, Northampton Co., VA, son of William (5) Andrews.

John Andrews, Northampton Co., VA, d. leaving a will dated 7 April 1688, proved 28 May 1688. To my bro. William Andrews my clothes and feather bed. To my nevoy [*sic*] Nathaniel Andrews, son of William Andrews, cow and calf at the plantation of John Mulls. To my bro. Obedience Andrews a mare called Towes in Old Plantation Neck. To my sister Grace Harmanson a mare called Fortune. To my bro. in law Thomas Harmanson, Jr. 600 lbs. of tobacco due from Andrew Stewart. To my sister Susanna Andrews one cow being at Ralph Pigot's plantation. To my aunt Mrs. Elizabeth Andrews for her trouble and expense in my sickness the tobacco due me from my dec'd uncle Andrew Andrews, and 441 lbs. of tobacco due me from (Capt.) Hillary Stringer. To my friend Isaac Hagamon whatever he owes me. To my bro. Robert Andrews my riding horse and working tools. Bro. Robert, exec. Witnessed by Lawrence Cranford, Walter Younge, Patrick Strelly. {Marshall:133}

9. ROBERT ANDREWS, prob. son of William (5) Andrews, m. (N) Shepherd, sister of Morris Shepherd.

Robert Andrews d. leaving a will dated 23 June 1718, proved 17 Sep 1718. To my son John Andrews. To my son Robert Andrews 280 a. in Accomack on the head of Nanduey Creek already given him by deed. To son Jacob (under 18) the 200 a. remainder of my land at Nanduey lying between the land of Mathew Hegher and the land that Philip Lecat formerly owned, on condition that Jacob make over his right to land given him (by his grandfather Sheapherd) to my sons John Andrews and Nathaniel Andrews, as soon as he is of age. To dau. Sarah Andrews silver bodkins, book called *The Soul's Espousall to Christ*, and half her mother's clothes. To son Southy Andrews (under 14), silver cup, books called *Ye Whole Duty of Man and Divine Banquets* (or *Sacremental Devotions*). Son Nathaniel to teach my son Southy to be a carpenter. To my dau. Rachell Andrews (under 14) half her mother's clothes, silver bodkins, and book called *Heaven Upon Earth*. My sons Robert and Nathaniel, residuary legatees and execs. My bro. Morris Shepherd to oversee. Witnessed by James Fairfax, Richard Booll, Thomas Gascoyne, Thomas James. {Marshall:214}

Robert was father of JOHN; ROBERT; JACOB; NATHANIEL; SARAH, m. (N) Gascoigne; SOUTHY; RACHEL, m. (N) Gascoigne.

10. WILLIAM ANDREWS, son of Andrew (6) Andrews.

William Andrews made a verbal will on 6 Oct 1712, proved 19 Feb 1711/12. He d. at the house of Mycall Halsbird on 28 Jan 1711/12, and gave all he had to his bro. Andrew Andrews. Witnessed by Mycall Halsbird, Antony Miceele. {Marshall:199}

11. ANDREW ANDREWS, son of Andrew (6) Andrews, m. Elenor Waterfield, dau. of William Waterfield.

In his will dated 12 April 1720, proved 17 May 1720 William Waterfield mentioned his dau. Elener Andrews. {Marshall:229}

Andrew Andrews d. leaving a will dated 1 Sep 1728, proved 8 Oct 1728. Mentioned: sons William, Andrew and John. My loving wife Eleanor residuary legatee and extx. Witnessed by John Luke, Silvannus Haggoman, Waterfield Dunton. {Marshall:264}

Andrew was father of WILLIAM; ANDREW; JOHN.

## Fourth Generation

12. MARCUS ANDREWS, son of William (7) Andrew, m. Rebecca (N).

On 4 Oct 1720, Marquis Andrews, Accomack Co., VA, presented and acknowledged a deed for land he sold to John Andrews. Rebeckah, wife of Marquis Andrews, acknowledged her relinquishment of dower. {ACCO 14:57}

Marcus Andrews of SO Co., made a deposition on 18 July 1722 in which he stated that he owned an Indian boy named James, a customary thing among the inhabitants of Ackamack in VA, and he sold Indian James to a gentleman in Philadelphia named Nicholas. {ARMD 25:390}

On 26 Jan 1722 (OS) Joseph MacCloster and his wife Isabell of SO Co. conveyed to Marcus Andrews of DO Co., *Racoon Point*, on s. side of Racoon Creek which issues out of Blackwater River, containing 244 a. {DOLR 2 Old 148}

On 27 Sep 1732 Marcus Andrews and his wife Rebecca of DO Co., planter, conveyed to James Robins of SO Co., mariner, part of a tract called *Raccoon Point* on s. side of Raccoon Creek on w. side of Blackwater River, containing 122 a. {DOLR 9 Old 13}

On 29 Aug 1740 John Willey, Senr., and his wife Catherine of DO Co., planter, conveyed to Marcus Andrews of the same co., planter, part of a tract called *Willeys Outlett* adj. land of Francis Willey, Senr., 52 a. {DOLR 10 Old 46} On 10 June 1741 Marcus Andrews of DO Co., planer, conveyed to Francis Willey the younger of the same co., *Willeys Outlett*, 52 a. {DOLR 10 Old 214}

At June Term 1744 Marcus Andrews, Edward Pritchett, Jr., and John Brawhawn of DO Co. were bound to William Pritchett, child and orphan of Zebulon Pritchett; and Ezekiel Pritchett, child of Zebulon Pritchett - to the amount of £51.12.10 each. {DOJR}

Marcus Andrews, DO Co., d. leaving a will dated 24 April 1750, proved 9 May 1750. To wife Rebeckah, extx., plantation and some slaves. To dau. Sarah, slaves. To son Daniel Andrews, furniture. To dau. Rebeckah, cattle. To sons Nathaniel and Marcus, land after death of wife. To son Isaac, slaves. Witnessed by Francis Willey, John Willey, Comfort Roe. {MWB 27:383}

The inventory of the estate was filed by Rebeckah Andrews, admx./extx. Signed as next of kin: Comfort Roe, Susannah Insley. {MINV 43:510}

On 8 Oct 1757 Rebecca Andrews of DO Co. gave to her son Marcus Andrews all her goods and chattels, after her death. Witnessed by Naboth Hartt, Joseph Andrews. {DOLR 15 Old 520}

Marcus was father of SARAH; DANIEL; REBECKAH; NATHANIEL; MARCUS; ISAAC.

13. NATHANIEL ANDREWS, son of William (7) Andrews, m. Elizabeth (N).

In 1715 Nathaniel Andrews purchased 200 a. in Accomack Co., VA, from Richard Lee of Northumberland Co., VA. {Whitelaw:1264}

Nathaniel Andrews, Accomack Co., VA, d. leaving a will dated 16 Feb 1720/21, proved 2 May 1721. Mentioned wife Elizabeth, extx.. To dau. Elizabeth (under age of 16), 200 a. near Pocomoke Road and should she die without issue to my bro. Isaac Andrews. Mentioned son in law Jabez Pitt, sister Dorothy Hastings. Friends Capt. John Bradhurst and Hancock Custis to assist wife. Witnessed by Robert Dalrymple, Martha Pitt, Elizabeth Morris, James Houlston, Thomas Merrill. {ACW}

Nathaniel was father of ELIZABETH and prob. step-father of Jabez Pitt.

14. ISAAC ANDREWS, b. c. 1703-1711, son of William (7) Andrews, m. c1734, Mary Stanaway, dau. of Joseph Stanaway. {A; MDAD 5:376}

Joseph Stanaway, DO Co., d. by 24 March 1723 when the admin. account of his estate was submitted by Nehemiah Misseck, admin./exec. Payments to Charles Ungle, Joseph Macklester of SO Co. and to Isaac Andrews who m. a dau. (unnamed). {MDAD 5:376}

In 1732 Isaac Andrews of DO Co. sold 50 a. of land in Accomack Co., left to him by his bro. Nathaniel, to William Sharpley and sixteen years later William Sharply, Jr., sold it back to Andrews. {Whitelaw:1264}

A land commission, 16 March 1733 - 3 June 1734, was appointed to perpetuate the bounds of Isaac Andrews' lands called *Ascumbs Outlett* in the possession of Solomon Chaplin and *Ferringtons Forrest* in the possession of said Andrews. {DOLR 9 Old 187}

Isaac Andrews, aged about 40 years, made a deposition before a DO Co. land commission, 14 June 1742 - 1 Aug 1743, regarding the bounds of Lot Pritchett's land called *Edenburrough* adj. *Northampton*. {DOLR 12 Old 167}

Isaac Andrews, aged about 40 years, made a deposition before a land commission, 14 June 1743 - 1 Aug 1743, regarding the bounds of Lot Pritchett's land called *Edenburrough*. {DOLR 12 Old 167}

On 9 Aug 1749 Peter Stokes of DO Co., shipwright, and Christian his wife, and James Stokes of DO Co., shipwright, conveyed to Isaac Andrews of the same co., part of a tract called *Honourable Division* on or near Blackwater River adj. *Anchor and Hope* and containing 200 a., being a resurvey of *Head Range* where David Shehawn now dwells. {DOLR 14 Old 363}

On 10 April 1757 Isaac Andrews conveyed to his dau. Betty League and her husband Samuel League, a Negro girl called Sabyna. Witnessed by Henry Brannock and Stephen Andrews. {DOLR 15 Old 464}

Isaac Andrews, DO Co., d. leaving a will dated 20 Dec 1757, proved 6 Jan 1758. Children: Joseph, Stephen, Mary and Bettey Andrews (Bettey League). Grandchildren: Isaac Losin, son of Betty League. Tracts: *Fergersands Forrest*, *Head Range*, *The Fork*, *Cree: Beaver Valley*. Execs. Stephen and Mary Andrew. Witnessed by James Jarrett(?), Henry Brannock, John Saulsbury. {MWB 30:468}

The inventory of the estate was filed by Mary Andrews and Stephen Andrews. Signed as next of kin: Naboth Hart, Comfort Tingle. {MDAD 65:407}

The admin. account was submitted on 31 [sic] April 1759 by execs. Stephen Andrews and Mary Keene wife of John Keene. Representatives: children Betty, Joseph, Mary, Stephen. {MDAD 43:225}

Distribution of the estate was made on 11 April 1759 by Stephen Andrews and Mary Keene to widow with residue to 4 children: Betty, Joseph, Mary, Stephen. {BFD 2:124}

Isaac was father of JOHN (pre-deceased his father); JOSEPH, b. c1730; STEPHEN, b. 10 May 1741, d. Spring 1772; MARY, m. John Keene; BETTY, m. by 10 April 1757, Samuel League.

15. NATHANIEL ANDREWS, son of Robert (9).

Nathaniel Andrews, Northampton Co., VA, d. leaving a will dated 31 Dec 1739, proved 12 Feb 1739/40. To my bro. Jacob my 300 a. plantation on Ockkahannock Creek where I now live, provided he makes over his own 200 a. plantation at the head of Nandewey in Accomack Co. which Hancock Beloat now lives upon to my bro. John Andrews. Mentioned: bro. Robert, sister Sarah Gascoigne, sister Rachel Gascoigne to whom he left £7. Bro. Jacob residuary legatee and exec. Witnessed by Isaac Smith, John Robert, Kelly Johnson. {Marshall:304}

16. SOUTHY ANDREWS, son of Robert (9) Andrews.

Southy Andrews d. by 8 Feb 1774 when the admin. of his estate was granted to Henry Harmanson. Approvers: William Cary, John Tankard, John Brickhouse, Hezekiah Brickhouse. {Marshall:426}

17. WILLIAM ANDREWS, son of Andrew (11) Andrews, m. Anne (N).

William Andrews d. leaving a will dated 13 July 1762. To loving wife Anne 100 a. near John Tankard's plantation during her life and then to my son Southy. At wife's death or marriage personal estate to be divided by all my children (unnamed). My wife and Andrew Andrews, execs. Witnessed by Michael Christian, John Smith, Andrew Andrews. {Marshall:393}

William was father of SOUTHY; OTHER CHILDREN.

18. ANDREW ANDREWS, son of Andrew (11) Andrews, m. Mary Waterfield, dau. of Jacob Waterfield.

In his will dated 2 Feb 1766, proved 14 Oct 1766 Jacob Waterfield mentioned daus. Francis Booll, wife of Nicholas and Mary Andrews, wife of Andrew Andrews. {Marshall:412}

Andrew Andrews d. leaving a will dated 24 Feb 1787, proved 10 April 1787. To dau. Smart Andrews, ½ my estate. To dau. Sarah Davis, ½ my estate. If both daus. die without heirs then estates to Molley Capell and William Waterfield. Friend William Waterfield, exec. Witnessed by Sally Hunt, Michael Dunton, Jr. {Marshall:491}

Andrew was father of SMART; SARAH, m. (N) Davis.

19. JOHN ANDREWS, son of Andrew (11) Andrews, m. Rebekkah (N).

John Andrew d. by 10 Nov 1741 when admin. of his estate was granted to Rebeckkah Andrews, relict of the dec'd. Approvers: Thomas Savage, Spencer Johnson, Robinson Custis, John Milby. {Marshall:281}

## Fifth Generation

20. DANIEL ANDREWS, son of Marcus (12) Andrews.

On 12 Aug 1751 Daniel Andrews of DO Co. conveyed to William Addams of the same co., *Willsons Swamp*, patented to James Smith, 87 a. on a branch on the northwest fork of Nanticoke River. {DOLR 14 Old 537}

Daniel Andrew patented 60 a. in DO Co. called *Andrew's Folly* on 10 Aug 1753. {MPL YS8:59; GS1:339}

21. REBECCAH ANDREWS, dau. of Marcus (12) Andrews, m. 1st George Ferguson, m. 2nd (N) Howard.

On 3 June 1753 Rebecca Howard, widow of George Ferguson, conveyed to Alexander Ferguson her lifetime 1/3 interest in part of a tract called *Norwhich*, 235 a. of which her said dec'd. husband d. possessed; said Alexander to be the owner after her decease. Witnessed by Marcus Andrews and Isaac Andrews. {DOLR 14 Old 718}

Rebecca Howard, DO Co., d. leaving a will dated 5 April 1760, proved 10 June 1760. To son Allen Howard, slaves, furniture. To dau. Reachel Howard, furniture. Exec. Naboth Heartt. Witnessed by Wm. Dean, Jr., Mark Andrews, Susanna Insley. {MWB 31:1117}

Rebeccah Howard (Haward), DO Co., d. by 3 Sep 1760 when the inventory of her estate was filed by Naboth Hart. signed as next of kin: Isaac Andrews, Markceis Andrews. {MINV 70:327}

Rebeccah was mother of ALLEN; REACHEL.

22. NATHANIEL ANDREWS, son of Marcus (12) Andrews.

Nathaniel Andrews patented 200 a. in DO Co. called *Providence* on 8 Oct 1747 and 432 a. in DO Co. called *Rubin's Beginning* on 30 Dec 1775. {MPL BT:126; T11:199; BC49:445; BC51:185}

On 13 June 1750 Nathaniel Andrews of DO Co., planter, conveyed to Marcus Andrews of the same co., planter, part of a tract called *Providence*, 100 a. {DOLR 14 Old 418}

On 14 June 1753 Francis Willey and his wife Margery of DO Co. conveyed to Nathanell Andrews of the same co., *Willeys Closure*, about a mile from the dwelling plantation of Marcus Andrews, 214 a. {DOLR 14 Old 706}

On 24 Oct 1765 John Gootee of DO Co., cooper, conveyed to Nathaniel Andrews of the same co., planter, part of *Cow Pasture* on s. side of Raccoon Creek and w. side of Blackwater River, 64 a., adj. Raccoon Point. {DOLR 20 Old 319}

On 12 July 1777 Nathaniel Andrews of DO Co., planter, conveyed to Andrew Insley of the same co., part of a tract called *Rubins Beginning*, between Rackoon Creek and Ceader Creek, containing 77 a. {DOLR 1 JCH 53}

23. MARCUS ANDREWS, son of Marcus (12) Andrews.

On 15 Nov 1764 Marcus Andrews of DO Co., planter, conveyed to Nathaniel Andrews of the same co., planter, part of a tract called *Providence*, 100 a. {DOLR 20 Old 293}

On 13 June 1765 Marcus Andrews of DO Co. conveyed to John Goutee of the same co., cooper, part of a tract called *Raccoon Point*, granted to Thomas Pattison 13 April 1683 for 50 a. and devised by the last will of Mark

Andrews, father of said Marcus Andrews, to his two sons Marcus and Nathaniel, located on Raccoon Creek which issues out of the w. side of Blackwater River and on Thoroughfare Creek, 12 ½ a. {DOLR 20 Old 153}

24. JOSEPH ANDREWS, b. c1730, son of Isaac (14) Andrews, m. 1st Rachel Insley, dau. of James Insley, m. 2nd Mary (N), prob. dau. of Massey Fountain..

At August Term 1744 John Fountain, son of Massey Fountain, chose Joseph Andrew his guardian. {DOJR}

Joseph Andrew(s) patented 36 a. called *Andrew's Desire* in DO Co. on 17 Aug 1752, later 158 a. called *Andrew's Desire* on 10 Oct 1754 and 23 a. called *Andrews' Desire* on 13 Feb 1761. {MPL BY3:525; YS7:280; GS2:96; BC1:45; BC13:665; BC14:229}

Joseph Andrews patented 45 a. in DO Co. on 5 Feb 1757 called *Andrew's Beginning*. {MPL BC11:36}

On 20 July 1761 Josiah Rotten of DO Co., planter, and his wife Ann, conveyed to Joseph Andrews of the same co., planter, part of a tract called *Stonewick* on Rottens Island and Piney Point Gut, containing 50 a. {DOLR 17 Old 403}

On 22 Oct 1761 land left by Capt. James Insley to his two daus. Rosana and Betty on Goose Creek near a house of Jacob Insley, was divided between Thomas Wingate and Joseph Andrews. {DOLR 17 Old 458}

On 24 Feb 1762 Joseph Andrew of DO Co., planter, and his wife Mary, conveyed to Solomon Chaplin of the same co., planter, *Andrews Desire* on the s.w. end of Ashcoms Island in DO Co. adj. *Stannaways Lucky Chance* and containing 23 ½ a. {DOLR 18:68}

On 9 June 1762 John Rumbley of DO Co. and his wife Betty conveyed to Joseph Andrews of the same co., 13 a. of *Andrews Fortune*, 47 a. of *Farum*, 74 a. of *Hampton*, and 38 a. of *Bettys Desire*. (See original record regarding proceedings in the Provincial Court.} {DOLR 18 Old 211}

On 15 Nov 1764 Joseph Andrews and his wife Mary of DO Co. conveyed to Vallintine Insley of the same co., 9 a., being ½ of *Horse Pasture* on the n. side of Ferm Creek in DO Co., for and during the term and right of said Joseph Andrews. {DOLR 19 Old 374}

The census of 1776 for Streight's Hundred shows a Joseph Andrews as head of household, aged between 40 and 50 with one male aged between 16 and 21, two males aged between 10 and 16, five males under age of 10, one female aged between 30 and 40, and one female under age of 10. {MD 1776 Census}

On 20 Nov 1777 Joseph Andrews of DO Co., planter, conveyed to Elija Andrews of the same co., planter, part of *Andrews Beginning* containing 21 ½ a. and part of *Andrews don* on a branch between Arthur Hart and Elija Andrew containing 18 a. {DOLR 1 JCH 62}

Joseph Andrews, aged about 55, made a deposition before a land commission, 14 June 1785 - 10 Jan 1786, regarding the bounds of the tracts *Racoon Ridge* and *Vale of Misery*, mentioning Mary Smith, dec'd. Other deponents were Job Slacum, aged c66 who mentioned James Insley, now dec'd.; Volentine Insley, aged c66; Arthur Hart, aged c38. {DOLR 5 NH 346}

On 7 Feb 1791 Thomas Wingate of DO Co., planter, conveyed to Naboath Hart of the same co., part of *Bettys Desier* on Feirm Creek adj. *Hog Quarter* and adj. lands of Joseph Andrews and Isaac Andrew, containing 9 a.; also part of *Feirm* on Feirm Creek containing 40 a.; also *Insleys Prevention* containing 51 a. {DOLR 3 HD 111}

Joseph and Rachel were parents of STANAWEA, b. 6 July 1752; ELIJAH, b. 7 Oct 1754; probable ISAAC. {Birth dates of the first two are recorded in DODO}

25. STEPHEN ANDREWS, b. 10 May 1741, d. Spring 1772, son of Isaac (14), m. Mary Medford, dau. of William Medford. {See The Medford Family, this volume.}

On 12 Nov 1766 Stephen Andrews of DO Co., planter, and John Keene and his wife Mary of the same place, conveyed to James Reed of SO Co., part of a tract called *Honorable Division* on or near Blackwater River adj. *Anchor and Hope* and near Henry Hooper's fence, and containing 200 a., the plantation where the said James Reed now dwelleth. {DOLR 21 Old 404; 23 Old 212}

On 9 Sep 1769 Stephen Andrews of DO Co., planter, conveyed to Henry Murray of the same co., physician, *Andrews Venture*, beginning at a marked oak in the woods to the northward of Whaitleys Swamp and near a path called John Andrews Cow Path, being the original bounder of the original *Deans Beginning* and containing 168 a. {DOLR 23 Old 442 ½} This was land that Stephen Andrews patented in 1768. {MPL BC34:486, 35:252}

Stephen and Mary were parents of MEDFORD, b. 19 Jan 1766, d. 9 Sep 1834. {Loose leaves found in Higgins Bible, owned by Mrs. Lester B. Kinnamon}

## Sixth Generation

26. ELIJAH ANDREWS, son of Joseph (24) Andrews.

On 1 April 1785 William Insley of DO Co., planter, conveyed to Elijah Andrews of the same co., a tract called *The Spreading Oak* adj. *Andrews Beginning*, containing 27 ½ a. {DOLR 5 NH 49}

27. ISAAC ANDREWS, prob. son of Joseph (24) Andrews, m. Mary (N).

On 27 Sep 1796 Isaac Andrews of DO Co., and his wife Mary, conveyed to Joice Insley of the same co. part of *Andrews Fortune*, conveyed to said Andrews by William Sotherin. Acknowledged by Isaac Andrews and Mary his wife. {DOLR 9 HD:531}

On 27 Sep 1796 Isaac Andrews and his wife Mary conveyed to Thomas Wingate of DO Co. parts of two tracts called *Ferm* and *Williams Prevention*, containing 50 a. {DOLR 9 HD:560}

On 27 Sep 1796 Isaac Andrews of DO Co. conveyed to John Insley (of Joseph) of the same co., land on the road from Firm Creek Bridge to Michael Todd's, adj. Thomas Wingate's land and land of Levi Insley. {DOLR 9 HD:562}

On 27 Sep 1796 Isaac Andrews of DO Co. and his wife Mary conveyed to Andrew Robinson of the same co., part of *Bettys Desire* left to said Isaac Andrews by Joseph Andrew by Last Will and Testament, adj. lands of Naboth Hart and Elijah Andrews. {DOLR 9 HD:563}

28. MEDFORD ANDREWS, b. 19 Jan 1766, d. 9 Sep 1834, son of Stephen (22) and Mary Andrews, m. 26 Jan 1794, Sarah Parker, dau. of Daniel Parker. {.Loose leaves found in Higgins Bible, owned by Mrs. Lester B. Kinnamon. Marshall's DO Co. Tombstone Records give the date of death as 14 Nov 1845}

On 23 Jan 1791 Richard Stanford, Celia Stanford and Elizabeth Stanford, acknowledged receipt of money paid them by Medford Andrews "in consideration of our full claim against a legacy left him by William Medford, late of Dorchester County deceased amounting to one hundred pounds six shillings current money of Maryland in virtue of a Judgement obtained by us against William Medford executor of said William Medford deceast." {DOLR 3 HD 42}

Medford Andrews of DO Co. conveyed to William Reed of the same co., *Honourable Division*, being a resurvey on a tract called *Head Range* on Blackwater, devised to said Medford Andrews in fee tail under the will of his grandfather Isaac Andrews and now conveyed in fee simple in accordance with Act of Assembly of 1782-83. Acknowledged by Medford Andrews and his wife Sarah. {DOLR 8 HD 65}

On 10 Aug 1796 James Steele and Mary, his wife of DO Co. conveyed to Medford Andrews of the same co. one a. of land adj. *Folkes Delight, Nevetts Addition* and *Bit by Chance*. {DOLR 9 HD:464}

On 16 April 179 Medford Andrews of DO Co. conveyed to Daniel Parker Senr. of the same co., Negro man named Dick. {DOLR 14 HD 28}

On 18 April 1798 Medford Andrews of DO Co. conveyed to James Edmondson Junior of the same county: one acre adj. *Folkes Delight, Nevetts Addition* and *Bit by Chance*. Acknowledged by Medford Andrews and Sarah his wife. {DOLR 14 HD 271}

Medford and Sarah were parents of JOSIAH, b. 29 Nov 1794, d. 15 July 1797; ELIZABETH, b. 8 March 1798, d. 1 July 1830; STEPHEN, b. 4 Sep

1801; MARY, b. 14 July 1804; ANNA, b. 7 July 1806; SARAH, b. 27 June 1808; CELIA, b. 22 Feb 1812. {Loose leaves found in Higgins Bible}

Buried at James Andrew's farm, Bobtown, Hurlock District: Medford Andrews, b. 19 Jan 1766, d. 14 Nov 1845; Elizabeth Andrews, b. 8 March 1798, d. 1 July 1830; Stephan P. Andrews, b. 6 Sep 1846, d. 22 Feb 1849; William W. Andrews, b. 27 Feb 1840, d. 9 Sep 1844. {Marshall's Tombstone Records of DO Co.}

29. STEPHEN ANDREWS, 4 Sep 1801, son of Medford (22) Andrews, m. 19 March 1839, Rebeckah Carrol, dau. of James Carrol. {Loose leaves found in Higgins Bible, owned by Mrs. Lester B. Kinnamon}

30. STANAWAY ANDREWS, b. 6 July 1752, d. 1814, son of Joseph (24) and Rachel Andrews, m. Mary Moore. {DO co. marr. lic. dated 31 Jan 1785}

Stanaway Andrews served as private in Capt. John Todd's militia Company. {RPDO:5}

The *Republican Star* dated 3 May 1814 referred to Benjamin Hart, admin. of Stanaway Andrews, DO Co., dec'd.

## THE JOHN ANDREW FAMILY of Dorchester County

This family settled in northeast Dorchester Co. that became Caroline Co.

See *British Roots*, pp. 17-18, for possible British origins. Barnes cites *Genealogy of the Andrews Family and Alliances with Biographical Sketches* by Robert Andrews. However he warns that this source must be used with care as there is little if any documentation.

1. JOHN ANDREW.

John Andrews patented the following tracts in DO Co.: *Hopewell* (200 a.) on 10 Nov 1695; *Iron Mine Neck* (100 a.) in 1704; *Andrews' Venture* (50 a.) on 14 Sep 1722; *Loss Regained* (50 a.) on 12 Dec 1732; *Andrews' Adventure Addition* (50 a.) on 10 Nov 1737. {MPL 40:577; CD4:156; FF7:388; PL5:94; PL8:737; AM1:188}

John was father of JOHN.

### Second Generation

2. JOHN ANDREW, b. c1685-89, son of John (1) Andrew, m. Jane (N).

John Andrew, aged 48 years, made a deposition before a DO Co. land commission, 18 Aug 1733 - 29 June 1734, regarding the bounds of Tench

Francis' land called *Parradice* and a re-survey of said land about 12-13 years earlier. {DOLR 9 Old 195}

On 28 Dec 1735 John Andrew of DO Co., carpenter, conveyed to Thomas Andrew of the same co., planter, *Loss Is Regained* on w. side of the northwest fork of Nanticoke, 50 a. {DOLR 9 Old 360}

On 16 Nov 1736 Henry Davis of DO Co., planter, conveyed to John Andrew of the same co., *Davis's Adventure* on s. side of Wolf Pitt Branch which issues out of the northwest fork of Nanticoke River, containing 100 a. {DOLR 9 Old 414}

John Andrew, aged about 50 years made a deposition before a DO Co. land commission, 11 March 1739-8 Nov 1740 in which he mentioned the bounder of *Hab Nab at a Venture*, described to him about 17 years earlier by Hezekiah Vickery. {DOLR 12 Old 128}

On 7 March 1742 John Andrews and his wife Jane of DO Co., planter, conveyed to William Shagnessy of the same co., planter, part of *Hopewell* on w. side of the northwest fork of Nanticoke River, 100 a. {DOLR 10 Old 373}

On 28 March 1748 John Andrew of DO Co., planter, conveyed to Zachariah Nicholls of the same co., *Andrews Venture* on a branch of Cakius's Creek, 50 a.; also *Addition to Andrews Adventure* on a road from Hunting Creek Church to the head of Watses Creek adj. *Andrews Adventure*, 50 a. {DOLR 14 Old 224}

On 14 July 1748 John Andrew of Choptank of DO Co. conveyed to Joseph Brand Junr. of the same co., part of a tract called *Davises Venture*, 43 a. and 182 perches, being all that part of said tract which is not taken away by land of Day Scott of Somerset called *Grantham*. {DOLR 14 Old 288}

On 18 Jan 1763 John Andrew of DO Co., planter, conveyed to Samuel Pritchet of the same co., carpenter, 97 a. of a 200 a. tract called *Hopewell*, being all of said tract not already sold to Wm. Shocknes, excepting 3 a. adj. *Addition to Hopewell*. {DOLR 18 Old 294}

On 18 Jan 1763 John Andrew of DO Co., planter, conveyed to Nancy Dawson of the same co., 3 a. of *Hopewell*, the remainder of the tract not sold to Wm. Shockneyshe. {DOLR 18 Old 380}

On 25 Jan 1763 John Andrew Senr. of DO Co., planter, conveyed to John Andrew 3rd of the same co., *Iron Mine Neck*, granted to John Taylor, 100 a. {DOLR 18 Old 278}

John Andrews, DO Co., d. leaving a will dated 10 June 1761, proved 15 June 1763. To children: John, Andrew, Jr., Thomas, Joseph, and Mary Griffith, household goods. To grandson Richard Norman, 100 a. on n.w. fork of Nanticoke River, being my part of the tract called *Hopewell*. To dau. Jean Cannon, 1 s. To son John Andrew, Jr., tract on the n.w. fork of Nanticoke River called *Iron Mine Neck*, 100 a. To William Andrew, James Andrew and Tamsy

Nuten, 1 s. Exec. John Andrew, Jr. Witnessed by Thomas Gray, Isaac Charles, Wm. Gray. MWB 31:935}

The inventory was filed on 26 Aug 1763 by John Andrew, Jr. Signed as next of kin: Thomas Andrew, Joseph Andrew. {MINV 82:169}

On 1 Nov 1763 the admin. account of his estate was submitted by John Andrew, Jr. Payments included those to John Andrew III for goods bought at the request of Mr. Andrew McGhee, Mr. James Murray and Mr. Charles Dickenson. A second account was submitted on 26 March 1764 by John Andrew, Jr. Representatives were of age (unnamed). {MDAD 50:148; 52:24}}

Distribution was made by John Andrew, Jr., on 26 March 1764. Legatees: Jane Cannon, William Andrew, James Andrew, Tamsey Nuton. Residue to (equally) John Andrew, Jr., Thomas Andrew, Joseph Andrew, Mary Griffith. {BFD 4:52}

John was father of JOHN; THOMAS, b. c1706; JOSEPH; MARY, m. (N) Griffith; JEAN (Jane), m. John Cannon, son of James Cannon; prob. WILLIAM; JAMES; TAMSY, m. (N) Newton. {See The Cannon Family, Vol. 3 of Colonial Families of Delaware}

## Third Generation

3. JOHN ANDREW, son of John (2) Andrew, m. Sarah (N).

On 11 Aug 1744 Littleton Ward and his wife Mary of TA Co., cooper, conveyed to John Andrew, Junr., of DO Co., *Marys Lott* at the head of the northwest fork of Nanticoke River near Wolf Pit Branch and Racoon Branch, 197 a. {DOLR 12 Old 41}

On 16 Feb 1774. John Andrew Junr. of DO Co., planter, leased to James Murray of the same co., for 500 years, *Iron Mine Neck*, containing 100 a. (mortgage). {DOLR 27 Old 231}

John Andrew, CA Co., d. leaving a will dated 15 Jan 1785, proved 23 Dec 1786. To wife Sarah, the free possession and use of 1/3 of all estate. To son Isaac Andrew, 100 a. of land whereon Isaac now lives, being part of a tract called *Marys Lott*. To son William Andrew, testator's dwelling plantation where testator now lives along with all lands not already given to him. Grandchildren: John, Elizabeth, James, Matthew, Jacob, Thomas, Andrew and Sarah Covey, 1/8 of personal estate. To dau. Sarah Covey. To grandchildren, children of son John Andrew: John, David, Edward, Samuel, Elijah, Sarah, Henry, L–y Andrew, 1/8 of personal estate. Sons Samuel, William and Isaac Andrew and dau. Jane Collins, dau. Esther Stafford, dau. Nancy Collins, remaining 6/8 share of personal estate. Witnessed by Anderton Eaton, Thomas Eaton, Jonathan Eaton. {CAW JB:52}

Isaac Andrew, aged 57, deposed before a CA Land Commission in 1798; mentioned his father John Andrew and John Sullivane.

John was father of ISAAC, b. c1741; WILLIAM; SARAH, m. John Covey, son of Matthew Covey; JOHN; SAMUEL; JANE, m. (N) Collins; ESTHER, m. (N) Stafford; NANCY, m. (N) Collins. {See The William Covey Family, this vol.}

4. THOMAS ANDREW, b. c1706, son of John (2) Andrew, m. 1st Mary, m. 2nd Elizabeth Nicholls, dau. of Isaac Nicholls..

On 26 Feb 1729 Jonathan Clifton of DO Co., cooper, conveyed to Thomas Andrew of the same co., carpenter, *Laytons Chance*, near the head of the northwest fork of Nanticoke River, containing 100 a. {DOLR 8 Old 299}

Thomas Andrews patented the following tracts in DO Co.: *Mill Land* (25 a.) on 2 April 1746; *Crooked Ridge* (191 a.) on 8 July 1752; *Scholarship* (320 a.) on 21 Oct 1758; *Scholarship Improved* (826 a.) on 29 Sep 1762; *Mill Land* (154 a.) on 29 Sep 1763. {MPL PT2:303; YS8:370; GS1:331; BC23:218; BC24:29; BC12:240; BC16:273; BC23:135; BC24:35}

On 15 March 1743 Thomas Andrew and his wife Mary of DO Co. conveyed to Josiah Trotter of the same co., *Loss is Regained* on w. side of the northwest fork of Nanticoke, 50 a. {DOLR 11 Old 135}

Isaac Nicholls, DO Co., d. leaving a will dated 3 Dec 1749, proved 23 April 1750. To dau. Elizabeth Andrew, wife of Thomas Andrew, certain slaves. To granddau. Betty Andrew, a tract called *Plain Dealing* of 100 a. with a proviso that should my son Isaac refuse to convey and make over to sd. Betty Andrew that parcel of land called *Richerson's Choice*, containing 111 a., then the devise to sd. Betty Andrew to be null and void. To grandson Thomas Andrew, son of Thomas Andrew, 1 head of cattle. To granddau. Rebecca Andrew, dau. of Thomas Andrew, 1 head of cattle. To bro. Isaac Nicholls, remaining part of estate. Son, exec. {MWB 27L381}

On 14 Nov 1758 John Nicolls and Isball Nicolls his wife, Isaac Nicolls; and Betty Andrew dau. of Thomas Andrew of DO Co., conveyed to Peter Edmondson of the same co., joyner, part of *Richardsons Choice* at the head of Marshecreek Branches adj. part of the same tract given to John Nicolls Junr. by his father John Nicolls; also adj. land . {DOLR 16 Old 109}

On 23 June 1759 the land of Isaac Nicols, son of John Nicols, dec'd., was valued - Thomas Andrew, guardian, part of a tract on Hunting Creek called *Hampton*, 80 ½ a. {DOLR 16 Old 225}

On 7 Sep 1764 Thomas Andrew and his wife Elizabeth of DO Co. conveyed to Levin Wright of the same co., part of a tract on Brights Branch[2] called *Mill Land* taken up by said Andrew, 91 a. {DOLR 19 Old 360}

---

[2] Today Brights Branch is known as Houston Branch.

On 28 Oct 1765 Thomas Andrew and his wife Elizabeth of DO Co. conveyed to his dau. Rebecca Brannock Andrew, part of a tract called *Schoolarship Improved* adj. *Venture* and *Theres or Mine*, 321 a. {DOLR 20 Old 369} On the same day Thomas Andrew and his wife Elizabeth of DO Co. conveyed to Anderton Brown and his wife Bettey of DO Co., part of *Schollership Improved* adj. *Venture* and *Crooked Ridge*, 237 a.; also part of *Lott*, 19 3/4 a., conveyed by deed between said Thomas Andrew and Joseph Andrew and Ann his wife, dated 6 Dec 1763. {DOLR 20 Old 404}

On 15 April 1768 Thomas Andrew and his wife Elizabeth of DO Co., planter, conveyed to Levin Wright of the same co., planter, 63 a. of *Mill Land* not already conveyed by said Andrew to said Wright. Located on the n. side of Brights Branch, on the e. side of the North West Fork of Nanticoke River. {DOLR 22 Old 316}

Thomas Andrew, aged about 62 years, deposed before a DO Co. land commission, 17 March 1768 - 9 Aug 1768, regarding the bounds of Isaac Nicols' land called *Rawley*; he mentioned Richard Borton about 29 years earlier and land bought by Mr. Nicols from John and George Collins called *Rawley*. {DOLR 22 Old 433}

In his deposition before a land commission, 9 Aug 1768 - 10 Oct 1768, John Caulk of DO Co. aged about 21 years recalled a bounder of the tract *Rings End* shown him sometime last spring by Thomas Andrew, now dec'd. {DOLR 23 Old 129}

On 13 March 1769 Rebecca Brannock Andrew of DO Co. leased to Samuel Griffith, son of John, of the same co., 50 a. of her part of *Scholarship Improved*, for 10 years. {DOLR 23 Old 165}

On 6 Oct 1772 Anderton Brown of DO Co. and his wife Betty, conveyed to James Murray of the same co., part of *Scollarship Improved* containing 237 a. and part of a tract called *Lott* containing 19 3/4 a., purchased by Thomas Andrew from his bro. Joseph Andrew by deed dated 6 Dec 1763. Both of said part of tracts were conveyed by Thomas Andrew and his wife Elizabeth by deed dated 28 Oct 1765. {DOLR 26 Old 189}

Thomas Andrew, Jr., DO Co., d. by 19 May 1774 when the inventory of his estate was filed by Elizabeth Andrew. Signed as next of kin: Betty Brown, Rebeccah Brown, Joseph Andrew, Isaiah Gray. {MINV 118:22}

On 19 Oct 1769 an admin. account of his estate was submitted by Elizabeth Andrew and again on 10 Dec 1773. {MDAD 62:55; 70:38}

Thomas was father of BETTY, m. Anderton Brown; THOMAS; REBECCA BRANNOCK, prob. m. (N) Brown .

5. JOSEPH ANDREW, son of John (2) Andrew, m. Ann (N).

On 21 July 1755 Joseph Andrew, brick layer, and his wife Ann, conveyed to Richard Lain of DO Co., part of a tract called *Andrews Desire* taken up and resurveyed by said Joseph Andrew, containing 93 a. {DOLR 15 Old 312}

On 6 Dec 1763 Joseph Andrew and his wife Ann conveyed to Thomas Andrew part of *Lott*, 19 3/4 a. {DOLR 19 Old 107}

On 4 June 1765 Joseph Andrew and his wife Ann of DO Co. conveyed to James Murray of the same co., part of a tract called *Andrews Desire*, excepting 97 a. sold to Richard Lane (65 a. hereby conveyed) and part of a tract called *Lott* whereon said Joseph Andrew now dwells, 226 a., excepting 19 3/4 a. heretofore sold to Mr. Thomas Andrew (206 1/4 a. hereby conveyed). {DOLR 20 Old 166}

Joseph Andrew, DO Co. d. by 22 May 1775 when the inventory of his estate was filed by Anne Martindall. Signed as next of kin: Joseph Andrew, John Andrew. {MINV 123:246}

Fourth Generation

6. WILLIAM ANDREW, son of John (3) Andrew, m. Mary (N).

William Andrew, son of John, d. leaving a will dated 2 March 1789, proved 28 April 1789. To sons John and Isaac Andrew all testator's land to be divided equally between them. Testator's two sons, when they come of age, to pay the daus. Selah, Starling and Sarah Andrew, £10 each. To wife Mary, her third of estate. Witnessed by Abraham Collins, Elijah, Curtis Beacham. {CAW JB:126}

William was father of JOHN; ISAAC; SELAH; STARLING; SARAH.

7. SAMUEL ANDREW, son of John (3) Andrew.

Samuel Andrews patented 101 a. in DO Co. called *Buck Hill* on 27 Feb 1761 and 50 a. called *Buck Hill Addition* on 26 June 1773. {MPL BC14:231; BC16:241; BC44:167; BC45:241}

Samuel Andrew d. seized of *Andrew's Fortune* and *Moore's Castle* leaving Thomas; Elizabeth; Sarah, wife of Jeremiah Dukes; Nancy; Esther; Samuel; Margaret; Nimrod - last three minors. {CA Land Commission of 1800. B:145}

Samuel was father of THOMAS; ELIZABETH; SARAH, m. Jeremiah Dukes; NANCY; ESTHER; SAMUEL; MARGARET; NIMROD.

8. THOMAS ANDREW, son of Thomas (4) and Elizabeth Andrew.

On 6 Oct 1772 Thomas Andrew and Elizabeth Andrew his mother of DO Co., planter, conveyed to William Dean Junr. of the same co., planter: part of a tract called *Crooked Ridge* on the n. side of said Andrew's dwelling plantations, containing 80 a. {DOLR 26 Old 126}.

Fifth Generation

9. NIMROD ANDREW, d. 1842, son of Samuel (6) Andrew, m. Sep 1826, Euphamy Patterson (b. c1785), they lived near Concord in Caroline Co.

The widow of Nimrod Andrew applied for bounty land on 17 Jan 1857 based on her assertion that Nimrod served as private in the company of Capt. Elijah Satterfield, 15-19 Aug 1813. Her statement was supported by William Wright of Caleb and Newton Andrew. In her claim on 17 Jan `1857 she said she was age 72. She m. Nimrod Andrew in DO Co. Sep 1826 by Rev. Paul Conaway. Nimrod d. 1842. {F. Edward Wright, Maryland Militia, War of 1812, vol. 1}

## THE RICHARD ANDREW FAMILY

1. RICHARD ANDREW m. Anne (N) who later m. Levin Smith.

Richard Andrew, Jr., DO Co., d. by 5 Aug 1747 when the inventory of his estate was filed by Anne Andrew. Mentioned Mark Andrew, Edward Billettor and William Perrey. {MINV 35:240}

On 16 Aug 1751 the admin. account of his estate was submitted by Levin Smith and his wife Ann. representatives: children (minors): Richard, Priscilla. {MDAD 31:191} On 7 Oct 1751 a second admin. account of his estate was submitted by Ann Smith, wife of Levin Smith. Payments to estate of Thomas Skidmore; Hugh Williams; Abraham Wynkoop; Mary Nicolls (minor, only representative of John Nicolls, dec'd. {MDAD 31:203}

Distribution was made by Levin Smith and Jane his wife, admins., on 16 Aug 1751 and 7 Oct 1751. Sureties: George Andrew and Richard Andrew. Due to Mary Nichols, dau. of John Nichols, dec'd., who is under age. 1/3 to widow. Two children: Richard and Priscilla Andrew, both minors. {BFD 1:12, 14}

Richard was father of RICHARD; PRISCILLA.

Second Generation

2. RICHARD ANDREW, prob. son of Richard (1) Andrew.

Richard Andrew, CA Co., d. leaving a will dated 31 Jan 1775, proved 1 Nov 1776. To grandson Richard Andrew Smith, son of dau. Ann Smith, 1 s. To grandson Levin Smith, granddau. Priscilla Right, grandson Thomas Smith, granddau. Rebecca Smith and granddau. Mary Dill, children of dau. Ann Smith, each 1 s. and their mother's share in full of the estate. Wife (unnamed) to have all estate goods and chattels for her natural life, and then to be divided among three children: Richard Andrew, Nehemiah Andrew, Rebecca Flowers. Richard to have the dwelling plantation and land where testator now lives after widow's decease. Richard, exec. Witnessed by William Covey, Henry Turner, Thomas Conner. Rebecca Wright. {CAW A:204}

Richard was father of ANN, m. (N) Smith; RICHARD; NEHEMIAH; REBECCA, m. (N) Flowers.

Third Generation

3. RICHARD ANDREW, prob. son of Richard (2) Andrew, m. Elizabeth (N).

Richard Andrew patented the following tracts in DO Co.: *Hobson's Choice* (150 a.) on 13 Dec 1740, *Taylor's Kindness* (291 a.) on 31 Oct 1755. {MPL LGB:252: LGC:71; BC3:123; BC4:24}

On 8 June 1742 Richard Andrew Junr. of DO Co. conveyed to Richard Dawson of the same co., 50 a. out of 150 a. called *Hobsons Choice*, to be laid out at the upper end of said land, located on the northwest fork of Nanticoke River. {DOLR 10 Old 324}

On 26 March 1767 Richard Andrew in the Fork of DO Co., planter, conveyed to Levin Smith of DO Co., planter, part of a tract called *Hobsons Choice* on the e. side of the main road that leads on the e. side of the stream from the North West Fork Bridge unto Marshahope Bridge, 36 a. Acknowledged by Richard Andrew and his wife Elizabeth. {DOLR 21 Old 352}

On 22 May 1764 Richard Andrew of DO Co. conveyed to Lambert Flowers of the same co., part of *Taylors Kindness* on s. side of the North East Branch of Hunting Creek, 13 3/4 a. {DOLR 19 Old 285}

On 1 Sep 1773 valuation of land of Thomas Smith was made; he was an orphan of Levin Smith, dec'd., now under the guardianship of Richard Andrew, Fork. Valued was part of a tract called *Levins Folly Inlarged*. {DOLR 27 Old 163}

Richard Andrew, Caroline Co., d. leaving a will dated 12 Oct 1780, proved 17 Nov 1780. To son William Andrew, all testator's wearing apparel and £40 to be raised out of the estate and to be deposited in the hands of Zabdiel Potter; to have all that tract lying in Sussex Co., DE, containing 100 a. called *Andrew's Bargain*; also small tract of 25 a. in same co. called *Andrew's Delay*. To wife Elizabeth, extx., maple desk and to enjoy all the lands. Daus. Nancy Andrew and Peggy Andrew each to have a cow and calf. Witnessed by Levin Noble, Joshua Wright, Thomas Smith. {CAW A:39}

Richard was father of WILLIAM; NANCY; PEGGY.

4. NEHEMIAH ANDREW, b. c1727, son of Richard (2) Andrew, m. Naomi (N).

Nehemiah Andrew patented the following tracts in DO Co.: *Pond Ridge* (6 a.) on 30 May 1759; *Pond Ridge* (208 a.) on 25 Feb 1762; *Timber Tree Ridge* (9 a.) on 20 July 1762. {MPL BC8:541; BC11:222; BC23:63; BC24:85; BC18:295; BC21:167}

On 6 April 1762 Nehemiah Andrew, son of Richard Andrew, Senr., and Naomi his wife conveyed to Lambert Flowers Senr part of *Pond Ridge*, 40 a. {DOLR 18 Old 179} On the same day Nehemiah Andrew, and his wife Naomi conveyed to Richard Andrew Junr. of the same co., part of *Pond Ridge*, 48 3/4 a. {DOLR 18 Old 181} On the same day Nehemiah Andrew and his wife Naomi conveyed to Thomas Cunaway of TA Co., part of *Pond Ridge*, 50 a. {DOLR 18 Old 200}

On 4 April 1763 Nehemiah Andrew and his wife Neomi of DO Co., conveyed to Solomon Camper of DO Co., planter, *Timber Tree Ridge* near said Andrew's dwelling plantation, adj. *Pond Ridge*, 9 a. {DOLR 18 Old 448}

On 4 April 1763 Nehemiah Andrew and his wife Naomi of DO Co. conveyed to Solomon Camper of DO Co., planter, part of *Pond Ridge* on s.w.side of the Pissimon Pond adj. the part of said tract belonging to Nehemiah's bro. Richard Andrew, 69 a. {DOLR 19 Old 2}

Nehemiah Andrew of DO Co., aged about 44 years, made a deposition before a land commission of DO Co., 13 Nov 1770 - 2 Aug 1771. He mentioned David Melvill, Edward Billiter, Isaac Kelly, Joseph Bland, Edward Ross and Thomas Wallace about 30 years ago; and Charles Dickinson about 4 or 5 years later. {DOLR 25 Old 26}

Nehemiah Andrew served as captain in the militia of Caroline Co., 14th Battn. by 13 Aug 1777; resigned 12 June 1781. {RPCA:5}

Unplaced

BEACHUM ANDREW, b. c1752.

At a General Court of the Eastern Shore of Maryland held 2nd Tuesday of April 1778 it was presented that Beauchamp Andrew, planter of Caroline Co., along with others being rioters, routers, and disturbers of the peace on 4 Sep 1777 did assemble and gather at the mansion house of Bromwell Andrew and did break and enter and take one gun being the property of the said Bromwell Andrew and other diverse guns to the number of 15, and 5 cartouche boxes and did carry them away. He was fined £5.

At September term 1778 of the Eastern Shore of Maryland General Court Beauchamp Andrew was ordered to appear before the court on 2nd Tuesday of April next to give evidence against Edward Russum, Moses Griffin, Darby Sullivane, and John Delahay for entering the house of Bromwell Andrew and taking out of the said house a number of guns being the public property.

Beauchamp (Beatchum) Andrew served as private in CA Co. militia, Capt. Nehemiah Andrew's Company, by 13 Aug 1777; 2nd lt., 17 Dec 1781. {RPCA:4}

Beachum Andrew, age 46, deposed before a CA Co. land commission, 1798; mentioned James Dawson, William and Thomas Gray; George Andrew. {CA Land Commissions B:105}

BROMWELL ANDREW m. Mary (N).

On 3rd Tues. of Nov 1777 Bromwell Andrew and his wife Mary were ordered to appear before the General Court of the Eastern Shore of Maryland to give evidence against persons for taking from afsd. Browell Andrew's dwelling house, guns and cartridge boxes, deposited there for the use of the militia then under marching orders to join the Continental regiments at camp.

Bromwell served as private in the militia of Caroline Co., 14th Battn., under Capt. Joseph Richardson by 13 Aug 1777. He was appointed ensign and served in Capt. Alexander Waddle's Company, 14th Battn., by 17 Dec 1781. {RPCA:4}

In his will dated 6 June 1782, Jonathan Greenhaugh, CA Co.,, left a heifer to Brumwell Andrew and to his son Russell Andrew he left clothes. {CAW A;82}

Bromwell was father of RUSSELL.

DANIEL ANDREW

On 19 Dec 1741 James Smith of DO Co., carpenter, conveyed to Daniel Andrews of the same co., planter, *Wilsons Swamp* adj. *Wales* on a branch of the northwest fork of Nanticoke, 87 a. {DOLR 10 Old 216}

ELIJAH ANDREW patented 20 a. in DO Co. called *Andrews' Venture* on 24 Oct 1752 and 50 a. in DO Co. called *Venture* on 30 March 1754. {MPL BY3:401; YS7:281; BC2:155; BC4:16} On 4 June 1765 Isaiah Gray and his wife Jemimah of DO Co. conveyed to James Murray of the same co., *Andrews Venture*, formerly the property of Elijah Andrew and given by him to the said Jemimah, now wife of Isaiah Gray, 20 a. {DOLR 20 Old 168}

FRANCIS ANDREWS

On 4 April 1771 Thomas John Marshall conveyed to Francis Andrew of Northampton Co.,VA, a Negro man named Peter, nowin the possession of Ezra Paremore in Northampton Co. Acknowledged in DO Co., MD. {DOLR 24 Old 282}

Francis Andrews d. by 1 Oct 1776 when the admin. of his estate was granted to James Taylor, Henry Guy. {Marshall:428}

GEORGE ANDREW, DO Co., m. 1st Eleanor (N), m. 2nd Mary (N).

George Andrews patented 100 a. in DO Co. called *Lancashire* on 20 July 1704 and 100 a. in DO Co. called *Hopewell* on 1 July 1723. {MPL CD4:197; FF7:418; PL5:328}

George Andrews and Elinor Andrews and Anne Billittor were witnesses to the will of Mary Molehorne (Malihom, Malohane) DO Co. dated 1 Aug 1721, proved 21 Oct 1721. Exec. Abraham Grifffeth. {MWB 17:46}

On 1 March 1738 Curtice Beachamp and his wife Mary of DO Co., planter, conveyed to George Andrew of the same co., planter, part of a tract called *Murpheys Addition* on s. side of Cockciacos Creek, 100 a. {DOLR 10 Old 111}

On 3 Oct 1745 Day Scott of SO Co. conveyed to George Andrew Senr. of DO Co., a moyety of a tract called *Grantham* between the northwest fork of Nanticoke and Great Choptank Rivers, 450 a. {DOLR 13 Old 24}

On 13 Nov 1745 George Andrew and his wife Eleanor of DO Co. conveyed to Thomas Andrew of the same co., *Hopewell* on a branch on the w. side of the northwest fork of Nanticoke River, 100 a. {DOLR 12 Old 206}

On 11 March 1746 George Andrew of DO Co. conveyed to his dau. Sarah Bran, wife of Joseph Bran Junr. of DO Co., *Grantham*, 100 a. in the freshes of Great Choptank. {DOLR 14 Old 109}

On 27 Jan 1747 George Andrew Senr. of DO Co. conveyed to Mark Andrew of the same co., part of a tract called *Grantham* on the e. side of the northwest fork of Nanticoke River, 347 a. {DOLR 14 Old 219}

On 11 May 1765 Joseph Bland Junr. and his wife Sarah conveyed to James Murray of DO Co., part of a tract originally called *Granthum*, formerly given to Sarah, wife of said Joseph Bland Junr. by her father George Andrews, containing 100 a., lately resurveyed and now called *Josephs Folly*; 103 a. of vacant land now included in *Josephs Folly*; part of *Davis's Venture*, 44 a.; and *Addition to Davis's Venture* containing 168 a. (268 a. excepting 100 a. heretofore sold to Abraham Collins. {DOLR 20 Old 160} On 28 Oct 1765 Joseph Bland Junr. of DO Co. conveyed to John Andrew of the same co., part of *Josephs Folley*, 90 a. {DOLR 20 Old 395}

On 17 Dec 1768 George Andrew Senr. of DO Co. conveyed to Joseph Bland of the same co., Negro man named Nase. {DOLR 23 Old 120}

George Andrew, Senr., DO Co. (proved in Caroline Co.), d. leaving a will dated 14 March 1773, proved 11 Aug 1773. To son William Andrew, exec., tract which is part of *Murpheys Addition*, 100 a., bought of Curtis Beauchamp, reserving to my wife Mary Andrew the dwelling plantation in her lifetime. Son William Andrew to pay to my 5 daus., Ann Millvill, Mary Connelly, Priscilla Connelly, Rebeccah Andrew and Esther Andrew, £10 each and to them at the death of my wife, my personal estate. Witnessed by Nathaniel Potter, George Andrew, Jr., Joshua Dilling. {MWB 39:546}

The inventory of the estate of George Andrew, now Caroline Co., was filed by William Andrew on 17 Feb 1774. Signed as next of kin: Mark Andrew, Mary Connelly. {MINV 121:317}

Joseph Bland deposed before a CA land commission, 1798, aged 80; mentioned William Spencer. {CA Co. Land Commissions}

William Andrew, aged 55 in 1797 made a deposition before a CA Co. land commission regarding the bounds of *Murphey's Addition*. {CA Land Commissions B:101}

George was father of WILLIAM, b. c1742; ANN, m. (N) Mellvill; MARY, m. (N) Connelly; PRISCILLA (N) Connelly; REBECCAH; ESTHER; SARAH, m. Joseph Bland (b. c1718)

GEORGE ANDREW, JR., b. c1710, bro. of Thomas Andrew.

George Andrew Jr. patented the following tracts in DO Co.: *William's Delight* (50 a.) on 17 April 1756; *Addition to William's Delight* (40 a.) on 28 Jan 1762; *Addition to William's Delight* (207 a.) on 29 Sep 1765. {MPL BC2:424; BC5:292; BC14:513; BC15:618; BC25:153; BC27:1}

George Andrew Jr., aged about 54 years made a deposition before a DO Co. land commission, 9 Aug 1763 - 31 March 1764 regarding the bounds of Moses Southwell's part of *Lemster*; he mentioned Wm. Layton who showed him a bounded tree abut 32 years earlier. Jacob Charles of DO Co., aged c56, mentioned Thomas Andrew and Charles Thompson about 8-9 years ago, and George Andrew, late of DO Co., dec'd. {DOLR 19 Old 418}

On 18 Oct 1765 George Andrew and his wife Mary of DO Co., farmer, conveyed to Elijah Cremeen of the same co., farmer, part of *Addition to Williams Delight*, 100 a. {DOLR 20 Old 433}

On 20 Dec 1766 George Andrew Junr. and his wife Mary of DO Co. conveyed to Abner Weatherly of the same co., part of two tracts called *Williams Delight* and *Addition to Williams Delight*, 102 ½ a. (15 3/4 a. of *Williams Delight* and 86 3/4 a. of *Addition to Williams Delight*. {DOLR 21 Old 288}

On 1 Aug 1769 George Andrew Junr. of DO Co., planter, conveyed to Isaac Henry of the same co., planter, 20 3/4 a. of *Williams Delight* and 13 1/4 a. of *Addition to Williams Delight*. {DOLR 23 Old 309}

On 25 March 1769 George Andrew Junr., aged about 58 years, stated that "about fifty years agoe he this Deponent lived with his Father in Kent County on Dillaway near a certain Henry Griffiths the Second he this Deponant sayeth that he often frequented the house of the afsd. Henry Griffith and this Deponant further sayeth that he was well acquainted with a gairl about the said Henry Griffiths house called Sarah Griffith which always while he this

Deponant was acquainted with the family he understood that she was a Daughter of the afd. Henry Griffith and this Deponant further sayeth that the afsd Sarah Griffith is wife of a certain John Needles of the afd Kent County." DOLR 23 Old 346}

George Andrew of DO co., aged about 62 years, deposed before a land commission of DO Co., 14 Nov 1769 - 6 Nov 1770, regarding the bounds of the tract *Wiltshire*, mentioning Elizabeth Cromean, now dec'd., and her son John about 17-18 years earlier. {DOLR 24 Old 308}

George Andrew of DO Co., aged about 63 years, deposed before a land commission of DO Co., 13 Nov 1770 - 2 Aug 1771, regarding the bounds of land of Deborah Nicolls and William Nicolls of Talbot County called *Painters Range.* He mentioned his bro. Thomas Andrew (now deceased), about 43- 44 years ago. {DOLR 25 Old 26}

George Andrew served as private in the militia of Caroline Co., Capt. Richard Andrew's Company by 13 Aug 1777. He provided wheat for the use of the military in Aug 1782. He subscribed to the Oath of Allegiancwe and Fidelity on 2 March 1778. {RPCA:4}

ISAAC ANDREWS m. Ann (N).

Isaac and Ann were parents of LEVING, b. 25 Nov 1756; DANIEL, b. 15 March 1758; MOLEY, b. 15 Aug 1759. {DODO}

JOHN ANDREW of Choptank patented 33 a. called *Good Luck* in DO Co. on 12 April 1753. {MPL YS8:385; GS1:326}

JOHN ANDREWS, Northampton Co., m. Elizabeth Dunton, dau. of Michael Dunton.

In his will dated 5 March 1754 and proved 12 March 1754 Michael Dunton mentioned his daus. Elizabeth Andrews and Leah Dunton to whom he left Negro girl Bet and Negro boy Nim when younger dau. is 20. he also mentioned son Elias and son in law John Andrews, execs. {Marshall:356}

John Andrews d. leaving a will dated 14 Jan 1766, proved 12 Aug 1766. To loving wife Betty use of whole estate, a Negro boy Nimrod and girl Jane during widowhood and then to be divided by my children, William, John, Anne, and Peggy. Wife and bro. in law Elias Dunton, execs. Witnessed by Zorobabell Downing, Berry Floyd, Absalom Dolby, Leah Dunton. {Marshall:411}

John was father of WILLIAM; JOHN; ANNE; PEGGY.

MAJOR ANDREWS, Northampton Co., VA, d. by 13 Sep 1774 when the admin. of his estate was granted to Moses Johnson. Approvers: Adial Milby, Thomas James, John Blair, John Wilkins. {Marshall:427}

NEHEMIAH ANDREW, b. c1756.

Nehemiah Andrew, Jr., served as private in Capt. Nehemiah Andrew's Company, 14th Battn., by 13 Aug 1777. He m. Anna Davis by license dated 23 Nov 1791. {RPCA:5}

Nehemiah Andrew deposed before a CA Co. land commission, 1798; mentioned Richard Lane, Francis Dean, Joshua Dilling, William Collins, Solomon Hobbs. {CA Land Commissions B:105}

PEAL ANDREWS, Northampton Co., VA, m. Tabby (N) who later m. Benjamin Kipp.

Peal Andrews d. by 8 Feb 1757 when the admin. of his estate was granted to Tabby Andrews. Securities: Abel James, Littleton Andrews. Approvers: Thomas Dewey, William Pettitt, William Christian, John White. {Marshall:364, 381}

On 14 May 1766 on the motion of Abel Savage the Court ordered Benjamin Kipp and Tabitha his wife, the admx., to be summoned. {Marshall:407}

RICHARD ANDREW, DO Co., m. Mary (N).

On 12 Nov 1744 Richard Andrew and his wife Mary and John Andrews of DO Co., conveyed to Thomas Canner, Junr., of the same co., cooper, *Lankershire* on a branch of the northwest fork of Nanticoke River, 100 a. {DOLR 13 Old 8}

RICHARD ANDREW m. Sarah (N).

On 27 Aug 1756 Richard Andrew Junr. of DO co., planter, and his wife Sarah, conveyed to John Richards of the same co., planter, *Addition to Andrews Venture*, 222 a. on e. side of the northwest fork of Nanticoke. {DOLR 15 Old 425}

RICHARD ANDREW, b. c1773.

Richard Andrew, aged 25 years, deposed before a CA Land Commission, 1798; mentioned William Nicols; Jacob Charles; Peter Taylor of DO Co. {CA Land Commissions B:105}

RUBEN ANDREWS.

Reuben Andrews served as private in Capt. John Todd's Militia Company of 1776. He was ensign as of 22 June 1778. {RPDO:5}

On 15 May 1780 Gustavus Scott of DO Co., attorney at law, conveyed to Reuben Andrews of the same co., *Bowebourk*, on Blackwater River, conveyed to said Scott by William Gootee and supposed to contain 100 a. Acknowledged by Gustas Scott and Margaret Hall Scott his wife. {DOLR 1 JCH 402}

SOLOMON ANDREW

On 21 July 1752 Edward Willibey of DO Co., planter, conveyed to Solomon Andrew of the same co., planter, part of *Chitles Lot*, 25 a. adj. lands of Beall and John Andrews' land. {DOLR 14 Old 637}

On 4 Nov 1755 Solomon Andrew, planter, conveyed to Henry Swiggett of DO Co., planter, part of *Shekels Lot* adj. *Rooses Venture* and on the s. side of *Good Luck*, 25 ½ a. {DOLR 15 Old 327} On the same day John Andrew of DO Co., planter, conveyed to Henry Swiget, *Good Luck*, 33 ½ a. {DOLR 15 Old 325}

## THE BOWDLE FAMILY of Dorchester County

This is a complete revision of The Bowdle Family of volume 5 of this series.

1. THOMAS BOWDLE, Calvert Co., later St. Peter's Parish, TA Co., m. Phebe (N).

Robert Barnes speculates that Thomas Bowdle may be the Thomas Bowdle who was son of Andrew Bowdler of Kerry Ireland who m. Joan, dau. of John Bury of Ballybegan, Ireland. {See British Roots II:27}

Thomas Bowdell was transported into the Province by 1662 and George and Simon Bowdell were transported by 1667. {MPL 5:64, 10:469} Thomas Bowdle of CV Co., taylor, was granted rights for service to William Parker by 1669. {MPL HH:246}

On 17 May 1679 Henry Michell, planter of Calvert Co. confirmed to Edward Turner, power of attorney to acknowledge 300 a. of *Michell's Hall* in Island Creek, Great Choptank River, to Thomas Bowdle of Calvert Co., planter. {TALR 3:317}

At TA Co. Court, August term of 1687, it was presented that Francis Harrison and Benony Porter, planters, on 13 April 1687 and at divers other days and times entered the plantation of Thomas Bowdell in Island Creek called *Mitcham Hall* and committed a breach of the peace. {TAJR}

At June Court 1689 Edmd. Bryant, servant to Tho. Bowdell, was judged to be 20 years old. {TAJR}

Recorded in the court records of TA Co., dated 17 March 1690/1, "I Thomas Bowdell doe give to my son Thomas Bowdel and my son Lofftus

Bowdell one maire called ... and one mair called ... young Bonney when Thomas comes of age of 21. {TAJR}

On 19 Sep 1693 Thomas Bowdell conveyed to his son Thomas Bowdle, a plantation in Island Creek, Great Choptank river called *Micham Hall*; to his dau. Phebe Bowdell, 400 a. at the head of Chester River called *Arcadia* and a cow. {TALR 7:29}

Thomas Bowdle (Boudle) d. 21 April 1696 {TAPE}, leaving a will dated 15 April 1697 and proved 27 July 1697. The heirs named were wife Feeebe (Phoebe), extx., to have life interest in all real estate except 300 a. on Chickencamako, which is bequeathed to Thomas Bowdle and Thomas Knightly, provided they serve their aunt four years. To son Loftes, plantation at death of wife, to be of age at 21 years. To son Thomas, *Timothy's Lott* on Tred Havan Creek. To dau. Feebe, 600 a. at Chester. To son Henry 300 a. at Cheekacon and interest in William State Town at 21 years of age. The will was witnessed by Jos. Leech, Ed. Corigan and Dennis Kelly. {MWB 7:303}

On 9 Nov 1696 John Kirke of DO Co. conveyed to Thomas Bowdle of TA Co., Gent., tract called *Grove* on e. side of the northwest branch of Nanticoke River, containing 300 a. {DOLR 5 Old 86}

At November Court 1696 Thomas Bowdle was allowed a levy for keeping and clothing Robert Million, a very poor decrepid man. {TAJR}

At November Court of 1696 a petition was submitted by Thomas Knight and Thomas Bowdle. It stated that they, about 7 years ago, were brought from their friends and relations out of England by Mr. Thomas Bowdle, the uncle of the petitioners, into this county and during his life did detaining the petitioners as servants who are still detained as servants by Mrs. Bowdle, relict of the said Mr. Bowdle. They conceive they ought to have served five years according to custom of the county and they pray for freedom. The court ordered them freed.

At June Court 1698 John O'Daley, servant to Mrs. Phebe Bowdle, was judged to be 17 years old. {TAJR}

Mrs. Phebe Bowdel d. leaving a will dated 17 Nov 1702 and proved Dec 1702. To son Thomas, exec., estate, real and personal, he to care for his brothers and sisters. Sons Loftus and Henry to share equally in estate with sd. son Thomas when he shall see fit to divide it. Witnessed by Dan'l. Walker, Jas. Bishop and Jane Bullock. {MWB 11:276}

The inventory was filed on 14 Jan 1702. Servants mentioned: John Odaley, John Hawood, Kamell Longo, Sarah Longo, Grace Longo, Elizabeth Vahane. Creditors or next of kin: Thomas Knight, Thomas Bowdle, Thomas Taylor, Joan Longo. {MINV 1:618}

Thomas was father of LOFTUS, THOMAS, b. after 1670, PHEBE; HENRY.

Second Generation

2. LOFTUS BOWDLE, son of Thomas (1) Bowdle, m. Elizabeth (N).

Phebe, dau. of Loftus and Elizabeth, d. 14 May 1720. {TAPE}

Loftus Bowdle d. 26 Dec 1723. {TAPE}

On 7 Sep 1724 Richard Gorsuch conveyed to Loftus Bowdle and his son Thomas Bowdle, 200 a. on n.w. side of Dividing Creek. {TALR 13:135}

Loftus was father of THOMAS; LOFTUS; PHEBE, m. William Martin 9 June 1709 {TAPE}

3. THOMAS BOWDLE d. 6 Nov 1725, son of Thomas (1) Bowdle, m. 1st 6 Dec 1709 Sarah Gorsuch (d. 12 May 1724). Thomas m. 2nd 19 Nov 1724 Mary Withgott, widow of Henry Wittgott.(Withcot) and dau. of Thomas and Eve (Rich) Delahay. Mary m. 3rd Edmund Fish.

Joseph Bowdle, son of Thomas and Sarah, b. 30 8ber 1710. {TAPE}

Sarah Bowdle d. 12 May 1724. {TAPE}

Mary Delahay, dau. of Thomas Delahay, m. Henry Wiothgott 25 Aug 1703. {TAPE}

At August Court 1706, Sarah Sango stated that during her time of service with Thomas Bowdle, she delivered of two children, and she not being free, said Bowdle detains the children, notwithstanding that the begetter of the children gave said Thomas a servant with 5 years to serve, in satisfaction of keeping the children. It was ordered that the petitioner's children be free from service of Thomas Bowdle. {TAJR}

Henry Withcot, TA Co., d. leaving a will dated 24 Nov 1720, proved 9 May 1721. To son Joseph, *Cornwell* and adj. tract *Joseph's Lott*. To son Henry and unborn child if a boy, *Gutterigs Chance* in DO Co. on s.e. side Cabin Creek, equally; should unborn child be not a boy sd. tract to son Henry. To wife Mary, extx., 1/3 personal estate. witnessed by Wm. Car, Edmd. Marsh, George Mordrik, Geo. Saile. {MWB 16:484}

An inventory was filed by Mary Withgirt, widow, on 26 Nov 1720. Approvers: John Carr, Mary Carr, Edmond Carr. A second inventory was filed on 20 Jan 1721 and a third inventory was filed on 17 Nov 1722. {MINCV 6:116, 7:168, 9;45}

An admin. account was submitted on 8 May 1722? by Mary Withgett, extx. and again on 4 April 1724. {MDAD 4:136B, 5:409}

Thomas Bowdle, TA Co., d. leaving a will dated 3 Oct 1726, proved 30 Nov 1726. The heirs named were 2 sons Joseph and Thomas, and unborn child and wife Mary. Sons afsd. to live with wife until 18 years of age. The execs. were wife Mary and son Joseph. Witnessed by Wm. White, John Feston (Feeston) and John Carr. {MWB 19:140}

The inventory was filed by Mary Bowdle, widow, on 8 May 1726, proved 12 July 1727. Signed as next of kin: Loftus Bowdle, Henry Bowdle. Note: Thomas Bowdle d 6 Nov 1725. {MINV 12:181; 13:98}

The admin account was submitted by Mary Bowdle on 24 April 1728. {MDAD 9:181}

Edmond Fish m. 4 Feb 1734, Mary Bowdle. {TAPE}

Edmund Fish, TA Co., d. leaving a will dated 10 Sep 1739, prov4ed 20 Dec 1740. Wife Mary extx., was devised 1/3 of the personal estate and dwelling plantation during her lifetime with the exception of 120 a. which testator left his grandson Edmund Carr, when he became of age. {MWB 22:285}

The admin. account was submitted by Mary Fish on 11 Nov 1743. Representatives (19 total): Mary Fish (accountant), Judith Carr wife of John Carr, Sarah Elston wife of Ralph Elston, Elizabeth Tumbleston, Sarah Withgot now wife of Thomas Delahay, Henry Withgot, Jonathan Culssell, Elizabeth Withgot, Grace Farrell wife of James Farrell, Joseph Gresham, Mary Gresham, Rachel Farrell, Moses Farrell, Mary Farrell, John Carr Jr., Elizabeth Carr (page torn), Moses Carr, Henry Carr. Note: Mary Farrell d. before the dec'd., aged 4 years. Payments to: Richard Gildart, Esq., Daniel Dulany, Esq., Thomas Bullen, John Bowdle (orphan of Thomas Bowdle (planter, dead)). {MDAD 20:15}

Mary Fish, DO Co., widow, d. leaving a will dated 4 Dec 1747, proved 1`748. To son Henry Withgot, 3 slaves. To son John Bowdle 2 slaves, but if he should die without heirs, to return to Henry Withgot. To dau. Sarah Dellehay, 1 slave until her son Thomas Dellehay comes of age 21. To dau. Elizabeth Littleton, 1 slave, and for default of heirs, to return to John Bowdel. To grandchild William Jones, Mary Withget, Mary Feaston, 1 ewe. To granddau. Mary Jones, 1 heifer. Slave woman to be sold. Son Henry Withgett, exec. Witnessed by John Anderton, William Jones, Mark Littleton, Jane Dellehay, Wm. Littleton. {MWB 25:372}

The inventory was filed by Henry Withget on 4 June 1748. Signed as next of kin: Sarah Dilehay, Elizabeth Littleton. {MINV 36:236}

The admin. account of the estate of Mary Fish was submitted by Henry Withgott on 22 Aug 1749. Payments to Thomas Delihay, James Delihay, John Bowdle, his portion of estate of his father Thomas Bowdle, John Carr, Ennalls Hooper, Jacob Hindman, Dr. Joseph Ennalls, Ennalls Hooper due to Daniel Dulany, esqr. Legatees: dau. Sarah Delihay, son John Bowdle, dau. Elizabeth Littleton, accountant. {MDAD 27:31}

Thomas was father of JOSEPH, b. 1710; THOMAS; JOHN.

4. HENRY BOWDLE, son of Thomas (1) Bowdle, probably m. 1st Mary Gouldsborough 23 June 1720 and m. 2nd Judith Armstrong 29 Nov 1736. {TAPE}

Henry and Mary were parents of Phebe, b. 18 Aug 1721; Thomas, b. 15 Feb 1722, d. 3 March 1722; Elizabeth, b. 15 Feb 1722, d. 4 March 1722. {TAPE}

Mary, wife of Henry Bowdle, d. 21 Nov 1729. {TAPE}

Henry Bowdle, TA Co., d. by 29 Jan 1738 when the inventory of his estate was filed by Robert Morris, admin./exec. Signed as next of kin: William Bowdle, Thomas Bowdle. {MINV 24:72}

The admin. account was submitted on 28 Feb 1739. Admin. Robert Morris, gent., for Foster Cunliffe, Esq. of Liverpool. {MDAD 17:470}

On 9 Aug 1750 Nicholas Bowdel, carpenter, son of Henry Bowdell, dec'd., conveyed to Samuel Chamberlaine, Gent., Lot No. 5 in Oxford. {TALR 17:346}

Henry was father of PHEBE, m. Phillip Martin 15 April 1742 {TAPE}; THOMAS, b. 1722, d. in infancy; ELIZABETH, b. 15 Feb 1722, d. in infancy; possibly HENRY and NICHOLAS.

5. LOFTUS BOWDLE, probable son of Loftus (2) Bowdle of TA Co., m. 27 Feb 1716, Ann Thomas, dau. of William Thomas. {TAPE. See also The Thomas Family, this vol.} Ann m. 2nd William Martin.

William Bowdle, son of Loftus Bowdle and Ann his wife, b. 1 Sep 1718. {TAPE}

Henry Loftus Bowdle, son of Loftus and Ann, b. 1 Jan 1720, d. – Oct 1721. {TAPE}

Henrey Bowdle, son of Loftis and Ann, b. — {TAPE}

Elizabeth, dau. of Loftus and Anne, b. 11 Jan 1723. {TAPE}

Loftis, son of Loftus and Anne, b. 12 Jan 1726. {TAPE}

Elizabeth, dau. of Loftus and Ann, d. 12 March 1727. {TAPE}

Loftus Bowdle, TA Co., d. leaving a will dated 6 Nov 1734, proved 21 June 1736. To wife Ann, dwelling plantation, *Mitchell's Hall* during her lifetime; at her decease one part thereof, meaning the manner plantation, extending to branch of Poplar Neck Cove at upper end of field by Peter Winsteloa's House, to son William; remainder to son Loftus. To son Thomas £5. To sons Loftus, Henry, Stephen, Trustram and John, personalty when they come of age. The extx. and residuary legatee was wife Ann. Overseers: William Sharp, Edward Needles and Henry Bowdle. Witnessed by Edward Needles, Richard Giles and Robert Martin. {MWB 21:624}

The inventory of the estate was filed by Anne Bowdle on 15 July 1736. Signed as next of kin: William Thomas, Jane Thomas, Henry Bowdells, Phebe Giets. {MINV 22:82} On 26 Aug 1741 Ann Martin, wife of William Martin filed a second inventory. Signed as next of kin: Thomas Bowdle, Phebe Giels. {MINV 26:267}

An admin. account was submitted by Ann Martin, wife of William Martin on 21 Dec 1741. Representatives: Ann (accountant, widow), 7 children: Thomas, William, Lofftis, Henry, Trustram, Stephen, John (now dead, aged 10 mos.). {MDAD 18:493} A second admin. account was submitted by Ann Martin, wife of William Martin, on 26 Sep 1746. Payments to Thomas Love (son of William Love (dec'd., who was security), Nicholas Love, Daniel Dulany, Esq. {MDAD 22:378}

William Martin m. Ann Bowdle, widow, 5 Aug 1737. {TAPE}

Loftus was father of HENRY LOFTUS, d. young; WILLIAM, b. 1718; LOFTUS; THOMAS; HENRY; STEPHEN; TRISTRAM; ELIZABETH, d. young; JOHN, d. 1741, aged 10 mos. {MDAD 18:493}

6. JOSEPH BOWDLE, b. c1710, son of Thomas (3) Bowdle, m. 16 Feb 1731, Elizabeth Boyce. {TAPE}

In the valuation of the land of the orphan William Perry, reference is made to the tract "*Alfords Paridice* where Joseph Bowdle lives." {DOLR 14 Old 635}

Joseph Bowdle, aged c51 made a deposition before a DO Co. land commission, 14 Aug 1759 - 11 March 1761, regarding the bounds of the tract *The Gore*, owned by Wm. Perry, son of Wm. Perry, dec'd. {DOLR 17 Old 376}

Joseph Bowdle, DO Co., d. leaving a will dated 29 Jan 1772, proved 31 March 1772. Wife Elizabeth, extx. Children: Henry, Sarah, John, Joseph. Legacy to James Grant. Bequeathal to granddau. Elizabeth Bowdle. Witnessed by James Shipley, Wm. Banning. MWB 38:569}

On 15 June 1772 the inventory of his estate was filed by Elizabeth Bowdle. Signed as next of kin: John Bowdle, Henry Bowdle. {MINV 110:16}

The admin. account was submitted by Elizabeth Bowdle on 24 Nov 1772. {MDAD 67:377}

Joseph was father of HENRY; SARAH, m. by license dated 8 March 1780, Anderton Blades {Caroline Co. marr. lic.}; JOHN; JOSEPH.

7. THOMAS BOWDLE, son of Thomas (3).

Thomas Bowdle, DO Co., d. by 6 May 1760 when the inventory of the estate was filed by Edward Smith. Signed as next of kin: Henry Bowdle, Mary Reach. {MINV 69:171}

Distribution was made by Edward Smith, 1/3 to widow and residue to Elizabeth Bowdle. {BFD 3:90}

Thomas was father of ELIZABETH.

8. JOHN BOWDLE, d. by 27 Aug 1778, son of Thomas (3) Bowdle, m. Elizabeth (N).

On 22 Aug 1778 Elizabeth Bowdle of DO Co., spinster, widow of John Bowdle, late of DO Co., dec'd., conveyed to Henry Bowdle, Thomas Bowdle and Mary Bowdle. sons and dau. of the said Elizabeth and John Bowdle: her thirds of the real and personal property of her said husband. "at the day that I shall join in Holy Matrimony with any Person." {DOLR 1 JCH 135}

On 9 Oct 1779 Elizabeth Bowdle of DO Co., widow, signed a bond to her children Henry Bowdle, Thomas Bowdle and Mary Bowdle, concerning slaves, livestock etc. taken by her as her thirds of the estate of her dec'd. husband John Bowdle, to be delivered to her said children at her death or remarriage. {DOLR 1 JCH 276}

John and Elizabeth were parents of HENRY; THOMAS; MARY.

9. HENRY BOWDLE, taylor, son of Henry (4) Bowdle, m. Elizabeth Skinner, dau. of Thomas Skinner..

On 3 Nov 1766 Henry Bowdle, taylor, and his wife Elizabeth, conveyed to Thomas Martin III, merchant, 61 a., part of *Hier Dier Lloyd*; mentioned a division line between Thomas Martin and Ann Bowdle; also 37 a., part of *Hard Measure*. {TALR 19:395}

Thomas Skinner, planter, TA Co., d. by 25 July 1765 when the inventory was filed by Peter Denny and Henry Bowdle. Signed as next of kin: Joseph Skinner, Mordecai Skinner. {MINV 103:342} On 10 Aug 1770 the admin. account of his estate was submitted by Peter Denny and Henry Bowdle, execs. No widow mentioned. Residuary legatees: Hester, wife of Peter Denny; Elizabeth, wife of Henry Bowdle; Joseph, age 18; Thomas, age 16; Ruth, age 14; Rose, age 12: Mary, age 10; William, age 8; Benjamin, age 6. {MDAD 63:207} Distribution of the estate was made on 10 Nov 1772 to children: Esther Denny, Elizabeth Bowdle, Joseph Skinner, Thomas Skinner, Ruth Skinner, Rose Skinner, Mary Skinner, William Skinner, Benjamin Skinner. {BFD 6:1, 147}

On 3 June 1794 the *Eastern Shore Herald* announced that Henry Bowdle, cabinet and chair maker, had opened a shop in Washington Street adj. Mr. Wilmot's (clockmaker), a little below Mr. Mullikin's tavern [in Easton].

Samuel Skinner Bowdle, aged 21 years, 7 mos., 25 days, d. 22 Sep 1797. {TAPE}

Henry Bowdle d. leaving a will dated 9 Oct 1797, proved 27 March 1798. To eldest dau. — Bowdle, a sum of money. To eldest son Loftis Bowdle, a Negro boy Ben, until he arrives at the age of 25 which will be 7 April 1810 and then to be freed; Negro girl Dafne until she arrives at the age of 21 which will be 20 Dec 1810; 2 plows with gear and 2 horses, and other items. To son

Henry Bowdle and son Tristram Bowdle, land near Coxes's Mill called *Part of Taylors Ridge*, and are instructed to sell the land with the advice of Loftis and all moneys arising from the sale to be divided between them. To Tristram Negro boy called Harry until he comes to the age of 25 which will be 24 Feb 1822. Henry to have the benefit of old Negro man Pompey and to let him have the benefit "of his labor and enjoy the privileges of freedom, but to be restrained by my said son henry from wicked and bad practices as I consider Pompey as not altogether capable to manage for himself. To dau. Elizabeth, Negro girl Rachel until she arrives at the age of 21 which will be on 18 Sep 1808. To Mary Skinner who now lives with me, Negro girl Meriah until she arrives at the age of 21 which will be 2 July 1814 and then to be freed. Mary to have a share of the personal estate which is also to be divided between Elizabeth and Rebecca n condition that Mary does not bring any account for services rendered to the family. To dau. Rebecca a walnut dish. Desires that the family stay together until the end of the year when the crop comes in. Witnessed by George Robins Hayward, Thomas Esgate, Moses Hopkins. {TAW JP5:264}

Henry was father of (N); LOFTIS; HENRY; TRISTRAM; ELIZABETH; REBECCA; SAMUEL SKINNER, b. 27 Feb 1776.

10. NICHOLAS BOWDLE, possible son of Henry (4) Bowdle.

On 4 June 1754 James Phillips, shipwright and his wife Ann, Joseph Fooks and his wife Mary, all of DO co., conveyed to Nicholas Bowdle of TA Co., carpenter, all their interest in a tract called *The Grove*. {DOLR 15 Ol 111} On 5 July 1754 Thomas Covington of DO co., planter, and his wife Sarah, conveyed to Nicholas Bowdle of TA Co., carpenter, all their interest in *The Grove*. {DOLR 15 Old 115}

On 5 July 1754 Nicholas Bowdle of TA Co. conveyed to Isaac Nicolls of DO Co. *The Grove*, containing 300 a. {DOLR 15 Old 110}

On 10 Nov 1766 Nicholas Bowdle of DO Co., waterman, conveyed to Stephen Bowdle of TA Co., taylor, one schooner with all equipment, and other personal property. {DOLR 21 Old 181}

11. LOFTUS BOWDLE, son of Loftus (5) Bowdle, m. Ann Martin, sister of Mary, Sarah and Richard Martin.

On 20 Oct 1750 Loftus Bowdle conveyed to Thomas Bowdle and William Bowdle, eldest son of Thomas, ½ (36 a. of a tract called *Shore Ditch* and ½ (27 a.) of *Swamp Tike*. {TALR 17:395}

Loftus d. leaving a will dated 10 March 1754, proved 7 May 1754. The heirs were wife Ann Bowdle, to whom he left Land I now dwell on being part of a tract called *Hier Dier Lloyd*, and land I bought of William Martin, Jr., on head of Schoolhouse Cove, or near it, during her life. Mentioned probably unborn child. If no child is born lands to my bro. Henry Bowdle at decease of my wife. If all should die without heirs, lands to bro. Tristram Bowdle. To sister Ann Bowdle, 2 slaves named Clow and Grace. Witnessed by Thos. Stevens, Sr., John Stevens, George Dudley and Thomas Stevens, Jr. {MWB 29:118}.

On 23 July 1754 the inventory of his estate was filed by Ann Bowdle, admx./extx. Mentioned Daniel Lowel, Henry Dickinson, Ann Martin, Henry Bowdle. {MINV 69:209}

A list of debts was filed on 14 Dec 1762. {MINV 79:303}

Ann Bowdle, TA Co., d. leaving a will dated 9 March 1767, proved 14 Feb 1769. In the will no children were mentioned. Mentioned were sisters Mary and Sarah Martin, and bro. Richard Martin. Execs.: James Berry, Robert Goldsborough, son of John, Nicholas Goldsborough. Witnessed by Thomas and Nicholas Martin and Sarah Blackshire. {MWB 37:14}

12. THOMAS BOWDLE, son of Loftus (5) Bowdle, m. 27 May 1740, Mary Mears. {TAPE}

On 22 Sep 1741 Thomas Bowdle and his wife Mary conveyed to Thomas Martin 58 a., part of *Hier Dier Lloyd*. {TALR 15:92}

On 15 July 1746 Thomas Bowdle and his wife Mary conveyed to Thomas Martin, Gent., 38 a., part of *Hier Dier Lloyd*. {TALR 16:297}

On 27 Feb 1769 William Bowdle, house carpenter, and Thomas Bowdle, his father, conveyed to Matthew Jenkins, 36 ½ a. of *Shore Ditch*; also 27 ½ a. of *Swamp Tike*. {TALR 20:12}

Thomas was father of WILLIAM.

13. STEPHEN BOWDLE, son of Loftus (5) Bowdle, m. Phebe Martin, widow of Philip Martin.

Philip Martin d. by 2 Oct 1758 when Phoebe Bowdle (late Phoebe Martin, wife of Stephen Bowdle), filed the inventory. Signed as next of kin: Jonas Martin, William Martin, Jr. {MINV 77:250}

On 15 Aug 1769 distribution of his estate was made by Phebe Bowdle, wife of Stephen Bowdle. To widow, 1/3 with residue to (equally) Nicholas Martin, Robert Martin. {BFD 6:317}.

In his will dated 8 Nov 1777 William Martin left a young mare to Mary Bowdle, dau. of Steven Bowdle. {TAW 3:81}

Stephen Bowdle d. leaving a will dated 23 April 1788, proved 20 June 1791. To Mary Turbutt he left a Negro woman Sydney. To grandson Nicholas Turbutt he left a Negro Levin. To wife Phebe, extx., the remainder of the estate. Witnessed by Samuel Thomas and Richard Coward. {TAW3:191}

Stephen was father of MARY, m. Samuel Turbutt.

14. TRISTRAM BOWDLE, son of Loftus (5) Bowdle, m. Sarah Eubanks.

Tristram Bowdle patented 180 a. in TA Co. on 17 March 1768 called *Hog Hole* and 5 a. on 23 Oct 1769 called *Hog Hole Addition*. {MPL BC32:500; BC37:67; BC36:494; BC40:21}

Tristram Bowdle was admin. of the estate of Elizabeth Dudley and filed the inventory of her estate on 5 Jan 1774. Signed as next of kin: Jane Barnett, Juliana Bowdle. A second inventory was filed on the estate of Elizabeth Dudley, relict of George Dudley by Tristram Bowdle on 7 Nov 1775. Signed as next of kin: Nancy Dudley. {MINV 118:126; 122:366}

On 21 June 1796 Tristram Bowdle, Easton, advertized for an apprentice to house carpenter and joiner business. {*Maryland Herald and Eastern Shore Advertiser*}

Tristram Bowdle, TA Co., d. leaving a will dated 10 March 1799, proved 4 May 1799. To wife Sarah, Negroes Robert, Lucretia and her two children; Hannah and her two children; and all the plate until son comes of age. To wife all land *Hoghole* and *Coxe's Remnant* for three years and then to have 1/3. Wife Sarah and either Tristram or James. To son Isaac above mentioned articles to be divided equally when he arrives at age; lands should both Tristram and James die without heirs;£300 to be putout to interest; Negroes Jacob, Levin, Stephen and Morris. To son Tristram at the end of three years, all lands *Hoghole* and *Coxe's Remnant* with exception of third left to widow; Negro woman Sarah and Negro boy Oliver; livestock To son James, all lands left to Tristram should he die without heirs; lot in Easton; sum of £260 which he had some time past and £100 that testator lent him in October of 1796; Negro man Toney. To dau. Elizabeth Jenkins, wife of George Jenkins: to her children, Negroes Rachel, Fanny, and Perry; furniture; and that silver table spoons "which you have got I desire shou'd be divided amongst her daughters ..." Witnessed by Thomas Stevens, John Porter, Samuel Small. {TAW JP5:339}

Sarah Bowdle d. leaving a will dated 12 June 1802, proved 24 Aug 1802, being in a very poor state of health. To niece Augusta Eubanks, $100. To Sally Stevens, dau. of Thomas Stevens, $100, ½ of wearing apparel to be divided with Augusta Eubanks, and the remainder to be divided among "my female black people." To son Isaac Bowdle, remainder of estate after debts are paid when he arrives at the age of 21. To bro. Edward Eubanks, exec., should testatrix's son Isaac die before arriving at age 21, remainder of the estate to him and his children. Witnessed by Francis Price, George Porter. {TAW JP6:470}

Tristram was father of TRISTRAM; JAMES; ELIZABETH, m. George Jenkins.

Tristram and Sarah were parents of ISAAC; RICHARD, b. 3 Sep 1796; TRISTRAM, b. 20 Sep 1800; ELEANOR ANN, b. 3 Nov 1802. {TAPE (birth dates of last three children)}

15. JOSEPH BOWDLE, son of Joseph (6) Bowdle, m. Polly Blades, by license dated 12 Feb 1791. {Caroline Co. marr. lic.}

On 17 Nov 1795 Joseph Bowdle, farmer, Caroline Co., conveyed to Thomas Baynard, a Negro woman Rachel and boy Robert. {CAD E:312}

16. HENRY BOWDLE, son of John (8) and Elizabeth Bowdle, m. Sarah Stevens, widow of William Stevens.

William Stevens, TA Co., d. by 5 July 1774 when Sarah Bowdle, wife of Henry Bowdle, filed a list of debts of the estate of William Stevens. {MINV 121:20} Distribution of the estate was made by Sarah Bowdle on 5 July 1774 to widow and 6 children (unnamed). {BFD 7:6}

Henry Bowdle served as private in Capt. John Mitchell's Company, 14th Battn., Caroline Co. militia, by 13 Aug 1777. He subscribed to the Oath of Allegiance before Hon. Peter Richardson on 28 Feb 1778 in Caroline Co. {RPCA}

On 29 Sep 1779 Stephen Fleharty, farmer, leased to Henry Bowdle 100 a., part of *Addition to Fleharty's Desire* for 12 years, beginning 1 Jan next with liberty to clear as much as he desires; build houses at his own cost; plant 100 apple and 200 peach trees. {CAD GFA:435}

On 20 March 1786 Henry Bowdle of DO Co. manumitted slaves. Witnessed by Benjamin Dixon. {DOLR 5 NH 354}

17. THOMAS BOWDLE, son of John (8) and Elizabeth Bowdle.

On 7 Feb 1784 Thomas Bowdle manumitted slaves Alice, age 37; Roger, age 18; Nelly, age 9. Witnessed by Freeborn Garrettson and Mary Bowdle. {2 NH 281}

On 25 Aug 1795 Thomas Bowdle of DO Co. manumitted Negro slaves. Witnessed by Edward White, Jr., and Henry Bowdle. {DOLR 8 HD 502}

Thomas Bowdle, DO Co., d. by 14 Nov 1760 when the admin. account of his estate was submitted by Edward Smith, Jr. Representatives: widow (unnamed0 and 1 child, Elizabeth. {MDAd 46:316}

Thomas was father of ELIZABETH.

18. MARY BOWDLE, dau. of John (8) and Elizabeth Bowdle.

On 7 Feb 1784 Mary Bowdle manumitted slaves Fan, age 16; Henny, age 13; and Isaac, age 11. Witnessed by Freeborn Garrettson and Thomas Bowdle. {DOLR 2 NH 282}

19. HENRY BOWDLE, possible son of Henry (9) Bowdle, m. 1795, Mary Chaplaine. {TA Co. marr. lic. dated 18 Feb 1795}

A newspaper obituary stated Henry Bowdle of this town (Easton) d. Saturday last after a tedious illness. On 2 April 1799 it was indicated that James Chaplain and Loftus Bowdle were admins. of the estate of Henry Bowdle, Junr., late of TA Co. {*Maryland Herald and Eastern Shore Intelligencer*, 19 March 1799, 2 April 1799}

20. MARY BOWDLE, dau. of Stephen (13) Bowdle, m. Samuel Turbutt.

Samuel Turbutt d. leaving a will dated 12 Feb 1821, proved 17 July 1821. To wife Mary, dwelling plantation, 106 a. and woodland containing 10 a. for her natural life provided she not marry; children to be maintained by widow. Execs. wife and sons William and Greenbury. To sons William Turbutt and Greenbury, lands left to widow after her decease or remarriage. William to be paid by Greenbury and three daus. $500. William and Greenbury named as trustees to three daus and their estates. Should William die without heirs, then daus. Henrietta Maria Turbutt, Sophia Turbutt and Eliza Turbutt, and Greenbury to divide land left to William. To son Nicholas Turbutt, Negro Levin now in his possession, and Negro boy Perry. {TAW JP8:6}

Samuel was father of WILLIAM TURBUTT; GREENBURY TURBUTT; HENRIETTA MARIA TURBUTT; SOPHIA TURBUTT; ELIZA TURBUTT; NICHOLAS TURBUTT. Nicholas was by Samuel's wife Mary.

21. ISAAC BOWDLE, son of Tristram (14) and Sarah Bowdle, m. Sarah (N).

Isaac Bowdle, TA Co., d. leaving a will dated 14 Sep 1816, proved 10 Oct 1816. To wife Sarah, extx., all estate. Witnessed by John Stevens, Jr., Robert Spedden, Levin Spedden. {TAW JP7:373}

Unplaced

(N) BOWDLE m. Katherine, dau. of Mary Sargent.

Mary Sargeant, QA Co., d. leaving a will dated 29 April 1711, proved 31 Aug 1711. To granddaus. Sarah Gibson, Katherine Emerson, Mary and Elizabeth Gouldsbrough and to Eliza: Cralchwood[3], personalty. Daus. Katharine

[3] Perhaps Elizabeth was dau. of Anna Maria Crotchawoodlan, spinster, servant to Eliza. Gouldesborough, widow. At August Court 1706 it was presented that Anna Maria Crotchawoodlan, spinster, servant to Eliza. Gouldesborough, widow, committed fornication with Thomas Bowdle and begot a bastard child. Ordered to receive 20 lashes, serve her master 15 additional months, and the child to serve James Laws until she attained the age of 21. {TAJU CR6399-1}

Bowdell and Priscilla Brewin, extxs. and residuary legatees. Witnessed by Robert Noble, Jr., Wm. Elbert, Thos. Emerson, Jr. {MWB 13:315}

At March Court 1713/14 Thomas Murphey, sawyer, was summoned to answer Mathew Errickson and his wife Katherine, late called Katherine Bowdle, one of the execs. of the last will of Mary Sergeant, widow, dec'd., and Priscilla B., co-extx. With a demand for 500 lbs. of tobacco owned to Mary Sergeant in her lifetime. {QAJR}

CARSON BOWDLE m. Juliana (N).

In the *Republican Star* of Easton, dated 23 April 1805, Carson Bowdle offered a reward for a Negro man, Jim, hired from David Kerr of Easton.

The *Republican Star*, dated 25 Oct 1808, announced that Carson Bowdle and Ruth Bowdle, admins. of Henry Bowdle, TA Co., dec'd., were to have a sale at late plantation of dec'd. below the Trappe, of his personal estate, consisting of household furniture, horses, cattle, sheep, hogs, flax, corn and corn fodder, wheat-straw, tobacco and farming utensils.

Carson and Juliana were parents of JULIANA, b. 20 Dec 1806; BENJAMIN, b. 1 Feb 1803; WILLIAM CARSON, b. 24 Jan 1805. {TAPE}

HENRY BOWDLE 2nd m. Ruth (N).

Henry Bowdle and Ruth Bowdle, TA Co.,were parents of WILLIAM, b. 27 March 1796; AARON, b. 29 April 1802; AMOS (Annos?), b. 13 Aug 1806.. {TAPE}

HENRY BOWDLE, admin./exec. filed the inventory of the estate of Jonathon Woods, TA Co., on 25 Oct 1769. Signed as next of kin: Mary Ann Walker, James Woods. {MINV 104:342}

JAMES BOWDLE

On 20 Nov 1792 *The Eastern Shore Herald* announced that James Bowdle, gold and silversmith, had removed from next to Owen Kennard's store into a house adj. Samuel Baldwin's store. [in Easton]. {*Maryland Herald and Eastern Shore Intelligencer*}

In 1797 he was Collector of Assessments for TA Co. {*Maryland Herald and Eastern Shore Intelligencer*, 18 July 1797}

MARY BOWDLE m. James Sisk by license dated 3 Jan 1791. {Caroline Co. marr. lic.}

LOFFS. (Loftis) BOWDLE served aboard and/or helped repair the vessel *Sturdy Beggar* in1776 under Capt. James Foster, as noted in the account book of John McKeel dated 13 Nov 1776 while at Fell's Point. {RPDO;15}

SALLY BOWDLE m. Thomas H. Handy, 16 Aug 1825. {DOGC}

## THE CONNERLY FAMILY

1. OWEN CONNERLY, m. Elizabeth (N).

On 8 June 1730 Peter Taylor of DO Co., Gent., and his wife Mary, conveyed to Owen Connerly of the same co., planter, part of a tract called *Taylors Neglect* on a branch of the northwest fork of Nanticoke River, 406 a.

On 26 Aug 1748 Owen Connerly of DO Co., planter, conveyed to Thomas Connerly and Patrick Connerly of the same co., cattle and other personal property. {DOLR 14 Old 270}

Owin Connerly, DO Co., d. leaving a will dated 3 Aug 1747, proved 15 March 1748. To son Thos. Connerly, that part of my land called *Taylor's* [*Taylor's Neglect*] lying to the eastward of the sd. tract containing 140 a. To son Patrick Connerly, my dwelling plantation, I live on with 165 a., it being the remainder of the tract called *Taylor's Neglect.* For as much as I had given eldest son Owing Connerly, 50 a. of my land in his lifetime, and by consent sold it to his bro. Thomas, I think not fit to give his hears any other lands. I give to Thomas, son of Owing Connerly, dec'd., 1 s. If any of my sons, Thomas, William or Patrick should not think fit to sell the said lands, they shall sell to his other bros. To grandson John Pain, the tract called *Cumbechance.* To son Thomas Connerly, my water mill now on Mill Creek. To dau. Rosanah Layton, furniture. To wife Elizabeth, remaining part of personal estate. To Ann Andrew, cattle. Wife, extx. Witnessed by Isaac Nicholls, Thos. Andrew, Isaac Nicholls, Jr. {MWB 27:285}

Owen was father of OWEN (eldest son, pre-deceased his father); THOMAS; PATRICK, b. c1721; WILLIAM; SARAH, m. Thomas Payne; ROSANAH, m. (N) Layton; prob. ANN, m. (N) Andrew..

### Second Generation

2. OWEN CONNERLY, son of Owen (1) Connerly, m. Martha [Marthew, Matthew] (N).

At August Court 1743, DO Co., Obediah Dawson was ordered to give evidence against Owen Connerly for cutting the ear of John Connerly. At

August term, 1744, it was presented that Owen Connerly, planter, of St. Mary's White Chapel Parish, assaulted John Connerly, planter on 10 June 1743. He was fined £10.{DOJR}

At DO Co. Court, June Term 1744, Richard Andrew, Jr., Owen Connerly, Jr., and William Nutter were bound to Mary Nicolls, child and orphan of John Nicolls in the sum of £44.19.0. to pay here when of age £22.9.6. {DOJR}

Owen Connerly, DO Co., d. by 21 May 1746 when the inventory of his estate was filed by Matthew [Marthew or Martha] Connerly. Signed as next of kin: Tom. Connerly, James Connerly.

The admin. account was submitted by Martha Connerly on 25 Nov 1746.

Owen was father of THOMAS; JAMES.

3. THOMAS CONNERLY, son of Owen (1) Connerly, m. Ann or Nancy (N).

Thomas Taylor in his will dated 17 Nov 1762 refers to Thomas Connerly, son of Thomas. {MWB 31:936}

On 15 Nov 1766 Thomas Connerly and his wife Nancy of DO Co., planter, conveyed to George Waters of the same co., merchant, part of a tract called *Norage*, surveyed for Thomas Ennalls for 300 a. in 1695, on w. side of the North West Fork of Nanticoke, 100 a. {DOLR 21 Old 307}

On 29 Dec 1770 John Richards, Thomas Connerly and his wife Ann, Isaac Charles and his wife Molly, and Mary Ann McKeel of DO Co., conveyed to Anthony Ross of DO Co., planter, *Black Levil* on Hopindoes Branch, on n.e. side of the Northwest Fork of Nanticoke River, 100 a. {DOLR 24 Old 334}

Thomas was father of THOMAS.

4. PATRICK CONNERLY, b. c1721, son of Owen (1) Connerly, m. Elizabeth (N).

Patrick Connerly, aged 43 years, made a deposition before a land commission of DO Co., 9 Aug 1763 - 31 March 1764. regarding the bounds of Moses Southwell's part of *Lemster*; he mentioned Nicols Layton, dec'd., who showed him Thomas Williams' bounder about 15-16 years earlier. {DOLR 19 Old 418}

Patrick Connerly, DO Co., d. by 4 July 1772 when the inventory of his estate was filed by Elizabeth Conerly. Signed as next of kin: Jeremiah Connelly, Terry Connelly. {MINV 110:302}

The admin. account was submitted by Elizabeth Connerly on 29 Nov 1773. representatives: widow (unnamed), 7 children: Terence, Saray, Jeremiah, William, Mary, Thomas, John.

On 29 Nov 1774 distribution of his estate was made by Mrs. Elizabeth Connerly to widow and 7 children (unnamed). {BFD 6:305}

Patrick was father of TERENCE (Terry); SARAY; JEREMIAH; WILLIAM; MARY; THOMAS; JOHN.

5. WILLIAM CONNERLY, son of Owen (1) Connerly, m. Mary (N).

On 16 Nov 1750 Joseph Ennalls of DO Co. conveyed to William Connerly of the same co., land bought by Ennalls from Merriday Williams on the northwest fork of Nanticoke River, 65 a. {DOLR 14 Old 496}

On 23 Dec 1751 William Connerly of DO Co., planter, and his wife Mary, conveyed to Robert Harden of DO Co., part of a tract called *Taylors Neglect*, devised to grantor by his father Owen Connerly, whereon said William Connerly formerly lived, 100 a. {DOLR 14 Old 570}

On 6 Dec 1755 William Connerly of DO Co., planter, and his wife Mary, conveyed to John McFarlin of the same co., planter, *Galloway*, on a branch of the northwest fork of Nanticoke formerly sold by Merida Williams to Col. Joseph Ennalls and supposed to contain 65 a.

William Connelly d. leaving a will dated 24 Aug 1777, proved 10 Feb 1778. To wife Mary, dwelling house and land, 35 a. and all personal estate. To sons Oen Connelly, Jesse Connelly, Rubin Connelly, after widow's decease land to be sold and money arising from sale to be divided among them equally. Owen, exec. To sons William Connelly, Allen Connelly and dau. Elinder Connelly - after widow's decease, personal estate to be divided equally among all children. Grandson John Connelly to have a heifer. Witnessed by Nathaniel Potter, John Chaffinch, James White Chaffinch. {CAW A:7}

On 14 May 1793 Jesse Connerly and his wife Elizabeth, Owen Connerly and his wife Elizabeth, and Reuben Connerly and his wife Rebecca, conveyed to John Dilling (Dillon) 35 a. called *Williams' Chance* on the Long Branch. {CAD D:300}

William was father of OWEN, m. Elizabeth (N); JESSE, m. Elizabeth (N); RUBIN, m. Rebecca Pritchett; ALLEN, b. c1738; ELINDER.

6. SARAH CONNERLY, dau. of Owen (1) Connerly, m. Thomas Payne.

On 6 Nov 1753 Thomas Payne of DO Co., planter, and his wife Sarah, conveyed to Robert Harden of the same co., planter, *Come by Chance* (or *Connerlys Chance*) containing 50 a. on a branch on w. side of the northwest fork of Nanticoke River, patented to Owen Connerly and devised by Connerly to John Payne, son of said Thomas Payne by Sarah his wife, dau. of the said Owen Connerly, dec'd., said John Payne not being of full age to convey the same. {DOLR 15 Old 55}

Sarah and Thomas were parents of JOHN PAYNE

Third Generation

7. JEREMIAH CONNERLY, son of Patrick (4) and Elizabeth Connerly, m. Mary Ann (N).

On 16 Dec 1777 Jeremiah Connerly and Mary Ann his wife, execs. of Richard Dawson dec'd.,conveyed to George Waters, *Security to Paint Point* and a Negro man slave called Sam. {1 JCH 65}

On 21 Dec 1779 Jeremiah Connelley and Maryann his wife of DO Co., planter, conveyed to James Wright of said co., 163 a., being the remaining part of a tract called *Taylors Neglect*. Elizabeth Connelley is mentioned as the mother of said Jeremiah, her right of 63 acres of said tract during her natural life being excepted. {DOLR 1 JCH 295}

8. WILLIAM CONNERLY (Connelly), b. c1760, d. 5 Dec 1813, son of Patrick (4) Connerly.

9. OWEN CONNERLY, son of William (5) Connerly, m. 1st (N), m. 2nd Elizabeth Layton. {CA Co. marr. lic. dated 25 Aug 1788}

Owen Connerly served a private in the militia of Caroline Co., 14th Battn., Capt. Joseph Richardson's Company by 13 Aug 1777. {RPCA:34}

Owen Connerly, CA Co., d. leaving a will dated 8 Nov 1789, proved 6 April 1796. To wife 1/3 of estate. Remainder of estate to be divided among the children: James Connerly, Andrew Connerly, Aaron Connerly, Peter Connerly, David Connerly, Lamsey (Tamsey?) Conncerly, Anne Connerly, Levina Connerly, Esther Connerly, Henrietta Connerly. Witnessed by William Andrew of George, James Waddell, J. V. Baker. Then came Elizabeth Connerly and Andrew Connerly and then came William Andrew of George. {CAW B:333}

Owen was father of JAMES; ANDREW; AARON; PETER; DAVID; LAMSEY (Tamsey?); ANNE; LEVINA; ESTHER; HENRIETTA.

10. JESSE CONNERLY, son of William (5) Connerly, m. Elizabeth (N).

On 25 Nov 1789 Jesse Conely and his wife Elizabeth conveyed to John Morriston 32 ½ a., parts of *Lloyd's Grove* and *Taylor's Rest*. {CAD C35}

Jesse Connelly d. leaving a will dted 2 Sep 1812, proved 9 Sep 1812. To son Jesse Connelly, testator's dwelling plantation whereon testator now lived lying on the w. side of the main road that leads from Hunting Creek to Fowling Creek and called *Painter's Ridge*; also to have that part of a tract purchased from William Potter on w. side of afsd. road. To son Caleb Connelly, the plantation that he now lives on which was purchased from Peter Willis and of Joseph Richardson and part of the land that testator purchased from the heirs of

Henry Willis, dec'd., beginning at the corner tree of Elijah Blades's land. Caleb to be exec and instructed to rent out the land for two years in order to pay off those lands left to James. To son James, that plantation whereon Newton Andrew now lives, it being the balance of the land testator purchased from the heirs of Henry Willis, not already given and to have the land purchased from William Potter, lying on the e. side of the aforementioned main road. Mentioned dau. Kitty Blades. Remainder of estate to be divided among testator's four children. Witnessed by Peter Willis, John Walker, Sally Towers. {CAW JB:211}

Jesse was father of JESSE; CALEB; JAMES; KITTY, m. (N) Blades.

11. REUBEN CONNERLY, son of William (5) Connerly, m. 1778, Rebekah Pritchett. {CA marr. lic. dated 13 Oct 1778}

Reubin Connerly served in the militia of Caroline Co. as a private, 14th Battn., Capt. Joseph Richardson's Company, by 13 Aug 1777. {RPCA:34}

12. ALLEN CONNERLY, b. c1738, son of William (5) Connerly, m. 1814, Margaret Davis. {CA marr. lic. dated 13 Oct 1778}

Allen Connerly, aged 47, made a deposition in 1785 before a CA Co. Land Commission.

Allin or Allen Connerly served as private in the Caroline Co. militia in Capt. Nehemiah Andrew's Company, 14th Battn., by 13 Aug 1777.

Unplaced

ANN CONNERLY

Ann Connerly d. by 13 Aug 1765, when the admin. account of her estate was submitted by Solomon Charles. Representatives (minors): Ann, James, Margaret. A second admin. account was submitted on 14 Oct 1765. A third admin. account was submitted on 28 Oct 1765. {MDAD 53:115, 116, 335}

Distribution of the estate was made by Solomon Charles on 28 Oct 1769 to Ann Connerly, James Connerly, Margaret Connerly, Legatees (children): Thomas, Mary. {BFD 5:136}

THOMAS CONNERLY, grandson of Owen Connerly.

On 4 March 1773 Thomas Connerly, mariner, grandson of Owen Connerly dec'd., of DO Co., conveyed to James Payne (son Daniel): part of a tract on the west side of the Northwest Fork of Nanticoke River called *Taylors Neglect*, agreeable to Owen Connerly's Will, exclusive of what was. sold to Thomas Taylor, containing 140 a. {DOLR 26 Old 287}

# THE WILLIAM COVEY FAMILY

Ref. A - Research by Jo Johnston of Willoughby, OH
Ref. B - Research by Joseph P. Moore of Greenfield, OH
*Editor's Note* : The Covey family was initially presented in Volume 11 of this series. Subsequent research and additional information submitted by Mrs. Johnston and Mr. Moore have resulted in the following revision.

1. WILLIAM COVEY, DO Co., b. c1660 in MD or MA, m. Mary (N) and d. 1713; she d. 1725. {A}

"Family tradition passed down through the generations that three brothers came from England. My line ended up in what is now known as Lee Co., VA. In my research I have found what I believe to be the three brothers often spoken about [the spelling of the surname varies as will be noted in different documents I have found]: James Couve, b. about 1615 in England, with his wife Mary, b. about 1619, and his two brothers, John, b. about 1624, and William, b. about 1625, came from England to Braintree, MA in 1639 [Old Calendar]. To date I have not found the ship and passenger list. On 26 Feb 1640 James received a grant of land for four heads, recorded in Braintree, MA. James later removed to Newport, Westerly, RI, where he lived and died 5 Sep 1712 (Sources: *Founders of Early American Families: Emigrants from Europe, 1607-1657*, by Meredith Colket, Jr. (1985); *The Pioneers of Massachusetts: A Descriptive List*, by Charles Henry Pope (1900); *Suffolk Deeds, Vol. 1 of the Probate Records*, transcribed by Elijah George). To my knowledge the various Covey researchers have not found anything about the whereabouts of John and William. Where did they go? Did they migrate to MD; if not, just where were these MD Coveys prior to their coming to MD? Many unanswered questions that hopefully time and further research will reveal." {Quoted from Ref: A}

*Commentary: Mrs. Johnston also states that the name Covey has been spelled and misspelled many ways in various records and it could be that the William and Mary Corry in SO Co. land records in the 1680s could actually be William and Mary Covey. Whether or not this is genealogically correct is subject to debate since the 1713 will of William Covey in DO Co. mentions only his son William by name, plus William's two bros. (prob. Richard and Matthew) and the rest of his children (unnamed). Be that as it may, Mrs. Johnston offers the following possibilities as to some of the other Covey children: John Corry, son of William and Mary Corry, b. 24 Sep 1686; Mary Corry, dau. of William and Mary Corry, b. 3 Jun 1688; William Currey, son of William and Mary Currie, b. 15 Jul 1688; Robert Currey, son of William and Mary Currey, b. 8 Sep 1691; James Currey, son of William and Mary Currie, b. 15 Oct 1693;*

*Richard Covey, b. c1695; and, Matthew Covey, b. c1700. Suffice it to say, additional research will be necessary before drawing any further conclusions.*

In September, 1690, DO Co., the fine against William Covey for not attending court was remitted. In November, 1690, William Covey was paid for serving the county. In March, 1692, William Covey served on a coroner's jury to inquire into the death of Joseph Shelly. {DOJR}

On 1 Jun 1697 William Covey, DO Co., acquired from Thomas Killman, DO Co., the 200 acre tract *Winfield's Trouble*. {DOLR 5 Old 94}

On 13 Sep 1712 William Covie and Mary Covie, DO Co., witnessed the will of John Willoby. {MWB 13:538}

William Cove (Covey), DO Co., d. leaving a will dated 30 Mar 1713, proved 11 Jun 1713. To wife (N), extx., plantation (N). To son William, plantation at marriage or death of wife and to give his 2 (N) bros. 2,000 lbs. of merchantable tobacco at age 21. To rest of children (N), residue equally (only the moll and great chest and couch shall never be removed from the house). {A; MWB 13:605}

On 24 Jan 1715/6 Mary Cove (Covey) filed an admin. acct. in the estate of William Cove, DO Co., dec'd., which was valued at £55.4.8. {INAC 37A:31, 38A:194}

On 1 Jun 1725 Mary Covey, DO Co., widow, conveyed all her goods and chattels to son Richard Covey. {DOLR 8 Old 86}

William was the father of: WILLIAM; RICHARD; prob. MATTHEW; poss. JOHN; poss. ELIZABETH; poss. OTHERS (N).

## Second Generation

2. WILLIAM COVEY, DO Co., son of William (1) Covey, prob. m. Mary Badley.

On 18 Sep 1750 William Covey, DO Co., witnessed a land conveyance. {DOLR 14 Old 528}

In 1761 William Covey and Mathew Covey, DO Co., appeared among many others in a long list of debts due the estate of Col. Joseph Ennalls. {MINV 76:200}

William Covey, DO Co., d. intestate by 11 Dec 1767 (date of inventory approval by admin. Zacharias Campbell). Next of kin were listed as Mary Covey and Mathew Covey. {MINV 96:13}

Richard Badley, DO Co., d. leaving a will dated 21 Oct 1771, proved 23 Jul 1773, and among those named were dau. Mary Covey (extx.) and granddau. Leah Covey. {MWB 39:553}

William was prob. the father of: LEAH; poss. OTHERS (N).

3. RICHARD COVEY, DO Co., b. c1695, son of William (1) Covey, m. 1st Elizabeth (N), m. 2nd Elizabeth (Wheeler) Soward, and d. 15 Nov 1755. {A}

On 8 Mar 1742/3 a land commission was appointed to perpetuate the land of Richard Covey, DO Co., called *Winfield's Trouble*. In November 1743, Richard Covey petitioned the court to settle the boundaries of said land. {DOLR 12 Old 166; DOJR}

Elizabeth (Wheeler) Soward, dau. of Charles Wheeler (d. 1746) and wife Sarah Worgin, m. 1st John Soward or Sowers (c1710-1748) and had 4 children: John, Sarah, Charles and Richard Sowers.

Richard Covey, DO Co., d. leaving a will dated 14 Nov 1755, proved 19 Nov 1755, naming wife Elizabeth (extx.) and children Richard, Nancy and Elizabeth. {MWB 30:6}

On 23 Mar 1756 the estate of Richard Covey, DO Co., dec'd., was appraised at £76.7.2 and approved by Elizabeth Covey (extx. of Richard Covey and also extx. of William Covey). Next of kin were listed as Elizabeth Covey and William Covey. {MINV 60:641}

On 8 Nov 1756 an admin. acct. was filed in the estate of Richard Covey, DO Co., dec'd., by extx. Elizabeth Covey. The named representatives were Elizabeth (widow and accountant) and children William (of age), Elizabeth (of age), John (of age), Mary (of age), Rachel (minor), Richard (minor), Nancy (minor), and Betsey (minor). {MDAD 40:226} On 16 May 1757 another admin. acct. listed the same representatives as those in 1756, but noted that Rachel was now of age and Betsey was referred to as Elizabeth the younger. {MDAD 41:177} It is not known if the 7 children were all of his 1st marriage; Elizabeth the younger may have been born of the 2nd marriage. {A}

Richard was the father of: WILLIAM; RICHARD; JOHN; ELIZABETH; RACHEL; NANCY; BETSEY (ELIZABETH THE YOUNGER). {A}; THOMAS. {B}

4. MATTHEW COVEY, DO Co. and CA Co., b. c1700, prob. son of William (1) Covey, m. Mary (N), poss. Mary Noble, and d. 1784. {A; B}

On 3 Mar 1752 Mathew Covey, DO Co., acquired from Edward and Barbara Billiter, a 100 acre part of the tract *Nancy's Delight* on the west side of the Northwest Fork of Nanticoke River. {DOLR 14 Old 571}

On 2 Dec 1758 Mathew Covey, DO Co., patented the 36 acre tract *Francis Hill* on the east side of the road that leads from Hunting Creek Church by Matthew Covey's place and between Matthew's land and Richard Andrew's land. {MPL BC11:223}

In 1761 Mathew Covey and William Covey, DO Co., appeared among many others in a long list of debts due the estate of Col. Joseph Ennalls. {MINV 76:200}

On 23 Jul 1764 Matthew Covey, DO Co., had a resurvey of the tract *Francis Hill* with 36 acres to be added to 64 acres of vacant land and reduced the whole into one tract now called *Battle Hill*, patented 30 Oct 1770. {A, citing Liber 31, folio 65}

On 15 Aug 1764 Mathew Covey, DO Co., planter, conveyed to John Covey, DO Co., planter, for £5, a 30 acre part of the tract *Nancy's Delight* adj. John Covey's land. {DOLR 19 Old 365}

On 30 Oct 1765 Mathew Covey, DO Co., patented the 100 acre tract *Battle Hill*. {MPL BC24:627, BC31:43}

Mathew Covey lived in the area of DO Co. situated on the road from Marshyhope Bridge to Cambridge which became part of CA Co. in 1773. {A}

Matthew, Noble, John, Francis, and William Covey took the Oath of Allegiance to the State of Maryland at Mellville Warehouse on the third Tues. in March, 1778, Great Choptank Hundred. {A, citing MSA CR44170, CA Co. Land Records, Census of 1778, p. 2}

On 17 Jun 1782 Matthew Covey, CA Co., conveyed to John Covey, for £30, the remaining part of *Nancy's Delight*. {CALR GFA:593}

Matthew, Noble, John, Francis, and William Covey appeared in the 1783 CA Co. tax list in Lower Choptank District. {A, citing MSA S1437, CA Co. Tax Assessments}

Matthew Covey, CA Co., d. leaving a will dated 29 Dec 1783, proved 25 Nov 1784. To son Noble, 1 sh. To son John, 1 sh. To son Francis, a negro called Robin and personalty. Residue of estate equally to son William (exec.), son Francis (exec.), and daus. Elizabeth Littleton, Ann Chilcod, Mary Gray, Sarah Dukes, and Rebekah Camper. Witnesses were Mary Hutton and Andrew Satterfield. Matthew Covey signed with his "X" mark. {B, CAW JRB:2}

Matthew Covey signed as next of kin on the inventory of William Noble, DO Co., in 1772 - perhaps they were brothers-in-law. Matthew's wife may have been a Noble; thus they named their son Noble.

The births of the children of Noble and Rachel are listed in the Nicholite record book. Noble's 2nd marriage is also recorded in the Nicholite book.

Matthew was the father of: NOBLE; JOHN; FRANCIS; WILLIAM; ANN, m. Thomas Chilcutt (d. 1797, CA Co.); MARY, m. (N) Gray); ELIZABETH, m. (N) Littleton); SARAH, b. 1746, m. Thomas Dukes, Jr.; REBEKAH, m. William Camper). {A; B}

5. ELIZABETH COVEY, DO Co. and TA Co., poss. dau. of William (1) Covey, m. John Higgins on 4 Jan 1727 in St. Peter's Parish, TA Co.; Elizabeth Higgins m. Alexander Winford on 19 Feb 1730; Elizabeth Winford m. Walter James on

29 Dec 1736; and, Elizabeth James m. James Plunket on 10 Feb 1743. {ESVR} Further research is needed before assuming these were marriages of the same Elizabeth. Note: John Higgins, TA Co., d. by 23 Sep 1730, when the inventory of his estate was filed by Elizabeth Higgins (relict) and Benjamin Bullock. Signed as next of kin: Elizabeth Higgins, Anna Cambel. {MINV 15:686}

Third Generation

6. RICHARD COVEY, DO Co., son of Richard (3) Covey.

On 28 Nov 1763 the real estate of Richard Covey, DO Co. (50 acres with house and buildings) was appraised at 50 lbs. of tobacco. {DOLR 19 Old 91}

On 1 Jun 1765 Richard Covey, DO Co., planter, conveyed to Joseph Byus, DO Co., planter, a 50 acre part of the tract *Windfield's Trouble* (whereon Daniel Frashure now lives) near the mouth of Great Choptank River at Brannock's Bay. {DOLR 20 Old 109}

On 11 Apr 1768 Richard Covey, DO Co., planter, acquired from Joseph Byus, DO Co., mariner, a 50 acre part of the tract *Windfield's Trouble* near the mouth of Great Choptank River at Brannock's Bay. {DOLR 22 Old 288}

On 16 Nov 1769 Richard Covey, DO Co., planter, leased to Joseph Byus, DO Co., mariner, part of *Winfield's Trouble* for 11 years and 5 months. {DOLR 23 Old 374}

On 17 Jun 1772 Richard Covey, DO Co., planter, conveyed to Joseph Byus, DO Co., mariner, a 50 acre part of *Winfield's Trouble* at the head of a creek issuing our of Great Choptank River at the mouth of Cook's Neck. {DOLR 25 Old 434}

In 1781 Richard Covey, DO Co., served as a private in the militia. {RPDO:45}

7. JOHN COVEY, DO Co., son of Richard (3) Covey.

John Covey, of Richard, DO Co., appeared among many others in a long list of desperate debts due the estate of David Murray circa 1765. {MINV 88:325}

8. NOBLE COVEY, DO Co. and CA Co., son of Matthew (4) Covey, b. c1734, was a Nicholite, m. 1st c1760, Rachel Bicham or Beauchamp (c1742-1774, dau. of Curtis and Mary Beauchamp), DO Co., m. 2nd Mary (Pegg) Beauchamp of Kent Co., DE, on 3 Apr 1775. She was the widow of Francis Beakham[4]

---

[4] Francis Beakham (Beauchamp), yeoman, d. leaving a will dated 23 March 1774, proved 23 March 1774. Heirs: wife Mary; sisters Elizabeth Pearson, Jean Ryley, Rachel Boming, Ann Baggs; heris of sister Mary Caffy. Execs. wife Mary and Vallentine Pegg. {Arch. A3:90. Reg. of Wills (Kent Co., DE) L:153}

(Beauchamp) (d. 1774) and sister of Martin and Valentine Pegg. Noble and Mary moved to Rowan Co., NC in 1784. He d. 1791; she d. 1807. {A; B; CANI}

On 27 Aug 1757 Noble Covey, DO Co., planter, acquired from Curtis Beecham, for £5, a 100 acre part of the tract *Cockiasses Field* [also *Coquesiess Fields* in 1758]. {DOLR 15 Old 517; Debt Books 1758, p. 24}

On 31 Mar 1761 Noble Covey, DO Co., patented the 25 acre tract *Noble's Lot* near the Deep Goose Pond and on the east side of a drain called Marsh Pond. {A, citing Rent Rolls 29:296; MPL BC14:237, BC15:180}

Nicholite birth records show Noble and Rachel were the parents of Ann (b. 10 Mar 1764), Rebecca (b. 10 Apr 1766), Sarah (b. 11 Jul 1771), and Rachel (b. 5 Nov 1774). Although the records do not show dau. Rhoda, she was named in her parents' wills. Noble and 2nd wife Mary had no children. One source indicated Ann and Rhoda Ann were the same person. {A; B; ESVR}

On 3 Apr 1775 Noble Covey, CA Co., m. Mary Bicham [Beauchamp] of Kent Co., DE. both Nicholites. {A; CANI}

On 6 Aug 1777 Noble Covey, CA Co., planter, acquired from Humphriss Brown, his wife Ebe Brown and his mother Elizabeth Goslen, DO Co., an 80 acre part of the tract *Addition to Hogg Quarter*. On that same day he acquired from Ambrose and Elizabeth Goslen, DO Co., a 24 acre part of the tract *Tryall* on the east side of the Northwest Fork of Nanticoke River. {DOLR 1 JCH 29-32}

On 4 Apr 1783 Noble Covey, CA Co., patented the 138 acre tract *Addition to Noble's Lot*. {MPL BC50:368}

On 24 Feb 1784 Noble Covey, CA Co., conveyed land as follows: to William Andrew, for £10, a 15 acre part of *Addition to Noble's Lott*; to John Beacham, for £75, a 50 acre part of *Addition to Noble's Lott*; to Nathaniel Fountain for £84 "gold half Joes," a 56 acre part of *Addition to Noble's Lott*; and, Noble and Mary Covey, and John and Sophia Beacham, conveyed to Nathaniel Fountain, for £311.7.6, the 174¼ acre tract *Cokiases Fields* on the southeast side of Phillypoes Creek Branch and just above Fountain's Mill Dam. {A, citing CALR GFA:711, 720, 749, 750}

On 27 Mar 1784 Noble and Mary Covey, CA Co., conveyed to Anthony Ross, CA Co., a 78½ acre part of *Addition to Hogg Quarter* and a 21½ acre part of tract *Tryall*. {DOLR 2 NH 307}

Rebecca Covey m. Levi Buckingham, Sarah Covey m. Newell Sapp, and Rhoda Covey m. Benjamin Shaw. The Coveys, Shaws, and Sapps removed to NC with the Nicholites. {A, citing "Another Look at the Nicholites," by Kenneth L. Carroll (1983), *The Southern Friend*, Vol. V, No. 2}

On 9 Aug 1787 Noble Cove (Covey) received State Grant No. 1473 for 352 acres (N) on Abbot's Creek, and on 15 Aug 1787 he acquired 160 acres (N) from Henry Davis. Noble Covey and others were also excused from attending as jurors in 1790. {A, citing Rowan Co., NC Court Minutes 11:347, 5:274, 5:282}

Noble Covey, Rowan Co., NC, d. leaving a will dated the 26th day of the 12th mo. 1790, proved Feb. Court 1791. To wife Mary, 205 acre home plantation; then to go to dau. Sarah. To dau. Rhoda Shaw and her husband Benjamin Shaw, £10. To dau. Rebecca Buckingham and her husband Levi Buckingham, £10. To dau. Sarah Sapp and her husband Newell Sapp, £10 and 350 acres bought from William David and 219 acres bought from Garrison & Caldwell. Witnesses were William Welborn and James Welborn. Noble Covey sign with his "X" mark. {A, B, citing Will Book C, n.p.}

Mary Covey, Rowan Co., NC, d. leaving a will dated the 21st day of the 6th mo., 1799, proved Feb. Court, 1807, naming the same three daus. and as her execs. her bros. Martin Pegg and Valentine Pegg. {A, citing Will Book A, n.p.}

Mary (Pegg) Beachum d. Feb 1807. In her will dated 20 Jun 1799, proved Feb 1807, she left Nowell Sapp her part of a wagon. To step dau. Sarah Sapp chest and fourth of wearing apparel. To sister Elizabeth Tharp remainder of wearing apparel. Children of her bros. and sisters to have remainder of estate. Execs.: bros. Martin Pegg and Valentine Pegg. {B}

Noble was the father of: RHODA ANN, m. Benjamin Shaw (d. 1820); REBECCA, m. Levi Buckingham; SARAH, m. Newell Sapp; RACHEL.

9. THOMAS COVEY, DO Co., prob. d. by 1756, son of Richard (3) Covey.

In 1749 Thomas Covey appeared among many others on a list of debts due the estate of Major Thomas Nevett, DO Co., dec'd. {MINV 42:145-166}

10. JOHN COVEY, DO Co. and CA Co., son of Matthew (4) Covey, m. 1st Sarah Andrew (dau. of John Andrew, Jr. and his wife Sarah) c1760 and m. 2nd Polly Covey circa 1780. {A; B. See also the John Andrew Family of Dorchester Co., this vol}

On 13 Aug 1760 John Covey, DO Co., patented the 50 acre tract *Billeter's Deceit*. {MPL BC14:468, BC17:488}

On 15 Aug 1764 John Covey, DO Co., acquired from Mathew Covey, DO Co., a 30 acre part of the tract *Nancy's Delight*. {DOLR 19 Old 365}

On 4 Jul 1768 John Covey, DO Co., acquired from Henry and Anne Hooper, DO Co., the 83 acre tract *Regulation* on Bechamp's alias Kockiakos's Branch which issues out of the south side of Great Choptank River. {DOLR 23 Old 115}

On 1 Apr 1771 John Covey, DO Co., planter, and wife Sarah, conveyed to Thomas Dukes, Jr., the 83 acre tract *Regulation*. {DOLR 25 Old 50}

On 26 May 1774 John Covey, DO Co., witnessed the will of Gideon Gamble. {MWB 39:897}

In 1776 John Covey, DO Co., Transquakin Hundred, was head of household with one white female aged between 40 and 50, one white female aged between 21 and 30, two white males aged between 21 and 30, and one white male aged under 10. {Brumbaugh's MD Records II:107}

John Covey, CA Co., served as a private in the militia in 1777 in Capt. Nehemiah Andrew's Company. {RPCA:38}

John Covey, CA Co., took the Oath of Allegiance at Mellville Warehouse, Great Choptank Hundred, on the third Tues. in March, 1778. {A; B}

On 17 Jun 1782 John Covey, CA Co., received from Matthew Covey more of the tract *Nancy's Delight* and in the 1783 assessment lists for CA Co., Lower Choptank District, he possessed tracts *Billiter's Deceit, Addition to Billiter's Deceit,* and *Nancy's Delight.* In 1784 he patented the 122 acre tract *Polly's Garden* in CA Co. {A, citing the 1783 Tax List and Land Patent Cert. No. 230}

John Covey, CA Co., d. leaving a will dated 28 Sep 1796, proved 8 Oct 1796. To wife Polly, extx. To sons John (eldest son), James, Jacob, Matthew, and Thomas Covey, and daus. Betsy Covey and Tamsey Dean (wife of Henry Dean), 1 sh. each. To son Joshua, half or moiety of my land (N) in CA Co. To son William, the other moiety or half of said land. To daus. Polly and Rebecca, and sons Peter and Francis Gardner Covey (youngest son living), my personal estate equally. Witnesses were Richard Willis, Richard Andrew, and J. Harrington. John Covey signed with his "X" mark. {A, B, citing CA Wills JRB:351-353}

The children of John Covey were, by 1st wife, John; Elizabeth or Betsy; James; Matthew; Jacob (m. Mary Camper by lic. dated 3 Jan 1793); Thomas; Andrew (m. 1st Sarah Morgan, 2nd Anna Camper, 3rd Dorothy (N) Covey, and d. 5 Mar 1845); and, Sarah. were, by 2nd wife, Polly; Rebecca (m. Thomas Wherrett by lic. dated 28 Jul 1802); Tamsey (m. Henry Dean by lic. dated 17 May 1796); Joshua; William; Peter (m. Peggy Eaton by lic. dated 29 Dec 1810); and, Francis Gardner (b. c1796, m. Elizabeth Arnett on 11 Jan 1820, TA Co., d. c1857, Union Co., OH). {A; B; Cranor's CA Co. Marr. Lic., 1774-1815}

John was the father of: JOHN: JAMES; MATTHEW; JACOB; THOMAS; ANDREW; JOSHUA; WILLIAM; PETER; FRANCIS GARDNER; ELIZABETH (BETSY); SARAH; POLLY; REBECCA; TAMSEY.

11. FRANCIS COVEY, DO Co. and CA Co., b. c1738, son of Matthew (4) Covey, m. Rebecca Hutton (dau. of George and Mary Hutton), and d. 1805 in Kent Co., DE. {A}

Francis Covey, CA Co., served as a private in the militia in 1777 in Capt. Nehemiah Andrew's Co. {RPCA:38}

In 1778 Francis Covey, CA Co., took the Oath of Allegiance at Mellville Warehouse, Great Choptank Hundred, on the third Tues. in March. {A}

In August, 1782, Francis Covey, CA Co., rendered material by supplying wheat for the use of the military. {RPCA:38}

In 1783 Francis Covey, CA Co., patented the 207 3/4 acre tract *Covey's Addition* on the DE State line. {A, citing Cert. No. 82}

In March, 1786, Francis Covey, CA Co., and wife Rebekah, conveyed to Brummel Andrew, Enoch Morgan and Samuel Collins, for £3, a 1 acre part of *Grantham*. {CALR}

In 1787 the will of Mary Hutton, CA Co., she named the children of Francis and Rebecca Covey as Margaret, Mary and John, but Hutton was not mentioned. {A, citing CA Wills JRB:98}

In 1790 Francis Covey was in Murderkill Hundred, Kent Co., DE. {1790 Census}

It was advertized in the *Republican Star* In 1805 that Peter T. Causey was admin. of the estate of Francis Covey, dec'd., of Kent Co., DE. {*Republican Star*, Easton, MD, 26 Mar 1805}

Francis was the father of: JOHN or JOHN GORDON; MARGARET; MARY; HUTTON, m. Mary (N). {A; B}

12. WILLIAM COVEY, DO Co. and CA Co., b. c1748, son of Matthew (4) Covey, m. Rebecca (N) (d. 14 Feb 1838 in Columbia, Maury Co., TN).

William Covey, DO Co., b. 1748, served as a private in the MD militia in 1781, m. Rebecca (N), moved to TN, and d. 14 Feb 1839. {RPDO:45; *DAR Patriot Index, Centennial Edition*, p. 681}

On 24 Nov 1775 William Covey, CA Co., acquired from his father Matthew Covey, the 100 acre tract *Battle Hill* (originally known as *Francis Hill*) on the road from Marshyhope Bridge to Cambridge, MD. {CALR GFA:162}

In 1778 William Covey, CA Co., took the Oath of Allegiance at Mellville Warehouse, Great Choptank Hundred, on the third Tues. in March. {A}

On 16 Jul 1781 William Covey enrolled in the Upper Battalion of militia in DO Co. pursuant to a late Act of Assembly for raising two battalions in MD. {ARMD 18:383, 402}

On 3 Aug 1781 William Covey was enlisted by Lt. Crawford for a term of 3 years in the 4th Regiment of the MD Continental Line. {ARMD 18:402}

On 30 May 1782 William Covey was paid £12 for his services by the Western Shore Treasurer of MD. {ARMD 48:178}

He remained in MD and five children were born to this union; more children were born in NC. Shortly before or after his dad died (Matthew's will 29 Dec 1783 - 25 Nov 1784) most likely after, he and Rebecca sold their land in April, 1784 (GFA 719) as did his brother Noble (four deeds on 24 February and one in March 1784). Evidently they were getting ready to leave MD as both were in NC before 1790, William in Guilford Co. and Noble in Rowan Co. He was in Guilford Co. by 20 Nov 1786 as he witnessed a deed and on 16 May 1787 he purchased 257 acres of land lying on Redyfork, the area of the Russell family. On the 17th of March 1791 he and son Noble witnessed a deed for Robert Russell. Tennessee offered land to the veterans on a first come first served basis. The veterans rushed in to claim the land and thus they were called the "Rush Soldiers." William and his family, except for two sons (one remaining in NC and another one (Noble) removing to Lee Co., VA) relocated in Maury Co., TN. He and Rebecca sold the land on Redyfork in Guilford Co., 25 Oct 1807 (Bk. 9, p. 282). In December, 1809, he was sworn as a juror for Maury Co., TN Court. In 1812 he was taxed for 244 a. at Hurrican and in 1816 taxed for 150 a., s. side of Deer Creek. He and Rebecca are buried at the Pleasant Garden Cemetery on Phiney-Murphy Road between Mooresville and Covey Hollow Road in Maury County. It is believed this cemetery is on the site of the earliest Methodist Church for which area he conveyed land. {24 Jul 1824, Bk. 16, p. 100); A}

The children of William and Rebecca Covey were as follows: William, Jr. (b. c1767, DO Co., m. 1st (N), m. 2nd Sarah Byard in Maury Co., TN, d. c1839, Maury Co., TN); Noble (b. c1768, DO Co., m. Mary Dougherty on 11 Mar 1793, Guilford Co., NC, d. 1848, Lee Co., VA); Thomas (b. c1771, DO Co.); Sarah (b. c1773, CA Co., m. Joseph John Fleming on 8 Jul 1799, Guilford Co., NC, d. c1869, Maury Co., TN); Lucaracy (b. c1774, CA Co., m. John Piper on 26 Dec 1792, Guilford Co., NC); Rebecca (b. c1775, CA Co., m. Abraham Piper on 17 Jun 1791, Orange Co., NC); Levin Lewis (b. 1776, CA Co., m. Sarah Edwards on 8 Oct 1798, Guilford Co., NC, d. 29 Sep 1842, Hardin Co., TN); Matthew George (b. c1780, CA Co.); Margaret (b. 2 Oct 1782, CA Co., m. Joseph Coe on 14 Aug 1805, Guilford Co., NC, d. 18 Feb 1858, Fayette Co., TN); Alla (b. c1783 in Guilford Co., NC, m. Avery Coe); and, Russell Ray (b. 1788, Guilford Co., NC, m. Rachel E. Davis on 21 Nov 1810, Maury Co., TN, d. c1862, Guilford Co., NC). {A; B}

William was the father of: WILLIAM, JR.; NOBLE; THOMAS; LEVIN LEWIS; MATTHEW GEORGE; RUSSELL RAY; SARAH; LUCARACY; REBECCA; MARGARET; ALLA.

13. REBEKAH COVEY, DO Co., dau. of Matthew (4) Covey, m. William Camper (who d. by 1824).

Rebekah (Covey) Camper was the mother of: JOHN CAMPER; MARY CAMPER (m. Jacob Covey). {B}

Fourth Generation

14. RHODA ANN COVEY, CA Co., b. 10 Mar 1764, dau. of Noble (8) Covey, m. Benjamin Shaw circa 1783 (prob. in DE), and d. 24 Jul 1820 in Guilford Co., NC. {B}

Benjamin Shaw was one of the largest land owners in Guilford Co., NC by 1815. He owned 1,420 a., valued at $2,840, in Deep River Township. Benjamin Shaw was b. c1760 prob. in DE, d. NC. Rhoda Ann Covey and Benjamin Shaw were parents of the following children: William Matthew (b. c1784 in DE), Sarah (b. c1786), John (b. c1784 in DE), James (b. 1786), Noble (b. 22 Apr 1787), Rhoda (b. c1789), Elizabeth "Betsy" (b. c1794), Aaron (b. c1796), and Mary (b. 31 Mar 1798). {B}

Rhoda (Covey) Shaw was the mother of: WILLIAM MATTHEW SHAW; SARAH SHAW; JOHN SHAW; JAMES SHAW; NOBLE SHAW; RHODA SHAW; ELIZABETH (BETSY) SHAW; AARON SHAW; MARY SHAW.

15. JACOB COVEY, CA Co., son of John (10) Covey, m. cousin Mary Camper (dau. of William Camper) by lic. dated 3 Jan 1793. {A}

In 1799 Jacob Covey, CA Co., purchased a 1 acre lot out of *Exeter* for £3.10, lying on the east side of the county road from Northwest Fork Bridge and near his present dwelling house, his most southerly parcel a part of *Sandy Hill*. {A, citing Horsey's *Origins of Caroline Co. from Land Plats*, Vol. 2, p. 8}

Jacob Covey, CA Co., served as an ensign in Capt. Peter Willis' Co., 19th Regt., from 15 Aug to 30 Aug 1813. {Wright's *MD Militia, War of 1812*, Vol. 1, p. 82}

Jacob Covey, CA Co., was named as a surety in the will of William Camper, Sr. on 8 Dec 1812 and his marriage to Mary Covey was implied. {A, citing CA Wills IRA:8}

William Camper, CA Co., d. by 1824 seized of tracts called *Griffith's Purchase* and *Brown's First Purchase* and among his heirs, all of legal age, was Mary, wife of Jacob Covey. {Harper's *Heirs and Legatees of Caroline County*, p. 34}

Jacob was the father of: MITCHELL; JACOB, JR.; JAMES; MARY P.; HEZEKIAH/HENRY; WILLIAM MATTHEW (m. Elizabeth Nichols, d. 1852). {A; B}

16. ANDREW COVEY, CA Co., b. c1775, son of John (10) Covey, m. 1st to Sarah "Sallie" Morgan (dau. of John Morgan) by CA Co. lic. dated 22 Jan 1800, m. 2nd to cousin Anna Camper (dau. of John Camper and Mary Dean) by lic. dated 21 Jun 1820, and m. 3rd to Dorothy "Dolly" Covey c1839. Andrew Covey d. 5 Mar 1845 and his widow Dorothy Covey m. Isaac Nichols on 29 Dec 1846. {A; B}

After the death of his 1st wife, Andrew Covey m. his cousin Anna Camper, dau. of John Camper (1785-1820) and wife Mary Dean (1787-1850). John Camper was the son of William Camper and Rebecca Covey, dau. of Matthew and Mary Covey. {A}

Andrew Covey, CA Co., served as a private in Capt. Peter Willis' Co., 19th Regt., from 15 Aug to 30 Aug 1813. Bounty land application was made by William Corkran on 19 Jun 1858 as guardian of the minor children of Andrew Covey, viz., Salley, Manda J., John and Richard Covey. Witnesses were Jacob Covey and William H. Charles, both of CA Co. The bounty land claim was rejected. {Wright's *MD Militia, War of 1812*, Vol. 1, pp. 82, 109}

Andrew Covey was the father of 4 children by his 1st wife: Rhoda (m. Thomas E. Edgell); Andrew, Jr. (b. 15 May 1810); Mary (m. Henry Camper); and, Thomas (b. 26 Apr 1814). Andrew was the father of 7 children by his 2nd wife: Peter (b. 17 Dec 1822); Uriah (b. 6 Feb 1824); Elizabeth (b. 4 Oct 1826); Enoch (b. -- Jan 1830, m. Deliah Nichols); Jacob (m. Elizabeth J. Lane); Amanda Jane (m. Benjamin Francis Cohee); Sarah Catherine (b. 25 Aug 1837, m. Lowder Hubbard). Andrew was the father of 2 children by his 3rd wife: John Henry (b. -- Mar 1841); Richard. {A; B}

Andrew was the father of: ANDREW, JR.; THOMAS; PETER; URIAH; ENOCH; JACOB; JOHN HENRY; RICHARD; RHODA; MARY; ELIZABETH; SARAH C.; AMANDA JANE.

17. WILLIAM COVEY, CA Co., b. c1792, son of John (10) Covey, m. 1st Milcah Corry and 2nd Margaret A. Bozman (1825-1910) in 1855 by Rev. Joseph H. Mann in Federalsburg, and d. near Federalsburg in 1857. (John H. Williams attended the wedding.) {1812 Bounty Land Claim}

William Covey, CA Co., served as a private in Capt. Peter Willis' Co., 19th Regt., from 15 Aug to 30 Aug 1813; born in CA Co., drafted at Denton where he was farmer; 5'10½" tall, black curly hair, blue or gray eyes, dark complexion. He applied for bounty land on 18 May 1855, aged 63; acquaintances: Newton Andrew and William Wright of Caleb, residents of CA Co. His widow applied for pension on 24 Jun 1879, aged 54, resident of Federalsburg; acquaintances: Thomas H. White, aged 81, and Elizabeth Wright, both of Smithville, stated they had known Margaret A. Covey for 50 years and 24 years respectively. Correspondence in 1880 showed that Margaret Covey was living two miles from the post office between Federalsburg, MD and Seaford, DE. She d. 1 Jul 1910 and in a letter dated 11 Jul 1910 at Federalsburg, John W. White wrote *"I am the only grant son or kin she got round here."* {Wright's *MD Militia, War of 1812*, Vol. 1, pp. 82, 109-110}

18. FRANCIS GARDNER COVEY, CA Co. and TA Co., son of John (10) Covey, m. Elizabeth Arnett on 11 Jan 1820, TA Co., and they had a son Samuel H. Covey (b. 12 Dec 1822). {B}

Francis was the father of: SAMUEL H.

19. JOSHUA COVEY, CA Co. and TA Co., prob. son of John (10) Covey.

Joshua Covey, TA Co., served as a private in the Easton Light Infantry Blues, 4th Regt., 1813-1814. {Wright's *MD Militia, War of 1812*, Vol. 1, pp. 85, 88, 92}

20. NOBLE COVEY, DO Co., b. c1768, son of William (12) Covey, m. Mary Dougherty (dau. of Charles Dougherty) on 11 Mar 1793 in Guilford Co., NC, and d. by September, 1848, at Sugar Run, Jonesville, Lee Co., VA. {A}

Noble was the father of: RANSOM (b. c1794); JANE (b. c1796, m. Joshua Muncy); WILLIAM MARMADUKE "DUKE" (b. 1800, m. Mourning Scott); ROBERT DOUGHERTY (b. 12 Jun 1804, VA, m. Jerusha Trotter on 25 Oct 1827, VA, d. 6 Sep 1884, IN); CHARLES B. (b. c1806, m. Diana Littrell on 7 Oct 1849, TN); ALFRED (b. 2 Dec 1808, m. Malinda T. Yeary on 3 Jun 1851, d. 28 Oct 1884, VA); MARY "POLLY" (b. 8 Nov 1812, m. Mark Cadle on 9 Aug 1838, TN). {A; B}

21. LEVIN LEWIS COVEY, CA Co., b. 1776, son of William (12) Covey, m. Sarah Edwards (b. 1780) on 8 Oct 1798 in Guilford Co., NC. {B}

Levin was the father of: WILLIAM (b. 1800, NC); EDWARD (b. 1805, NC); NOBLE (b. 1809, NC); ARCHIBALD (b. 1810, TN); LEVIN GREEN W. (b. 1820); SARAH; JANE; MARY; REBECCA; ELIJAH.

## Fifth Generation

22. ELIZABETH SHAW, b. c1794, dau. of Rhoda Ann (14) Covey and Benjamin Shaw, m. 7 Aug 1815 in Guilford Co., NC to Robert Nordyke (b. 18 Jul 1796, NC - d. c1846, IN), was disowned for marrying outside the Quaker church, removed to Tippecanoe Co., IN c1830, was dismissed or disowned for operating a still, removed to White Co., IN, and d. in 1862 in Seafield, IN. {B}

Elizabeth (Shaw) Nordyke was the mother of: LEVI NORDYKE; ADEN NORDYKE; ISRAEL NORDYKE; MARY ANN NORDYKE; AARON NORDYKE; NOBLE NORDYKE; BENEJAH ROBERT NORDYKE; RHODA NORDYKE; PARIS L. NORDYKE.

23. AARON SHAW, b. c1796, son of Rhoda Ann (14) Covey and Benjamin Shaw, m. 1st by 1816 in Guilford Co., NC to Phebe Nordyke (17 May 1798 - 19 Jun 1821), was disowned for marrying "out of unity" by the Quaker church, m.

2nd to Sally Morton on 3 Jul 1824 in Guilford Co., NC, removed to Indiana, and d. 9 Dec 1833 in Pike Co., IL. {B}

Aaron was the father of: (by 1st wife) MARTHA SHAW; RHODA SHAW; (by 2nd wife) EMILY SHAW; RUFFEN SHAW.

24. MITCHELL COVEY, CA Co. and DO Co., b. 1807, son of Jacob (15) Covey, m. 1st Elizabeth Sarah Stack (24 Mar 1809 - 23 Nov 1849, DO Co.) on 12 Sep 1830, m. 2nd Martha B. Neal or Harris (1821 - 1 Oct 1877), and d. 26 Aug 1877; bur. in Covey Family Cem. on Rt. 318, Federalsburg, MD. {A; B}

Mitchell was the father of: MARTHA KATHERINE; ELIZA ELLEN (1851-1916); ANGELINE (d. 1836); CELONA or SALONA (m. Christopher R. Gillingham).

25. JACOB COVEY, JR., CA Co., b. 1810, son of Jacob (15) Covey, m. Lucinda Turner (1824 - 24 Mar 1886, Linkwood, MD) on 6 Sep 1842, and d. 21 Oct 1876, Greensboro, MD. {A; B}

Jacob was the father of: ANNIE V. (1843-1930); ISABELLE F. (1847-1924).

26. MARY P. COVEY, CA Co., b. c1811, dau. of Jacob (15) Covey, m. Zachariah White (1819-1854) on 10 Dec 1834; bur. in Union Meth. Ch. Cem. in Federalsburg, MD. {A; B}

Mary (Covey) White was the mother of: MARY WHITE; JAMES POLK WHITE.

27. HEZEKIAH/HENRY COVEY, CA Co., b. c1816, son of Jacob (15) Covey, m. Elitha Eaton on 15 Nov 1843. {B}

Hezekiah/Henry was the father of: JAMES; LUTHER W.; JOSEPHINE; JOHN M.; LEWIS.

28. ANDREW COVEY, JR., CA Co., b. 15 May 1810, son of Andrew (16) Covey, m. 1st in January, 1833 to Sarah Jane White (15 May 1817 - 25 May 1864, bur. in Friendship Meth. Ch. Cem.), m. 2nd on 18 Jan 1866 to Elizabeth Dyer (b. c1820, d. 22 Jan 1899, bur. in Concord Meth. Ch. Cem.), and d. 20 Apr 1901; bur. in Friendship Meth. Ch. Cem. {A; B}

Andrew was the father of: JAMES HENRY; JOHN WESLEY (b. 31 Dec 1836); WILLIAM L. (1838-1869); ELIZA; MARY M. (1843-1862); ANN EMILY (b. 25 Apr 1845); SARAH E.; FRANCIS.

29. MARY COVEY, CA Co., b. 1813, dau. of Andrew (16) Covey, m. Henry Camper (c1791-1860), and d. 22 May 1877. {B}

Mary (Covey) Camper was the mother of: WILLIAM H. CAMPER (b. 1841).

30. THOMAS COVEY, CA Co., b. 26 Apr 1814, son of Andrew (16) Covey, m. Mary Satterfield (12 Dec 1822 - 8 Sep 1849) on 2 Jan 1843, and d. 1 Feb 1884; bur. in Covey-Satterfield Cem. in Hynson, MD. {A; B}

Thomas was the father of: SARAH M.; ANDREW THOMAS (1845-1940); JOSHUA FRANCIS.

31. PETER COVEY, CA Co., b. 17 Dec 1822, son of Andrew (16) Covey, m. Elizabeth Satterfield (21 Jun 1824 - 21 Apr 1896) on 29 Dec 1845, and d. 12 Jan 1897; bur. in Fairmount Cem. in Preston, MD. {A; B}

Peter was the father of: SPENCER; MARY ANN (b. 1849); MARTHA P. (1856-1878); JAMES PETER (b. 1867). {B}

32. URIAH COVEY, CA Co., b. 6 Feb 1824, son of Andrew (16) Covey, m. Susan Nichols (3 May 1825 - 30 Jan 1910) on 17 Feb 1846, and d. 5 Jan 1888; bur. in Nichols-Williamson Family Cem., Federalsburg, MD. {A; B}

Uriah was the father of: CAROLINE (1847-1915); SAMUEL (b. & d. 1848); SOLOMON (b. 1850); NICHOLS (b. 1853).

33. ELIZABETH COVEY, CA Co., b. 4 Oct 1826, dau. of Andrew (16) Covey, m. 21 May 1844 to Peregrine DeRochebrune Taylor (b. 25 Mar 1819, CA Co., MD or 24 Apr 1819, KE Co., DE, d. 12 Dec 1896, CA Co., MD), and d. 11 Jul 1908. {A; B}

Elizabeth (Covey) Taylor was the mother of: JOHN F. TAYLOR (1845-1847); ROBERT P. TAYLOR (b. 25 Mar 1848); ALEXINE TAYLOR (b. 1849); MARTHA TAYLOR (6 Mar 1851 - 27 Jan 1887); ANNA TAYLOR (b. 1853); EMILY TAYLOR (b. 9 Sep 1854); THOMAS TAYLOR (b. 21 Aug 1856); GEORGE MERRILL TAYLOR (b. 27 Sep 1858); ELIZABETH TAYLOR; SARAH IDA TAYLOR; WALTON P. TAYLOR (b. 1864); MARY A. TAYLOR; AMANDA B. TAYLOR (b. -- Apr 1869); C. HOWARD TAYLOR (1871-1873). {B}

34. ENOCH COVEY, CA Co., b. -- Jan 1830, son of Andrew (16) Covey, m. Deliah Nichols (26 Oct 1837, CA Co. - 24 Jan 1899, TA Co.) on 25 Aug 1846, and d. 14 Oct 1901, Baltimore City; bur. in Spring Hill Cem., CA Co., MD. {B}

Enoch was the father of: SAMUEL J. (b. 29 Jun 1857); LAURA E. (b. 1863); HENRY M. (b. 21 Jul 1866); RHODA (b. c1869); ALEXINE (1875-c1900).

35. JACOB COVEY, CA Co., b. c1832, son of Andrew (16) Covey, m. Elizabeth J. Lane on 31 Jan 1854, and d. after 1870. {B}

Jacob was the father of: ASA (b. 11 Sep 1855); MARY.

36. SARAH CATHERINE COVEY, CA Co., b. 25 Aug 1837, m. Lowder Hubbard (7 Mar 1835 - 30 Jan 1908) on 29 Nov 1855, and d. 8 Dec 1914. {B}

Sarah (Covey) Hubbard was the mother of: EMMA HUBBARD; ALBERT HUBBARD; MARY E. HUBBARD; EMMA JANE HUBBARD; ANNA ALICE HUBBARD; LEWIS O. HUBBARD; GEORGE R. HUBBARD; ALONZO F. HUBBARD; SARAH R. HUBBARD.

37. JOHN HENRY COVEY, DO Co. and CA Co., b. -- Mar 1841, DO Co., son of Andrew (16) Covey, m. 1st on 8 Mar 1860 to Eliza J. Bowdle (c1834-c1880) in CA Co., m. 2nd on 25 Dec 1882 to Martha Jane Webber (31 Mar 1864 - c1934) in CA Co., and d. 19 Jul 1893, Hurlock, DO Co., MD. {A; B}

John was the father of: (by 1st wife) SARAH F.; (by 2nd wife) DAISY PEARL; LEOLA B.; LULU ESTELLE; WILLIAM T. CARL; HATTIE VIRGINIA MAUDE.

Unplaced

CATHERINE COVIE, CA Co., received payment from the estate of John Brabron, dec'd., on 16 Jul 1740. {MDAD 18:22}

ELIZABETH COVEY, DO Co., m. William McCallister on 20 Jan 1781. This could be the William McAllister or McCallister, DO Co., b. 23 Mar 1762, who served in the MD Militia, m. Elizabeth Covey, moved to NC, m. 2nd to Henrietta Shipley in 1828, and d. 3 Oct 1842 in Bradley or McMinn Co., TN. {MD Marriages; Rev. War Pension W2239}

HENRY COVEY, DO Co., rendered material aid by supplying wheat for the use of the military on 1 Oct 1782. {RPDO:45}

HENRY COVEY, TA Co., served as a private in the militia in 1777-1778 and also took the Oath of Allegiance in 1778. {RPTA:46}

HENRY COVEY, TA Co., took the Oath of Allegiance in 1778 and served in the militia in 1780-1781. {RPTA:46}

HENRY COVEY and THOMAS COVEY, DO Co., appeared among many others in a long list of desperate debts due the estate of Daniel Killum, dec'd., in 1773. {MINV 113:50}

TOMMY COVEY, DO Co., was mentioned in the will of John LeCompte, of Philemon, DO Co., written 9 May 1768, as "a boy who lives with me." {MWB 36:561}

## THE DAGG FAMILY

1. ANDREW DAGG of unknown connection to Andrew Dagg (below).

On 11 Nov 1747 Andrew Dagg of DO Co., planter, conveyed to Matthew Driver of the same co., Gent., *End of Strife*, 50 a. on main road from Ingrams Branch to the head of Great Choptank River. {DOLR 14 Old 186}

Andrew Dagg was exec. of the estate of Edward Evans, DO Co., who d. leaving a will dated 1 April 1749, proved 1 Oct 1750. To son in law Andrew Dagg he left 40 a., being part of the tract called *Evenses Chance*, the plantation that the sd. Dagg lived on, first settled by James Clark. To grandson Evens Clark, son of James Clark and his wife Sarah, the dwelling plantation with the remaining part of the land called *Evenses Chance*, and if Andrew Dagg should die without issue, then sd. land to grandson Evens Clark. If both should die without issue sd. and to fall to grandson James Charles Craft. To grandson Evens Clark, furnishings. To dau. Elizabeth Charles Craft, 1 s. Andrew Dagg to possess the land until the boy comes of age 16. {MWB 27:386}

On 11 May 1761 Andrew Dagg of Sussex Co., PA, conveyed to Richard Dawson, son of Obadiah Dawson, 40 a. of *Evans Chance*. {DOLR 17 Old 431}

On 18 June 1774 William Willey, Sussex Co., conveyed to Jacob Coverdal, Sussex Co., 300 a., being a place first settled and improved by Andrew Dagg, 300 a., taken up by a warrant in the name of William Willey and sold to Andrew Dagg. {SUDELR M12:150}

Andrew was father of ANGUS.

2. ANGUS DAGG, son of Andrew (1) Dagg, m. 24 Nov 1774, Lydia Rodney.

Angus Dag m. 24 Nov 1774, Lydia Rodney, "after two bastards" at Wm. Rodney's. {Lewes and Coolspring Presbyterian Church, Lewes, DE}}

On 7 April 1774 Angus Dagg of Salem Co. in West New Jersey, blacksmith, son and heir at law of Andrew Dagg late of DO Co., dec'd., conveyed to Benjamin Sherman of DO Co., planter: part of a tract called *Evans's Chance* devised by the Last Will and Testament of Edward Evans deceased to the said Andrew Dagg, containing 40 a. (100 acres in the entire tract). {DOLR 27 Old 319}

Unplaced

ANDREW DAGG m. Catharine (N).

Andrew Dagg patented 74 a. in DO Co. called *Hap at a Venture* on 10 April 1715. {MPL EE6:146; RY1;419}

Andrew Dagg, DO Co., d. by 8 Aug 1715 when a list of debts was filed. On 4 Sep 1715 Catherine Dagg, admx. filed a list of payments. {INAC 36c:87, 88}

Catharine Dagg,, DO Co., d. leaving a will dated 15 June 1743, proved 4 May 1749. To dau. Christey Brown of a Black born in the Kingdom of Scotland, 1 tract or parcel of land called *Batchelor's Hope*, 122 a. lying in the co. afsd., and if she dies without issue then sd. land I give to my bro. William Lowe, if living. My friend Capt. John Eccleston, would of his utmost endeavor to make the best enquiry he can for my afsd. dau. and bro., and if they should be found then or any of their heirs are alive, then my request is that my friend, John Eccleston, would sell the sd. land and remit the effects to them or their heirs, but if after such inquiry be made, and none of the afsd. should be found, then my will is that sd. land I give to the afsd. John Eccleston. John Eccleston, exec. Witnessed by Thos. Ennalls, Tristm. Thomas, Mary Thomas, Elizabeth Ennalls. {MWB 27:287}

JOHN DAGG

In his deposition before a DO Co. land commission William Littleton, aged about 70 years, located bounds of the tract *Canawhy*, owned by Mary Moore, as at the head of a branch of Cabbin Creek, near where John Dagg formerly lived. Nehemiah Hubbert, aged about 41 years, mentioned Catherine Dagg, now dec'd. who showed him a bounded tree and told him that a particular oak was John Dagg's bounder which Col. John Rider scared him the sd. John Dagg out of and then the said John Dagg moved his survey or warrant and laid it on Ingrams Creek. {DOLR 19 Old 293}

# THE DAIL FAMILY of Dorchester County

Ref A.: Bible in possession of Herbert Hall Dail and published in Nellie Marshall, *Bible Records of Dorchester County, Maryland 1612 - 1969 and Baptismal and Marriage Records, 1855-1866 Zion United Methodist Church Cambridge, Md.* Dorchester County Historical Society, 1971.

1. WILLIAM DAIL m. 1st 11 Dec 1762, Frances Dingle. {DODO}
James Dail, son of William, b. 9 Sep 1763. {DODO}
William Dail, son of William, b. 11 March 1767. {DODO}
Moses Dail, son of William and Frances, b. 7 Nov 1768. {DODO}
Nancy, dau. of William and Frances, b. 6 Oct 1770. {DODO}
Sarah, dau. of William and Frances, b. 21 April 1775. {DODO}
Rosanna Dail, dau. of William and Frances, b. 25 April 1777. {DODO}
Elizabeth Dail, dau. of William and Frances, b. 21 Jan 1780. {DODO}

On 4 July 1772 Solomon Vickars of DO Co., planter, and Ann Vickars his mother conveyed to William Dail of. the same county, blacksmith, *Addition to Harwich*, near the head of Fishing Creek, excepting part thereof sold by John Vickers and Ann his wife, father and mother of said Solomon, to William Jones, containing 159 a. {DOLR 26 Old 91}

On 14 Nov 1774 William Ross, son of John, of DO Co., planter, and Nancy (Anne) his wife conveyed to William Dail of the same co., blacksmith: part of two tracts on the south side of Little Choptank River near the head of Sharps Creek, called *Rosses Purchase* and *Williams Chance*, containing 128 a. {DOLR 27 Old 379}

William and Frances were parents of JAMES, b. 9 Sep 1763; WILLIAM, b. 11 March 1767; MOSES, b. 7 Nov 1768; NANCY, b. 6 Oct 1770; SARAH, b. 21 April 1775; ROSANNA, b. 25 April 1777; ELIZABETH, b. 21 Jan 1780.

## Second Generation

2. JAMES DAIL, b. 9 sep 1763, d. 8 Jan 1823, son of William (1) and Frances Dail, b. 9 Sep 1763.

On 14 Nov 1785 Gustavus Scott of DO Co. conveyed to James Dail of the same co., Negro boy named Charles. {DOLR 5 NH233}

On 14 Feb 1786 James Mace of DO Co., planter, leased to James Dail of the same co., blacksmith: part of *Head Range* at the head of Fishing Creek, which was formerly in the possession of Robert Ewing, containing 2 a., {DOLR 5 NH 287}

On 3 Aug 1792 James Murray and his wife Sarah of Annapolis to James Dail of DO Co., parts of *Cornwell* and *Head Range*, at the head of

Fishing Creek, containing 74 a., agreeably to deed of 15 Aug 1753 between John Mace and Mary his wife and Jean Fishwick, dau. of William Fishwick. {DOLR 4 HD 90}

On 5 Nov 1793 Thomas Colsten of Dorchester Co., Trustee of Thomas Kallender, conveyed to James Dail of the same co., planter, part of *Tootles Venture* (lot No. 4), containing 89 ½ a. {DOLR 6 HD 139}

Died at his residence on Church Creek, DO Co., Wednesday, 8th inst., James Dail, in the 63rd year of his age. {*Easton Gazette*, 18 Jan 1823}

3. WILLIAM DAIL, b. 11 March 1767, son of William (1) and Frances Dail, m. 1785, Ann (Nancy) Barnes. {DO Co. marr. lic. dated 29 Sep 1785}

On 23 May 1786William Dail of DO Co. conveyed to his dau. Elizabeth Dail, a Negro girl slave named Henny. {DOLR 5 NH 418}

On 23 May 1786 John Stewart of Ann of DO Co. conveyed to Rosanna Dail, dau. of William Dail, a Negro girl slave named Rondah. {DOLR 5 NH 421}

On 4 Nov 1791 William Vans Murray, Attorney at Law, of DO Co., conveyed to Thomas James Pattison of the same co., planter, parts of *Hailes's Choice*, *Stokes's Priviledge*, *Stokes Adventure* and *Addition to Skinners Choice* and part of a late resurvey called *Hay-Land*, made by R. Goldsborough, conveyed to Wm. Dail and by him to said Murray exchanged for 50 a. of equal value. {DOLR 3 HD 329}

On 10 Aug 1791 Charles Goldsborough, exec. of Robert Goldsborough dec'd., conveyed to William Dail of the same co., 50 a. of *Hayland* adj. *Hails Choice*, in accordance with the Will of said dec'd. {DOLR 3HD 395}

On 6 Feb 1792 Thomas Colsten, carpenter, of DO Co., Trustee for Thomas Kallender, conveyed to William Dail, blacksmith, of the same co., part of *Tootles Venture* and part of *Busicks Range*, adj. *Outlett* and containing 94 ½ a. {DOLR 4 ED 41}

On 3 Sep 1792 William Vans Murray and Charlotte his wife of DO Co. to William Dail of the same co., part of *Murrays Settlement* on the e. side of the main road from the meeting house towards Wright's store (at the head of Fishing Creek), adj. *Addition to Harwick* and containing 51 a. {DOLR 4 HD 151}

On 23 Oct 1792 Richard Goldsborough of DO Co. conveyed to William Dail of the same co., part of a tract formerly called *Lee Grand* but now by resurvey called *Bell Field*, on the main road from Cambridge to the head of Fishing Creek, adj. *Murrays Settlement* and containing 112 a. {DOLR 4 HD 259}

On 23 Aug 1793 James Arnett and Mary Ann his wife conveyed to William Dail of DO Co.: part of *Bellfield* on the road from the Meeting House to Arthur Wheatley's, adj. Wm. Vickars' part of *Bellfield* and John Blair's part of said tract and containing 18 a. {DOLR 6 HD 78}

On 18 Nov 1793 William Dail and Nancy his wife of DO Co. conveyed to William Vans Murray of the same co., part of *Hayland*, lately conveyed to said Dail by Charles Goldsborough, exec. of Robert, near Fishing Creek and the farm of James Patison, adj. *Hailes Choice* and containing 51 a. {DOLR 6 HD 203}

On 13 Jan 1798 John Draper and Betty his wife, both of DO Co. conveyed to James Ross of the same co., 13 head of cattle and a crop of tobacco made last year on Wm. Dail's farm by the said John Draper. Witnesses: Thomas Vickars, Alexander Willson. {DOLR 12 HD 503}

On 21 May 1798 Levin Jones of DO Co. and his wife Nancy conveyed to William Dail of the same county, part of *Jones's Beginning*,, adj. *Harwick* and *Murrays Settlement* and containing 16 ½ a. {DOLR 14 HD 101}

William was father of ELIZABETH; ROSANNA; prob. THOMAS.

4. MOSES DAIL, b. 7 Nov 1768, son of William (1) Dail, m. Mary (N) (d. 25 Feb 1826).

Died in Dorchester on Tuesday night, 14th inst., Mrs. Mary Dail, consort of Moses Dail. {*Easton Gazette*, 25 Feb 1826}

## Third Generation

5. THOMAS DAIL, b. 17 July 1789, d. 5 May 1853 or 1858, prob. son of William (3) and Ann (Barnes) Dail, m. 31 Dec 1807 Elizabeth Smith (b. 9 June 1789, d. 5 March 1855). {A; Marshall's Tombstone Rcds, Vol. 1}

6. WILLIAM BARNES DAIL, b. 25 Feb 1809, d. 13 March 1879, prob. son of William (3) and Ann (Barnes) Dail, m. 1st, Catharine Bain (b. 27 Jan 1807, d. 11 April 1846), dau. of Daniel Bain. {Marshall's Tombstone Rcds, Vol. 1}

William B. Dail m. 2nd Emily A. Corkran (b. 25 Nov 1821, d. 23 May 1880), dau. of Samuel Corkran. {Emily A., relict of William B. Dail, dau. of the late Somuel Corkran, b. 25 Nov 1821, d. 23 May 1880. {Marshall's Tombstone Rcds, Vol. 1}

LEVIN A., son of Wm. B. and Catharine Bain Dail, b. 17 March 1840, d. 20 March 1899. {Marshall's Tombstone Rcds, Vol. 1}

## Fourth Generation

7. JAMES SMITH DAIL, son of Thomas (5) and Elizabeth Dail, d. 11 Sep 1813. {A}

8. JOHN W. DAIL, b. 25 Oct 1812, d. 27 March 1767, prob. son of Thomas (5) and Elizabeth Dail, m. Caroline (b. 24 Nov 1814, d. 10 March 1876) (N). {Marshall's Tombstone Rcds, Vol. 1}

<u>Unplaced</u>

BETSEY DAIL m. 20 April 1800, Levin Rawleigh. {DODO}

CHARLOTTE DIAL m. 30 Aug 1800, George Robinson. {DODO}

## THE LEVIN DENWOOD FAMILY

1. LEVIN DENWOOD, of England and Northampton-Accomack Co., VA, b. c1602, m. Mary Cutting, and d. c1664. {OSES; Mowbray I:31}

Levin Denwood was in Virginia possibly as early as 1633. {Jones:303 cites genealogical notes by Dr. Christopher Johnson}

In January, 1635/6, Northampton Co. court records indicated Leavin Denwood was about 33 years old. {*Colonial Residents of Virginia's Eastern Shore*, p. 28}

On 18 Jun 1636 Levin Denwood patented 150 acres of land on Old Plantation Creek in Accomack Co., VA for transporting William Allison, Thomas Harrison and Robert Lawson into the province. {Cavaliers & Pioneers I:43}

A certificate was issued to Levin Denwood on 23 Mar 1640 for 550 acres due him for transporting himself, his wife and others into the province {Northampton Co. Rec., Lib. I, fol. 162; Jones:303}

At Court 23 Nov 1640 Living Denwood stated that he was due 50 acres for the transportation of John Jarvas. This is to be certified by the Governor and Counsell at James City. {County Court Records of Accomack-Northampton, Virginia, 1640-45:46}

At Court 11 Jan 1640/1 Liveing Denwood was ordered "to aske George Traviler forgiveness in open Court for some scandolous wordes which he the said Denwood have raysed upon said Traveler and fined 5 shillings and court costs." {*County Court Records of Accomack-Northampton, Virginia*, 1640-45:60}

Levin Denwood was "a man of means and high social position (at one time a magistrate of Northampton Court) who was certainly most friendly to the Quakers. He most probably became a member of their 'Society' and is reported to have erected (about 1657) the first Quaker Meeting House on the 'Eastern Shore' of Maryland - a simple log structure on Nassawaddox Creek. This elder Levin Denwood, we are told, was 'a receiver of Quakers' who were imported into Northampton County, Virginia, by the celebrated Henry Vaux who, under pretense of transporting them to Patuxent in Calvert County, Maryland, would land them at Nassawaddox Creek in Virginia." {Quoted from OSES:99}

Thomas Hicks and Henry Hooper of DO Co. were bros.-in-law of Nehemiah Covington, Jr., all three having married sisters of Levin Denwood, Jr. {ASOS}

Leving Denwood was fined in Accomack Co., VA on 16 Dec 1664 for failure to provide powder and shot. On 18 Dec 1665 Thomas Summers made oath to the will of Mr. Lyving Denwood and it was recorded. {ACCO 1:107, 136; however, said will is not extant}

Jane Hartree, widow, Northampton Co., VA, d. leaving a will dated 11 Mar 1665, proved 10 Apr 1666, and mentioned several persons of no given relationship, including Mary Denwood, Sr., Elizabeth Denwood, Rebeckah Denwood, Susanna Brown, Jane Severne, Ann Tilney, Priscilla Jacobs, and others. {Marshall:75}

Levin was the father of: ARTHUR; THOMAS; LUKE; LEVIN; SUSANNA (m. Thomas Browne); MARY, m. Roger Woolford; ELIZABETH, m. Henry Hooper; REBECCA, m. Nehemiah Covington; SARAH, m. Thomas Hicks. {OSES; Jones:303-304}

## Second Generation

2. THOMAS DENWOOD, son of Levin (1) Denwood.

In 1666 Thomas Denwood and Levin Denwood recorded their cattle marks in SO Co. land records. {COES:34}

Thomas Denwood, Elizabeth Denwood, Mary Denwood, and Rebecca Denwood were transported into Maryland by 1664 The early land patents show that they were transported in 1667 or earlier. {MPL 11:229}

On 24 Jan 1669 a 250 acre tract called *Denwood's Lott* was surveyed for Thomas Denwood, SO Co., on the Chicamacomico River in DO Co.. However, "Rent Roll Record L10 F456 shows no heirs to be found and no patent taken out." {Mowbray I:31}

3. LUKE DENWOOD, son of Levin (1) Denwood.

At Accomack County Court on 18 Jan 1663/4 John Wolford of Monoakin assigned power of attorney to his friends George Watson and Luke Denwood in order to demand and receive of John Turnor all debts owed to Wolford, or in case of nonpayment, to sue. Signed 24 Nov 1663 by Roger Wolford. Witnesses by Lyving Denwood and John Yeo. {ACCO 1:62}

At Accomack County Court on 12 Mar 1663/4 it was determined that Richard Pim, servant of Luke Denwood, was 13 years old. {ACCO 1:74}

No record has been found that Luke Denwood migrated to Maryland as did his siblings; he apparently died in Virginia.

4. LEVIN DENWOOD, of Accomack Co., VA and SO Co., MD, b. c1646, son of Levin (1) Denwood, m. Priscilla (N), and d. 1726. He initially came into Maryland in 1664 and later returned to Virginia. By 1671 Leven Denwood and

Sarah Denwood (prob. his sister) were transported into Maryland from Virginia. {MPL 8:486}

In 1666 Levin Denwood and Thomas Denwood recorded their cattle marks in SO Co. land records. {COES:34}

Levin Denwood seated a large tract of land called *Hackland* on the south side of Great Monie Creek and at the headwaters thereof. {OSES:98-99}

"The young Levin Denwood seems to have spent some of his time with his brother-in-law Roger Woolford in Somerset before finally going there to reside permanently, appearing as having been transported to Maryland by Woolford in 1665 [actually by 1664], when he was about 17 years old. However, young Denwood evidently married in Accomack County, Virginia and there is a record of a son having been born there to him and his wife in November, 1670. In this same month he obtained land rights in Somerset County for having transported his wife Priscilla into the province of Maryland." {OSES:99. See this source for more description of the Denwood family; see also MPL 8:486, 16:13, 16:302}

Living Denwood, son of Living and Prissilla Denwood, born at Naswadocks in Accomack in Virginia 6 Nov 1670; Arthur Denwood, son, born at Many 25 Feb 1671/2; Betty Denwood, daughter, born at Many 7 May 1674; and, Mary Denwood, daughter, born at Many 2 May 1677. {ESVR}

Levin Denwood, son of Levin, was a member of the Somerset Grand Jury in 1671/2, overseer of highways in 1675, and pressmaster for providing provisions for the militia in Monie Hundred in 1676. {OSES}

Levin Denwood owned several slaves as evident by the following births of *"nigroes belonging to Mr. Living Denwood"* recorded in SO Co. land records: Pegg, dau. to Boobo and Tockoe, b. Sep 1684; Rose, dau. to Boobo and Tockoe, b. Aug 1686; Sarah, dau. to Gola and Nan, b. Feb 1686/7; Dominick, son to Gola and Nan, b. May 1689; Sue, dau. to Tony and Jane, b. May 1690; and, Sampson, son to Tom and Ginny, b. Jun 1690; plus, the following salves belonged to *"Livin Denwood, Senr."* as well: Moll, a negro girl, b. last Jul 1695; James, a negro boy, b. 10 Feb 1696/7; and Will, a negro boy, b. 1 Apr 1697. {ESVR}

On 7 Nov and 17 Nov 1685 Richard Acworth and wife Sarah, SO Co., conveyed the 150 acre tract *Nutters Delight* and the 210 acre tract *First Choice* to Levin Denwood. {SOLR}

On 17 Nov 1686 James Weatherly and wife Ann, SO Co., conveyed the 150 acre tract *Weatherly's Chance* to Levin Denwood. {SOLR}

On 18 Dec 1686 Levin Denwood, SO Co., merchant, patented the 300 acre tract *Denwood's Den* and on 6 Mar 1687 the 21 acre tract *Denwood's Inclusion*. {MPL 25:278, 282}

On 28 Jun 1697 John Frissell, SO Co., planter, conveyed to Levin Denwood, Sr., of same co., the 50 acre tract *Gallway* on west side of Tedious Creek, DO Co. {DOLR 5 Old 96}

On 26 Aug 1700 Levin Denwood and wife Priscilla conveyed to Thomas Dashiell the 108 acre tract *Lott's Wife* which Denwood had owned in 1685 from William Right. {SOLR}

On 7 Nov 1709 Levin Denwood, SO Co., patented the 300 acre tract *Stonridge* [i.e., *Stony Ridge*]. {MPL DD5:543, PL3:392}

In 1710 Livin Denwood, SO Co., stated in a deposition that he was about 64 years old. {MDEP:51}

On 10 Apr 1716 Levin Denwood, SO Co., patented the 1,116 acre tract *Arthur & Betty*. {MPL EE6:285, CE1:234}

On 18 Jun 1723 the SO Co. tax list for Munney [Monie] Hundred showed Levin Denwood as head of household. Listed with him was taxable Francis Graden and 14 negroes, viz., Hercules, Brissa, Joe, Samson, Ceasar, Munday, Peter, Robin, Jacob, Henny, Pallina, Merando, Penelopy, and Holiday. {COES:4}

Levin Denwood, SO Co., d. leaving a will dated 21 Apr 1725, proved 9 May 1726. To dau. Betty Gale 100 acre dwelling plantation *Hack Land* on Manny Creek, *Stony Ridge* adj., and all other lands adjacent to either of said tracts and ½ of lands on or near The Upper Straights in DO Co. To grandsons Thomas and George Denwood the other ½ of lands at The Upper Straights and plantation on Manocan where son Arthur lived, with all other lands adj. and share of Forest land not before disposed of. To sis. Sarah Hicks and sis. Rebecca Covington 1 guinea each. To dau. Betty Gale, and Elizabeth Waters, £15 to be disposed of among Friends; also 1 acre between Wiccocomico and Manny where the Quaker Meeting House stands, with the Meeting House to be kept for that purpose. To Martha and Mary (2 daus. of cous. Levin Woolford) 2 tracts between Rock Creek and the Devils Island (bought with late bro.-in-law Woolford); To Thomas Hill a tract in The Forrest bought of testator by James Hill late of afsd. county. To daus. Betty Gale and Mary Hill each 1/3 of residue of estate. To grandchildren Thomas, George, Betty and Mary Denwood, Esther King and Priscilla Gillis, and great-grandchild Levin Denwood (if he shall live to age of 18) £100 and residue of 1/3 of estate equally. Execs. dau. Betty Gale and grandson Levin Gale. {MWB 18:507}

The estate of Mr. Levin Denwood, SO Co., was appraised at £1740.3.8 on 13 Jun 1726 and approved on 29 Oct 1726 by Levin Gale. Next of kin were listed as Henry Hill and Mary Hill. {MINV 11:595}

Levin was the father of: LEVIN; ARTHUR; ELIZABETH or BETTY (m. George Gale); MARY (m. Henry Hill).

5. SUSANNA DENWOOD, dau. of Levin (1) Denwood, m. Thomas Browne, a devout Quaker and son of John Browne of Northampton Co., VA. {OSES}

John Brown and wife Ursula were transported into Virginia in 1646. In 1656 John Browne (wife Ursula) left to his son John 1000 acres in Northampton Co., VA near Dalby's Creek or Phillips' Creek. In 1662 the personal estate of John was divided between his bro. Thomas, sis. Elizabeth, and William Smith who had m. his sis. Sarah. His bro. Thomas inherited the land. In 1705 Thomas Browne (wife Susanna Denwood) left the north half to his dau. Sarah (who m. Arthur Upshur II) and the south half to his dau. Anne (who m. 1st Joseph Preeson and 2nd Andrew Hamilton). {*Cavaliers & Pioneers* I:163, 194; Whitelaw:469}

In 1671 Levin Denwood sold 600 acres in Northampton Co. to his bro.-in-law Thomas Browne who later in the year bought the title to another 100 acres. In 1705 Thomas Brown (wife Susanna) left the 600 acres "whereon I now live" to his dau. Elizabeth, wife of Thomas Preeson. The next year the Preesons gave it to their son Zorobabel and when he later died without a will it passed to his son Thomas. In 1759 Thomas Preeson left it to his wife Esther (Cable) and nine years later she m. Isaac Avery. In 1768 he Averys deeded it in trust to James Henry, they to enjoy the property as long as they lived, but if they died without issue, it was to go to Esther's sis. Sarah, the widow of William Parsons. In 1789 Avery alone deeded it to Thomas Parsons, son of Sarah and William, provided Parsons would deed back to him a fee simple title to 125 acres, which was done. {Whitelaw:441}

Susanna (Denwood) Browne was the mother of: SARAH BROWNE (m. Arthur Upshur II); ANNE BROWNE (m. 1st Joseph Preeson and 2nd Andrew Hamilton); MARY BROWNE (m. 1st Southy Littleton and 2nd Hancock Custis). {Whitelaw:441; *Of Purse and Person*:580}

6. MARY DENWOOD, dau. of Levin (1) Denwood, m. Roger Woolford on 1 Mar 1660/1. {Mowbray I:184. See also The Woolford Family in Volume 14 of this series}

"Mary Denwood's marriage to Roger Woolford who settled in SO Co. was prob. the connection that determined the removal of the Denwood family from Virginia to Maryland. The following entries from the Land Office at Annapolis throw light upon their removal: 10th July 1665, Roger Woolford enters these rights, Levin and Sarah Denwood, John Wells, Martha Robinson, and Owen Mackara (Lib. 8, fol. 486). 13th February 1667, Roger Woolford, of SO Co., proved rights for transporting Mary, Thomas, Elizabeth and Rebecca Denwood, Richard Prinum, Barbara Gilbert, Thomas Somers, and Elizabeth Gradwell (Lib. 11, fol. 229; Lib. 12, fol. 359). 17th November 1670, Liveing Denwood, of SO Co., proved his right to 50 acres for transporting his wife Priscilla (Lib. 16, fol. 13). 13th June 1671, Levin Denwood, of SO Co., proved his rights to 50 acres for transporting his son Levin out of Virginia into this province (Lib. 16, fol. 302)." {Quoted from Jones:303}

Roger Woolford was in Northampton Co., VA, [by] March 1660/1 when he married Mary Denwood, dau. of Levin Denwood of Northampton and Accomack Cos., VA, and sister of Levin Denwood of SO Co., MD. Roger Woolford came to Manokin in 1664 and settled in the north side of the Manokin River, east of Goose Creek. He was a surveyor of highways (1666), a justice of the peace (1676-1697), and a member of the Maryland Assembly (1671, 1674, 1682). He died testate by 26 Feb 1701/2. {BDML II:908; Mowbray I:184}

The children of Roger Woolford and Mary Denwood whose births were recorded in SO Co. were: Elizabeth (b. at Manokin 8 Feb 1664/5); Rosannah (b. at Manokin 1 Mar 1666/7); Roger (b. at Manokin 20 Jul 1670); Sarah (b. at Manokin 8 Mar 1672/3); Ann (b. 1675); James (b. at Manoakin 9 Sep 1677); and, Living or Levin (b. 20 Sep 1683). {ESVR; OSES}

Mary (Denwood) Woolford was the mother of: MARY WOOLFORD (m. Henry Hooper); ELIZABETH WOOLFORD (m. Thomas Ennalls); ROSANNAH WOOLFORD; ROGER WOOLFORD (m. Elizabeth Ennalls); SARAH WOOLFORD (m. Govert Loockerman); ANN WOOLFORD; JAMES WOOLFORD (m. Grace Stevens); LEVIN WOOLFORD. {Mowbray I:184. See also The Woolford Family, Volume 14 of this series.}

7. ELIZABETH DENWOOD, SO Co. and DO Co., dau. of Levin (1) Denwood, m. Henry Hooper of DO Co. on 4 Jul 1669 by Capt. William Thorne, Justice of the Peace, SO Co. {ESVR. See also The Henry Hooper Family, Volume 7 of this series}

Henry Hooper (1643-1720), son of Henry, migrated to CV Co. with his father in 1652 and they subsequently moved to DO Co. Like his father he served as a justice of DO Co. and also served as a delegate to the Maryland Assembly. He married Elizabeth Denwood, dau. of Levin Denwood, SO Co., on 4 Jul 1669 and they had three children: Richard, Mary and Elizabeth. After Elizabeth died Henry married Mary Woolford, dau. of Roger Woolford, and they had eleven children: Henry, Thomas, John, Robert, James, Anne, Mary, Rosanna, Sarah, Rebecca, and Priscilla. {Mowbray I:69}

Elizabeth (Denwood) Hooper was the mother of: RICHARD HOOPER (m. Anne Dorrington); MARY HOOPER (m. Henry Ennalls); ELIZABETH HOOPER (m. Matthew Travers).

8. REBECCA DENWOOD, dau. of Levin (1) Denwood, m. Nehemiah Covington, Jr. (d. 1713) on 15 Nov 1679 by Capt. David Browne. {ESVR; Mowbray I:27 incorrectly states they married in 1676}

Nehemiah Covington was an Indian interpreter. {ARMD 13:251}

The children of Nehemiah Covington and Rebecca Denwood were: Nehemiah (b. 8 Feb 1680 at 10 at night); Levin (18 Apr 1685-1725, of PG Co.); Elizabeth (m. Benjamin Wailes); Priscilla (m. Robert King); Sarah (m. 1st Edward Lloyd of TA Co. and 2nd James Hollyday of QA Co.). {OSES; ESVR}

Nehemiah Covington, SO Co., d. leaving a will dated 14 Feb 1710/1, proved 5 Aug 1713. To wife Rebecca (extx.) tracts *Covington's Vineyard* and *Covington's Comfort* (450 acres altogether). To son Levin (exec.), dau. Sarah Lloyd, and dau. Elizabeth Wailes, said tracts after wife's decease (should differences arise to be settled by bro. Levin Denwood, bro. Thomas Hicks, cous. George Gale, and Samuel Worthington). To son Levin 513 acre *Covington's Chance* in DO Co. To dau. Elizabeth Wailes 420 acre *Addition to Collins Adventure*. To dau. Priscilla 500 acre *Collins Adventure*. The 200 acre tract *Snow Hill* to be sold and proceeds given to Maj. Gen. Edward Lloyd for benefit of his son (testator's grandson) Philemon Lloyd, Jr. {SOWB EB9:48; MWB 13:549}

Rebecca (Denwood) Covington was the mother of: NEHEMIAH COVINGTON (III); LEVIN (LIVIN) COVINGTON; ELIZABETH COVINGTON (m. Benjamin Wailes); SARAH COVINGTON (m. 1st Edward Lloyd (Governor of MD) and 2nd James Hollyday); PRISCILLA COVINGTON (m. Robert King).

9. SARAH DENWOOD, dau. of Levin (1) Denwood, m. Thomas Hicks, DO Co., in 1679. {OSES}

By 1714 Thomas Hicks, DO Co., was an extensive land owner, having acquired approx. 5,000 acres of land in the vicinity of Vienna. He died testate in 1722 and his wife Sarah died in 1731/2. {BDML I:440; Mowbray I:65. See also The Thomas Hicks Family of Dorchester County in this volume}

Thomas Hicks, DO Co., d. leaving a will dated 24 Jul 1720, proved 6 Aug 1722. To son Levin, 453 acre tract *Hicks Lott*. To son Thomas, tract *Hicks Field* where he now lives. To son-in-law John Rider, 450 acre tract *The Reserve* and 150 acres (N) adj. To granddau. Ann (eldest dau. of son Levin), tracts *The Forrest* and *The Addition to Bartholomew's Close*. To dau. Ann Ryder, grandson John Rider, granddaus. Sarah Rider and Sarah Hicks (dau. of son Thomas), personalty. To wife Sarah (extx.), residue of personal estate and use of dwelling plantation. {MWB 17:310}

On 21 Apr 1725 Levin Denwood, SO Co., wrote his will and in it he bequeathed 1 guinea each to his sisters Sarah Hicks and Rebecca Covington. {MWB 18:507}

Sarah (Denwood) Hicks was the mother of: THOMAS HICKS, JR. (m. Elizabeth Woolford); LEVIN HICKS (m. Mary Hooper and d. 1732); DENWOOD HICKS; WILLIAM HICKS; HENRY HICKS; ANN HICKS (1684-1733, m. John Rider).

## Third Generation

10. LEVIN DENWOOD, b. 1670, son of Levin (4) Denwood, d. 1703, unm.

He may have been the Levin Denwood who purchased 200 acres in Accomack Co., VA from Francis Moore in 1691. Two years later Levin Denwood, SO Co., MD, sold the land to John Travally. {Whitelaw:1210}

Levin Denwood, SO Co., d. in 1703 (exact date not given) at which time his estate was inventoried. {Vernon L. Skinner, *Other Wills in the Prerogative Court for Somerset and Worcester Counties, 1664-1775* states "inventory unreadable" and cites Liber 3, fol. 686}

On 22 Sep 1705 the estate of Levin Denwood, Jr., SO Co., was appraised at £431.19.7 and admin. by Arthur Denwood, Henry Hill and George Gale. {INAC 25:110}

11. ARTHUR DENWOOD, son of Levin (4) Denwood, b. 1671/2, m. Esther Robins (dau. of John Robins of Northampton Co., VA), and d. 1720. {OSES}

On 18 Aug 1696 John Taylor and wife Dorothy, DO Co., conveyed to Arthur Denwood, SO Co., Gent., 1,500 acre tract *Hogg Yard* on the east side of the River Fork of Nanticoke River adj. land of Col. Lee. {DOLR 5 Old 79}

Arthur Denwood, SO Co, was owner of the following slaves: negro Frost b. 20 Jan 1703, negro Bess b. 16 Apr 1704. {ESVR}

In his will dated 5 Dec 1707, proved 28 May 1709, Major John Robins, Gent., mentioned his dau. Esther, wife of Arthur Denwood, SO Co., and he bequeathed a silver spoon to his six grandchildren: Esther, Levin, John, Prissilla, Arthur and Betty Denwood (sons and daus. of Arthur and Esther). {Marshall:184}

On 10 Oct 1708 Arthur Denwood, SO Co., patented the 40 acre tract *Unexpected*. {MPL DD5:578, PL2:342}

On 7 Mar 1714 Zebulon Pritchett and wife Rachell, DO Co., conveyed to Arthur Denwood and Betty Gale, SO Co., 25 acre part of tract *Apes Hill* on the upper side of the upper straits of Hungar River. {DOLR 6 Old 235}

On 2 Sep 1714 Arthur Denwood, SO Co., patented the 1,362 acre tract *Hog Yard*. {MPL EE6:102; CE1:149}

The estate of Mr. Arthur Denwood, SO Co., was appraised at £1222.3.0 on 19 Aug 1720 and was admin. by Esther Denwood on 6 Sep 1723. Next of kin in 1720 were listed as Esther King, John Denwood, and Betty Denwood. {MINV 7:129; MDAD 5:320}

In 1723 the SO Co. tax list for Manokin Hundred showed Mrs. Esther Denwood (widow) as head of household. Listed with her were negroes Jack, Jacob, and Toney. {COES:9}

Esther Denwood, SO Co., d. leaving a will dated -- Aug 1724, proved 21 Sep 1724. To dau. Esther King use of £40 from estate; at her decease to her 3 children Arthur, Planer, Jesse and Priscilla King. To son John personalty on condition he pay to son Thomas £50 at age 21. To grandson Levin and cous. Richard Hill and cous. Levin Gale £10 each. To dau. Priscilla Gillis £50, part thereof to be divided at her decease between her son and dau. Levin and Betty Gillis and her unborn child. To daus. Betty and Mary and son George £50 each; sons Thomas and George to be kept at school until 15 years of age; cous. Richard Hill to have tuition and charge of son Thomas, and son Thomas Gillis charge of son George; sis. Betty Gale tuition and guardianship of dau. Mary until 21 years of age or marriage; should said sis. not live so long, cous. Levin Gale to have charge of her. To sons Thomas and George, residue of estate equally. Execs. sons John Denwood and Thomas Gillis, and cous. Levin Gale. {MWB 18:334}

The estate of Esther Denwood, SO Co., was appraised at £656.19.8 on 2 Oct 1724 and approved on 15 Jul 1725 by Levin Gale and Thomas Gillis. On 28 Feb 1727 Richard Hill was named as a legatee. Next of kin in 1724 were listed as Betty Denwood and Mary Denwood. {MINV 11:73; MDAD 9:148}

Arthur was the father of: LEVIN (d. young); JOHN (b. c1699, m. Mary Elizabeth Hack (she m. 2nd John Waters), d. by 21 Apr 1725); THOMAS (b. c1710, m. 1st Mary Waters and 2nd Mary (N), d. by 26 Jan 1761); GEORGE; ARTHUR (d. young); ESTHER (m. 1st Upshur King and 2nd William Turpin); PRISCILLA (b. c1701, m. Thomas Gillis on 22 Sep 1720, d. c1743); BETTY (b. 5 Feb 1706/7, m. David Wilson, d. 27 Jun 1742); MARY (b. c1708, prob. m. a Ballard); LEVIN (b. c1714, d. young). {*Of Purse and Person*:406; *The Littleton Heritage* by Matthew M. Wise}

12. ELIZABETH (BETTY) DENWOOD, dau. of Levin (4) Denwood, b. 7 May 1674, m. Col. George Gale, and d. 1736. {OSES}

"This daughter of his [Levin Denwood], Madam Betty Gale, was a factor to be reckoned with in Somerset; a woman of splendid executive ability, concerned in large affairs in the administration of a great estate; a veritable regent in the social realm; and the mother of four gifted sons whose ability was not traceable only to their paternal ancestor." {OSES:105}

George Gale, SO Co., d. leaving a will dated 26 Jul 1712, proved 20 Aug 1712. To wife Betty, one-half of personal estate and joint exec. together with bro. Matthew Gale of Great Britain. To children (N), residue of estate, real and personal, when youngest is 18 years of age; they to be brought up by Protestants. One of the witnesses was Esther Denwood, Jr. {MWB 13:438}

In 1713 the estate of Col. George Gale, SO Co., was appraised at £3263.12.10 and approved by Levin Denwood and Arthur Denwood; also mentioned bros. John and Mathias Gale, and father John Gale. {INAC 34:131}

On 29 Jul 1715 the estate of Col. George Gale was admin. by Mrs. Betty Gale, extx. {INAC 36B:237}

On 18 Jun 1723 the SO Co. tax list for Munney [Monie] Hundred showed Betty Gale as head of household. Listed with her were taxables George Gale, Dennis Foley, and 4 negroes, viz., Jemy, Ceaser, Bess, Pheby, and Rose. {COES:4}

Betty Gale, SO Co., d. leaving a will dated 15 Apr 1727, proved 31 May 1736, To son Levin tract *Father's Care* on Wiccocomico Creek and some lands contiguous to lands of her dec'd. husband George Gale. To sons Levin, George, John and Mathias (execs.), residue of estate. {MWB 21:600}

Elizabeth (Denwood) Gale was the mother of: LEVIN GALE; GEORGE GALE; JOHN GALE; MATHIAS GALE; MILDRED GALE (d. infancy). {See The George Gale Family in Volume 8 of this series}

13. MARY DENWOOD, dau. of Levin (4) Denwood, b. 2 May 1676, m. Henry Hill, AA Co. (son of Richard Hill) on 16 Nov 1697, and d. 9 Dec 1735. Henry Hill m. 2nd to Sarah Galloway on 14 Nov 1738. {Mowbray I:67; Jones:304; Peden's *Quaker Records of Southern Maryland, 1658-1800*}

On 19 Dec 1699 Henry Hill, mariner, AA Co., acquired the 1,000 acre tract *Jordan's Point* (later called *Hill's Point*) in DO Co. {DOLR 5 Old 148}

Henry Hill, AA Co., d. leaving a will dated 10 Feb 1738, naming wife Sarah, daus. Mary Gilliss, Milcah Gale, Priscilla Dorsey, sons Joseph and Levin Hill, grandson Henry Hill (son of son Richard and wife Deborrah), granddaus. Mary Hill (dau. of son Richard) and Priscilla and Mary Hill (daus. of son Levin and wife Elizabeth), and grandson Henry Dorsey. {MWB 22:106}

Mary (Denwood) Hill was the mother of: RICHARD HILL (m. Deborah Moore in 1720/1); LEVIN HILL (m. Elizabeth Hopkins in 1722/3, d. 1748); JOSEPH HILL (b. 1705, m. Sarah Richardson in 1724, d. 1761); MARY HILL (m. a Gilliss); MILCAH HILL (m. a Gale); PRISCILLA HILL (b. 1718, m. Caleb Dorsey in 1735, d. 1782). {Peden's *Quaker Records of Southern Maryland*; Dorsey & Nimmo's *The Dorsey Family*}

14. ANN HICKS, b. 1684, dau. Thomas Hicks and Sarah (9) Denwood, m. Col. John Rider (b. 1686, son of John Rider of England and Anne Hutchins of DO Co.) on 23 Jan 1706/7 and she d. 1733. John m. 2nd to Mary (Hooper) Hicks (widow of Levin Hicks and dau. of Henry Hooper) in 1734 and he d. by 9 Apr 1740. {Mowbray I:78; BDML II:680. See The Thomas Hicks Family in this volume and also The John Rider Family in Volume 13 of this series}

Ann (Hicks) Rider was the mother of: HUTCHINS RIDER [#1] (b. & d. 1706); JOHN RIDER, JR. (III), 1708-c1733; CAPT. CHARLES RIDER (1716-1741, unm.); HUTCHINS RIDER [#2] (1718-1732); (N) TWIN SONS (b. & d. 1724); SARAH RIDER (b. 1710, m. 1st Thomas Nevitt, 2nd William Fishwick, and 3rd Robert Darnall); ANNE RIDER (1713-1756, m. 1st Major

James Billings and 2nd Govert Loockerman); DOROTHY RIDER (b. 1725, m. John Henry). {BDML II:680; DOLR 14 Old 375, 15 Old 403, 17 Old 357, 367, DOLR 23 Old 247}

15. LEVIN HICKS, son of Thomas Hicks and Sarah (9) Denwood, m. Mary Hooper, dau. of Henry Hooper, and d. 1732. She m. 2nd to John Rider, widower of Ann Hicks, her sister. {See The Thomas Hicks Family in this volume and also The John Rider Family in Volume 13 of this series}

Liven Hicks, DO Co., d. leaving a will dated 25 Feb 1731/2, prove 16 Mar 1731/2. To eldest son Liven, part of dwelling plantation *Hinchman's Neck* adj. land of John Rider. To son Henry, residue of afsd. tract and *Crooked Ridge*. To son John, lands on Chickacone River. To youngest son Denwood, tract (N) by Chiconocomoco Upper Bridge and tract (N) at Marshahope. To dau. Ann Travers, 20 sh. To wife (N) and 6 children Liven, John, Henry, Denwood, Mary and Sarah, personal estate equally. Execs.: wife (N) and son Liven. {MWB 20:331}

Mary (Hicks) Rider, DO Co., d. leaving a will dated 18 Nov 1755, proved 6 Jan 1757, naming son Levin Hicks, son Denwood Hicks, son Henry Hicks (exec.), dau. Ann Travers (wife of Henry), Mary Parker (wife of Richard), and dau. Sarah Hicks. {MWB 30:228}

Levin was the father of: LEVIN; JOHN; HENRY; DENWOOD; ANN (m. Henry Travers); MARY (m. Richard Parker); SARAH.

16. THOMAS HICKS, JR., b. c1688, son of Thomas Hicks and Sarah (9) Denwood, m. Elizabeth Woolford (b. 29 Feb 1691/2, dau. of Roger Woolford and Elizabeth Ennalls). {Mowbray I:66, 184. See The Thomas Hicks Family in this volume. See also The Woolford Family in Volume 14 of this series}

Thomas Hicks, Great Choptank Parish, DO Co., was a captain by 1729 (aged about 42 in 1729 and aged about 47 in 1735). {MDEP:91}

In a deposition taken in 1757 Thomas Hicks, DO Co., stated he was about 69 years old. {DOLR 15 Old 522}

On 18 Feb 1760 Thomas Hicks, DO Co., Gent., conveyed 82 acre part of *Partnership* to his son Thomas Hicks, Jr. {DOLR 17 Old 57}

On 26 Dec 1760 Thomas Hicks, DO Co., conveyed livestock and other personal property to his son John Hicks of said co. {DOLR 17 Old 234}

John Hicks, DO Co., d. leaving a will dated 9 Feb 1765, proved 4 Mar 1765, naming wife Sarah, sons William, John and Thomas, and father Thomas Hicks; also mentioned tracts *Hicks Fields* and *Darby*. {MWB 33:78}

In a deposition taken in 1767, regarding the tract *Maiden's Forest*, Hooper Hodson, DO Co., stated "three or four years ago being on the said land in company with Capt. Thomas Hicks, then of said county, aged 77 years as he himself said, but now deceased." {DOLR 21 Old 382}

Thomas was the father of: THOMAS HICKS, JR. (III); JOHN HICKS (d. 1765).

Fourth Generation

17. JOHN DENWOOD, son of Arthur (11) Denwood, b. c1699, m. Mary Elizabeth Hack (who m. 2nd John Waters), and d. 1725.

In 1723 the SO Co. tax list for Manokin Hundred showed John Denwood as head of household (living next to Mrs. Esther Denwood, widow). Listed with him were negroes Will, Harry, and Sue. {COES:9}

John Denwood, SO Co., d. intestate by 12 May 1725 at which time his estate was appraised at £234.12.8 and approved on 7 Jul 1725 by admx. Mary Elisabeth Denwood. Next of kin were listed as Betty Gale and Levin Gale. {MINV 11:60}

On 18 Mar 1737 the estate of John Denwood was admin. by Mary Elisabeth Waters, wife of Mr. John Waters, with payments made to Levin Denwood left by his grandmother and in the hands of John Denwood (among many others who were paid and also with distribution made to Levin Denwood). {MDAD 16:110}

On 16 Jan 1747 Levin Denwood, son of John Denwood, son of Arthur Denwood, of DO Co., conveyed 40 acre tract *Unexpected* to David Wilson. {SOLR}

John Waters, SO Co., d. leaving a will dated 27 Mar 1760, proved 28 Apr 1761, and, among others, he bequeathed slaves to his wife Mary Elizabeth Waters and John Denwood, son of Levin Denwood; also mentioned his right to land called *Hogg Land* in DO Co. on the Northwest Fork of Nanticoke River. {MWB 31:295}

John was the father of: LEVIN.

18. DR. THOMAS DENWOOD, son of Arthur (11) Denwood, b. c1710, m. 1st Mary Waters (dau. of John Waters and Mary Maddox) who d. circa 1752. Thomas m. 2nd Mary (N) and d. 1760. Mary Denwood later m. Hon. William Winder (1714/5-1792). {RPSO}

On 16 Sep 1740 he and bro. George divided the lands of their grandfather Levin Denwood, and Thomas sold his land to George.

William Caldwell, SO Co., merchant, d. leaving a will dated 31 Jul 1742, proved 14 Aug 1742, and directed his exec. John Elzey to pay the bill due to Dr. Denwood. {MWB 8:181}

On 6 Aug 1742 Thomas Denwood, SO Co., Gent., conveyed to Levin Gale of the same co., Gent., 279 acre part of *Arthur and Betty* near Bishops Head, the entire lot having been patented to Levin Denwood, late of SO Co., dec'd., for 1,108 acres of which one-half was devised by said Levin Denwood to his grandsons Thomas and George Denwood. {DOLR 10 Old 280}

In 1746 Thomas Denwood patented 410 acre tract *Brownstone*. {SOLR}

On 12 Nov 1750 Thomas Denwood witnessed the will of David Wilson, SO Co., who had named one of his sons Denwood Wilson. {MWB 27:441-445}

The estate of Dr. Thomas Denwood, SO Co., was appraised at £810.16.6 on 26 Jan 1761 and approved on 13 Sep 1763 by Mary Denwood, admx. Next of kin were listed as Mary Ballard and Esther Turpin. {MINV 81:198}

On 23 Sep 1765 a distribution of the estate of Dr. Thomas Denwood was made by Mrs. Mary Denwood (admx.) to "representatives unknown to this office." {BFD 4:142}

On 31 Oct 1765 the estate of Dr. Thomas Denwood was again admin. by Mary Denwood (widow) and payments were made to numerous people. {MDAD 53:273A}

On 23 Feb 1770 a Chancery Court Bill of Complaint filed by Thomas Gantt Denwood stated that Thomas Denwood, late of SO Co., was the father of the complainant and was indebted to Ephraim Wilson as exec. of David Wilson, dec'd. Thomas Denwood died intestate in March 1760, leaving Thomas Gantt Denwood, his eldest son an infant, and Mary his widow. Said Mary intermarried with William Winder of SO Co. {Hooper:124 cites MSA Vol. 13, p. 343}

On 20 Jul 1772 John Denwood, SO Co., Gent., stated he was aged about 24 and that he was a son of Thomas Denwood. {MCHR 13:359}

On 20 Jul 1772 John McGrath, SO Co., planter, stated he was aged about 43 and that John Jones married Priscilla Denwood. {MCHR 13:360}

On 17 Aug 1772 Mary Ann Woolford, SO Co., widow, stated she was about 25 and that one of the children of Thomas and Mary Denwood was Betsey Denwood who left her mother and went over the bay. This deponent has not received her distributive share. {MCHR 13: 368}

On 17 Aug 1772 Mary Winder, SO Co., spinster, aged about 48, and Denwood Wilson, SO Co., planter, aged about 32, were deposed in the above case (no details given). {Hooper:125 cites MSA Vol. 13, pp. 375-376}

On 25 May 1781 William Winder and wife Mary stated that Thomas Denwood died intestate leaving 8 children, 5 of which were infants. Thomas Denwood, the son, was of full age in 1759. One of the children was Priscilla Denwood, now Jones. {MCHR 13:345}

The above Chancery Court case of Thomas Gantt Denwood, SO Co., mariner vs. Thomas Denwood's adms., Ephraim Wilson, James Wilson and William Winder, continued on with many depositions taken in 1772 and 1781. No final disposition of the case was indicated. In the Records of SO Co., admin. papers list representatives of Thomas Denwood-Mary Denwood, Thomas Sloss and Charles Woolford bound unto Thomas Denwood, Priscilla Jones, Elizabeth Denwood, John Denwood, Leah Denwood, Mary Denwood, Mary Ann Woolford, and Levin Denwood, representatives of Thomas Denwood, dec'd., {MCHR 13:388}

Mary Winder, relict of Capt. William Winder, SO Co., d. leaving a will dated 19 Feb 1798, proved 11 Jan 1799, naming son Levin Denwood and his 3 children (N); grandson Peregrine Leatherbury (son of John and Leah Leatherbury); granddaus. Mary Ann Jones, Mary Ann Denwood, Rigby Jones, and Milcah Jones (daus. of John and Mary Ann Jones); grandson Benjamin Jones (son of John and Mary Ann Jones); and, 5 children (N) of dau. Mary Jones, dec'd. Execs.: John Holland, Esq. and son-in-law John Leatherbury. {SOWB EB1:701-703}

Thomas was the father of: THOMAS GANTT; JOHN; LEVIN; ELIZABETH (BETSEY); MARY ANN (m. Charles Woolford); PRISCILLA (m. John Jones); LEAH (m. John Leatherbury); MARY aka MARY ANN (m. John Jones).

19. GEORGE DENWOOD, son of Arthur (11) Denwood, m. Mary Lindow, dau. of James Lindow.

On 16 Sep 1740 George Denwood and Thomas Denwood divided the lands of grandfather Levin Denwood. On 16 Sep 1741 George Denwood conveyed 420½ acres of tracts *Nutters Delight, Brownstone, Weatherly's Chance, First Choice* and *Denwood's Inclusion* to David Wilson. {SOLR}

On 18 Sep 1741 George Denwood, SO Co., joyner, conveyed to Levin Gale of the same place, Gent., 279 acre part of *Arthur and Betty* in DO Co., at a place called *Bishops Head*, devised to said George Denwood by Levin Denwood, late of SO Co., dec'd. {DOLR 10 Old 240}

Margaret Lindow, SO Co., d. leaving a will dated 11 Nov 1742, proved 17 Nov 1742, and mentioned dau. Mary Denwood, wife of George Denwood, among other daus. Mary Denwood and Elizabeth Wilson were listed as next of kin in 1744. {MWB 23:36; MINV 29:192}

On 6 Dec 1742 George Denwood, of Kent Co., DE, and wife Mary Denwood, dau. of James Lindow, sold 350 acre part of *Piney Point* to John Dennis. {WOLR:478}

On 19 Jan 1746 the estate of Margaret Lindow, SO Co., was admin. by Samuel Willson, acting exec. The named legatees were Elisabeth Wilson Lindow, Mary Smith, and Mary Denwood, wife of George Denwood per Thomas Chaice & Mary McDaniel allowed by Daniel Dulany, Esq. per Henry Ballard for use of William Cumming. Distribution was also made to 3 youngest children (N). {MDAD 23:136}

George Denwood and Margaret Gale were listed as next of kin when the estate of Capt. Matthias Gale, SO Co., was appraised on 24 Mar 1748 and also when the estate of Levin Gale, Esq., was appraised on 15 Feb 1749. {MINV 45:215-217}

Rebecca Lindow, SO Co., d. leaving a will dated 26 Dec 1753, proved 21 Aug 1755, and mentioned bro.-in-law Thomas Denwood and wife Mary (who also witnessed the will), and 3 children (N) of sis. Mary Denwood, wife of George Denwood. Codicil dated 29 Dec 1755, Pocomoke River, WO Co., bro.-in-law Arnold Elzey exec. {MWB 30:18}

George was the father of: MATHEW; NEWTON; ARTHUR; ELIZABETH. {*The Littleton Heritage*, by Matthew M. Wise, cites Leslie P. Dryden in naming children as "?Arthur and Elizabeth"}

20. PRISCILLA DENWOOD, dau. of Arthur (11) Denwood, m. Thomas Gillis (or Gilliss) on 22 Sep 1720, Stepney Parish, WI Co. {ESVR}

Priscilla (Denwood) Gillis was the mother of: LEAH GILLIS (b. 1 Apr 1726); BETTY GILLIS (b. 25 Dec 1727); THOMAS GILLIS (b. 14 Nov 1729); MARY GILLIS (b. 20 Jul 1731); PRISSEE GILLIS (b. 16 Mar 1732/3); SARAH GILLIS (b. 26 Jan 1734/5); NELLY GILLIS (b. 7 Oct 1736). {See The Thomas Gilliss Family in Volume 12 of this series}

21. ESTHER DENWOOD, dau. of Arthur (11) Denwood, m. 1st Upshur King and 2nd William Turpin. {*Of Purse and Person*:406}

Upshur King, SO Co., d. leaving a will dated 3 Jan 1727/8, proved 26 Jun 1728, naming eldest son Arthur, son Zerebel, son Planner, son Jesse, and wife (N) extx. {MWB 19:458}

Esther (Denwood) King was the mother of: ARTHUR KING; ZEREBEL (ZEROBABLE) KING; PLANNER KING (d. 1738); JESSE KING; PRISCILLA KING. {MWB 19:458, 20:921, 22:6. See also The William Turpin Family in Volume 8 of this series and The King Family, Vol. 17 of this series.}

22. COL. GEORGE GALE, SO Co., son of George Gale and Betty (12) Denwood, m. Elizabeth (N) by 1736, and d. in 1772. {BDML I:335}

George Gale, SO Co., d. leaving a will dated 11 Jan 1768, proved 11 Jan 1772, naming nephews Levin Gale (son of John) and Henry Gale, and Margaret Denwood, Levin Gale the elder, Leah Gale (wife of Levin), Mary Willson (wife of Samuel), Cornelia Forman (wife of Joseph), Milcah Gale, George Gale, Elizabeth Gale and Leah Gale, children of deceased nephew George Gale. {MWB 38:614}

George and Elizabeth Gale had no surviving children. {See The George Gale Family in Volume 8 of this series}

23. LEVIN HILL, AA Co. and DO Co., son of Henry Hill and Mary (13) Denwood, m. Elizabeth Hopkins (b. 16th day of 1st mo. 1703/4, dau. of Gerrard and Margaret Hopkins) at West River MM in AA Co. on 10th day of 11th mo. January, 1722/3. Elizabeth Hill d. 27th day of 2nd mo., 1772, age 69, AA Co. {Peden's *Quaker Records of Southern Maryland, 1658-1800*, pp. 4, 26}

Levin Hill, DO Co., Gent., d. leaving a will dated 13 Nov 1748, proved 5 Dec 1748. To wife Elizabeth my lands in westward of a tract of land called *Chink* now in possession of bro. Joseph Hill in AA Co. near the mouth of Severn River. My lands eastward of tract called *Chink* I order to be sold by bro. Joseph Hill as I have ordered in a letter to him [dated 13 Nov 1748 and indicating he was "very weak with pluracy"]. To wife Elizabeth my whole estate and to be my extx. with my bro. Joseph to be an assistant. {MWB 27:51}

On 13 Nov 1752 Elizabeth Hill, DO Co., widow and extx. of Levin Hill, late of DO Co., dec'd., sold slaves to Joseph Hill, AA Co., in order to enable her to pay a judgment rendered in the Provincial Court for Thomas Lancaster against the said Levin Hill in his lifetime. {DOLR 14 Old 651}

## Fifth Generation

24. LEVIN DENWOOD, SO Co. and DO Co., son of John (17) Denwood, b. c1722, m. Isabell Stringer by 1744 (dau. of Jacob and Elishe Stringer). They separated by March 1753 and he d. by Dec 1757. Isabell Denwood m. 2nd Ezekiel Selby on 17 Dec 1758. {MD Marriages; *Maryland Gazette*; *The Littleton Heritage*:277}

Elishe Nottingham, Northampton Co., VA, widow [of Jacob Stringer and Robert Nottingham], d. leaving a will dated 15 Mar 1744/5, proved 9 Apr 1745, and mentioned daus. Mary Marshall, Elizabeth Harmanson, Elishe Bell, and Isbell Denwood. {Marshall:316}

On 16 Jan 1747 Levin Denwood, son of John Denwood, son of Arthur Denwood, of DO Co., conveyed 40 acre tract *Unexpected* to David Wilson. {SOLR}

On 29 Apr 1749 Levin Denwood witnessed the will of Charles Hodson, DO Co. {MWB 27:54}

On 13 Feb 1752 Levin Denwood, DO Co., Gent., granted power of attorney to Capt. Henry Hooper and Isabel Denwood, wife of said Levin Denwood. Signed by said Denwood in the Colony of Virginia. {DOLR 14 Old 615}

In the *Maryland Gazette*, 20 Aug 1752, the following notice appeared: "Levin Denwood has land for sale in Dorchester County on the North West Branch of Nanticoke River." {Karen Green, *The Maryland Gazette, 1727-1761*, p. 109}

On 13 Oct 1752 Levin Denwood, DO Co., Gent., conveyed to John Waters, Sr., SO Co., planter, a 1,000 acre part of tract *Hogyard* on the north side of the Northwest Fork of Nanticoke River, formerly surveyed for and granted to

Arthur Denwood, late of SO Co., grandfather of said Levin Denwood, adj. Lee's land and now called by the name of *Salem*. {DOLR 14 Old 631}

In the *Maryland Gazette*, 29 Mar 1753, the following notice appeared: "Levin Denwood, of Dorchester County, says that his wife, Isabel Denwood, has left him for another man. He will no longer honor her debts." {Karen Green, *The Maryland Gazette, 1727-1761*, p. 117}

Levin Denwood, SO Co., d. leaving a will dated 20 Feb 1757, proved 27 Dec 1757, leaving stepchildren John and Betty Denwood, children of my wife, and bros. George, John and Spencer Waters, tracts of land (N) in DO Co. on Nanticoke River. {MWB 30:486}

The estate of Levin Denwood, SO Co., was appraised at £66.4.0 on 19 Apr 1758 and approved on 14 Jul 1758 by Spencer Waters. Next of kin were listed as John Waters, Jr. and William Waters.

Levin was the father of: JOHN; BETTY.

25. JOHN DENWOOD, son of Thomas (18) Denwood.

The Sessional Record of Manokin Presbyterian Church, SO Co., 1747-1750, registered John Denwood as a pewholder. {COES:85}

On 22 Jul 1776 the Council of Maryland ordered the Treasurer to pay £300 to John Denwood for the use of the Committee of Observation in SO Co. He also may have been the John Denwood who took the Oath of Allegiance in 1778. {RPSO}

26. THOMAS GANTT DENWOOD, mariner, son of Thomas (18) Denwood.

On 1 May 1772 Thomas G. Denwood witnessed the will of Charles Woolford, SO Co. {MWB 38:684}

Thomas Gantt Denwood was a mariner by 1775. {*The Littleton Heritage*:276}

On 19 May 1781 the Chancery Court case of Thomas Gantt Denwood, SO Co., mariner vs. Thomas Denwood's adms., Ephraim Wilson, James Wilson and William Winder, was tried. The Bill of Complaint dated 23 Feb 1770 stated that Thomas Denwood, late of SO Co., was the father of the complainant and was indebted to Ephraim Wilson as exec. of David Wilson, dec'd. Thomas Denwood died intestate in March 1760, leaving Thomas Gantt Denwood, his eldest son an infant, and Mary his widow. The said Mary Denwood intermarried with William Winder of SO Co.{MCHR 13,:343}

On 25 May 1781 William Winder and wife Mary stated that Thomas Denwood died intestate leaving 8 children, 5 of which were infants. Thomas Denwood, the son, was of full age in 1759. One of the children was Priscilla Denwood, now Jones. {Hooper:125 cites MSA Vol. 13, p. 345}

27. LEVIN DENWOOD, prob. son of Thomas (18) Denwood, was a doctor who served as surgeon to the 7th Maryland Line in 1780. {Peden's *Maryland Public Service Records, 1775-1783*, p. 83}

28. MARY ANN DENWOOD, dau. of Thomas (18) Denwood, m. Charles Woolford.

Charles Woolford, SO Co., d. leaving a will dated 1 May 1772, proved 21 Jul 1772, naming wife Mary Ann and sons Thomas, John, Tubman, and William Pitt Woolford. Witnesses: Thomas G. Denwood, James Wilson, John Winder. {SOWB EB4:183}

Mary Ann Woolford pre-deceased her mother Mary Denwood Winder who d. testate in 1799 and mentioned Mary Ann (dec'd.) and Mary Ann's 5 children (N) in her will. {SOWB EB1:701-703}

Mary Ann (Denwood) Woolford was the mother of: THOMAS WOOLFORD; JOHN WOOLFORD; TUBMAN WOOLFORD; WILLIAM PITT WOOLFORD; (N) WOOLFORD.

29. ARTHUR DENWOOD, prob. son of George (19) Denwood.

Arthur Denwood, SO Co., took the Oath of Allegiance in 1778 and served as a private in the Somerset Militia, Salisbury Bttn., Capt. Henry Gale's Quantico Co., 1778/1780. {RPSO:81}

## Sixth Generation

30. JOHN DENWOOD, prob. son of Levin (23) Denwood.

John Denwood served as a first lieutenant in the Somerset Militia, Princess Anne Bttn., Capt. John Jones' Princess Anne Co., from 22 Sep 1777 to at least 24 Jul 1780. {RPSO}

On 21 May 1782 John Denwood, SO Co., received a receipt from the Purchasing Agent for furnishing pork for the use of the state. {Peden's *Maryland Public Service Records*, p. 83}

He may have been the John Denwood who was High Sheriff of SO Co. in 1787. {SOLR}

## Unplaced

(N) DENWOOD, m. Mary Rigby, dau. of Lewis Rigby.

In 1716 a 300 acre tract was surveyed in SO Co. for Levin Denwood who then conveyed the said tract (called *Elzey's Care*) to Frances and Elizabeth Elzey. Frances Elzey married Francis Crowder and Elizabeth Elzey married Lewis Rigby. They later assigned the said tract to Col. Levin Gale, Judge of the Land Office, in 1734. {MPL EI3:308}

On 29 Oct 1744 Mary Rigby (alias Mary Denwood), Elizabeth Rigby (widow), and John Rigby (admin.) received equal payments (one-third each) from the estate of Lewis Rigby, SO Co., dec'd. {MDAD 21:78}

WILSON DENWOOD, SO Co., m. Margaret Skirvin on 31 Aug 1758. {MD Marriages}

## THE DORSEY FAMILY of Dorchester County

1. WILLIAM DORSEY m. Mary (N).

On 4 Jan 1679 William Jump of TA Co., carpenter, conveyed to William Dossey of DO Co., planter, *End of Controversie* on Little Choptank River and Fishing Creek near *Teverton*, 200 a. {DOLR 4 Old 12}

On 7 Aug 1689 William Dossey of DO Co., planter, and his wife Mary, conveyed to Thomas Ennalls, mariner of DO Co., *Dossey's Choice* on Chicanocomoco River adj. *Causes Lott* and land formerly laid out for Thomas Smithson, Bartholomew Ennalls and William Dolsbury, and the land of Adam Moxson. {DOLR 1 Old 104}

It was presented at DO Co Court, September Term 1691, that William Dossey of Fishing Creeke Hundred and his wife Mary, on or about 21 Dec 1691, assaulted Elizabeth Nowland [and apparently place her] in to the woods in an obscure place where she died from lack of food and raiment and other sustenance. The jury found ignoramus. {DOJR}

On 4 June 1700 William Dossey of DO Co., planter, conveyed to Joshua Kennerly of the same co., land on the s.w. side of Teverton Creek, 17 a., being part of *End of Controversy*. {DOLR 5 Old 164}

William Dossey, DO Co., d. leaving a will dated 29 Nov 1703, proved 4 Dec 1703. to sons William and John, execs., all lands equally. In event of either son dying without issue, survivor to inherit deceased's portion. Both sons dying without issue, estate to pass to daus. named below. To sons afsd. and daus., viz., Isabell, Dorothy and Mary, personalty. Witnessed by Wm. Campbell, Thos. Brannock, Thos. Park. {MWB 3:7}

The admin. account of the estate was submitted by William Dossey on 24 July 1707. {INAC 27:181}

William was father of WILLIAM; JOHN; ISABELL; DOROTHY; MARY.

Second Generation

2. WILLIAM DORSEY, son of William (1), m. Elizabeth Wright (b. 1692), dau. of Edward Wright. {See The Wright Family, Volume 11 of this series.} Elizabeth m. 1st William Dorsey, m. 2nd William Mills, m. 3rd James Jarrard.

On 14 March 1712 William Dossey of DO Co., planter, conveyed to his bro. John Dossey, ½ of a tract formerly belonging to Wm. Dossey, dec'd., father of said Wm. and John, on Fishing Creek at the head of *Teverton*, called *End of Controversy*. {DOLR 6 Old 203}

On 11 June 1713 William Dossey and John Dossey of DO Co., planters, conveyed to Joshua Kenerly of the same co., Gent., the southernmost part of a tract of land called *The End of Controversy* lying on the s. side of Teverton Creek, 83 a. Elizabeth was mentioned as wife of Wm. Dossey. {DOLR 6 Old 208} William Dossey, planter, DO Co., d. leaving a will dated 25 April 1714, proved 18 Dec 1714. To son William, residue of *The end of Controversy*. To son John, 50 a., *Olive Branch*. To son Edward, personalty and tract afsd. devised to son William, should he die without issue. To wife, extx., residue of estate. Witnessed by Joshua Kennerly, Thos. (Viegers) Vickers, Waller Campbell, John Vinson. {MWB 14:57}

The inventory of the estate was filed on 30 Dec 1714. {INAC 36B:210}

William Mills, Jr., DO Co., d. by 8 Feb 1724 when the admin. account of his estate was filed by James Jarrard and his wife Elizabeth. {MDAD 6:272}

James Jarrard, DO Co., d. leaving a will dated 10 Nov 1734, proved 27 Jan 1734. To son James, *Hardhip*. To dau. Betty, *Jerrard's Desire*. To son Thomas, *Thomas His Chance*. Wife Elizabeth, extx., and after her decease if children are not of age, bro. Mathew to act; sons to be of age at 18. Witnessed by Andrew Taylor, William Grantham, Sarah Grantham, Mary Meddise. {MWB 21:287} On 30 Jan 1735 the admin. account of his estate was submitted by Elizabeth Jarrard, extx. {MDAD 14:138} A second admin. account was submitted by Elizabeth Jarrard on 22 Oct 1737. Payees included Walter Campbell, William Mills and Goovert Mills and Right Mills (children of William Mills (dead, accountant's former husband)), Richard Bennett, Esq., and Mr. Samuel Hyde, Daniel Dulany, Esq. {MDAD 14:453} The admin. account was submitted by Elizabeth Jarrart on 10 June 1736.

Edward Wright d. by 10 Nov 1737. The admin. account mentioned dau. Elizabeth Jarrard. {See The Wright Family, Volume 11 of this series.}

On 30 Oct 1757 Elizabeth Jarret, age 65, made a oath that Andrew Telfer (his will dated 17 Sep 1754) desired that Edward Dossey should have his horse, bridle and saddle. {MWB 30:392}

Elizabeth Jarrard, DO Co., d. leaving a will dated 4 Oct 1759, proved 9 Feb 1760. Children: James Jarrard, John Dorsey, Edward Dorsey, Wm. Mills,

Wright Mills, Betty Williams. Grandchildren: Levin Dorsey, Frederick, Susannah, Kezziah and Amelia Mills. Exec. James Jarrard. Witnessed by Isaac Patridge, James Stokes. {MWB 30:830}

The inventory of her estate was filed by James Jarett before 11 Aug 1760. Signed as next of kin: Edward Dossey, Elizabeth Williams. {MINV 70:321}

Admin. accounts of Elizabeth Jarrett, DO Co. were submitted by James Jarrett on 15 Aug 1760 and 14 April 1761. {MDAD 46:220; 47:45}

Distribution of her estate was made by James Jarrett on 1 Aug 1760 and on 14 Aug 1761 to (equally): Edward Mills, Betty Williams, James Gerrard. Legatees: John Dorsey, Edward Dorsey, Betty Williams, William Mills, Wright Mills, Levin Dossey, Frederick Mills, Lurana Mills, Hezekiah Mills, Amilla Mills, James Jerrrd. BFD 3:87; 3:97}}

Elizabeth Chezum, aged about 60 years, deposed before a land commission of DO Co., 11 Oct 1790- - 22 March 1791, regarding the bounds of Richard Keene's land, part of *End of Controversy*. She mentioned her bro. Edward Dorsey[5] about 42 years earlier. Also deposed were William Vickarse of Sarah, aged about 63 years, and Levin Mills, aged about 50 years, who, about 19 years ago, were chain carrier when the said land was divided between Robt. Goldsborough, dec'd., Levin Dorsey and Ezekl. Keene, guardian to Richard Keene. The bounded post near the dwelling houses of John Dorsey and Richard Keene were located. {DOLR 3 HD 168}

William was father of WILLIAM; JOHN; EDWARD.

## Third Generation

3. JOHN DOSSEY, son of William (2) Dossey, m. Mary (N) (b. c1705).

On 7-26 Nov 1683 John Dossey, planter of Little Choptank in DO Co., leased to Daniell Willard of the same place, planter, *Old Field*, being part of *Preston* on e. side of Little Choptank for the lifetime of said Williard and if he should die leaving a widow, then the widow to have the use of the land for two years after his death. {DOLR 4 Old 99}

On 10 Aug 1734 William Twyford of DO Co., hatmaker, conveyed to John Dorsey of the same co., carpenter, ½ of *Barrel Green* on w. side of Davis Creek which issues out of Slaughter Creek on n. side thereof near the head on Taylors Island, 200 a. {DOLR 9 Old 208}

On 11 March 1736 John Dorsey of DO Co. conveyed to Thomas Vickers of the same co., ½ of *Oliver Branch* at the head of Fishing Creek on s.

---

[5] Elizabeth was a half-sister to Edward by their mother Elizabeth and her father James Jarrard. Elizabeth m. 1st (N) Williams and m. 2nd (N) Chezum.

side of Little Choptank River adj. *Humphreys Fortune*; also adj. land taken up by Henry Turner called *The Devise*, 50 a. {DOLR 9 Old 431}

On 11 March 1736 John Dossey of St. Marys Co., joyner, conveyed to William Murray of DO Co., chyrurgeion, ½ of *Oliver Branch* on Fishing Creek, 50 a. near the land where Sarah Ryan lived and near where William Stoakes now dwells. {DOLR 9 Old 427}

On 28 Jan 1749 John Dorsey of St. Marys Co., Gent., conveyed to William Hughlet of VA, Gent., part of a tract called *Barrel Green* adj. land of Richard Chapman, 100 a. on Taylors Island. {DOLR 14 Old 571}

Mary Dossey, QA Co., age about 54, deposed March 1759. {MD Deponents vol. 3:70}

John Dorsey, QA Co., d. by 29 July 1761 when the first admin. account was submitted by Mary Dossey. Payees included son Levin Dossey, his portion; Nathan Hammond, Jr. who m. widow (unnamed) and extx. of John Raitt, Esq. of AA Co. {MDAD 46:396}

On 23 Aug 1762 the second admin. account of his estate was submitted by Mrs. Mary Dorsey, admx. {MDAD 48:136}

On 6 Sep 1762 a third admin. account was submitted on 6 Sep 1762 by Mrs. Mary Dossey. Payeees included Jacob and Thomas Winchester (under age, 2 of the orphans of Jacob Wincheser (dec'd. m. widow (unnamed); Sarah (orphan of said Jacob) already paid; Jacob and Thomas Winchester (due per marriage contract made by William Stavely (former husband of accountant)). {MDAD 48:214}

On 1 Oct 1763 the fourth admin. account was submitted by Mrs. Mary Dossey. Payees included Levin Dossey, only son, representative and accountant, her portion, and others. {MDAD 49:550}

John was father of only son LEVIN, b. 1735, d. 1781.

4. EDWARD DORSEY, son of William (2) Dorsey.

On 19 Oct 1752 Edward Dossey of DO Co. conveyed to his bro. John Dossey of St. Marys Co., *End of Controversy* on Fishing Creek adj. *Teverton*, 100 a. {DOLR 14 Old 675}

## Fourth Generation

5. LEVIN DORSEY, b. 1735, d. Oct 1781,son of John (3) Dorsey, m. Elizabeth or Betty Keene.

Nancy Cooper Dossey, dau. of Leven and Betty Dossey, b. 18 Oct 1764. {DODO}

On 27 Feb 1773 Levin Dorsey of DO Co., planter, released a mortgage on *Jarards Desire* on Fishing Creek, given by Wm. Chizum and his wife Betty to said Dorsey, the said Chizum and wife having now sold the land to Robert

Gouldsborough, who has paid off the mortgage. It has been mortgaged on 17 Jan 1771. {DOLR 25 Old 16; 26 Old 251}

Levin Dorsey was killed at the "battle of Vienna," MD, 1781, by the British. He was bur. at the Old Trinity Churchyard. {Marshall's Tombstone Recds Vol. 1} According to Jones, "In the year 1781, when the English in barges harassed the Eastern Shore of Maryland, the home guards were called on to defend Vienna. Where the British landed to maraud the town, Levin Dorsey responded and was killed during the fight there while attempting to repel the invaders. He would have been buried at Vienna had not his only son John, a boy of about fifteen years, begged his body of the English officer, who, touched by his appeal, granted the lad's request.

"His remains were conveyed in a wagon to 'Controversey,' a distance of twenty miles, guarded by his young son and an old slave." {Elias Jones, *History of Dorchester County:306*}

On 11 March 1782 valuation was made of the land of John Dorsey, orphan son of Levin Dorsey dec'd., under the guardianship of Joseph Robinson: land called *Controversie* on Fishing Creek. Elizabeth Dorsey, widow of said Levin Dorsey and mother of the orphan, lives on the said land and is entitled to her 1/3 right of dower. {DOLR 28 Old 414}

Levin was father of NANCY COOPER, b. 18 Oct 1764; JOHN, b. 1766.

Fifth Generation

6. NANCY COOPER DORSEY, b. 18 Oct 1764, dau. of Levin (5) and Elizabeth Dorsey.

Nancy Cooper Dossey, aged about 21, made a deposition before a DO Co. land commission, 14 June 1785 - 11 Nov 1785. {DOLR 5 NH 241}

7. JOHN DORSEY, b. c1766, d. 24 Nov 1821, son of Levin (5) and Elizabeth Dorsey, m. Martha (N).

On 11 Feb 1795 John Dossey manumitted Negro slaves. {DOLR 8 HD 291}

On 23 May 1795 Thomas Kallender of DO Co. conveyed to John Dorsey, William Geoghegan, Capewell Keene, John Fooks, Ezekiel Vickars, Henry Ennalls, Levin Keene, Ezekiel Johnson and Thomas Brierwood, Trustees for the Methodist Church, part of *White Haven* at the head of Church Creek, ½ a., for a Meeting House. {DOLR 8 HD 329}

Died 24th ult., at his residence in Fishing Creek, DO Co., Rev. John Dorsey, in the 55th year of his age. {*Easton Gazette*, 15 Dec 1821}

John was father of JAMES LEVIN.

Sixth Generation

8. JAMES LEVIN DORSEY, son of Rev. John (7) Dorsey, m. Sarah A. W. Richardson (b. 9 May 1822, d. 10 Feb 1898), dau. of Levin and Elizabeth Richardson.

James Levin Dorsey, son of Martha and Rev. John Dorsey, b. 17 Sep 1808, d. 30 Aug 1892. Sarah A. W. Dorsey, wife of James L. Dorsey, dau. of Elizabeth and Levin Richardson, b. 9 May 1822, d. 10 Feb 1898. George Edwin, son of James L. and Sarah a. W. Dorsey, b. 26 Jan 1851, d. 10 Jan 1882. Sallie Webster Dorsey, dau. of James L. and Sarah A. W. Dorsey, b. 5 April 1860, d. 5 Aug 1937. Mary Virginia Dorsey, dau. of James L. and Sarah A. W. Dorsey, b. 30 June 1858, d. 4 Oct 1947. {Marshall's Tombstone Rcds Vol. 1:93 - Taken from tombstone inscriptions of Old Trinity Churchyard}

James and Sarah were parents of GEORGE EDWIN, b. 26 Jan 1851, d. 30 Aug 1892; SALLIE WEBSTER, b. 5 April 1860, d. 5 Aug 1937; MARY VIRGINIA, b. 30 June 1858, d. 4 Oct 1947.

Unplaced

HANNAH DOSSEY, SM Co., d. by 3 May 1756 when the admin. account was submitted by John Dossey. {MDAD 40:18}

JAMES DOSSEY

On 23 June 1743 James Dossey and his wife Mary of Calvert Co., conveyed to Charles Goldsborough of DO Co., *Horn* on Great Choptank River where said Charles now dwells. {DOLR 12 Old 8}

RICHARD DORSEY m. 18 March 1798, Rebecca Willis. [DODO}

## THE GEOGHEGAN FAMILY

Ref. A: Bible in possession (17 Aug 1959) of Mrs. Jefferson Geoghegan and her dau., Mrs. Paul Gunby, 3108 Cheverly Ave., Cheverly, MD, Nellie Marshall, *Bible Records of DO Co., Maryland 1612 - 1969 and Baptismal and Marriage Records, 1855-1866 Zion United Methodist Church Cambridge, Md.* DO Co. Historical Society, 1971.

1. WILLIAM GEOGHEGAN, b. c1704, m. Levina LeCompte, dau. of Moses and Levina (Pattison) LeCompte. {See The LeCompte Family, vol. 14}

William Geoghegan is said to have been born in Dublin and to have come to DO Co. as a teacher for the LeCompte family. {Mowbray:46}

William Geoghegan, aged c49 years, deposed before a DO Co. land commission, 13 March 1753 - 2 June 1753, regarding the bounds of Moses LeCompte's land called *Padan Arm*. {DOLR 15 Old 134}

On 8 March 1768 Moses LeCompte Senr. of DO Co., planter, conveyed land to his three grandsons. To Levin Cator, ½ of *Lecomptes Addition* on James Island, 34 ½ a. To William and Moses Geoghegan, the eastern half of *Lecomptes Addition*, 34 ½ a., and part of a tract called *The Grove* on James Island, 75 a. Levina Geoghegan was mentioned as dau. of said Moses LeCompte, Senr. {DOLR 22 Old 222}

On 17 March 1778 Moses LeCompte Senr. of DO Co. planter, gave to his two granddaus. Levina Smith and Sally Geoghegan, a Negro girl called Savy, except the use of the afsd. Negro girl to my Daughter Levina Pattison during her natural life. {DOLR 1 JCH 87}

On 11 Dec 1778 Moses LeCompte of DO Co., planter, conveyed to William Geoghegan of the same co., planter, land on James Island called *Armstrongs Folly*, 100 a., except 15 sq. feet whereon the father and mother of Thomas Patison are buried. {DOLR 1 JCH 158}

On 11 Dec 1778 Thomas Phillips and Sarah Jones, wife of Morgin Jones of DO Co., planter, conveyed to William Geoghegan and Moses Geoghegan of the same co., planters, land on Little Choptank near the head of St. Stevens Creek called *Morgins Venture*, 62 a. {DOLR 1 JCH 159}

William and Levina were parents of MARY, b. 30 Oct 1733, m. (N) Smith; PHILEMON, b. 14 April 1735, d. 4 Jan 1810; LEVINAH, b. 10 Sep 1739; WILLIAM, b. 14 April 1742; SARAH, b. 27 Nov 1749; MOSES, b. 19 May 1747; ANNE, b. 27 Nov 1749; ESTHER, b. 13(?) June 1752. {A, Mowbray:46 - also lists children John and Elizabeth who m. (N) Jones}

## Second Generation

2. PHILEMON GEOGHEGAN, b. 14 April 1735, d. 4 Sep 1774, son of William (1) and Levina Geoghegan, m. Penelope Pattison, dau. of St. Leger and Mary Pattison. {A, Mowbray:46}

They were parents of WILLIAM, b. 2 Oct 1772 (1773?); JOHN P., b. 22 June 1774; PHILEMON, b. Jan 1775. {A}

3. WILLIAM GEOGHEGAN, b. 14 April 1742, son of William (1) and Levina Geoghegan, m. Rebecca (N).

On 23 Feb 1793 William Geoghegan of DO Co. and his wife Rebecca conveyed to John Geoghegan of the same co., *Armstrongs Folly* on James Island, 100 a., land the said John Geoghegan now lives on. Also part of *The Grove*, 5 a. {DOLR 4 HD 444}

4. MOSES GEOGHEGAN, b. 19 May 1747, son of William (1) and Levina Geoghegan, m. 1st Rose Pattison, dau. of John Pattison, and m. 2nd Rebecca Ferguson. {See The Pattison Family, Vol. 14 of this series. Mowbray:46}

A marriage license was granted to Moses Geoghegan and Rebecca Ferguson 18 Feb 1784. {DO Co. marr. lic.}

Third Generation

5. WILLIAM GEOGHEGAN, b. 2 Oct 1772, d. 10 Dec 1822, son of Philemon (2) and Penelope Geoghegan, m. 17 Dec 1803, Martha Geoghegan (b. 13 Dec 1783, d. 6 Jan 1820), dau. of John and Dinnah Geoghegan.

Martha Geoghegan, consort of William Geoghegan, d. 6 Jan 1820, aged about 38 years. William Geoghegan, son of Phillimon and Penelope Geoghegan, d. 10 Dec 1822, aged 50 years. Both are buried at *Grass Reeden* in Susquehanna Neck, Madison District. {Marshall's Tombstone Records:27}

They were parents of SUSANNAH, b. 1 March 1805; HENRY, b. 28 Sep 1806; JOHN WILLIAM, b. 3 March 1808; PHILEMON, b. 17 Dec 1809; GEORGE WASHINGTON, b. 17 March 1814; THOMAS JACKSON, b. 22 Jan 1816; JOHN P., b. 22 June 181-; EMMA DIANA, b. 8 April 1817; MARY REBACA, b. 9 April 1819; JAMES, b. 29 Jan 181-. {A}.

6. PHILEMON GEOGHEGAN, b. Jan 1775, d. 10 Feb 1840, aged 64 years, son of Philemon (2) and Penelope (Pattison) Geoghegan, m. Elizabeth (N).

Philimon Geoghegan, d. 10 Feb 1840, aged 64, buried at *Grass Reeden* (patented to Stephen Gary in Aug 1662) in Susquehanna Neck, Madison District, DO Co. Buried nearby is Elizabeth Geoghegan, wife of Philemon Geoghegan, d. 11 Oct 1849, aged 71 years. {Marshall's Tombstone Records:27}

## THE THOMAS HACKETT FAMILY

1. THOMAS HACKETT, of England and DO Co., came into this province in 1674, m. Elizabeth (N), and d. 1717; his widow m. 2nd John Tench.

*Commentary: Thomas Hackett of DO Co. was transported into this province in 1674 and there was a Theo Hackett in AA Co. by 1679. Although their relationship is undetermined, it is interesting to note that Thomas Hackett's son Oliver named one of his son's Theophilius. {MPL 18:291; ARMD 50:301. See also The Hackett Family of TA and QA Cos. in Volume 5 of this series.}*

From genealogical notes by Prof. Charles W. Hackett (1860-1941) written circa 1920: "In the Maryland Archives and in other historic records many references are found to Hacketts in various counties of Maryland during the colonial and early national periods of our history. From information on record in the State Land Office at Annapolis, and painstakingly compiled for the writer by Mrs. George W. Hodges, however, it appears that the founder of the Dorchester County family of Hacketts settled there in 1674. On March 17 of that year á tract of 3,350 acres of land was assigned to one Richard Angell for having brought over from England in the Dover sixty-seven colonists, among whom was one Thomas Hackett. That Thomas Hackett was a man of good standing in his community is indicated by the fact that his name frequently appears as that of bondsman for various administrators of estates and as an administrator of estates himself." {Quoted from Jones:327}

On 25 Dec 1682 Thomas Hackett, DO Co., leased from Daniel Jones the 100 acre tract *Riccarton* for 4 years. {DOLR 4 Old 90}

On 6 Aug 1689 Thomas Hackett and wife Elizabeth, DO Co., conveyed to Jeremiah Hooke the 100 acre tract *St. Johns* on the east side of the northwest branch of Nanticoke River. {DOLR 4 Old 249} It should be noted that Nicholas Hackett (undetermined relationship to Thomas Hackett) once owned and sold 500 acres of the tract *St. Jones* in 1674 (See Unplaced, below).

Thomas Hackett, Sr., DO Co., blacksmith, d. leaving a will dated 9 June 1716, proved 12 Nov 1716. To wife Elizabeth, 103 acre part of tract *Neighborly Kindness*. To sons Oliver and Thomas, personalty and residue of real estate equally. To grandson Theophilus (son of Oliver Hackett), personalty. To granddau. Litia (dau of Thomas Hackett), personalty. To granddau. Elizabeth (dau. of Oliver Hackett), personalty. Execs.: wife Elizabeth Hackett and son Oliver Hackett (who renounced his exec. on 12 Nov 1716). {MWB 14:417}

The estate of Thomas Hackett, DO Co., dec'd., was appraised at £39.14.0 on 12 April 1717. Signed as next of kin were Oliver Hackett and Thomas Hackett. {INAC 37B:150}

On 7 Feb 1717/8 the estate of Thomas Hackett, DO Co., was admin. by Elisabeth Tench (extx.), wife of John Tench (who d. intestate by 9 May 1723; Elisabeth Tench, admx.). {MDAD 1:120; MINV 8:321}

Thomas was the father of: OLIVER; THOMAS.

## Second Generation

2. THOMAS HACKETT, DO Co., b. c1689, son of Thomas (1) Hackett, m. Rebecca (N).

Thomas Hackett and Oliver Hackett signed as next of kin on the inventory of the estate of Thomas Hackett, DO Co., dec'd., filed 12 April 1717. {INAC 37B:150}

Thomas Hackett and Edward Wright appraised the estate of Thomas Harpin, DO Co., dec'd., on 15 April 1717; John Tench, admin. {INAC 37B:22; MDAD 1:122}

From genealogical notes by Prof. Charles W. Hackett (1860-1941) written circa 1920: "On March 23, 1730 there was surveyed for, and on November 13, 1732, by order of the Lord Proprietor, Charles Calvert, there was patented to Thomas (II) Hackett a tract of 60 acres of land known as *Hackett's Adventure* which began 'at a marked white oak standing on the south side of Puckhama branch that issueth out of the Northwest Fork of Nanticoke River.' The greater part of this tract of land has ever since been in the possession of some member of the Hackett family, and at present is owned by Luke Hackett, the great-great-grandson of the original patentee. Furthermore, entries in the Debt Books of the Lords Proprietary of Maryland show that two shillings and five pence were paid annually by Thomas (II) Hackett and his heirs as quit rent on this tract of land from 1734 until 1770, or until only six years before the beginning of the Revolution." {Quoted from Jones:328}

On 13 Nov 1742 Thomas Hackett, DO Co., patented the 60 acre tract *Hackett's Adventure* and on 20 July 1743 the 70 acre tract *Friendship*. {MPL PL8:712, EI6:612}

In a deposition taken in 1744 regarding the bounds of *Piney Ridge* owned by William Fishburn in the freshes of DO Co., Thomas Hackett stated that he was about 55 years old. {DOLR 12 Old 250}

In a deposition taken in 1745 regarding land called *Rehoboth* owned by Francis Lee in DO Co., Thomas Hackett stated that he was about 56 years old and he was shown the bounded tree about 30 years ago. {DOLR 14 Old 48}

In a deposition taken in 1746 regarding land called *Traverse Purchase* owned by John Travers in DO Co., Thomas Hackett stated that he was about 57 years old and he was shown the bounded tree about 40 years ago. {DOLR 14 Old 102}

In the *Maryland Gazette*, 5 Sep 1754, the following article appeared: "A Negro fellow attacked his master, John Reed, of Dorchester County, on Saturday the 27th of August. The slave then went to the house of Thomas Hackett, an elderly man, and nearly murdered Hackett's wife. Hackett's daughter killed the slave." {Karen Green, *The Maryland Gazette, 1727-1761*, p. 144}

From genealogical notes by Prof. Charles W. Hackett (1860-1941) written circa 1920: "In his final will and testament, written on July 30, 1753, Thomas (II) Hackett mentions his wife Rebecca, an adult son by the name of Oliver, and two young children - Thomas who was born on October 16, 1742 and Betty who was born on May 27, 1745. Litia, who was mentioned in the will of her grandfather Thomas (I) Hackett, is not mentioned in the will of her father Thomas (II) Hackett. From this and from other facts given in the will of Thomas (II) the writer infers that Litia and Oliver (II) were children of Thomas (II) by an early marriage, that Litia died without issue prior to the date of her father's will (1753), and that Thomas (III) and Betsy were children of Thomas (II) by a second marriage. In his will Thomas (II) Hackett gave his occupation as that of planter. All of his 'land and houses and dwelling plantation' were willed to his son Thomas (III); to his wife he willed all his personal property and household goods; and provision was made that if his wife died during the minority of Thomas (III) and Betsy that his son Oliver was to be the executor of his estate and also the guardian of Thomas (III) and Betsy. Thomas (II) Hackett died in the latter part of 1765 and his will was filed for probate by his widow Rebecca on April 24, 1765. One of the sureties on the administratrix's bond of Rebecca Hackett was Oliver Hackett who, apparently, was her step-son. Legal appraisers of the Thomas (II) Hackett estate included two nearest kin, namely Theoples and Thomas Hackett. The former was most likely the nephew and the latter the son, then twenty-two years old, of the deceased." {Quoted from Jones:328-329}

*Commentary: It must be noted, however, that the abstract of Thomas Hackett's will by Jane Baldwin Cotton is slightly different than that of Charles W. Hackett. Cotton stated that Thomas Hackett, DO Co., d. leaving a will dated 30 July 1763, proved 10 Dec and 17 Dec 1764, and he bequeathed to his wife Rebecca his whole estate and his children Thomas, Jr., Oliver, and Betsy Hackett were to receive the estate upon her death. {MCW 13:65; MWB 33:96}*

The estate of Thomas Hackett, DO Co., dec'd., was appraised at £47.19.9 and approved on 24 April 1765 by Rebecca Hackett, admx. Signed as next of kin were Theophilus Hackett and Thomas Hackett. An account was filed by his widow Rebecca Hackett on 11 March 1767; no other heirs were named. Her sureties were Oliver Hackett and David Harper. {MINV 86:344; MDAD 56:137; BFD 5:22}

In a deposition taken in DO Co. in 1771 Rebecca Hackett stated that she was about 70 years old and mentioned her husband Thomas Hackett, dec'd. Billinder Stevens was also deposed at that time and stated she was about 49 years old and her father was Thomas Hackett. {DOLR 25 Old 238}

Thomas was the father of: THOMAS, JR.; OLIVER; LITIA; BETSY or ELIZABETH (unm.); BILLINDER, m. (N) Stevens); poss. MARGARET, m. William Ross.

3. OLIVER HACKETT, DO Co., son of Thomas (1) Hackett, m. Frances (N).

Oliver's father Thomas Hackett, Sr., DO Co., blacksmith, d. leaving a will dated 9 June 1716, proved 12 Nov 1716. To wife Elizabeth, 103 acre part of tract *Neighborly Kindness*. To sons Oliver and Thomas, personalty and residue of real estate equally. To grandson Theophilus (son of Oliver Hackett), personalty. To granddau. Litia (dau. of Thomas Hackett), personalty. To granddau. Elizabeth (dau. of Oliver Hackett), personalty. Execs.: wife Elizabeth

Hackett and son Oliver Hackett (who renounced his executorship on 12 Nov 1716). {MWB 14:417}

In 1728 Oliver Hackett, DO Co., was among those who witnessed the marking of the bounds of *Pinder's Lodge*. {DOLR 8 Old 247}

The estate of Oliver Hackett, DO Co., dec'd., was appraised at £127.15.5 and approved on 28 Sep 1741 by Frances Hackett, admx. Next of kin were listed as Thomas Hackett and Theophilus Hackett. {MINV 26:397}

On 5 April 1743 the estate of Oliver Hackett, DO Co., was admin. by Mrs. Frances Hackett (admx.) and the sureties were Theophilus Hackett and John King. {MDAD 19:396}

In 1752 Frances Hackett and Mary Cratcher were listed as next of kin when the estate of Barterton or Barleton Fletcher, DO Co., was appraised. In 1755 an account was filed by admx. "Mary Fletcher by Theophilus Hacket" and payments were made to the decedent's five children (N). {MINV 52:1; MDAD 38:319}

In 1757 Frances Hackett, mother of Theophilus Hackett, was entitled to live on *Neighbourly Kindness* for her lifetime. {DOLR 15 Old 505}

In a 1759 deposition Mary Cratcher, DO Co., stated she was about 74 years old and also mentioned Thomas Hackett. {ARMD 31:355}

In a 1770 deposition Jemima Stainton, DO Co., aged about 27, wife of Charles Stainton, dec'd., stated that her grandmother was Frances Hackett, dec'd., wife of Oliver Hackett, dec'd., and Frances was a reputed sister to Mary Cratcher. {DOLR 24 Old 9}

In a 1771 deposition Rosanna Williams, DO Co., stated that she was about 50 years old and mentioned her father Oliver Hackett, dec'd., her uncle Thomas Hackett the Elder, dec'd., and her grandfather Thomas Hackett, dec'd. {DOLR 26 Old 50}

Oliver was the father of: THEOPHILUS; THOMAS; ELIZABETH; ROSANNA (b. c1721, m. a Williams).

## Third Generation

4. THOMAS HACKETT, JR., DO Co., son of Thomas (2) Hackett, m. Sarah Hubbert (dau. of John Hubbert), and d. 1754. Sarah Hackett m. 2nd to John Safford. {MWB 39:690}

On 13 June 1750 Thomas Hackett, Jr., DO Co., acquired from John Griffith the 50 acre tract *John's Hill* on the west side of the Northwest Fork of Nanticoke River. {DOLR 14 Old 419}

On 15 Sep 1753 Thomas Hackett, DO Co., planter, and wife Sarah conveyed to Andrew Willis a 28 acre part of the tract *Friendship*. {DOLR 14 Old 738}

The estate of Thomas Hackett, DO Co., dec'd., was appraised at £35.16.11 on 10 June 1754 and approved on 12 Aug 1754 by Sarah Hackett, admx. Next of kin were listed as John Hubbart, Solomon Hubbart, Theophilus Hackett, and Mary Hackett. {MINV 57:285}

On 9 March 1757 the estate of Thomas Hackett, Jr., DO Co., was admin. by Sarah Safford, admx. and wife of John Safford. The named representatives were his children Margaret, Betty, Frances, and Tommy Hackett. {MDAD 41:150; BFD 2:65}

Thomas was the father of: THOMAS (TOMMY); MARGARET; BETTY; FRANCES.

5. OLIVER HACKETT, DO Co. and CA Co., b. c1719, son of Thomas (2) Hackett, m. Rosannah Kirkman (b. c1725), dau. of George Kirkman. {MDAD 31:176; DOLR 24 Old 9. See also The George Kirkman Family in Volume 7 of this series}

On 16 Dec 1745 Oliver Hackett, DO Co., acquired the 65 acre tract *Hoghole* at the head of the Northwest Fork of Nanticoke River. {DOLR 13 Old 16}

On 4 Nov 1752 Thomas Orrell, DO Co., conveyed to James Kirkman, DO Co., the 50 acre tract *Hog Pen Ridge*. It was noted that Rosannah Hackett, wife of Oliver Hackett, has a dower interest in said land, which said Kirkman has bought from the said Hackett and wife. {DOLR 14 Old 650}

On 29 Sep 1763 Oliver Hackett, DO Co., patented the 182 acre tract *Hackett's Venture*. {MPL BC23:82, BC24:78}

On 15 Oct 1770 Oliver Hackett, Jr. and James Kirkman, Jr., DO Co., witnessed the leasing of *Salley's Plains*. {DOLR 24 Old 187}

In a deposition taken after March 1771 regarding the bounds of the tract *Rehobeth* owned by Edward and John Smoot in DO Co., Oliver Hackett stated that he was about 51 years old and his father was Thomas Hackett, now dec'd. In another deposition taken later that year Oliver stated he was about 52 years old. {DOLR 25 Old 238}

Oliver Hackett, Sr. and Oliver Hackett, Jr., both of CA Co., rendered material aid by furnishing wheat for the use of the military on 5 June 1782. {Peden's *Maryland Public Service Records, 1775-1783*, p. 130}

Oliver was the father of: OLIVER, JR.; prob. OTHERS (N).

6. BILLINDER HACKETT, DO Co., b. c1722, dau. of Thomas (2) Hackett, m. (N) Stevens.

In a deposition taken between March 1771 and Nov 1771 Billinder Stevens, DO Co., stated that she was about 49 years old and her father was Thomas Hackett. {DOLR 25 Old 238}

7. ELIZABETH (BETSY) HACKETT, DO Co., dau. of Thomas (2) Hackett.

On 5 Nov 1772 Elizabeth Hackett, DO Co., spinster, and William Ross (of James) and wife Margaret, DO Co., conveyed to John Douglass, Chester Co., PA and William Douglass, DO Co., iron masters, 50 acre tract *John's Hill* and 60 acre tract *Hackett's Fortune* in DO Co., formerly the property of Thomas Hackett, Jr., late of DO Co., dec'd. {DOLR 26 Old 172}

8. THOMAS HACKETT, DO Co., son of Oliver (3) Hackett.

On 26 Feb 1742/3 Thomas Hackett, DO Co., witnessed a power of attorney. {DOLR 10 Old 369}

On 7 Oct 1747 Thomas Hackett, son of Oliver Hackett, DO Co., patented the 60 acre tract *Hackett's Fortune*. {MPL BT:307}

9. THEOPHILUS HACKETT, DO Co., b. c1712, son of Oliver (3) Hackett, m. (N).

On 13 Jan 1734 Theophilus Hackett, DO Co., witnessed the sale of *Walter's Lott* on the north side of Puckam Branch on the east side of the Northwest Fork of Nanticoke River. {DOLR 9 Old 251}

On 23 Nov 1738 Theophilus Hackett, DO Co., patented the 50 acre tract *Theophilus's Choice* and on 10 Aug 1743 the 200 acre tract *Neighbourly Kindness*. {MPL EI6:67, LGB:671}

On 11 Nov 1747 Theophilus Hackett, DO Co., acquired from John and Mary Traverse a 29 acre part of the tract *Travers Purches*. {DOLR 14 Old 188}

On 7 Feb 1748 Theophilus Hackett, DO Co., conveyed to John Wallis a 100 acre part of the tract *Neighbourly Kindness*. {DOLR 14 Old 326}

On 4 Oct 1755 Theophilus Hackett, DO Co., patented the 102 acre tract *Theophilus's Choice*. {MPL BC6:442}

On 10 Aug 1757 Theophilus Hackett, DO Co., conveyed to his dau. Levinah Bramble, wife of David Bramble, a 100 acre part of the tract *Neighbourly Kindness*. Frances Hackett, mother of Theophilus, to have possession of the plantation where she now lives for her lifetime. {DOLR 15 Old 505}

On 30 Jan 1765 Ebenezer Alexander, DO Co., conveyed livestock to Theophilus Hackett. {DOLR 19 Old 411}

In a 1770 deposition Jemima Stainton, DO Co., aged about 27, wife of Charles Stainton, dec'd., stated that her grandmother was Frances Hackett, now dec'd., was the wife of Oliver Hackett, dec'd. Also deposed was Theophilus Hackett, aged about 57, son of Oliver Hackett, dec'd., and he mentioned Mary Cratcher, Moses Lord, Daniel Hill and Thomas Hackett, all late of DO Co., dec'd. {DOLR 24 Old 9}

In a deposition taken between Nov 1771 and April 1772 Theophilus Hackett, DO Co., stated that he was about 59 or 60 years old and mentioned his father (N) and uncle Thomas Hackett. {DOLR 26 Old 50}

Theophilus Hackett, DO Co., took the Oath of Allegiance in 1778 and rendered material aid by supplying wheat for the use of the military on 1 Nov 1782. {RPDO:89}

In a deposition taken some time between 11 March 1783 and 29 June 1785 regarding the bounds of *Pinder's Lodge* in DO Co., Theophilus Hackett stated that he was about 72 years old and mentioned his father Oliver Hackett and Thomas Hackett about 30 years ago. {DOLR 5 NH 162}

On 2 Feb 1788 George Stanton and wife Mary Stanton (alias Mary Hackett) of Rockingham Co., NC, conveyed to Ann Ennalls, widow and extx. of Henry Ennalls, DO Co., dec'd., a 94 acre part of two tracts, *Theophilus Choice* and *Travers's Purchase* or *Lott*. {DOLR 2 HD 120}

Theophilus was the father of: LEVINAH (m. David Bramble); MARY (m. George Stanton); JEMIMA (m. Charles Stainton); prob. OTHERS (N).

10. ROSANNA HACKETT, DO Co., b. c1721, dau. of Oliver (3) Hackett, m. (N) Williams.

In a 1771 deposition Rosanna Williams, DO Co., stated that she was about 50 years old and mentioned her father Oliver Hackett, dec'd., her uncle Thomas Hackett the Elder, dec'd., and her grandfather Thomas Hackett, dec'd. {DOLR 26 Old 50}

## Fourth Generation

11. THOMAS (TOMMY) HACKETT, DO Co., son of Thomas (4) Hackett, Jr., m. Lovey (N).

Thomas Hackett, DO Co., rendered material aid by supplying wheat for the use of the military on 1 Nov 1782. {RPDO:89}

On 26 April 1788 Thomas Hackett, DO Co., acquired from Eben Hill the 21½ acre tract *Conclusion* which adj. *Hackett's Adventure*. On that same day Thomas Hackett and wife Lovey conveyed to Eben Hill a 13 acre part of *Hackett's Adventure* [which was once owned by Thomas Hackett, Jr.]. {DOLR 9 NH 518}

Thomas was the father of: LUKE (m. Nancy Darby). {Jones:329}

12. OLIVER HACKETT, JR., DO Co. and CA Co., son of Oliver (5) Hackett, m. Ann Wilson circa 18 July 1777. {Cranor's *Marriage Licenses of Caroline Co., MD, 1774-1815*, p. 7}

On 15 Oct 1770 Oliver Hackett, Jr., DO Co., witnessed the leasing of *Salley's Plains*. {DOLR 24 Old 187}

Oliver Hackett, CA Co., was a private in Capt. John Stafford's Militia Co., 14th Bttn., by 13 Aug 1777. {RPCA:70}

Oliver Hackett, Jr., CA Co., rendered material aid by furnishing wheat for the use of the military on 5 June 1782. {Peden's *Maryland Public Service Records, 1775-1783*, p. 130}

13. LEVINAH HACKETT, DO Co., dau. of Theophilus (9) Hackett, m. David Bramble.

On 10 Aug 1757 Theophilus Hackett, DO Co., conveyed to his dau. Levinah Bramble, wife of David Bramble, a 100 acre part of the tract *Neighbourly Kindness*, and Frances Hackett, mother of Theophilus, to have possession of the plantation where she now lives for her lifetime. {DOLR 15 Old 505}

Hackett Bramble, DO Co., prob. son of David and Levinah Bramble, enlisted as a private in the 2nd MD Line on 4 May 1778 and served to at least 1 Nov 1780. Hackett Bramble married Elizabeth Butler before 1790 in North Carolina. On 21 April 1819 Hackett or William Bramble of Cumberland Co., NC applied for a pension (R1151) and in 1820 he was age 61. He died on the first Sunday in September 1837, leaving a widow Elizabeth who died 1 March 1840. A son William Bramble was aged 65 in 1855 and was their only living child. {RPDO:16}

In December, 1793, David Bramble, DO Co., leased from Thomas Sears a 50 acre tract of woodland (N) in the Northwest Fork of Nanticoke River for 15 years. {DOLR 4 HD 611}

Levinah (Hackett) Bramble was prob. the mother of: HACKETT; DAVID; prob. OTHERS (N).

14. MARY HACKETT, DO Co., MD and Rockingham Co., NC, dau. of Theophilus (9) Hackett, m. George Stanton.

On 2 Feb 1788 George Stanton and wife Mary Stanton (alias Mary Hackett) of Rockingham Co., NC, conveyed to Ann Ennalls, widow and extx. of Henry Ennalls, DO Co., dec'd., a 94 acre part of two tracts, *Theophilus Choice* and *Travers's Purchase* or *Lott*. {DOLR 2 HD 120}

15. JEMIMA HACKETT, DO Co., b. c1743, dau. of Theophilus (9) Hackett, m. Charles Stainton.

In a 1770 deposition Jemima Stainton, DO Co., age about 27, wife of Charles Stainton, DO Co., dec'd. (son of Thomas Stainton, DO Co., dec'd.), stated that her grandmother was Frances Hackett, DO Co., dec'd. (wife of Oliver Hackett, dec'd.), and said Frances Hackett was a reputed sister to Mary Cratcher. {DOLR 24 Old 9}

Charles Stainton, DO Co., d. by 15 July 1768 at which time his estate was admin. by his widow Jemima Stainton. Charles left behind two minor children, William and Major Stainton. {MDAD 58:279}

Jemima (Hackett) Stainton was the mother of: WILLIAM STAINTON; MAJOR STAINTON.

Unplaced

NICHOLAS HACKETT, DO Co. and TA Co., b. c1642 in England, immigrated into this province by 1665 and m. Mary Woolchurch, dau. of Henry Woolchurch. {MPL SR8203, EE:35-6; Transcript 9:37 [SR7351]}

Nicholas Hackett and William Travers acquired from Timothy Goodridge 300 acres (N) on Nanticoke River in DO Co. near Broad Marsh on 20 July 1668. One moiety of 150 acres in this parcel of land was acknowledged by William Travers to Nicholas Hackett on 6 Sep 1670. {DOLR 1 Old 85}

Nicholas Hackett and Robert Gold conveyed 300 acres (N) on Nanticoke River to James Jones on 1 June 1670. {DOLR 1 Old 185}

Nicholas Hackett, TA Co., planter, conveyed to William Jones, Bristol, England, merchant, 500 acre tract *St. Jones* on Phillips Creek in DO Co. on 2 Nov 1674. {DOLR 3 Old 74}

On 3 June 1686 in a deposition regarding a survey of land on Nanticoke River, Nicholas Hackett stated that he was about 44 years old. {DOLR 5 Old 36}

## THE JOHN HENRY FAMILY

1. REV. JOHN HENRY, a Presbyterian minister from Dublin, Ireland, graduated from the University of Edinburgh and was ordained by the Presbytery of Dublin. He came to this province from Ireland in 1710, settled near *Rehoboth* on the Pocomoke River, SO Co., and served as minister of Pocomoke Church. John m. Mary Jenkins (1674-1744), widow of Francis Jenkins (d. 1710) and dau. of Robert King), and d. in 1717. His widow, Mary Henry, m. 3rd to Rev. John Hampton, a Presbyterian minister of Snow Hill Church. {Mowbray I:64; BDML I:435, 437. See also The Robert King Family, Vol. 17 of this series.}

Mr. John Henry and wife Mary Henry (admx. of Col. Francis Jenkins) were admins. of the estate of Richard Williams, SO Co., dec'd., on 11 July 1711. {INAC 32C:156}

On 10 Dec 1713 John Henry, SO Co., patented the 50 acre tract *Henry's Addition*. {MPL EE6:26}

John Henry, of Pocomoke, SO Co., d. leaving a will dated 1 Oct 1715, proved 20 June 1717. To bro. Hugh Henry and sisters Jannet and Helen, £15 sterling, to be paid to Rev. Alexander Sinclaire in Plumked St., Dublin; if he be dead, to the Rev. Messrs. Francis Iredale or Cragehead in Cable St., Dublin. To son John, ½ of tract *Buckland* on St. Martin's River, division to be bro. (N) King's line; also ½ of storehouse and lot at Snow Hill and 100 acre tract *Pershoar* on Whorekill Creek; if bro. Robert disturbs him or his male heirs then to son John the other ½ of *Buckland* also at decease of wife, and 1/3 personal estate. To son Robert Jenkins, two tracts of 930 acres and 640 acres on Morattock River in North Carolina; also 400 acre dwelling plantation *Mary's Lot* and adj. 50 acre tract *Henry's Addition*; also 150 acre tract *Joshemon* lying above Snow Hill and 200 acre tract *Providence* at Dividing Creek; also the southernmost half of *Buckland* under afsd. condition; also ½ of a lot at Snow Hill and a tract called *Necessity* on Pocomoke where Thomas Ellis now lives; all other real estate not herein mentioned and 2/3 of personal estate at decease of wife. To wife Mary (extx.), the use of entire estate during life. Sons to have an education such as their genius inclines them to. Desire bro. Robert King and Epr. Wilson to be counsellors to wife. Should either die before said sons become of age, desire neighbor Robert Mills to join with survivor and also Rev. John Hampton. {MWB 14:408-409}

It should be noted that source BDML I:435 mentions a dau. (first name unknown) who d. in 1722; however, she is not mentioned in Rev. John Henry's will in 1715 nor in Rev. John Hampton's will proved on 2 Feb 1721/2, but Rev. Hampton's will does mention his wife Mary and sons-in-law [i.e., stepsons] Robert Jenkins Henry and John Henry. {MWB 17:121}

On 10 Sep 1718 the estate of Rev. John Henry, SO Co., dec'd., was appraised at £1898.17.7 and approved on 10 Sep 1719 (admin. not named). Next of kin was listed as Robert King. {MINV 3:116}

Mary Hampton, SO Co., d. leaving a will dated 26 Feb 1741, proved 13 Dec 1744. To son Robert Jenkins Henry (exec.), tracts *Mary's Lot, Henry's Addition, Lembreck, Cyprus Swamp, Conveyance, Cyprus Neck, Highland, Whitely, Dickenson's Hope, Goose Marsh, Cow Marsh, Providence*, and *Friend's Assistance*, plus 200 acres bought from bro. Robert King; my grist mill near William Stephens' Ferry and another at Rehoboth Town and all my lots in said town; one moiety of a lot in Snow Hill Town and ½ of the stone house on said lot no. 2; one moiety of tract *Pershore* in Delaware Bay near Horn Kill Creek in Sussex Co., DE. To son John Henry, tracts *Spring Hill, Gold's Delight, Buckland, Jasemine*, and *Sister's Gift* which I bought of my bro. Robert King. To Rev. Thomas Fletcher, tract *Ignoble Quarter*. To bro. Robert King, £10. To 2 nephews, sons of said bro., and nephew and niece, sons of my sister Eleanor

Ballard, dec'd., 20 sh. To Mr. Edward Round and wife Katherine Round, 20 sh. To Elizabeth Jones, wife of William Jones, of Menikin [Manocan], 1 slave. To Mary Jones, dau. of William Jones, some cattle. {MWB 24:44-47}

John was the father of: ROBERT JENKINS; JOHN.

Second Generation

2. REV. HUGH HENRY, a Presbyterian minister (poss. nephew of Rev. John (1) Henry who had a bro. in Ireland named Hugh Henry), received an A.B. degree from the College of New Jersey (now Princeton University) in 1748 and was ordained and served at Pocomoke Church, Rehobeth, SO Co., in 1751 (plus other churches in SO Co., DO Co., and Laurel, DE). Hugh Henry m. Sarah Handy (dau. of Isaac Handy) and d. in 1763. Sarah Henry m. 2nd John Darby, DO Co., in 1775. {BDML I:435}

In 1759 Rev. Hugh Henry was holder of pew no. 18 in Rocawakin Presbyterian Church (SO Co., now WI Co.); Col. John Henry held pew no. 12; and Col. Isaac Handy held pew no. 25. {Peden's *A Collection of Maryland Church Records*, p. 300}

On 21 Nov 1761 a number of negroes were distributed from the estate of Thomas Dashiells, SO Co., dec'd., and among those listed was Sarah Handy, wife of Hugh Henry, who received negro Fra. {MDAD 47:370}

Hugh Henry, SO Co., d. leaving a will dated 8 Nov 1762, proved 16 March 1763, naming wife Sarah; son Isaac Henry, lands (N) and to be under care of his grandfather Isaac Handy, Gent. [who also died in 1763 and in his will named, among others, Rev. Hugh Henry and Col. Robert Jenkins Henry as guardians of his son Isaac Handy]; son Hugh Henry (under 21); son James Henry (under 21); son William Blair Henry (under 21); dau. Nancy Henry; and, my bro. James Henry. {MWB 31:940-942; SOWB EB4:105-106}

The estate of Rev. Hugh Henry, SO Co., dec'd., was appraised at £686.0.5 and approved on 23 March 1764 by Sarah Henry, extx. Next of kin were listed as Isaac Henry and William Handy. {MINV 83:168}

On 8 Oct 1766 the estate of Rev. Hugh Henry, SO Co., dec'd., was admin. by Sarah Henry (admx.) with distributions made to Sarah Henry (accountant, 1/3) and residue to Nancy Henry, James Henry, Hugh Henry, and William Blear Henry (paid to his guardian James Henry). {MDAD 55.24}

On 23 Jan 1775 Sarah Henry, SO Co., filed a bond concerning her intention to marry John Darby, DO Co. {DOLR 5 NH 426}

On 10 April 1775 Isaac Henry, SO Co., filed a bond concerning slaves and chattels that he held for the use of his mother Sarah Darby, [now] wife of John Darby, DO Co. {DOLR 5 NH 426}

Hugh was the father of: ISAAC (m. Dorothy Henry); HUGH; WILLIAM BLAIR; JAMES; NANCY.

3. COL. ROBERT JENKINS HENRY, SO Co., b. c1712, son of John (1) Henry, m. Gertrude Rousby (dau. of John Rousby of SM Co.) in May, 1746, and d. in October, 1766, of the gout at the house of his bro. John Henry in DO Co. on his return home from a meeting of the Assize Court. {BDML I:438}

Robert Jenkins Henry served in the Maryland Legislature (Lower House, 1738-1756), in the Maryland Council (1756-1766) and served successively as a Justice of the Court of Oyer and Terminer and Gaol Delivery, Justice of the Provincial Court, Judge of the Assize Court, and Naval Officer at Pocomoke, 1762-1766. He was a captain by 1735, major by 1745, and colonel by 1752. {BDML I:438}

In 1747 Major Robert Jenckins Henry, SO Co., was elected a member of the MD Assembly in place of William Stoughton, Esq., who had resigned. {*MD Gazette*, 16 June 1747}

Col. Robert Jenkins Henry, SO Co., patented the 646 acre tract *Long Meadow* on 4 Oct 1747, the 585 acre tract *Fair Meadow* on 12 Sep 1748, and the 72 acre tract *Glasgow* on 28 Feb 1749. {MPL TI4:240, BY2:264, 266}

In 1756 Col. Robert Jenckins Henry, a SO Co. representative, was one of His Lordship's Honorable Council of State. {*MD Gazette*, 27 May 1756}

At the time of his death in 1766 Robert Jenkins Henry was an extensive land owner, having acquired over 3,964 acres of land in SO, WO and CV Cos., and Sussex Co., DE, plus lots in Rehobeth, SO Co. He resided at *Mary's Lot* which estate came to be known as *Hampton* in later years. {BDML I:439; OSES:370}

Robert Jenkins Henry, SO Co., d. leaving a will dated 21 July 1764, proved 14 Nov 1766. To wife Gertrude, lands (N) and her thirds. To son Robert Jenkins Henry (now about age 9), 400 acre tract *Mary's Lot* where I now live, being part of *Rehobeth*; 50 acre tract *Henry's Addition*; 138½ acre part of tract *Manlove's Lot*; 1/3 of tract *Limbrick*, being part of *Son's Choice*; 72 acre tract *Glasgow*; 245 acre tract *Whitley Rectified*, part of *Hignet's Choice* and all lands at mouth of Morumsco Creek; 646 acre tract *Long Meadow*; lands in WO Co. at *Cypress Neck*; land on Pocomoke River devised me by the will of Col. Robert King, purchased by him and my dec'd. mother Mary Hampton; also my wife's portion at her death. To son Edward Henry, 535 acre tract *Fair Meadow Rectified*; tract *Petshore* [or *Pershore*] left me by my mother on Hornkill Creek in Sussex Co., DE on Delaware Bay; 640 acre tract *Hororotson* on Merottuck River in Chowan Precinct, North Carolina, being part of land purchased by my dec'd. father John Henry; if he dies to daus. Mary King Henry, Ann Henry, Elizabeth Henry, and Gertrude Henry. To dau. Mary King Henry, 278 acre tract *Golden Lyon* on Morumsco Creek and 20 acre marsh adj. *Long Meadow*. To dau. Ann Henry, 400 acre tract *Providence* at Dividing Creek. To dau. Elizabeth Henry, 300 acre tract *Friend's Assistance*; if no issue, to dau. Gertrude. To friend James Sherod of Terryl Co., North Carolina, tract *Hununtok* when he pays up bond dated 25 March 1763. To William Allen, WO Co., 51 acre tract *Security* if he agrees to pay debt due me from Francis Porter, if not, exec. to sell land. To the people of the congregation of Pocomoke, the land whereon the Presbyterian meeting house now stands in Rehobeth. To the people of Coventry Parish, the parcel whereon the parish church now stands. To the public use, the parcel whereon the Inspection House now stands at Rehobeth. To my daus., the negroes given me by the Honorable Col. Edward Lloyd. My friends Isaac Morris and Levin Gale and bro. John Henry to settle the accounts of the brig *Friendship* and company. Littleton Dennis and bro. John Henry to settle affair about *Cypress Swamp*, that is ¼ part of tract *Newfoundland* in WO Co. Also mentioned Martha Hall, a young woman who has lived in my family; bro. John Henry and his wife Dorothy; bro. Lloyd and cousin Betsy Lloyd; kinsman Nehemiah King; and, named Hon. Edward Lloyd of TA Co., Col. John Henry of DO Co., and my wife Gertrude Henry, execs. {SOWB EB4:119-121}

The estate of Col. Robert Jenkins Henry, SO Co., dec'd., was appraised at £6135.16.7 and admin. on 23 Nov 1767 by Gertrude Henry, extx. {MDAD 58.10}

On 5 March 1767 the estate of Col. Robert Jenkins Henry, SO Co., dec'd., was admin. by Gertrude Henry, extx. Next of kin were listed as Mary King Henry and Ann Henry. {MINV 93:294}

On 23 Sep 1770 the estate of Robert Jenkins Henry, SO Co., was admin. by John Bacon (adm. de bonis non) and distribution was made to Gertrude Henry (widow, 1/6) retained by accountant in right of his wife (N), with residue in equal amounts to wife (N) of Edward Rounds, to Mary King Whittington, and to Robert Jenkins Henry, Elizabeth Henry, Gertrude Henry, and Edward Henry (paid to their tutor Col. John Henry). {MDAD 64:195}

*Commentary: It must be noted that in the aforementioned account in 1770 the widow Gertrude Henry received one-sixth of the estate even though there were apparently 8 named legatees (i.e., the widow and 7 children). Only 5 children were mentioned by name, viz., Mary, Robert, Elizabeth, Gertrude and Edward, but the account also mentioned a dau. (N) who married John Bacon and a dau. (N) who married Edward Rounds. This makes a total of 7 children; however, the only other known dau. was Ann, but she was not mentioned by name in that account. Ann Henry prob. married Edward Rounds because an Edward Rownd of WO Co. d. testate in 1773 and named his wife Ann in his will (WOWB JW4:200). Still, all other sources consulted about this family indicated Robert Jenkins Henry had 6, not 7, children. Therefore, additional research will be necessary before drawing conclusions.*

Robert was the father of: ROBERT JENKINS; EDWARD; MARY KING (m. William Whittington who d. 1769); ANN (m. Edward Rounds); ELIZABETH; GERTRUDE (m. William Purnell, son of Capt. John Purnell, had

5 children (N), he d. 1798, and she d. 1831) {BDML I:666, II:946}; poss. (N) DAU. (m. John Bacon).

4. COL. JOHN HENRY, SO Co., WO Co. and DO Co., b. c1714, son of John (1) Henry, m. Dorothy Rider (b. 1725, dau. of Col. John Rider and Ann Hicks), and lived at *Weston* in DO Co. {OSES:371; DOLR 14 Old 375. See also The John Rider Family in Volume 13 of this series}

Col. John Henry, Deputy Surveyor, WO Co., was an extensive landowner, having patented the 1,793 acre tract *Security* on 23 May 1743, the 1,793 acre tract *Buckland* on 23 May 1744, and the 34 acre tract *Bald Eagle Point* on 10 Aug 1745, all tracts located in SO Co. {MPL EI6:680, LGC:453, PT1:161}

On 25 June 1750 John Henry, WO Co., Gent., and wife Dorothy, WO Co., to Robert Jenckins Henry, SO Co., Esq., and Robert King the younger, WO Co., Gent., a 1,144 acre part of *Weston* on the north side of Nanticoke River and a 120 acre part of *Marsh Pasture*, to the use of said John Henry and Dorothy his wife for their lifetimes, and then in trust for the benefit of Charles Rider Henry, eldest son of said John and Dorothy, for his lifetime, and after the death of said Charles Rider Henry to the use of his heirs, and for the default of such issue to the use of Francis Jenkins Henry, second son of said John and Dorothy, and to the use of his heirs, and for default of such issue to the use of John Henry, third son of said John and Dorothy, and his heirs, and to all and every other son and sons of the body of the said Dorothy by the said John Henry begotten and the heirs of the body or bodies of all and every of such son and sons issuing severally and successively as such sons shall be in seniority and priority of birth, and for default of such issue to the use of the daughters and their heirs, and for default of such heirs to the heirs of said Dorothy. {DOLR 14 Old 434-435}

Ann Loockerman, DO Co., widow of Govert Loockerman, d. leaving a will dated 2 June 1755, proved 10 June 1756, naming nieces Jean Fishwick (dau. of sister Sarah Darnal) and Charlotte Henry and Keturah Henry (daus. of sister Dorothy Henry). {MWB 30:148}

In 1759 Col. John Henry was holder of pew no. 12 in Rocawakin Presbyterian Church (SO Co., now WI Co.), and Rev. Hugh Henry held pew no. 18. {Peden's *A Collection of Maryland Church Records*, p. 300}

Col. John Henry, DO Co., patented the 31 acre tract *Second Addition* in WO Co on 28 June 1766, the 1,793 acre tract *Buckland* in DO Co. on 30 Oct 1769, the 234 acre tract *Addition to Pasture Neck* in DO Co. on 13 Sep 1773, and the 320 acre tract *Marsh Meadow* in DO Co. on 30 Nov 1782. {MPL BC29:451, BC37:420, BC45:264, BC50:296}

At the time of his death in 1781 John Henry owned about 5,700 acres in DO, SO, and WO Cos., MD and in DE, plus a moiety of 2 lots in Vienna, DO Co. {BDML I:436}

John was the father of: CHARLES RIDER (d.s.p.); FRANCIS JENKINS (d.s.p.); JOHN, JR.; CHARLOTTE (m. William Winder, Jr.); KETURAH (prob. the Katura Henry who m. John Brown, DO Co., in June, 1784) {RPDO:23; her name was misspelled as "Niturah" in some sources}; DOROTHY (m. Isaac Henry, son of Rev. Hugh Henry); NANCY; SARAH.

Third Generation

5. ISAAC HENRY, SO Co., son of Rev. Hugh (2) Henry, m. cousin Dorothy (8) Henry, dau. of John (4) Henry. He served in the Maryland Legislature (Lower House, 1779-1780), was a Trustee of Washington Academy, 1779-1801, and d. by 17 Nov 1802. {BDML I:435}

Isaac was the father of: HUGH (m. Harriet Gale); MATILDA (m. Dr. Thomas Handy); SARAH ANN (m. 1st George Roberts and 2nd Dr. Thomas Handy); JOHN (m. Rebecca (N); ROBERT (m. Mary Mitchell); WILLIAM (m. Jane Hutton); CHARLES (m. Juliana Fassett); MARY ANN (m. Peter Franklin); JAMES. {RPSO:137, citing "Henry Family" by Gale J. Belser in MGSB 29:2 (1988)}

6. REV. HUGH HENRY, SO Co., son of Rev. Hugh (2) Henry, patented the 12 acre tract *Henry's Meadow* on 16 Oct 1775. {MPL BC49:421}

7. HON. JOHN HENRY, b. c1750 at *Weston* near Vienna, DO Co., son of John (4) Henry, m. Margaret Campbell (dau. of John Campbell and Elizabeth Goldsborough of CA Co.) on 16 March 1787. Margaret Henry d. in 1789 and John Henry d. 16 Dec 1798. {BDML I:436}

John Henry attended West Nottingham Academy in CE Co., MD, graduated from the College of New Jersey (now Princeton University) in 1769, and studied law for several years in this country and about 2½ years in London, England at Middle Temple (member of the Robin Hood Club which debated the issues of separation of American and Great Britain). In 1777 he was elected to the Maryland Legislature and served successively in the Continental Congress, the U. S. Senate, and as Governor of Maryland in 1797 until shortly before his death in 1798. John also served as a captain in the militia, 1778-1781. He was buried at *Weston*, the place of his birth (burned by the British in 1780). His body was later removed to Christ Church Cemetery, Cambridge, MD, where a monument was erected by his descendants in his memory. {Mowbray I:64; BDML I:436; RPDO:101}

At the time of his death John Henry in 1798 was an extensive land owner, having acquired at least 4,226 acres of land in SO, DO and CA Cos. {BDML I:437}

John was the father of: JOHN CAMPBELL HENRY (1787-1857, m. Mary Nevett Steele); FRANCIS JENKINS HENRY (1789-1810).

8. HON. FRANCIS JENKINS HENRY, WO Co. and DO Co., son of John (4) Henry, m. Frances (Fanny) Purnell (dau. of Walton Purnell) and resided in Buckingham Hundred. He took the Oath of Allegiance in 1778, served in the Maryland Legislature, 1786-1788, was a county justice, 1794-1795, and d. testate by June, 1796. At the time of his death he owned about 2,100 acres of land in WO and DO Co. {RPDO:100; BDML I:434, II:946}

9. DOROTHY (DOLLY) HENRY, SO Co., dau. of John (4) Henry, m. Isaac (5) Henry, son of Rev. Hugh (2) Henry, and had no issue. {BDML I:435}

Unplaced

FRANCIS HENRY, DO Co.

On 6 June 1745 Francis Henry and Stephen Henry, DO Co., were listed as next of kin when the estate of Thomas Winstandley, DO Co., dec'd., was appraised. {MINV 31:108}

On 4 Nov 1758 Francis Henry, of St. Mary's White Chapel Parish, DO Co., planter, conveyed livestock and other personal property to Dr. William Murray of said co. {DOLR 16 Old 113}

ISAAC HENRY, DO Co., m. Mary (N).

On 3 Jan 1767 Isaac Henry, DO Co., planter, and wife Mary conveyed a 50¼ acre part of *Henry's Right* to Elijah Dean of same co. {DOLR 21 Old 258}

On 30 Sep 1770 Isaac Henry, DO Co., patented the 73 acre tract *Privilege in Partnership*. {MPL BC39:326}

On 20 Dec 1771 Isaac Henry, DO Co., planter, and wife Mary, conveyed parts of two tracts, *William's Delight* and *Addition to William's Delight*, containing 136½ acres, to Peter Eaton, DO Co. {DOLR 25 Old 308}

JOHN HENRY, SO Co., was among those who received payment from the estate of William Innis, SO Co., dec'd., on 23 Oct 1697. {INAC 15:283}

JOHN HENRY, SO Co., m. Frances (N).

John Henry, Sr., SO Co., d. leaving a will dated 10 Feb 1757, proved 3 Jan 1758, naming wife Frances, sons John Henry, Jr. (exec.), Robert Henry, and Hugh Henry, dau. Martha Wiley, and granddau. Frances Wiley. {MWB 30:233}

The estate of John Henry, SO Co., dec'd., was appraised at £50.3.2 and admin. on 21 Feb 1758 by John Henry, exec. The named legatees were Frances Wiley, Robert Henry (in Carolina), Hugh Henry (in Roan Oak) [Roanoke,

Virginia], and Martha Willen [Willey?]. Distribution was made to Frances Henry (widow, 1/3) and residue to John Henry (accountant). {MDAD 41:344}

John was the father of: JOHN, JR.; ROBERT; HUGH; MARTHA (m. a Wiley).

JOHN HENRY, SO Co., patented the 39 acre tract *Henry's Lot* on 7 June 1770 and 80 acre tract *Marsh Meadow* on 13 Sep 1773. {MPL BC39:261, BC45:302}

LAZARUS HENRY, SO Co., patented the 200 acre tract *Henry's Lot* on 10 Sep 1716. {MPL PL4:322}

MARTIN HENRY, WO Co., d. by 18 Feb 1758 at which time his estate was appraised at £40.2.4 and approved on 7 May 1758 by admx. Isabell Henry (widow).

MARY HENRY, DO Co., acknowledged owing the Proprietary £5 in 1733 and she was ordered to appear before the court in August next to give evidence against William Barnett for committing fornication with her and begetting a bastard child. {DOJR 1733-1734, p. 86}

STEPHEN HENRY, DO Co., m. Elizabeth (N).

On 6 June 1745 Stephen Henry and Francis Henry, DO Co., were listed as next of kin when the estate of Thomas Winstandley, DO Co., dec'd., was appraised. {MINV 31:108}

On 8 Feb 1765 Stephen Henry, DO Co., and wife Elizabeth conveyed a 50 3/4 acre part of *Henry's Folly Enlarged* to Solomon Jones, TA Co. {DOLR 20 Old 23}

On 17 Oct 1765 Stephen Henry, DO Co., and wife Elizabeth conveyed a 314 acre part of *Henry's Folly Enlarged*, whereon said Stephen Henry dwells, to James Murray of same co. {DOLR 20 Old 365}

WOLSTON HENRY, SO Co., was among those who received a payment from the estate of Joshua Hitch, SO Co., dec'd., on 25 July 1774. {MDAD 71:191}

## THE THOMAS HICKS FAMILY

1. THOMAS HICKS, b. 1659, White Haven, England, immigrated into this province by 1671, m. Sarah Denwood (youngest dau. of Levin Denwood and Mary Cutting) in 1679, DO Co., and d. 1722. {MPL 16:170; Jones:342; Mowbray I:65; Barnes' *British Roots* II:93. See also The Levin Denwood Family in this volume}

On 9 Nov 1678 Thomas Hicks, DO Co., witnessed a land conveyance on the Nanticoke River between Ann Coppen (widow) and Charles Hutchins, Gent. {DOLR 3 Old 144}

On 30 Sep 1683 Thomas Hicks, DO Co., carpenter, patented the 75 acre tract *Poplar Neck*. {MPL 25:124, 32:402}

On 8 June 1687 Thomas Hicks and Jeremiah Davis, DO Co., acquired the 769 acre tract *Seckter* [also spelled *Sector*] on a branch of the Chicacomoco River and the adj. 100 acre tract *Cambre Lake* from Thomas Smithson. {DOLR 4 Old 68, 171}

On 8 Feb 1687/8 Jeremiah Davis conveyed to Thomas Hicks, DO Co., the 100 acre tract *Camber Lake* and one-half moiety of the tract *Sector* containing 388 acres. {DOLR 4 Old 204}

On 11 July 1698 Major Thomas Hicks and Lt. Col. Thomas Ennalls, Magistrates of DO Co., were appointed by the Governor and Council of Maryland to decide differences between the English colonists and the Nanticoke Indians. {ARMD 23:457}

By 2 Sep 1690 Thomas Hicks was a court justice of DO Co. {DOLR 4½ Old 9}

On 10 Nov 1695 Thomas Hicks, DO Co., carpenter, patented the 100 acre tract *Forest* and the 165 acre tract *Bartholomew's Choice*. {MPL 40:451, 453}

Major Thomas Hicks and wife Sarah were named in the will of Col. Charles Hutchins, DO Co., dated 29 June 1699. Ann Rider, dau. of Thomas Hicks, received 500 acre tract *Apinforis* and her son John Rider (testator's grandson) was bequeathed Hutchins' entire estate after the death of Hutchins' wife. {MWB 11:127}

On 10 May 1706 Thomas Hicks, DO Co., patented the 100 acre tract *Addition to Bartholomew's Choice*. On 10 Oct 1707 he patented the 19 acre tract *Crooked Ridge* and the 430 acre tract *Hicks Fields*. {MPL WD:528, DD5:194, PL2:270}

On 10 Aug 1713 Thomas Hicks, DO Co., patented the 186 acre tract *Cow Lane*, on 27 April 1714 the 17 acre tract *Levin Hicks Lot*, on 10 April 1715 the 13 acre tract *Bear Quarter*, and on 6 Aug 1718 the 50 acre tract *Brother's Adventure*. {MPL DD5:805, EE6:34, 254, PL3:69, CE1:45, FF7:228, PL4:258}

On 3 May 1714 Thomas Hicks, DO Co., Gent., and wife Sarah, conveyed to Edward Hoggens, SO Co., planter, the 75 acre tract *Poplar Neck* on Nanticoke River. {DOLR 6 Old 217}

On 24 Aug 1719 Thomas Hicks, Sr., and wife Sarah, DO Co., conveyed the 17 acre tract *Hicks Lott* (patented to Thomas Hicks on 5 June 1687 on the north side of Nanticoke at the mouth thereof) to Elias Venalson (or Venatson); acknowledged before John Rider and Levin Hicks, justices. {DOLR 2 Old 59, 8 Old 3}

By the time of his death in 1722 Thomas Hicks, DO Co., was an extensive land owner, having acquired approx. 5,000 acres in the vicinity of Vienna, near the Nanticoke and Chicamacomico Rivers. His home plantation was made up of the tracts *Sector*, *Cambre Lane* and *Luck By Chance*, all adj. at the head of Chicamacomico River. (Gov. Thomas Holliday Hicks was born on this plantation). Major Thomas Hicks served as a DO Co. justice, Provincial Court justice, and a delegate to the Maryland Assembly (1694-1700, 1710-1711). He died testate in Vienna in 1722 and his wife Sarah died in 1731/2. {BDML I:440; Mowbray I:65-66}

Thomas Hicks, DO Co., d. leaving a will dated 24 July 1720, proved 6 Aug 1722. To son Levin, 453 acre tract *Hicks Lott*. To son Thomas, tract *Hicks Field* where he now lives. To son-in-law John Rider, 450 acre tract *The Reserve* on north side of Chicacone River and 150 acres (N) adj. To granddau. Ann (eldest dau. of son Levin), tracts *The Forrest* and *The Addition to Bartholomew's Close*. To dau. Ann Ryder, grandson John Rider, granddau. Sarah Rider and granddau. Sarah Hicks (dau. of son Thomas), personalty. To wife Sarah (extx.), residue of personal estate and use of dwelling plantation during life. {MWB 17:310-312}

On 2 Feb 1722/3 the estate of Major Thomas Hicks, DO Co., was appraised at £722.18.11 and approved by Sarah Hicks, extx. Next of kin were listed as Livin Hicks and Thomas Hicks. An admin. account was filed on 22 Nov 1723 by Sarah Hicks, extx. {MINV 8:2; MDAD 5:286}

Thomas was the father of: LEVIN (m. Mary Hooper); THOMAS, JR. (m. Elizabeth Woolford); DENWOOD; WILLIAM; HENRY; ANN (m. John Rider).

## Second Generation

2. LEVIN HICKS, DO Co., b. c1680, son of Thomas (1) Hicks and Sarah Denwood, m. Mary Hooper (dau. of Henry Hooper), and d. by 16 March 1731/2. She m. 2nd to John Rider, widower of Ann Hicks who was Mary's sister. {MWB 16:159; DOLR 8 Old 296. See The Henry Hooper Family in Volume 7 and also The John Rider Family in Volume 13 of this series}

On 3 March 1713 Levin Hicks, DO Co., patented the 25 acre tract *Levin's Chance*. {MPL DD5:783, RY1:41}

Levin Hicks, Great Choptank Parish, DO Co., was a captain by 1715, a justice of DO Co. by 2 Feb 1718/19, and was styled major by 1730 (although an account filed in 1732 still referred to him as captain). {DOLR 2 Old 16; ARMD 25:529; SOJR III:66}

On 8 March 1719/20 Levin Hicks, DO Co., Gent., conveyed to Hugh Handley, DO Co., planter, the 25 acre tract *Levin's Chance*, adj. *Sector* on the Chicamocomico River. {DOLR 2 Old 18}

Henry Hooper, Sr., DO Co., d. leaving a will dated 27 March 1720, proved 30 Aug 1720, and bequeathed 1 sh. to each of his daus., including Mary Hicks. {MWB 16:159}

In depositions taken in DO Co. in June, 1729, Capt. Levin Hicks stated he was about 49 years old and Capt. Thomas Hicks stated he was about 42 years old. {DOLR 8 Old 296}

Liven Hicks, DO Co., d. leaving a will dated 25 Feb 1731/2, proved 16 March 1731/2. To eldest son Liven, part of dwelling plantation *Hinchman's Neck* adj. land of John Rider. To son Henry, residue of afsd. tract and *Crooked Ridge* [also spelled *Crucked Ridge*]. To son John, lands (N) on Chickacone River. To youngest son Denwood, tract (N) by Chiconocomoco Upper Bridge and tract (N) at Marshahope. To dau. Anne Travers, 20 sh. To wife (N) and 6 children Liven, John, Henry, Denwood, Mary and Sarah, personal estate equally. Execs.: wife (N) and son Liven. {MWB 20:331}

On 29 Sep 1732 the estate of Capt. Levin Hicks, DO Co., dec'd., was appraised at £718.9.9 and approved by extx. Mary Hicks. Next of kin were listed as Thomas Hicks and Thomas Hooper. {MINV 16:599}

On 15 July 1735 John Rider, DO Co., Gent., gave a negro named Batt to his kinswoman Sarah Hicks, dau. of Levin Hicks, dec'd., and he gave a negro named Boaz to his kinsman Denwood Hicks, son of Levin Hicks, dec'd. {DOLR 9 Old 297}

Mary Rider, DO Co., d. leaving a will dated 18 Nov 1755, proved 6 Jan 1757, naming son Levin Hicks, son Denwood Hicks, son Henry Hicks (exec.), dau. Ann Travers (wife of Henry), Mary Parker (wife of Richard), and dau. Sarah Hicks. {MWB 30:228}

Levin was the father of: LEVIN; JOHN; HENRY; DENWOOD; ANN (m. Henry Travers); MARY (m. Richard Parker); SARAH.

3. THOMAS HICKS, JR., b. c1687, son of Thomas (1) Hicks and Sarah Denwood, m. Elizabeth Woolford (b. 29 Feb 1691/2, dau. of Roger Woolford and Elizabeth Ennalls). {Mowbray I:66, 184. See also The Woolford Family in Volume 14 of this series}

On 21 Aug 1729 Thomas Hicks, DO Co., patented the 50 acre tract *Privilege*. {MPL PL7:284, ILA:773}

Thomas Hicks, Great Choptank Parish, DO Co., aged about 42, was a captain by 1729. {MDEP:91; ARMD 25:529}

On 7 Oct 1730 Roger Woolford, DO Co., wrote his will and in it he bequeathed 20 sh. each to his daus. Mary Pitts (wife of John Pitts) and Elizabeth Hicks (wife of Thomas Hicks). {MWB 20:119}

On 4 Nov 1731 Thomas Hicks, DO Co., patented the 50 acre tract *Hicks Marshes*. {MPL PL8:246, ILB:435}

By 6 Sep 1732 Thomas Hicks was a court justice of DO Co. {DOLR 9 Old 1}

On 31 Oct 1732 John Lemee, DO Co., wrote his will and in it he requested Thomas Hicks to have care of grandson James Lemee and his estate until able to act for himself. Thomas Hicks witnessed the will as Capt. Thomas Hicks. {MWB 20:640}

On 13 Nov 1732 Thomas Hicks, DO Co., patented the 80 acre tract *Hicks Forest*. {MPL PL8:721, AM1:165}

On 22 April 1734 Thomas Tackett, DO Co., wrote his will and in it he bequeathed personalty to Mrs. Elizabeth Hicks. One of the named execs. was Capt. Thomas Hicks. {MWB 21:123}

On 7 Dec 1734 Capt. Thomas Hicks, DO Co., Gent., stated he was about 47 years old; mentioned his father Thomas Hicks 20 years ago. {DOLR 9 Old 293; MCHR *6:444*}

On 15 June 1735 Thomas Hicks, DO Co., Gent., and wife Elizabeth, conveyed to John Hubbert, DO Co., planter, the 80 acre tract *Hicks Forest* adj. *Johns Hills* on the west side of the Northwest Fork of Nanticoke River. {DOLR 9 Old 529}

On 23 July 1744 John Hicks, Elizabeth Hicks, Mary Hicks, and Roger Pitt witnessed the will of Benjamin Ball, DO Co. (who was the son of Benjamin Ball of CV Co.), which stated, in part, that in consideration that my eldest son Thomas Ball has a plantation given him by his grandfather Thomas Hicks, I give him no part of my land. Testator also mentioned his wife Elizabeth Ball, sons Benjamin and Levin Ball, and dau. Betty Ball. {MWB 24:26}

In a 1745 deposition Thomas Hicks, DO Co., stated he was about 57 years old. {DOLR 14 Old 44}

On 26 March 1754 Thomas Hicks, DO Co., conveyed to son John Hicks a 330 acre part of *Hicks Fields*, excluding 100 acres formerly given to Thomas Ball. {DOLR 15 Old 60}

In a 1757 deposition Thomas Hicks, DO Co., stated he was about 69 years old. {DOLR 15 Old 522}

On 18 Feb 1760 Thomas Hicks, DO Co., Gent., conveyed 82 acre part of *Partnership* to his son Thomas Hicks, Jr., and 100 acre part of *Hicks Fields* to Thomas Ball. {DOLR 17 Old 55-57}

On 26 Dec 1760 Thomas Hicks, DO Co., conveyed livestock and other personal property to his son John Hicks of said co. {DOLR 17 Old 234}

John Hicks, DO Co., d. leaving a will dated 9 Feb 1765, proved 4 March 1765, naming wife Sarah, sons William, John and Thomas, and father Thomas Hicks; also mentioned tracts *Hicks Fields* and *Darley*. {MWB 33:78}

In a 1767 deposition regarding the tract *Maiden Forest*, Hooper Hodson, DO Co., stated "three or four years ago being on the said land in company with Capt. Thomas Hicks, then of said county, aged 77 years as he himself said, but now deceased." {DOLR 21 Old 382}

Thomas Hicks apparently lived to a great age because he was 77 years old circa 1764 and he was still living in 1771, at which time he was about age 84. {BFD 6:81}

*Commentary: Thomas Hicks was prob. dec'd. by 1777 although no inventory or admin. account has been found for him (and after which time probate records are not extant for DO Co. due to the 1852 courthouse fire).*

Thomas was the father of: THOMAS, JR. (III); JOHN (d. 1765); ELIZABETH (m. 1st Benjamin Ball and 2nd (N) Hodson); poss. MARY.

4. ANN HICKS, b. 1684, dau. Thomas (1) Hicks and Sarah Denwood, m. Col. John Rider (b. 1686, son of John Rider of England and Anne Hutchins of DO Co.) on 23 Jan 1706/7 and she d. 1733. John Rider m. 2nd to Mary (Hooper) Hicks (widow of Levin Hicks and dau. of Henry Hooper) in 1734 and he d. testate by 9 April 1740. {MWB 22:157; Mowbray I:78; BDML II:680. See also The John Rider Family in Volume 13 of this series}

Col. Charles Hutchins, DO Co., d. leaving a will dated 29 June 1699, proved 23 Oct 1700. To wife Ann Hutchins (extx.), sole legatee and entire estate during life. To grandson John Rider (exec.), entire estate after wife Ann's death; if he should die without heirs, the following bequests are made: To Major Thomas Hicks (overseer), Sarah Hicks his wife, and Stephen Tully, personalty. To Ann [Rider], dau. of said Thomas Hicks, 500 acre tract *Apinforis*. To Thomas Thacker, 100 acre tract *Fulham*. Also named Col. Thomas Evans, guardian for infant exec. {MWB 11:127}

John Rider and Thomas Hicks, Sr., were named as trustees in the will of John Gladstone, DO Co., on 30 April 1709. {MWB 12:219, Pt. 2}

John Rider was a justice of DO Co. by 24 Aug 1719. {DOLR 2 Old 59}

On 25 July 1720 John Rider and wife Ann, DO Co., conveyed the 361 acre tract *Doublin* to William Nutter who in turn conveyed the 700 acre tract *Hansel*, lying in Chicacone Indian Town, to John and Ann Rider; acknowledged before Henry Ennalls and Levin Hicks, justices. {DOLR 2 Old 52}

John Rider, DO Co., d. leaving a will dated 15 Feb 1739/40, proved 9 April 1740. To dau. Dorothy, 725 acre tract *Rider's Forest*. To dau. Sarah, 332 acre tract *Discovery* and 50 acre tract *Hope*. To William Housley, tract *Scotch Folly*. To Mary Housley, personalty. To Denwood Hicks, 1/3 of tract *Three Brothers*. To Capt. Thomas Hicks, 1/3 of tract *Three Brothers*. To wife Mary, either her dower or 1/3 of estate but not both; the 1/3 real estate to consist of life interest in 400 acre tract (N) on Wappermando Creek. To son Charles (exec.), residue of real estate and ½ of personal estate. To daus. Ann, Sarah and Dorothy (to be under care of said Ann and Sarah until she reaches age 16), residue of personal estate. {MWB 22:157}

Ann (Hicks) Rider was the mother of: HUTCHINS RIDER [#1] (b. & d. 1706); JOHN RIDER, JR. (III), 1708-c1733; CAPT. CHARLES RIDER (1716-1741, unm.); HUTCHINS RIDER [#2] (1718-1732); (N) TWIN SONS (b. & d. 1724); SARAH RIDER (b. 1710, m. 1st Thomas Nevitt, 2nd William Fishwick, and 3rd Robert Darnall); ANNE RIDER (1713-1756, m. 1st Major James Billings and 2nd Govert Loockerman); DOROTHY RIDER (b. 1725, m. John Henry). {BDML II:680; DOLR 14 Old 375, 15 Old 403, 17 Old 357, 367, DOLR 23 Old 247}

Third Generation

5. LEVIN HICKS, DO Co., b. 1713, son of Levin (2) Hicks, m. Mary (Hooper) Ennalls, widow of Bartholomew Ennalls and dau. of Col. Henry Hooper, on 25 Jan 1744. {Jones:342. See also The Henry Hooper Family in Volume 7 of this series}

Mary Hicks, dau. of Levin and Mary Hicks, b. 5 March 1745, m. Zachariah Campbell in 1765, d. 1779. Levin Hicks, son of Levin and Mary Hicks, b. 17 Aug 1748, d. unmarried. {Jones:342}

Levin Hicks, DO Co., d. leaving a will dated 23 May 1753, proved 16 Aug 1753. To son Levin Hicks, my part of 585 acre tract *Copartnership* on Chicacone River; if no heirs, to dau. Mary Hicks, and for want of heir of her then to bro. Denwood Hicks. To dau. Mary, the plantation (N) where my mother now lives, and my part of tract *Hinchman's Neck* except 50 acres to be sold. To bro. Henry Hicks, certain lands devised to children if they have no heirs. To wife Mary Hicks, 1/3 part of real estate. {MWB 28:533}

On 22 Feb 1758 Ennalls Hooper, DO Co., and wife Mary, conveyed to Mary Hicks (widow), 1/3 of the land called *The Woodyard* (formerly given by Col. Thomas Ennalls to Bartholomew Ennalls) for the lifetime of said Mary Hicks. {DOLR 15 Old 558}

On 28 March 1759 John Hicks, DO Co., Gent., and wife Betty, conveyed to Mary Hicks (widow), 1/3 of the lands called *Hoghole* and *Clifton* on Great Choptank River and Jenkins Creek which had been purchased by Col. Thomas Ennalls from William Dorrington, dec'd., whereof Henry Ennalls, son and heir of Bartholomew Ennalls, was seized at the time of his death. {DOLR 16 Old 152}

On 21 March 1760 Henry Ennalls, Jr., DO Co., conveyed to Mary Hicks (widow), 75 acres of tract *The Woodyard* which had been purchased by said Henry Ennalls, Jr. from Ennalls Hooper and wife Mary. {DOLR 17 Old 81}

On 17 June 1765 Richard Glover, DO Co., and wife Elizabeth, conveyed to Mary Hicks (widow), 100 acres being parts of tracts *Clifts, Clifton,*

*Busby* and *Hoghole* on the east side of Jenkins Creek and Indian Cabbin Cove. {DOLR 20 Old 150}

On 20 Feb 1770 Mary Hicks, relict and executrix of Levin Hicks, late of DO Co., dec'd., and Levin Hicks, son and heir of the afsd. Levin Hicks, conveyed to Zacharias and Mary Campbell a 50 acre part of *Hinchman's Neck* devised by the will of said dec'd. to be sold. {DOLR 23 Old 468}

In 1777 Benjamin Ball, DO Co., was deposed regarding the tract *Partnership* and stated he was about 41 years old; mentioned his grandfather Capt. Levin Hicks (now dec'd.) about 16 or 17 years ago; also mentioned Thomas Hicks, son of Capt. Thomas Hicks. {DOLR 1 JCH 82}

Levin was the father of: LEVIN (d. unmarried); MARY (m. Zachariah Campbell); prob. (N) DAU. (m. a Ball).

6. DENWOOD HICKS, DO Co., son of Levin (2) Hicks, m. Anne Hooper, dau. of Gen. Henry Hooper and Ann Ennalls.

On 9 Nov 1747 Denwood Hicks, DO Co., witnessed a land conveyance in DO Co. {DOLR 14 Old 180}

On 15 Jan 1747/8 Anne Hicks and Henry Hooper, DO Co., witnessed a conveyance of land on the Northeast Fork of the Nanticoke River. {DOLR 14 Old 206}

On 28 March 1748 Denwood Hicks and Henry Hooper, DO Co., witnessed a conveyance of land on a branch of Cakius Creek and another tract on a road from Hunting Creek Church to the head of Watses Creek. {DOLR 14 Old 224}

On 25 Jan 1755 Denwood Hicks, DO Co., Gent., and wife Anne, conveyed to Ezekiel Pritchet, DO Co., planter, the 50 acre tract *Brother's Adventure* on the northwest side of the northeast branch of Nanticoke River. {DOLR 15 Old 192}

Henry Hooper, DO Co., d. leaving a will dated 15 April 1767, proved 4 May 1767, bequeathing, in part, To dau. Ann Hicks, wife of Denwood Hicks, the plantation whereon the said Denwood Hicks now lives, with remaining part of afsd. tract *Warwick Fort Manor* [which he bequeathed to his son Henry Hooper], divided by north and by west line afsd., to said Ann Hicks, wife of Denwood Hicks, plantation whereon said Denwood Hicks now dwells. Remaining part of said *Warwick Fort Manor*, divided by the north and by west line afsd., to said Ann Hicks and heirs; for want of such issue, to son Henry Hooper and heirs. Testator also bequeathed to daus. Mary and Ann Hicks, silver. Residue of personal estate to be disposed of as follows: one half to son Henry Hooper; the other half to daus. Mary and Anne Hicks. {MWB 35:382}

Denwood Hicks, DO Co., was head of household in Transquakin Hundred in 1776, aged between 50 and 60, with one male aged between 21 and

30, one male aged between 10 and 16, one male under age 10, one female aged between 30 and 40, one female aged between 16 and 21, and one female aged between 10 and 16, plus 27 negroes. {1776 Census}

On 24 May 1776 Denwood Hicks was a captain in the DO Co. militia and took the Oath of Allegiance in 1778. {RPDO:102}

Denwood was the father of: (N) 3 SONS; (N) 2 DAUS.; prob. ELIZABETH HOOPER HICKS (m. William Barrow in 1786). {RPDO:9}

7. HENRY HICKS, DO Co., son of Levin (2) Hicks, m. (N).

On 23 Oct 1754 Henry Hicks, Gent., late of DO Co., but now of Carolina, conveyed to John Beerd, DO Co., planter, 100 acre part of *Luck by Chance* on the west side of Nanticoke River. Said tract had been conveyed by John Russell to Thomas Hicks, grandfather of said Henry Hicks, and it was subsequently devised by said Thomas Hicks to his son Levin Hicks and by said Levin to his son the said Henry Hicks. {DOLR 15 Old 139}

On 28 Sep 1758 Henry Hicks, DO Co., mariner, acquired from James Galloway and William Phillips, DO Co., the 127 acre tract *Galloway's Fancy* in Meekins Neck. {DOLR 16 Old 125}

On 15 Nov 1769 Henry Hicks, DO Co., mariner, conveyed the 19 acre tract *Crooked Ridge* to Darby Hurley, DO Co., planter. {DOLR 23 Old 389}

Some time between 9 Aug 1767 and 28 Aug 1773 Henry Hicks, DO Co., was deposed and stated he was about 54 years old; mentioned his uncle Thomas Hicks, now dec'd.; also mentioned his grandfather Thomas Hicks who he understood had given all his land in Nanticoke Indian Town to his dau. Ann Hicks who intermarried with Col. John Rider, now dec'd. {DOLR 26 Old 436-438}

Henry Hicks, DO Co., d. leaving a will dated 13 May 1775, proved 29 Sep 1775. To son Baptist, my real estate (N) provided his 4 sisters, Sarah, Dulcybella, Anne and Louisa, are allowed to live with him until married. To dau. Louisa, £60 to be paid by her bro. Baptist over her share. To afsd. son and 4 daus., residue of personal estate equally. To dau. Mary Dawson, stock and £5. Execs.: dau. Sarah and Capt. Robert Dawson. [Dawson subsequently refused to act as exec. of the will]. {MWB 40:438}

On 17 Oct 1776 the estate of Henry Hicks, DO Co., was appraised at £391.5.6 and admin. by Sarah Farguson, wife of Philip Farguson. Payment to George Lock for schooling his son John Baptist Hicks paid by Capt. Dawson. {MDAD 72:322}

Henry was the father of: JOHN BAPTIST; SARAH (m. Philip Farguson); DULCYBELLA; ANNE; LOUISA; MARY (prob. m. Robert Dawson).

8. JOHN HICKS, DO Co., son of Levin (2) Hicks, m. Betty Ennalls, dau. of Col. William Ennalls. {DOLR 114 Old 451, 740}

On 30 Nov 1747 John Hicks, DO Co., witnessed the conveyance of an infant negro girl named Sary (b. April 1747) from Edward Trippe to John Hodson 4th. {DOLR 14 Old 198}

On 13 July 1750 a division of the lands of Col. William Ennalls, DO Co., dec'd., was conveyed between Ennalls Hooper and wife Mary, and Henry Hooper, Jr. and wife Ann, and John Hicks and wife Betty, said Mary, Ann and Betty being daus. of said Col. William Ennalls. The 100 acre tract *Ennalls' Regulation* was conveyed to John and Betty Hicks. {DOLR 14 Old 451-452}

On 21 Feb 1752 John Hicks and wife Betty, and Ennalls Hooper and wife Mary, and Henry Hooper, Jr. and wife Ann, and John Stewart, Sr. and wife Ann, all of DO Co., conveyed the 300 acre tract *Porpeham* to James Hooper and the 100 acre tract *Crow's Nest*, both lands on the west side of Transquakin River. {DOLR 14 Old 574}

On 14 March 1752 John Hicks, DO Co., acquired the 200 acre tract *Hooper's Outlet* from Henry Hooper, DO Co. {DOLR 14 Old 595}

On 28 June 1756 John Hicks, DO Co., and wife Betty, conveyed to James Sulivane, DO Co., the 200 acre tract *Hooper's Outlet*. {DOLR 15 Old 372}

On 29 March 1762 John Hicks, DO Co., and wife Betty, conveyed to John Darby, of the Colony of Virginia, tracts *John's Lane* and *Hodson's Regulation* on Chickamacomico River at Black Walnut Landing containing 422 acres. {DOLR 18 Old 106}

9. ANN HICKS, DO Co., dau. of Levin (2) Hicks, m. Henry Travers or Traverse.

Henry Travers was a justice of DO Co. by 1752. {DOLR 14 Old 595}

On 20 July 1771 the estate of Henry Traverse, DO Co., was admin. by Ann Travers, Levin Travers, Henry Travers and John Hicks Traverse. The named legatees were Sarah Hooper, Nancy Philips, Emelia Traverse, Priscilla Traverse, William Hicks Travers, Nancy Travers, Henry Hicks Travers, Nancy and Emelia and Mary Tucker. Distribution was made to widow (N), her third, with residue equally to Levin Traverse, Henry Traverse, John Hicks Traverse, William Hicks Traverse, Mary Tucker, Nancy Phillips, Rebecca Traverse, Priscilla Traverse, and Amelia Travers. {BFD 6:42}

Anne Traverse, DO Co., d. leaving a will dated 4 June 1773, proved 22 July 1773. To dau. Prissilla Traverse, negroes Jim, Kate and Anna. To grandson Frederick Traverse (son of Henry), negro Harry. To grandson Henry Tucker, negro Jem. To granddau. Terrissa Traverse (dau. of Thomas and Amillia), negro Creasa. To granddau. Lavisa Traverse (dau. of William and Rebeckah), negro

Sall. To dau.-in-law Priscilla Traverse (widow of son Hicks Traverse), bed and furniture. To dau. Molly Tucker, bed, furniture and 1 sh. To dau. Priscilla Traverse and dau.-in-law Priscilla Traverse (widow of Hicks Traverse), residue of moveable estate. One shilling each to son Levin Traverse, son Henry Traverse, son John Hicks Traverse (exec.), dau. Sarah Hooper (wife of Henry Hooper), dau. Rebecca Traverse (wife of William Traverse), dau. Nancy Phillips (wife of Levin Phillips), and dau. Amillia Traverse (widow of my son Thomas Traverse). To grandson Henry Traverse Phillips, son of Leavin Phillips, negro not for Lavissa Traverse, dau. of William Traverse, but for said grandson Henry Traverse Phillips [note written at end of the will]. {MWB 39:554-555}

Ann (Hicks) Traverse was the mother of: HENRY HICKS TRAVERSE (m. ----); THOMAS TRAVERSE (m. Amillia ----); WILLIAM HICKS TRAVERSE (m. Priscilla ----); LEVIN TRAVERSE; JOHN HICKS TRAVERSE; REBECCA TRAVERSE (m. William Traverse); SARAH TRAVERSE (m. Henry Hooper); MARY (MOLLY) TRAVERSE (m. ---- Tucker); NANCY TRAVERSE (m. Levin Phillips); PRISSILLA TRAVERSE.

10. THOMAS HICKS, JR., son of Thomas (3) Hicks, prob. m. Mary (N).

On 12 Aug 1755 a DO Co. land commission was created to perpetuate the bounds of the land of Thomas Hicks and Mary Hicks called *Sidney*. {DOLR 15 Old 512}

On 13 March 1762 Thomas Hicks, Jr., DO Co., patented the 49 acre tract *Addition to Partnership*. {MPL BC14:485, BC17:476}

In 1777 Thomas Hicks, DO Co., was deposed regarding the tract *Partnership* and stated he was about 47 years old; mentioned his father Thomas Hicks; also mentioned his bro. John Hicks. {DOLR 1 JCH 82}

Thomas Hicks, DO Co., took the Oath of Allegiance in 1778. {RPDO:103}

On 4 April 1792 Henry Hicks, DO Co., son of Thomas, conveyed to David Smith a 6¼ acre part of the tract *Partnership* on the east side of the main road from Vienna to Crotcher's Ferry. {DOLR 3 HD 537}

Thomas was the father of: HENRY; OTHERS (N).

11. JOHN HICKS, DO Co., son of Thomas (3) Hicks, m. Sarah (N).

On 23 July 1744 John Hicks, Elizabeth Hicks, Mary Hicks, and Roger Pitt witnessed the will of Benjamin Ball, DO Co., which stated, in part, that in consideration that my eldest son Thomas Ball has a plantation given him by his grandfather Thomas Hicks, I give him no part of my land. {MWB 24:26}

On 26 Dec 1760 Thomas Hicks, DO Co., conveyed to his son John Hicks, DO Co., slaves, livestock and other personal property. {DOLR 17 Old 234}

John Hicks, DO Co., d. leaving a will dated 9 Feb 1765, proved 4 March 1765, naming wife Sarah, sons William, John and Thomas, and father Thomas Hicks; also mentioned tracts *Hicks Fields* and *Darley*. {MWB 33:78}

On 17 Sep 1766 the lands of William, John and Thomas Hicks, orphans of John Hicks, dec'd. (now under the guardianship of Sarah Hicks, widow), were valuated, namely *Hicks Fields* (330 acres of which belongs to said orphans) and *Darley*. {DOLR 21 Old 183}

On 10 June 1767 Sarah Hicks, DO Co., conveyed a negro girl named Mintia to Isaac Henry. {DOLR 21 Old 348}

On 3 May 1768 the following was directed to Sarah Hicks by Isaac Lloyd, DO Co.: "I do require and demand of you the negroes and other effects that were removed out of my possession by virtue of an Order of Court granted to Sarah Hicks, executrix of the testament and last will of John Hicks who in his lifetime was one of the suretys for Mary Hodson, admx. of Roger Hodson, and that you deliver the same to my brother Thomas Lloyd in as ample a manner and in as good condition as at the time they were taken out of my possession and he the said Thomas Lloyd will satisfie to the guardian of the said children their distributive share or dividend of their father Roger Hodson's estate and the said Thos. Loyd's rect. shall sufficiently indemnifie you and each you agt. yrs. etc." William Stevens and James Hodson, sureties for Sarah Hicks. {DOLR 23 Old 268}

On 10 June 1768 Sarah Hicks (widow), DO Co., conveyed negro slaves to John Hodson, Jr. {DOLR 22 Old 358}

On 17 Nov 1768 the estate of John Hicks, DO Co., was appraised at £1547.5.3 and admin. by Sarah Hicks (extx.) at that time and again on 14 June 1769 and 8 July 1771. Sureties on all three dates were Thomas Hicks and Thomas Ball. {MDAD 60:140, 62:217, 66:96}

On 8 July 1771 final distribution of the estate of John Hicks, DO Co., was made by extx. Sarah Hicks. Thomas Hicks, father of the deceased, was a named legatee. Distribution was made to the widow (her third) with residue equally to his children (N). {BFD 6:81}

John was the father of: WILLIAM; JOHN; THOMAS.

12. ELIZABETH HICKS, DO Co., dau. of Thomas (3) Hicks, m. 1st Benjamin Ball and 2nd (N) Hodson.

On 23 July 1744 John Hicks, Elizabeth Hicks, Mary Hicks, and Roger Pitt witnessed the will of Benjamin Ball, DO Co. (who was the son of Benjamin Ball of CV Co.), which stated, in part, that in consideration that my eldest son Thomas Ball has a plantation given him by his grandfather Thomas Hicks, I give him no part of my land. Testator also mentioned his wife Elizabeth Ball, sons Benjamin and Levin Ball, and dau. Betty Ball. {MWB 24:26}

In a deposition taken circa 1766-1767 in DO Co., Elizabeth Hodson stated she was about 53 years old and mentioned her father Capt. Thomas Hicks and her son Thomas Ball about 2 years ago regarding the bounds of Thomas Hodson's land (part of *Maiden's Forest*). {DOLR 21 Old 382}

In 1777 Benjamin Ball, DO Co., was deposed regarding the tract *Partnership* and stated he was about 41 years old; mentioned his grandfather Capt. Levin Hicks (now dec'd.) about 16 or 17 years ago; also mentioned Thomas Hicks, son of Capt. Thomas Hicks. {DOLR 1 JCH 82}

On 22 Oct 1779 William Hicks, DO Co., Gent., leased ½ of the tract *Darley* to Benjamin Ball, DO Co., planter, for 14 years, but said lease to be voided if John Hicks, bro. of the said William Hicks, should be living and return here before the expiration of the said term. {DOLR 1 JCH 282}

Elizabeth (Hicks) (Ball) Hodson was the mother of: THOMAS BALL; BENJAMIN BALL; LEVIN BALL; BETTY BALL.

13. MARY HICKS, DO Co., b. 1745, dau. of Levin (5) Hicks, m. Zachariah Campbell in 1765, and d. 1779. {Jones:342}

Zachariah Campbell came from Glasgow, Scotland and first settled in Virginia. He later came to Vienna in DO Co. where he m. Mary Hicks, a niece of Gen. Henry Hooper. {Jones:342}

On 20 Feb 1770 Mary Hicks, relict and executrix of Levin Hicks, late of DO Co., dec'd., and Levin Hicks, son and heir of the afsd. Levin Hicks, conveyed to Zacharias and Mary Campbell a 50 acre part of *Hinchman's Neck* devised by the will of said dec'd. to be sold. {DOLR 23 Old 468}

In 1776 Zacharas Cammel was head of household in Nanticoke Hundred, DO Co., aged between 30 and 40, with one male aged between 16 and 21, one male under age 10, two females aged between 30 and 40, and four females under age 10, plus 13 negroes. {1776 Census}

Zachariah Campbell, DO Co., was a captain in the militia, Transquakin Company, on 10 Feb 1776 and served as Naval Officer of the Sixth District until his death (exact date not given) when he was replaced by Adam Muir on 25 Feb 1779. {ARMD 11:147, 21:308}

Mary Hooper Hicks survived her dau. Mary Hicks Campbell and son-in-law Zachariah Campbell. Their children (N) were left to the guardianship of Dr. William Ennalls Hooper, eldest son of Gen. Henry Hooper, a most intimate friend and cousin to Mary Hicks Campbell, their mother. {Jones:343}

Mary (Hicks) Campbell was the mother of: MARY CAMPBELL; ISABELLA CAMPBELL; ELIZABETH CAMPBELL; LEVIN HICKS CAMPBELL {Jones:342}; OTHERS (N).

Fourth Generation

14. JOHN HICKS TRAVERSE, DO Co., son of Henry Traverse and Ann (9) Hicks, m. Anne (N), d. by 1795, and she m. 2nd Thomas Walters.

On 15 Aug 1795 Thomas Walters, DO Co., and wife Anne conveyed to Thomas Hicks the dower interest in *Maiden's Forest, Traverse's Honeysucker*, and three other tracts (N), all lying in DO Co. near Vienna, formerly the property of John Hicks Traverse, late of DO Co., dec'd., former husband of the said Anne, and now in the tenure and occupation of Matthew Traverse, son of the said John Hicks Traverse. {DOLR 8 HD 537}

John Hicks Traverse was the father of: MATTHEW TRAVERSE.

15. HENRY HICKS, DO Co., b. c1760, son of Thomas (10) Hicks.

On 4 April 1792 Henry Hicks, DO Co., son of Thomas, conveyed to David Smith a 6¼ acre part of the tract *Partnership* on the east side of the main road from Vienna to Crotchers Ferry. {DOLR 3 HD 537}

Some time between 22 Oct 1792 and 21 June 1794 Henry Hicks was deposed and stated he was about 33 years old. {DOLR 8 HD 22}

16. WILLIAM ENNALLS HICKS, DO Co., son of John (11) Hicks, m. Sarah (N), and d. by 1789.

On 23 Aug 1771 the lands of William Ennalls Hicks, son of John Hicks, DO Co., dec'd., were valuated (Levin Kirkman was the guardian of said William): 500 acre tract *Darley*, 17 acre tract *Woolford's Inheritance*, and 100 acre tract *Ennalls' Regulation*. {DOLR 25 Old 209}

On 17 March 1779 William Ennalls Hicks, DO Co., and wife Sarah, conveyed a 40 acre part of tract *Ennalls' Regulation* (which adj. the tract *Partnership*) to John Scott and another 41½ acre part of said tract on Transquakin River to Joseph Ennalls, Jr. {DOLR 1 JCH 196, 199}

William Ennalls Hicks, DO Co., took the Oath of Allegiance in 1778 and was a second lieutenant in the militia, Upper Bttn., 1779-1782. {MD Militia:87; MHS MS.1814}

On 1 March 1786 William Ennalls Hicks, DO Co., Gent., conveyed to Priscilla Ball, DO Co., widow, a 43 acre part of the tract *Hicks Fields*. {DOLR 5 NH 453}

On 6 April 1787 William Ennalls Hicks and Thomas Hicks, DO Co., Gent., conveyed to John Scott a 175 acre part of the tract *Darley* (also mentioned Sarah Hicks, wife of Thomas). {DOLR 3 HD 173}

On 8 June 1789 Thomas Hicks, son of Thomas Hicks and guardian of John Hicks, orphan of William Ennalls Hicks, DO Co., leased to Thomas Smith two-thirds of the land on Chiccacone Creek (now in the possession of Leah Kirkman) for 14 years. On that same day Dr. James Tootell, DO Co., leased to

Thomas Smith all his right of dower to certain lands and premises lying and being in DO Co. on Chiccacone Creek and now in the occupancy of Leah Kirkman formerly the property of John Hicks by which his wife claims her dower and was bequeathed to William Ennalls Hicks and lately devised by said William Ennalls Hicks to his son John Hicks, ward of Thomas Hicks. {DOLR 1 HD 338-339}

William was the father of: JOHN.

17. JOHN HICKS, JR., DO Co., son of John (11) Hicks.

On 23 Dec 1773 the lands of John Hicks, son of John Hicks, DO Co., dec'd., were valuated (Levin Kirkman, guardian of said John), namely the 330 acre tract *Hicks Fields* of which 1/3 belongs to said minor. {DOLR 27 Old 277}

John Hicks was a private in the Maryland Line, 1782-1783. {ARMD 18:540}

18. THOMAS HICKS, DO Co., son of John (11) Hicks, m. Sarah Wall by license dated 31 Jan 1784. {DO Marriages:59}

On 26 July 1787 Thomas Hicks, DO Co., Gent., and wife Sarah, conveyed to John Scott a 175 acre part and a 126 acre part of the tract *Darley* on Blackwater River. {DOLR 9 NH 345}

On 21 July 1794 Thomas Hicks, DO Co., and wife Sarah, conveyed to Samuel W. Pitt, DO Co., a 414 acre part of the tract *Darley* which had been granted and released to said Thomas Hicks by his bro. William Ennalls Hicks pursuant to the Last Will and Testament of their father John Hicks. {DOLR 6 HD 525}

On 15 Aug 1795 Thomas Hicks, DO Co., and wife Sarah mortgaged all their lands in DO Co. and elsewhere to Peter Rea. {DOLR 8 HD 586}

19. THOMAS BALL, DO Co., son of Benjamin Ball and Elizabeth (12) Hicks, m. Priscilla (N).

On 17 Nov 1768 the estate of John Hicks, DO Co., dec'd., was admin. by Sarah Hicks (extx.) and admin. again on 14 June 1769 and 8 July 1771. Sureties on all three dates were Thomas Hicks and Thomas Ball. {MDAD 60:140, 62:217, 66:96}

On 22 April 1775 the estate of Thomas Ball, DO Co., was admin. by Priscilla Ball. The representatives were his widow (N) and 7 children, viz., John, Mary, Thomas, Betsy, Priscilla, Rebecca, and James Ball. {MDAD 71:210}

On 1 March 1786 William Ennalls Hicks, DO Co., Gent., conveyed to Priscilla Ball, DO Co., widow, a 43 acre part of the tract *Hicks Fields*. {DOLR 5 NH 453}

Thomas Ball was the father of: JOHN BALL; THOMAS BALL; JAMES BALL; MARY BALL; BETSY BALL; PRISCILLA BALL; REBECCA BALL.

20. LEVIN HICKS CAMPBELL, DO Co., b. 1774, son of Zachariah Campbell and Mary (13) Hicks, m. 1st in 1797 to Mary Troup, dau. of Dr. John Troup of County Kincardineshire, Scotland; she d. 1811 and he m. 2nd to Anna Maria Davis, dau. of Dr. William Worthington Davis. {Jones:342}

Levin Hicks Campbell was the father of the following children by his 2nd wife: LEVIN HICKS CAMPBELL, JR.; ANNA MARIA CAMPBELL. {Jones:343}

Unplaced

GILES HICKS m. Mary Broadaway.

On 7 May 1754 James Broadaway, DO Co., wrote his will and in it he named his sister Mary Hicks and bro.-in-law Giles Hicks as guardians to his dau. Sarah Broadaway. {MWB 30:619-621}

On 5 Aug 1765 Giles Hicks, QA Co., patented the 81 acre tract *Hicks Discovery*. {MPL BC26:314}

In 1782 Giles Hicks III, CA Co., served as a Commissary Agent. {Peden's *MD Public Service Records, 1775-1783*}

JAMES HICKS, DO Co., was a private in the Upper Bttn., Select Militia, on 23 Aug 1781. {RPDO:102}

JAMES HICKS, JR., CA Co., received a receipt from the Purchasing Agent for furnishing wheat on 17 Aug 1782. {Peden's MD Public Service Records}

JOSEPH HICKS, DO Cc., m. (N).

Joseph Hicks, DO Co., joyner, was granted power of attorney by Price Higgins, of Lewis Town in Sussex Co. on Delaware, on 23 Jan 1764 to collect debts due to said Higgins from William Byus. One of the witnesses was Joseph Hicks, Jr. {DOLR 19 Old 255}

Joseph Hicks, DO Co., patented the 480 tract *Hicks True Dealing* on 25 March 1764. {MPL BC22:342}

On 14 Aug 1766 Joseph Hicks, DO Co., planter, conveyed to Joseph Richardson, AA Co., Gent., the 480½ acre tract *Hicks True Dealing* near the tract *Money's True Dealing*. {DOLR 21 Old 103}

On 20 Oct 1767 Joseph Hicks, DO Co., conveyed to Benjamin Cave, SO Co., a 220 acre part of *Addition to Mazareen Hall*, which noted in part, "upon which a Fieri Facias was Levyed by Charles Eccleston and by virtue of his Lordship the Right Honble. the Lord Propry. his Writ of Venditione Exponas was sold to the said Joseph Hicks." {DOLR 22 Old 89}

JOSEPH HICKS, JR., DO Co., joyner, son of Joseph Hicks, DO Co., joyner, acquired a 400 acre part of tract *Money's True Dealing* on 4 June 1761. {DOLR 17 Old 317}

SARAH HICKS, DO Co., m. John Patterson by license dated 21 July 1784. {DO Marriages:62}

TABITHA HICKS, DO Co., conveyed personal property to Henry Hooper on 11 Oct 1784. {DOLR 2 NH 572}

THOMAS HICKS, DO Co., m. Amelia Newton by license dated 12 May 1789. {MD Marriages}

## THE MCGEE/MCGHEE FAMILY

1. ANDREW MCGEE, b. in Ireland.

On 24 Sep 1759 Robert Darnal of DO Co., Gent., leased to Andrew Magee of the Province of PA, merchant, land on Hunting Creek where Robert Hargaton now lives for 10 years. {DOLR 16 Old 233}

A land commission, 10 Nov 1767 - 10 Aug 1768, was appointed to perpetuate bounds of Andrew McGhee's land called *Mill Security* adj. *Folks Delight* and *Nevetts Addition*. {DOLR 23 Old 1}

On 6 Sep 1768 Isaac Nicolls Junr. and his wife Elizabeth of DO Co. conveyed to Andrew McGhee of the same co., merchant, part of a tract called *Hampton* adj. part of the same tract formerly bought by said McGhee from the said Isaac Nicolls and from Levin Nicholls, 16 3/4 a. conveyed. {DOLR 23 Old 19}

On 24 March 1769 Andrew McGhee of DO Co., merchant, conveyed to Rev. Philip Walker of the same co., Hampton on s. side of Hunting Creek, also Mill Security n branches of Hunting Creek. {DOLR 23 Old 185}

On 5 March 1770 Andrew McGhee of DO Co., merchant, conveyed to Andrew Mein of TA Co., merchant, Negro man slave named Busbey. {DOLR 23 Old 477}

On 30 May 1770 Alexander Ross, mariner, conveyed to Andrew McGhee, Gent., the sloop *Two Sisters*, about 20 tons burthen, riding at anchor in Hunting Creek. {DOLR 24 Old 39}

Andrew McGhee, DO Co., merchant, d. leaving a will dated 25 Feb 1773, proved 17 March 1773. To 2 nephews Samuel and John McGhee, sons of John McGhee, living in North Carolina, Guilford Co., all my lands, part of tract I bought of Levin Nicholls, *Hampton*, 81 ½ a.; part of three tracts bought of Isaac Nicolls, Jr., the 1st containing 3 ½ a., the 2nd 16 3/4 a. called *Hampton*; the 3rd called *Mill Security*, 9 a., with all improvements including the mill; also 3 tracts bought of Robert Hardekin, *Purel*, 5 a.; *Hardekins Beginning*, 1 ½ a.; *Conclusion*, 27 a.; part of the tract *Richardsons Choice*, 100 a.; 8 Negroes - provided they pay to my bro. William McGhee of Ireland, £50; my bro. Joseph of Ireland, £25; John McGhee of North Carolina, £25. To above nephews residue of personal estate. To Frances Dulany, £10 yearly for 10 years. To Peter Richardson, exec., stock. Witnessed by James Thomson, Edward Smith, Isaac Nicolls, Jr. {MWB 39:537}

The inventory of the estate was filed on 26 March 1773 by Peter Richardson. {MINV 115:165}

The admin. account was submitted on 8 Oct 1774 by Peter Richardson. {MDAD 70:295}

## Second Generation

2. JOHN MCGEE, bro. of Andrew (1) McGee, b. in Ireland.

On 20 Aug 1773 John McGee of Gilford Co., NC, granted to William Edmondson of DO Co.: Power of Attorney to manage lands in DO Co. or elsewhere in Maryland left by Will of Andrew McGee, brother of said John McGee, to the said John McGee's two sons Samuel and John McGee. {DOLR 27 Old 188}

John was father of SAMUEL; JOHN.

## Third Generation

3. SAMUEL MCGGEE, son of John (2) McGee.

Samuel served in the Lower House, from DO Co., 1779-1780 (resigned on 11 April 1780, during the 2nd session of the 1779-1780 Assembly. {BDML}

On 2 Feb 1785 Samuel McGee and John McGee of DO Co. conveyed to Edward Noel Junr., John Eccleston and Joseph Richardson of the same co., lands on Hunting Creek called *Puzzle* containing 5 a.; *Mills Security*, 9 a.; part of *Hampton* or *Hamton*, 80 ½ a.; and other parts of *Hampton*. {DOLR 5 NH 41}

On 31 Dec 1794 Samuel McGhee of DO Co. and John McGhee of Fayette Co., NC, Gent., conveyed to James Murray of the City of Annapolis, physician, *Hardekins Conclusion* on e. side of Hunting Creek, containing 27 a. and *Hardekins Beginning* on e. side of Hunting Creek, ½ a. {DOLR 2 NH 557}

4. JOHN MCGEE, son of John (2) McGee.

John McGee of Randolph Co., NC, manumitted Negro girl named Rose. {DOLR 9 NH 384}

## THE MCNEMARA FAMILY

1. TIMOTHY MCNEMARA d. by 13 May 1710, m. Sarah Griffin, widow of Lewis Griffin and dau. of John Prout.

Timothy Macknemarrough was transported into the province in 1664. {MPL EE:166} Skordas shows that Timothy Macknemarra of Calvert Co. was granted a patent for service in 1674. {MPL 17:635}

Timothy McNemara patented the following tracts in DO Co.: *Batchelor's Fancy* (50 a.) on 18 March 1680; *Galloway* (100 a.) on 2 July 1702; *Timothy's Prevention* (57 a.) on 16 March 1681; *Turkey Range* (50 a.) on 19 Oct 1695; *Turkey Ridge* (50 a.) on 10 Nov 1695; *West Chester* (200 a.) on 1 April 1680. {MPL 24:198, 204, 254, 259; 28:283, 308; 29:99; 35:370; 37:282, 283}

Lewis Griffin, DO Co., d. by 17 Feb 1680 when Sarah Macknemarra, wife of Timothy Macknemarra and relict of dec'd., filed the inventory of the estate. The inventory indicated she m. immediately after the death of Lewis Griffin. {INAC 7A:377}

In Aug 1677 Richard Meekins and his wife Joanna of DO Co., planter, conveyed to Timothy MacNamara of SO Co., planter, *Apes Hill* at the mouth of Hungar River, 50 a. On 1 April 1679 Timothy McNamara conveyed this land to John Pritchett of the same co. {DOLR 3 Old 138, 156}

On 8 Jan 1678 Lewis Griffin of Do Co. conveyed to Timothy McNemara of the same co., planter, 50 a. near the mouth of Transquakin River, originally patented to Henry Hooper. {DOLR 3 Old 159}

On 30 May 1685 Timothy McNamara of DO Co. conveyed to John People of the same place, *Batchelors Fancy* on a branch of the Blackwater River, 50 a. {DOLR 4 Old 142}

On 3 Aug 1685 Timothy McNamara and his wife Sarah conveyed to Robert Pope *Buck Valley* near Transquakin Bay, 50 a. {DOLR 4 Old 123}

At November Court 1691 Arthur Hart was appointed constable of Armitage Hundred in place of Timothy Macknamarra. {DOJR}

John Proutt, Hungar River, DO Co., d. leaving a will dated 21 Oct 1699, proved 22 Nov 1699. To wife Catherine, 1/3 of estate during life. Timothy MacNemara and his wife Sarah, execs., residuary legatees of estate; to possess entire estate at death of wife afsd. Witnessed by George Staplefort, Jno. Griffin, Mary Staplefort. MWB 6:385}

Timothy Macknemarr, DO, d. by 13 May 1710 when the inventory of his estate was filed. Approvers: Mary Macknemarr, Sarah Macknemarr. {INAC 31:174}

Timothy was prob. father of TIMOTHY.

## Second Generation

2. TIMOTHY MCNEMARA b. c1676, d. by 27 May 1758, son of Timothy (1) McNemara, m. Jane Read, widow of William Read and dau. of Henry and Alice Wheeler and a sister of Mary Stewart wife of John Stewart II and m. 2nd 1717/ 1720, Jane Lake, widow of Robert Lake and dau. of John Pritchett. {Mowbray. See also The John Pritchett Family, vol. 14 of this series.}

William Read d. by 21 Dec 1697 when the admin. account was submitted by Jane Read. {INAC 15:303} A second admin. account was submitted by Jane Read on 21 Nov 1699. {INAC 19½A:125}

Timothy McNemarra patented the following tracts in DO Co.: *Bachelor's Range* (50 a.) on 10 Dec 1714; *Nabb's Quarter* (25 a.) on 13 May 1715; *Macnemarra's Meadows* (50 a.) on 10 June 1734; *Nab's Quarter Addition* on 18 March 1747; *Sandy Ridge* (107 a.) on 10 June 1734; *Timothy's Bear Garden* (13 a.); *Macnemara's Meadow* (65 a.) on 2 Feb 1751. {MPL EE6:155; CE1:205; EE6:237; CE1:26; EI1:477; EI3:198; EI2:583; EI3:535; T14:736; BY5:298}

On 18 May 1733 Timothy MacNamarrah and his wife Jane conveyed to William Robbinson, Junr., of the same co., planter, *Obscurity* on a branch of Blackwater River, 50 a. {DOLR 9 Old 91}

On 27 May 1733 Timothy MacNamarrah of DO Co., planter, and his wife Jane, conveyed to their son in law William Robbinson Junr. and his wife Mary of the same co., planter, *Luck* on the w. side of the northwest branch of Blackwater and on a branch of Meekins Creek, 50 a.; and *Boarns Landing* on s. e. side of Slaughter Creek adj. *Peaknell* and containing 100 a. {DOLR 9 Old 89}

On 29 June 1739 Timothy Macnamara was mentioned as guardian to the minor William Evans, son of William Evans, dec'd. {DOLR 11 Old 73}

On 24 Sep 1744 Timothy Macnamar of DO Co., planter, conveyed to his son John Macnamar of the same co., planter, a Negro man called Sam, aged about 20 years. {DOLR 10 Old 415}

Timothy Macknimar, aged about 67 years, deposed before a land commission of DO Co., 14 June 1743 - 1 Aug 1743, regarding the bounds of Lot Pritchett's land called *Edenburrough*. {DOLR 12 Old 167}

Timothy Macnemara patented the following land in DO Co.: *Macnemarra's Meadows* (50 a.) on 10 June 1734; *Macnemara's Meadow* (65 a.) on 2 Feb 1751. {MPL T14:736; BY5:298}

Timothy Macknamara, DO Co., d. leaving a will dated 20 Oct 1756, proved 11 April 1757. Wife Jean. Children: John, Timothy, Jr., Sarah Mannin.

Grandchildren: John, Timothy and Levin Macknamara. Exec. John Macknamara. Witnessed by James Cannon, Wm. Willey, Robert Scott. {MWB 30:327}

On 27 May 1758 Jane Macnamar of DO Co., widow, gave to her dau. Mary Robinson of the same co., widow, slaves, livestock and other personal property. {DOLR 16 Old 37}

On 29 Sep 1759 The admin. account of the estate of Timothy McNemara was submitted by exec. John McNemara. {MDAD 44:111}

Timothy was father of JOHN; TIMOTHY; poss. MARY who m. William Robinson (Robertson); SARAH, m. Thomas Manning, son of Richard Manning. {See The Thomas Manning Family, vol. 14 of this series.}

Third Generation

3. JOHN MCNEMARA, b. c1736, son of Timothy (2) McNemaera, m. Mary Stewart, dau. of John Stewart.

John Macnamara patented the following tracts in DO Co.: *Conclusion to Whole* (235 a.) on 29 July 1763; *Indian Cabin Range* (9 a.) on 4 Aug 1763; *Macnemara's Privilege* (174 a.) on 10 Aug 1753; *Greenland* (18 a.) on 5 July 1768; *Liberty* (6 a.) on 26 July 1768; *Squirrel Point Neck* (50 a.) on 10 Nov 1769. {MPL BC23:181, 203; BC24:103, 126; BC33:258; BC35:109; BC37:11, 18; BC38:373; BC40:9; YS6:143; GS1:404}

Timothy, son of ---- Macnamar — and Mary his wife, b. 20 April 1742. {DODO}

In 1745 John Macnamar was appointed constable of Streights Hundred. {DOJR}

On 6 Oct 1748 John Stewart of DO Co., Gent., conveyed to his son in law John McKnamar and his wife Mary, grantor's dau.: slaves. {DOLR 14 Old 255}

On 14 Aug 1750 Sarah Messick and Nemiah Messick of DO Co., planters, conveyed to John McNamar of the same co., planter, part of two tracts called *Great Wadlin* and *Merideths Chance* on Charles Creek and Hungar River adj. land where Patrick Colings formerly lived, now in the possession of said John Macnamar, 50 a. {DOLR 14 Old 437}

On 29 Nov 1759 Peter Wingate of DO Co., Gent., conveyed to John McNemara of the same co., planter, 26 a. of *Wingates Inclosure* and 26 a. of *Wadles Desire* on the s.w. side of Goose Creek. {DOLR 17 Old 106}

On 12 Aug 1761 John Bramble of DO Co. planter, conveyed to John Macnamara of the same co., planter, 104 a. of *Fair Dealing*; 50 a. of *Waxford*; and 25 a. of *Haverwell* on Goose Creek whcih issues out of Fishing Bay. {DOLR 17 Old 427}

On 9 Jan 1769 John McNamara of DO Co., planter, conveyed to Levin McNamara, his son, of the same co., 104 a. a a tract called *Fair Dealing*; also part of *Wasford*, 12 ½ a.; part of *Wingates Inclosher*, 27 a.; part of *Waddles Desier*, 25 a.; and part of *The Conclusion to the Whole*, 15 a. {DOLR 23 Old 138}

On 17 Jan 1772 a division was made between John McNamara Junr. and Timothy McNamara of lands devised by Timothy McNamara, deceased to their father during his life and to them after his decease, to which said lands their father has resigned his claim. Land located on a branch of Fox Creek, adj. *Buck Ridge* and adj. *Addition to Nabs Quarter*; and *Bornes Meadows* adj. *Healand Bumstead.* Witnesses: Dan Fallin, Levin McNamara, James Cannon, William Willey. "This above Division agreed to by me - John McNemara Sener." {DOLR 25 Old 421}

On 31 Dec 1773 John McNemara of DO Co., planter, conveyed to his sons John McNemara Junr. and Timothy McNemara: *Buck Ridge* containing 100 a.; *Buck Ridge* containing 50 a.; *Heland Bumstead*, containing 50 a.; *Browns Meadows*, 50 a.; *Nabs Quarter*, 25 a.; *Addition to Nabs Quarter*, 46 a..; *McNemars Meadows,* 50 a.; and *McNemars Meadows Again*, 65 a. {DOLR 27 Old 98}

The 1776 census shows John McNemara as head of household in Straits Hundred, DO Co. Living in the household were 1 male between the ages of 30 and 40, 2 males under the age of 10; 1 female between the ages of 40 and 50 and 1 female between the ages of 21 and 30. Also in Straits Hundred is Timothy McNamara with 1 male between the ages of 21 and 30, 3 males under 10, 1 female between 21 and 30, and 1 female under the age of 10. Levin McNamara was head of household in Straits Hundred, with 1 male between the age of 21 and 30, 2 males below the age of 10 and 1 female between the ages of 16 and 21.

On 15 Aug 1776 John McNemara of DO Co., planter, conveyed to his son Thomas McNemara, part of a tract called *Coles Venture*, 108 a.; and part of *Coles Regulation* containing 214 a.; also *Greenland* of 18 a. and *Liberty* of 6 a. {DOLR 28 Old 191}

On 27 Dec 1781 John McNemara of DO Co., planter, conveyed to his children John Stuart McNemara, Sarah McNemara, Caroline McNemara and Nancy McNemara: Negro slaves. {DOLR 28 Old 384}

At September Term, 1782, John Stewart Macnamarra, Thomas Macnemara, Edward Pritchett, John Stewart M. Pritchett and Edward Pritchett, Jr., was found guilty in that they did unlawfully assemble and riot upon Thomas Vickars, Sr. and stabbed Vickars with a bayonet; assaulted Elizabeth Vickars; and assaulted Thomas Vickars, Jr. Thomas Macnemara was fined a total of £6. John Stewart Macnamarra was fined a total of £24.

John was father of TIMOTHY, b. 20 April 1745; LEVIN, b. 4 Nov 1746; JOHN STEWART, b. c1755, d. 1823; THOMAS; SARAH; CAROLINE; NANCY; prob. MARY STEWART.

Fourth Generation

4. JOHN STEWART MCNEMARA[6], b. c1755, d 8 July 1823, son of John (3) McNemara, m. Lovey Lake (d. 17 Nov 1843, aged 77).

On 30 Nov 1770 James Cannon of DO Co., planter, and his wife Alethea, conveyed to John McNamara, Junr., of the same co., part of a tract called *Buck Valley* on Gum Branch, 9 a. {DOLR 24 Old 208}

On 31 Dec 1773 John McNemara Junr. of DO Co., planter, conveyed to Timothy McNemara of the same co., planter: part of *Buck Valley* on w. side of Goose Creek and e. side of Honger River, containing 8 a. {DOLR 27 Old 102}

On 11 Jan 1772 John McNemarra Junr. and Timothy McNemarra made a bond to John McNemarra Senr., concerning lands called *Batchlers Range* and *Beargarden*, on e. side of Blackwater River. {DOLR 2 NH 344}

John Stewart McNamara served at 1st lt. in the militia of DO Co., in the Friends to America Company, 20 March 1776 to at least 24 June 1778 when commissioned again. He subscribed to the Oath of Allegiance and Fidelity in 1778. {RPDO:161}

On 28 Feb 1784 John McNemarra of DO Co., conveyed to John Stewart McNemarra of the same co., *Batcheldors Range* containing 52 a., on the e. side of Blackwater River near Walls Creek. {DOLR 2 NH 331}

On 1 June 1784 John McNemara of DO Co. conveyed to Jacob Insley and James Todd. of the same co., *McNemaras Meadows*, containing 115 a. {DOLR 2 NH 417}

On 28 Feb 1784 John Stewart McNemara of DO Co., Gent., conveyed to John Bestpitch of the same county, planter, *Sandyridge*, containing 65 a.; *Addition to Sandyridge*, containing 40 a.; *Squarel Point Neck*, containing 50 a.; and *Batchelders Rainge*, containing 52 a. *Sandyridge* is located on the Beargardin which issues out of the east side of Blackwater River; *Addition to Sandyridge* begins about ½ mile from Ezekiel Keene's dwelling house; and *Squarel Point Neck* is located on n. side of Blackwater Marsh, adj. *Keens Eleventh Purchase*. {DOLR 2 NH 296}

On 26 Aug 1784 John Stewart McNemara and Lovey his wife of DO Co. conveyed to John Kirwan of the same co., *McNemaras Previledge* on a gut which makes out of Jones Creek, containing 24. {DOLR 2 NH 468}

---

[6] It is not clear that John Stewart McNemara and John McNemara, Junr., are the same person. Note for example that John McNemara, Jr., conveyed a bond to John McNemara, Sr. in 1772. Based on the data that he was born in 1755, this makes him age 17 at the time of the transaction. For the time being was have assumed that this is one and the same person.

A Land Commission of DO Co., 9 March 1784 - 26 June 1784, was appointed to perpetuate bounds of John Stewart McNemara's lands called *Merediths Chance* and *Kendels Chance*. Deposition was given by Matthew Kirwan, aged about 51 years, concerning a survey about 30 years ago by Jeremiah Pritchett. Also deposing was Thomas Wrotton, aged about 71 years. {DOLR 2 NH 519}

John S. McNamara d. 8 July 1823, in 68th year of his age; hie remains were removed to Christ Church Graveyard in Cambridge. Lovey McNamara d. 17 Nov 1843, aged 77. Both were bur. on the farm of Denard Johnson in Lake District. Also buried here were John McNamara, d. 27 May 1854, age 74; Eliza McNamara, wife of William, d. 3 April 1837, age 40; Henry L. McNamara, b. 30 April 1803, d. 27 Dec 1844. {Marshall's Tombstone Records:8}

The *Republican Star* announced on 24 Nov 1812 the marriage of Job Slacum to Miss Ann McNemar, all of DO Co., on Thursday, 12th inst. by Rev. James Ridgaway.

The *Easton Gazette* announced on 26 July 1823: Died - Col. John S. McNamara on Tuesday 8th inst., at his residence in Dorchester Co., in the 68th year of his age, leaving a wife and 8 children.

John Stewart McNemara was father of prob. JOHN, b. c1780; ANN, m. 12 Nov 1812, Job Slacum; prob. HENRY L., b. 30 April 1803; 5 OTHER CHILDREN.

5. TIMOTHY MCNEMARA, son of John (3) McNemara.

Timothy McNemarra patented 36 a. in DO Co. called *Buck Ridge Addition* on 21 Nov 1769. {MPL BC39; bc40:15}

On 31 Dec 1770 John McNemara of DO Co., planter, conveyed to Timothy McNemara of the same co., planter: part of a tract called *Conclusion to the Whole*, on a branch of Fox Creek, near where Jacob Bramble formerly lived, containing 10 a. {DOLR 27 Old 95}

6. LEVIN MCNEMARA, b. 4 Nov 1746, d. 29 April 1831, son of John (3) McNemara, m. Sarah Ross., dau. of Thomas Ross Junr.

On 31 Dec 1773 Levin McNemara of DO Co., planter, conveyed to Timothy McNemara of tho same co., planter: part of *Faredealing*, on w. side of Goose Creek which issues out of Fishing Bay, containing 11 a. {DOLR 27 Old 100}

Levin McNemara signed the Oath of Allegiance and Fidelity in 1778. {RPDO:162}

At April term 1783 of the General Court of the Eastern Shore of Maryland it was presented that Levin McNemara, yeoman of DO Co., as a rioter, router and disturber of the peace on 10 Jan 1781 did assemble and gather together and so being assembled assaulted Thomas Vickars along with Edward

Pritchard, Sr. beat, wound and ill treat Elizabeth Vickars, and assault Thomas Vickars, Jr. and stabbed him with a bayonet. He was fined £3.

On 12 March 1800 Rebecca Ross, Levin McNemara, Jacob Todd, Lowder Mister, Amelia Ross and Nancy Insley, all of DO Co., manumitted Negro man named Joe, aged 31 years, late the property of Thomas Ross Junr., dec'd. {DOLR 15 HD 563}

Levin McNamara, aged 84 years, 5 mos., 25 days, d. in this county, 29th ult. {*Cambridge Chronicle*, 14 May 1831}

Levin and Sarah were parents of CLEMENT, b. 1790, m. Sarah Cooper; LEVIN; TIMOTHY; CALEB, m. Mary Foxwell; JOHN, m. 1st Elizabeth Tyler, m. 2nd George [sic] Jones. {RPDO}

7. THOMAS MCNEMARA, son of John (3) McNemara.

On 16 April 1792 Abraham Lewis of Thomas of DO Co. conveyed to Thomas McNamara of the same co., *Coles Regulation*, *Coles Venture* and *Brambles Hope*. {DOLR 3 HD 541}

8. CAROLINE MCNEMARA, dau. of John (3) McNemara, m. John Barns. {DO Co. Marr. lic. dated 7 Jan 1786}

On 8 June 1784 Caroline McNemara of DO Co., manumitted Negro slaves: Rebechah, aged about 22 years; and Reuben, aged about 40 years. Witness: Henry Lake. {DOLR 2 NH 425}

On 14 Sep 1784 Caroline McNamara of DO restated her manumission of Negro slaves Reubin, aged about 40 years, and Beck, aged about 20 years: Witnesses: Benjamin Todd, Jacob Todd. {DOLR 5 NH 32}

9. NANCY MCNEMARA, dau. of John (3) McNemara.

Nancy McNamara m. 30 July 1801 John Gootee. {DOGC}

10. MARY STEWART MCNAMARA, prob. dau. of John (3) McNemara, m. Edward Pritchett, son of William Pritchett. They were parents of BETSY PRITCHETT, b. 3 Nov 1774. {DOGC. See The John Pritchett Family, vol. 14 of this series.}

Fifth Generation

11. LEVIN MCNAMARA, son of Levin (6) McNamara, m. 27 April 1802, Mary (Polly) Robinson (Robertson).

Levin McNamara m. 27 April 1802 Mary (Polly) Robertson. {DOGC}

Levin and Polly McNamara were parents of SALLY, b. 1 Sep 1804. {DOGC}

Unplaced

CORNELIUS MCNEMARA

Cornelius Macknemarrow was transported into the province by 1679. {MPL WC2:10, 17}

At November Court (DO Co.) in 1691 Honour Fitzgerald was presented for having of her body a bastard child and by her oath layd this child to Bryan Fitzpatrick. Came Cornelius Macknamarra and faithfully promised to pay Honour Fitzgerald's fine of 500 lbs. of tobacco. {DOJR}

MARY MCNEMARA m. 18 Dec 1790,.Arthur Pritchett. {DOGC}

MARY MCNAMARA m. 14 Dec 1819, David Barnes. {DOGC}

MOLLY SLACOM MCNAMARA m. 16 Sep 1791, Joseph Wheeler. {DOGC}

REBECCA MCNAMARA m. 27 May 1802, Isaac Moore. {DOGC}

THOMAS MCNAMARA and TIMOTHY MACNAMARA.

*Turkey Range* was surveyed for Thomas Mcnamara on 11/28/1694 - lying on the head of the Great Beaverdam Branch of the Blackwater, 50 a. It was possessed by George Valentine of AA Co. and conveyed to John Griffin. It was included in a tract called *World's End* . On 11/23/1694 *Turkey Ridge* was surveyed for Timothy Macnamara, lying in a swamp near a great beaverdam branch of the Blackwater. It too was later possessed by George Valentine of AA Co. and included in *World's End* when re-=surveyed for John Griffin.{DO Co. rent rolls, 1688 - 1707}

## THE MEDFORD FAMILY of Dorchester County

Ref. A: Loose leaves found in Higgins Bible, owned by Mrs. Lester B. Kinnamon.

1. ROBERT MEDFORD, b. c1700, m. Mary (N).

Robert Medford and Mary his wife immigrated into Maryland from England sometime before 1710. {A}

On 18 Aug 1733 Robert Medford and Mary Medford each proved 6 days attendance in the court case against Peter Taylor, John Sullivant and Thos. Sumers in which the latter (of Great Choptank Parish) three were found guilty of assaulting Thomas Corson and his wife Sarah and each fined 5 shillings. {DOJR:21}

On 15 Aug 1744 it was presented that Robert Medford of St. Mary's White Chapel Parish on 10 Sep 1743 assaulted Rachel Medford and was fined 40 shillings. {DOJR:46}

Robert Medford and William Medford signed as next of kin on the inventory of the estate of Sarah Cavendor, filed on 20 Jan 1739 by Solomon West, admin. {MINV 24:427}

William and Robart Medford signed as next of kin to the inventory of the estate of Solomon West, dated 7 July 1749. Rosannah West was admx. {MINV 40:300}

Robert Medford, aged c61, made a deposition before a land commission, 9 Nov 1762 - 13 Aug 1764, regarding the bounds of Mary Moore's land called *Canawhy* adj. *Batchelors Hope.*

Robert Medford, DO Co., d. leaving a will dated 13 Oct 1766, proved 2 Feb 1767. To sons Robert and William, two tracts of land, one called *Medford's Chance*, the other *Medford's Hazard*, to be equally divided between them. To son James, 1 shilling. To daus. Lidia, Mary and Esther, 1 shilling. Mentioned dau. Ann. Exec. son Robert. Witnessed by James Barns, Annakin West, John Davis. {MWB 35:2}

The inventory was filed on 19 Feb 1767 by Robert Medford. Signed as next of kin: Lydia Russell, William Medford. {MINV 94:37} A list of debts was filed on 4 March 1768. {MINV 95:262}

The admin. account was submitted on 9 March 1768 by Robert Medford. {MDAD 58:129}

They were parents of WILLIAM, b. 1711, d. 30 Jan 1784 {A}; ROBERT; JAMES; LIDIA, m. (N) Russell; MARY; ESTHER; ANN..

Second Generation

2. WILLIAM MEDFORD, b. 1711, d. 30 Jan 1784, son of Robert (1) Medford, m. Jan 1740, Ann Thomas (b. 10 Sep 1724, d. Dec 1788), dau. of Mary Thomas. {A}

On 28 March 1739 Peter Taylor of DO Co., Gent., conveyed to William Medford of the same co., planter, part of a tract called *Fair Dealing* on the road from Cabin Creek Mill to the plantation of Thomas Williams, containing 154 a. {DOLR 10 Old 29}

On 24 Feb 1764 Edward West and his wife Elizabeth of DO Co. conveyed to William Medford, son of Robert Medford, part of *Sandwick* containing 22 3/4 a. {DOLR 19 Old 161}

On 13 Aug 1766 William Medford, son of Robert of DO Co. conveyed to Robert Medford Junr., part of a tract called *Sandwick* and 1/4 a. as also to include ½ of a gress mill now built and standing on the said land. {DOLR 21 Old 83}

On 16 March 1764 Bartholomew Ennalls of DO Co. conveyed to William Medford, part of *Endeavour* containing 168 a. on the main road from said Wm. Medford's plantation to James Murray's plantation adj. land taken up by Painter called *Grove*. {DOLR 19 Old 188}

On 18 Sep 1770 George Maxwell of Charles Co., merchant, conveyed to William Medford and Robert Medford of DO Co., planters, two parts of *Addition* containing 200 a.; also part of *Hope* adj. *Addition,* on Cabin Creek adj. *Mill Land* or *Addition to Mill Land* and containing 77 a.; also *Sandy Hill* taken up by Henry Trippe by escheat containing 80 a. and the grist water mill located thereon; also part of a tract on n. side of Cabin Creek called *Trippes Security* containing 10 3/4 a.; also land on the branch of Cabin Creek called *Addition to Mill Land* containing 150 a. except 8 a. which runs into an elder survey called *The Hope*. {DOLR 24 Old 134}

On 18 Feb 1775 John Richardson of Caroline Co., planter, conveyed to William Medford and Robert Medford of the same co., planter, *Addition,* excepting 66 a. sold by said John Richardson to George Maxwell of Charles Co. {DOLR 27 Old 423}

On 23 Jan 1791 Richard Stanford, Celia Stanford and Elizabeth Stanford, acknowledged receipt of money paid them by Medford Andrews in consideration of our full claim against a legacy left him by William Medford, late of DO Co. deceased amounting to one hundred pounds six shillings current money of Maryland in virtue of a Judgement obtained by us against William Medford, exec. of said William Medford deceast. {DOLR 3 HD 42}

William and Ann were parents of MARY, b. 7 Feb 1745. {A}

3. ROBERT MEDFORD, son of Robert (1) Medford.

On 20 Dec 1771 William Medford, son of Robert, miller, and Sarah his wife; and Robert Medford, son of Robert, miller, and Elizabeth his wife, of DO Co., conveyed to Isaac Henry of the same co., planter, part of *Medfords Hazzard* adj. *Ramseys Folly*, on a path leading from William Eccleston's to Charles Eccleston's containing 251 al {DOLR 25 Old 224}

Robert was father of WILLIAM, m. Sarah (N); ROBERT, m. Elizabeth (N).

## Third Generation

4. MARY MEDFORD, b. 7 Feb 1745, d. 7 Feb 1766, dau. of William (2) Medford, m. 24 March 1763, Stephen Andrews (b. 10 May 1741, d. Spring 1772), son of Isaac Andrews. {A. See also The William Andrews Family, this vol.}

Mary and Stephen were parents of MEDFORD ANDREWS, b. 19 Jan 1766, d. 14 Nov 1845. {Marshall's DO Co. Tombstone Records 249}

5. WILLIAM MEDFORD, prob. son of Robert (3) MEDFORD, m. Sarah (N).

On 17 Dec 1781(?) William Medford Junr. of DO Co. manumitted Negroes Rhoda, Charles and Adam. {DOLR 28 Old 408}

William Medford supplied wheat for the use of the military on 1 Oct 1782. {RPDO:163}

On 16 April 1799 William Medford of DO Co., miller, conveyed to Henry Dean of the same co., part of *Medfords Chance*, 100 a. {DOLR 15 HD 202}

Unplaced

CHARLES MEDFORD m. Ruth Perry. {DO marr. licenses dated 27 Aug 1800}

JAMES MEDFORD m. Amelia Henry. {DO Co. marr. license dated 26 April 1796}

JOHN MEDFORD m. Margaret Brodess. {DO Co. marr. license dated 15 March 1796}

LURANA MEDFORD m. James Henry. {DO Co. marr. license dated 15 Feb 1796}

MARY MEDFORD m. Elisha Wright. {DO Co. marr. license dated 4 June 1787}

NANCY MEDFORD m. Isaac Henry. {DO Co. marr. license dated 29 March 1796}

NATHANIEL MEDFORD, b. 10 Jan 1758, d. 10 May 1826. He supplied wheat for the use of the military no 1 Oct 1782. {RPDO:163}

Buried on James Andrews' farm, Bobtown, Hurlock District are Nathaniel Medford, b. 10 Jan 1758, d. 10 May 1826, adj. the grave of Rebecca Medford, b. 12 Aug 1755, d. 23 July 1852. {Marshall's DO Co. Tombstone Records 249}

PETER MEDFORD m. Betsey Medford. {DO Co. marr. license dated 25 Jan 1797}

REBECCA MEDFORD m William Grainger. {DO Co. marr. license dated 5 Feb 1790}

WILLIAM MEDFORD m. Charlotte Grainger {DO Co. marr. license dated 1 Jan 1791}

# THE WILLIAM MERCHANT FAMILY

1. WILLIAM MERCHANT, DO Co., came into MD from VA by the 1660s and was a servant to Thomas Skinner. He m. Mary (N) who was prob. the Mary Saunders he had subsequently transported into this province. William had at least two children, William and Ellinor. After his death (date not known; no probate records found), Mary Merchant m. 2nd to John Stoker and both d. in 1694. {MPL 28:469; Mowbray I:105; MINV 13A:381; MWB 7:55}

*Commentary: There appears to have been two men named William Merchant in DO Co. in the late 1600s. There was also a William Marchant who was transported into Charles City Co., VA by William Calvert before 26 Jan 1663. {Nugent's Cavaliers & Pioneers I:493} One William Merchant and James Mossley had the 100 acre tract Cedar Point on Little Choptank River surveyed on 24 June 1666. {Mowbray's Early Settlers of Dorchester County and Their Land I:70, citing Land Grant No. 115C} MD Rent Rolls show this tract in the possession of William Pollard. {RR L10 F358} Another William Merchant was a servant to Thomas Skinner about this time. One William was born circa 1632 (age about 70 when deposed in 1702), had a wife named Rachell (m. by 1674) and a dau. named Mary, and he was still living in 1702. {DOLR 5 Old 230} The other William had a wife named Mary and two children named William and Ellinor, and he died in the late 1680s; his widow married John Stoker. Recent attempts to determine the relationship, if any, between these two William Merchants in DO Co. have been unsuccessful. In fact, one was called "Jr." in 1673, prob. to distinguish the younger William from the older William rather than their actually being father and son. {DOLR 3 Old 7} Therefore, some of the information that follows may pertain to either William Merchant. Additional research will be necessary before drawing any conclusions.*

On 29 Jan 1669 William Merchant and James Ogg, DO Co., planters, acquired from James Selby, DO Co., the 100 acre tract *Selby's Desire* at the head of Blackwater River. {DOLR 1 Old 9}

On 2 Aug 1669 William Merchant, DO Co., planter, and Henry Turner, DO Co., carpenter, acquired from Daniel Clarke, Gent., the 100 acre tract *Clarke's Outlett* on Salt Marsh Creek. {DOLR 1 Old 61}

On 6 Feb 1671/2 William Merchant and Henry Turner, both of DO Co., conveyed to Richard Keene, CV Co., innholder, the 100 acre tract *Clark's Outlett* on the Little Choptank River and Salt Marsh Creek. {DOLR 3 Old 242}

On 1 Aug 1672 William Merchant and James Agg [Ogg?], both of DO Co., acquired from Thomas Pratt, AA Co., the 100 acre tract *Congum*. {DOLR 3 Old 254}

On 1 June 1673 William Merchant, Jr. witnessed a bond of sale between Thomas Oliver and William Killman, both of DO Co. {DOLR 3 Old 7}

On 8 July 1674 William Merchant, DO Co., planter, acquired from Henry Turner, DO Co., Gent., the 132 acre tract *Ipswich* on the Blackwater River. {DOLR 3 Old 44}

On 4 Oct 1674 William Merchant, DO Co., planter, acquired from John Rawlings, DO Co., boatwright, the 150 acre tract *Merchant's Adventure* on Transquakin River. {DOLR 3 Old 59}

William Merchant (Marchant), DO Co., was a soldier circa 1675 and was paid for his services in the late expedition against the Nanticoke Indians in 1678. {ARMD 7:93}

On 5 March 1676 William Merchant, DO Co., planter, acquired from William Ford, DO Co., Gent., the 550 acre tract *Hereford* on Blackwater Creek. {DOLR 3 Old 130}

On 1 March 1679 William Merchant, DO Co., planter, conveyed to Bartholomew Ennalls, DO Co., the 150 acre tract *Merchant's Adventure* on Transquakin River. {DOLR 4 Old 1/2, 21, 6 Old 242}

On 4 Nov 1679 William Merchant, DO Co., and wife Rachell, conveyed to James Agg [Ogg?], DO Co., the assignment of lands (N) previously assigned to William Merchant by Thomas Pratt, AA Co. {DOLR 3 Old 192}

On 7 Feb 1681 William Merchant, DO Co., acquired from Henry Aldred, DO Co., the 16 acre tract *Stow* on the south side of Southey's Beaverdam branch of Blackwater River. {DOLR 4 Old 51}

On 13 Jan 1682 William Marchant, DO Co., patented the 50 acre tract *Marchant's Lot* and on 2 May 1682 he patented the 60 acre tract *Mount Silly*. {MPL 24:429, 28:485}

On 28 Nov 1683 William Marchant and Thomas Oliver, both of DO Co., acquired from William Trego, DO Co., mariner, the 50 acre tract *Refuge* on the northwest branch of Transquakin River. {DOLR 4 Old 100}

On 2 Jan 1684 William Marchant, DO Co., planter, conveyed to John Button, DO Co., cooper, part of the tract *Hereford* on Blackwater River. {DOLR 4 Old 101}

On 4 Nov 1684 Mary Marchant, dau. of William Marchant, DO Co., planter, acquired from John Pearson, DO Co., the 100 acre tract *Havre de Grace* in the fork of Blackwater River. {DOLR 4 Old 119}

John Stoker (Stoaker), DO Co., d. by 4 June 1694 when his estate was inventoried and approved on 14 Dec 1694; no heirs or next of kin were mentioned in that account. {MINV 13A:381-382}

Mary Stoker, DO Co., widow, d. leaving a will dated 11 Sep 1694, proved 22 Oct 1694. To son (by first husband) William Marchant and eldest dau. Ellinor Marchant, personalty. To children John Stoker, Michael Stoker and Mary Stoker, certain cattle (marked with the mark of William Kirke, DO Co.)

equally at age 21. Humphrey Hubert and Charles Powell were her execs. {MWB 7:55}

William was the father of: WILLIAM, JR.; ELLINOR; MARY.

Second Generation

2. WILLIAM MERCHANT, JR., DO Co., son of William (1) Merchant, m. (N).

In November Court 1691, DO Co., John Orithason(?) was bound out to serve Will Marchant until he reached the age of 21. {DOJR}

On 15 April 1696 William Merchant, DO Co., owned the 108 acre tract *Mount Silly*. {MPL 40:583}

On 3 Oct 1702 William Merchant, DO Co., witnessed the will of John Button. {MWB 13:347}

On 30 Jan 1711 William Merchant, DO Co., planter, conveyed to Rev. Thomas Howell et al., the tracts *Ipswich* and *Marchant's Range* for the use of Thomas Hunt and his heirs. {DOLR 6 Old 182}

William Merchant, DO Co., planter, d. leaving a will dated 30 Jan 1711, proved 23 Sep 1717. To son Joseph, the 50 acre tract *Merchant's Outlett* and a 200 acre part of tract *Herriford*; should he fail to have issue, said tracts to grandson Thomas Wall. To grandsons Alexander and William Wall, residue of tract *Herriford* and land called *Slow* equally between them; should they fail to have issue, said land to pass to rightful heirs. To son-in-law Alexander Wall, exec., and wife Mary, residue of personalty; they to be the guardians of son Joseph until he reaches age 21. To son-in-law John Stanford, Jr., 108 acre tract *Mount Silley* during lifetime; after his decease to granddau. Margaret Stanford; should she fail to have issue, said tract to lawful heirs of John Stanford afsd. {MWB 14:325}

On 27 Sep 1717 the estate of William Merchant, DO Co., dec'd., was appraised at £27.12.6 by John Ford and Thomas Cook; admin. not named. Next of kin mentioned at that time was "only an orphan boy (unnamed)." {MINV 39C:7}

On 11 Aug 1718 the estate of William Merchant, DO Co., dec'd., was admin. by Richard Pearson, Sr. Additional accounts were filed on 13 June 1720 and 14 March 1721 by Richard Pearson. {MDAD 1:256, 3:92, 4:69}

William was the father of: JOSEPH; MARY (m. Alexander Wall); (N) DAU., prob. ELIZABETH (m. John Stanford, Jr.).

Third Generation

3. JOSEPH MERCHANT, DO Co., b. 1700, son of William (2) Merchant, m. Elizabeth (N), prob. Elizabeth Pearson.

In 1712 Joseph Merchant was listed as a servant boy to Richard Feddeman, TA Co., dec'd. {MINV 34:219}

On 27 Sep 1717 the estate of William Merchant, DO Co., dec'd., listed his next of kin as "only an orphan boy (unnamed)." {MINV 39C:7}

On 11 Aug 1718 Joseph Merchant was among those who received payment from the estate of Alexander Wall, DO Co., dec'd. {MDAD 1:268}

In 1728 Joseph Merchant, DO Co., was deposed and stated he was about 28 years old. In 1732 he stated he was about 32 years old. {DOLR 8 Old 328, 9 Old 64}

On 8 March 1728/9 the estate of Richard Pearson, Jr., DO Co., dec'd., was inventoried and the next of kin were listed as Noah Pearson and Joseph Merchant. {MINV 14:50}

On 14 May 1734 the estate of Joseph Merchant, DO Co., dec'd., was appraised at £32.11.9 and approved by Elizabeth Merchant, admx. Next of kin were listed as Richard Pearson and William Wall. {MINV 19:23}

On 4 Aug 1740 Edward Marders, late of DO Co., but now of Bath Co., NC, granted power of atty. to Thomas Maid to sell his land in DO Co. Witnesses were Joseph Marchant and Warner Chance. {DOLR 10 Old 220}

Joseph was prob. the father of: JOSEPH.

4. MARY MERCHANT, DO Co., dau. of William (2) Merchant, m. Alexander Wall, son of Thomas and Alse Wall. {MWB 14:325. See also The Thomas Wall Family in Volume 11 of this series.}

Alexander Wall, DO Co., d. by 28 Sep 1717 at which time his estate was appraised at £23.4.2; admin. not named. Next of kin were listed as Richard Pearson, Jr. and James Merchant. {MINV 1:136}

On 11 Aug 1718 the estate of Alexander Wall, DO Co., dec'd., was admin. by Richard Pearson, Jr. {MDAD 1:268}

Mary (Merchant) Wall was the mother of: ALEXANDER WALL, JR.; WILLIAM WALL; THOMAS WALL.

5. ELIZABETH MERCHANT, DO Co., prob. dau. of William (2) Merchant, m. John Stanford, Jr.

Margaret Stanford was named as granddau. when William Merchant, DO Co., wrote his will on 30 Jan 1711, but he did not mention his dau. (her mother) who was prob. Elizabeth. {MWB 14:325}

John Stanford, DO Co., d. leaving a will dated 17 April 1725, proved 6 April 1727, naming wife Elizabeth (extx.) and minor children John (eldest son), William, Elizabeth, and Margaret; mentioned tracts called *London, Benjamin's Mass, Stanford's Addition* and *Stanford's Preventur*; also mentioned wife to have use of afsd. lands during minority of son John; should she marry, her dower only. Witnesses were John Marchant, William Stanford, Charles Stanford, John Ford, and Thomas Cook. {MWB 19:132}

Elizabeth (Merchant) Stanford was the mother of: JOHN STANFORD; WILLIAM STANFORD; ELIZABETH STANFORD; MARGARET STANFORD.

Fourth Generation

6. JOSEPH MERCHANT (MARCHANT), DO Co., prob. son of Joseph (3) Merchant.

On 4 Aug 1740 Edward Marders, late of DO Co., but now of Bath Co., NC, granted power of atty. to Thomas Maid to sell his land in DO Co. Witnesses were Joseph Marchant and Warner Chance. {DOLR 10 Old 220}

Joseph Merchant, DO Co., d. by 27 Sep 1752 at which time there was a division of his lands as follows: 50 acre *Priviledge*, 50 acre *Outlet*, and the lower part of *Hereford* to Thomas Staplefort and wife Sarah; the middle part of *Hereford* to Thomas Wallace and wife Rebeccah; and, the upper part of *Hereford* and 16 acre *Stow* to William Pritchet and wife Jochebed. {DOLR 14 Old 627}

On 29 Sep 1756 Rebecca Marchant, DO Co., patented the 100 acre tract *Partnership* on 29 Sep 1756. {MPL BC2:497}

On 3 Jan 1758 the 100 acre tract *Partnership* was divided between Thomas Staplefort, William Pritchett and Rebeckah Marchant. {DOLR 16 Old 27}

Unplaced

ANN MERCHANT, CA Co., m. David Craig by lic. dated 15 Feb 1778. {Cranor's CA Co. Marr. Lic., 1774-1815, p. 8}

CATHARINE MERCHANT, WO Co., was among those who received payment from the estate of Robert Nairn, dec'd., in 1768. {MDAD 60:8}

ELIZA MARCHANT and Attalanta Britt, SO Co., were listed as next of kin to Mrs. Katherine Billings, dec'd., in 1742. {MINV 27:436}

JOHN MERCHANT, CA Co., m. Phener Jackson by lic. dated 3 Oct 1789. {Cranor's CA Co. Marr. Lic., 1774-1815, p. 20}

MARGARET MARCHANT, SO Co., m. Bell Maddux in 1753 by Nathaniel Whitaker in Coventry Parish. {ESVR}

STERLING MERCHANT, WO Co., was among those who received payment from the estate of Simon Smith, dec'd., in 1766. {MDAD 55:73}

WILLIAM MERCHANT, WO Co., was among those who received payment from the estate of Stevens White, dec'd., in 1772. {MDAD 69:333}

ZOROBABEL MARCHANT, WO Co., was among those who received payment from the estate of Moses Chaille, dec'd., in 1773. {MDAD 69:347}

## THE JAMES MOWBRAY FAMILY

1. JAMES MOWBRAY, DO Co., m. Mary (N), poss. Mary Cook.

On 4 Oct 1766 James Mowbray, DO Co., witnessed a conveyance of land between James Muir and Charles Muir. {DOLR 21 Old 140}

On 28 Nov 1768 James Mowbray, DO Co., valuated the land of William Bonner called *The Inspection*. {DOLR 23 Old 150}

On 14 June 1769 James Mowbray, DO Co., witnessed the sale of negro slaves between Benjamin Ball and Robert Dowson. {DOLR 23 Old 280}

On 18 Aug 1769 James Mowbray, DO Co., merchant, and wife Mary, acquired from Henry Hooper, DO Co., planter, a 310 acre part of the tract *Goodridge's Choice* on Cabin Creek. On that same day they acquired another 310 acre part of said tract from James Hooper and then they reconveyed a 310 acre part to Henry Hooper and a 310 acre part to James Hooper. {DOLR 23 Old 357-360, 433-436}

On 29 Aug 1791 James Mowbray, Henry Mowbray and Nathan Harrington, DO Co., sold to Edward Anderson and Joseph Anderson a negro woman named Daphne. {DOLR 3 HD 257}

James was prob. the father of: HENRY; JAMES; poss. COOK; poss. MARY.

### Second Generation

2. HENRY MOWBRAY (MOBRAY), DO Co., prob son of James (1) Mowbray, m. Mary Hooper by lic. dated 14 April 1791. {MD Marriages}

On 29 Aug 1791 Henry Mowbray, James Mowbray and Nathan Harrington, DO Co., sold to Edward Anderson and Joseph Anderson a negro woman named Daphne. {DOLR 3 HD 257}

On 6 Dec 1791 Henry Mobray, DO Co., conveyed to Nathan Harrington, DO Co., a 310 acre part of the tract *Goodridge's Choice* on the north side of Cabin Creek. {DOLR 3 HD 460}

3. JAMES MOWBRAY, DO Co., prob. son of James (1) Mowbray, m. Sarah Applegarth by lic. dated 24 Dec 1798. {MD Marriages}

James Mobray, DO Co., was a private in Capt. Charles K. Bryan's Co. in the Extra Bttn., 12-25 May 1813, 3-10 Aug 1813, and 10-15 July 1814. {MD Militia, War of 1812, Vol. 1, p. 77}

4. COOK MOWBRAY, DO Co., poss. son of James (1) Mowbray, m. Margaret Breerwood by lic. dated 19 Dec 1791. {MD Marriages}

5. MARY MOBRAY (MOBERRY, MOBOROUGH)), CA Co., poss. dau. of James (1) Mowbray, m. Nathan Harrington by lic. dated 21 Jan 1783, and/or Robert Sherwin by lic. dated 29 July 1785, and/or Solomon Richardson by lic. dated 19 May 1792. {Cranor's CA Co. Marr. Lic, 1774-1815, pp. 15, 16, 24} Additional research will be necessary before assuming this is the same Mary.

## THE WILLIAM MOWBRAY FAMILY

1. WILLIAM MOWBRAY (MOBRAY), of Scotland and DO Co., m. Mary (N).

"At the Battle of Preston a Jacobite rebel by the name of William Mowbray was captured. He was transported (along with 79 others, most of them Scotsmen) to MD aboard the vessel *Friendship*. He arrived in Annapolis on 24 Aug 1716 and was indentured to Henry Trippe of DO Co. for seven years." It should be noted that the list of "rebbells names" actually spelled his name "William Mobbery." His arrival date was 20 Aug 1716, and his "purchaser's name" was spelled "Henry Tripp." {Mowbray I:110; Note from Boyer's *Ship Passenger Lists: The South (1538-1825)*, p. 13}

On 20 Dec 1722 William Mowbray (Mowbery), DO Co., witnessed the will of Charles Ross, DO Co. {MWB 18:75}

On 11 Nov 1731 William Mowbray, DO Co., witnessed a conveyance of land on Rosses Neck between Edward Ross and John Trippe. {DOLR 8 Old 448}

On 8 Feb 1736 [1746?] Henry Trippe, DO Co., acknowledged receipt of £50 paid by William Mowbray for 50 acres of land (N). {DOLR 14 Old 187}

On 14 Aug 1740 William Mobray (Mowbray), DO Co., planter, acquired from Henry Trippe, DO Co., Gent., a 50 acre part of the tract *Trippe's Regulation* on the south side of the Great Choptank River near Mitchell's Cove. {DOLR 10 Old 50}

In DO Co. Court, Nov 1743, William Moubrey signed a petition with other inhabitants on the west side of the North West Fork of Nanticoke River "in want of a road from the upper bridge of the said fork to the lower bridge for the conveniency in carting or travelling from one bridge to the other once cleared but now is stopt up." {DOJR}

On 10 Nov 1748 William Mowbray, DO Co., acquired from Joshua Beall, PG Co., a 115 acre part of the tract *Danby* on a branch of Watts Creek adj. land of Robert Bishop, DO Co. {DOLR 14 Old 261}

On 4 Aug 1751 William Mowbray, DO Co., appraised the estate of Roger Childerston, dec'd., on 16 July 1752 he appraised the estate of Margret Brannock, dec'd., and on 23 March 1756 he appraised the estate of Richard Covey, dec'd. {MINV 48:500, 50:28, 60:641}

On 2 Feb 1755 William Mowbray, DO Co., was among those who received payment from the estate of Thomas Wing, dec'd. {MDAD 39:35}

William Moubray (Mowbray), DO Co., d. leaving a will dated 28 April 1760, proved 8 Dec 1760. To wife Mary, extx., land (N). To Charles Hubbard, 1 sh. To dau. Clare Beckwith, 1 sh. To sons Aaron and Thomas, tract (N) on branches of Wattses Creek equally. To son William, dwelling plantation (N); if he dies without issue, to son Thomas. To daus. Anna and Milcah, personalty. {MWB 31:159}

*Commentary: In his will William Mowbray mentions Milcah Mowbray. "It is believed that Milcah was his dau.-in-law, wife of his son William. This belief is buttressed by a reference to a deposition dated 6 Feb 1797 in the land records of DO Co. (12 HD 15) which shows that Milcah Mowbray had a son named William; this latter William would be the grandson of the original William." {Mowbray I:110} However, this appears not to be the case since Anna Mowbray and Milcah Mowbray were actually named as daus. in William's will and they were subsequently mentioned as daus. of William Mowbray in a 1761 account. {BFD 3:96}*

On 20 Feb 1761 final distribution of the estate of William Mowbry, DO Co., dec'd., was to be made to Anna Mowberry and Milcah Mowberry after their mother's decease or widowhood. The named legatees were Charles Hubbard, Clare Beckwith, Aaron Mowberry, Thomas Mowberry and William Mowberry; extx. Mary Mowbry. {BFD 3:96}

On 20 Jan 1761 the estate of William Mobray (Mowbray), DO Co., dec'd., was appraised at £75.17.9 and approved on 20 Feb 1761 by Mary Mobray (Mowbray), extx. The admin. account mentioned William Moobray and Ann Moobray; Nehemiah Beckwith and Thomas Cook were sureties; also mentioned payment to Dr. Charles Leith. {MINV 73:146; MDAD 47:36}

William was the father of: AARON; THOMAS; WILLIAM; ANNA (m. Henry Beckwith); CLARE (m. Nehemiah Beckwith, Jr.); MILCAH.

### Second Generation

2. AARON MOWBRAY, DO Co. and CA Co., son of William (1) Mowbray, m. Nancy or Ann (N), and d. 1789.

On 15 Aug 1771 Aaron Mowbray and Richard Soward, DO Co., were listed as sureties when the estate of Rheubin Phillips, DO Co., dec'd., was admin. and distributed. {MDAD 66:105; BFD 6:98}

By 13 Aug 1777 Aaron Mowbrey, CA Co., was a private in the 14th Militia Regt., Capt. John Stafford's Co. {RPCA:117}

In March, 1778, Aaron Mobury, CA Co., was listed as a taxable in Bridgetown Hundred. {Tax List}

On 20 May 1789 Nancy Mowbray was admx. of the estate of her dec'd. husband Aaron Mowbray. Sureties were Henry Swiggate and Solomon Warren. {CA Co. Admin. Bonds JRA:83}

Aaron was prob. the father of: AARON; WILLIAM.

3. WILLIAM MOWBRAY (MOBERY), DO Co., b. c1730, son of William (1) Mowbray.

In a deposition taken some time between 12 Oct 1784 and 18 Nov 1785 William Mobery, DO Co., stated he was about age 54. {DOLR 5 NH 263}

## Third Generation

4. AARON MOWBRAY, DO Co., prob. son of Aaron (2) Mowbray, m. Sarah Dorrington on 11 April 1811 in Great Choptank Parish.

Aaron Mowbray was third corporal in the Extra Bttn. stationed at Cook's Point, DO Co., 14-17 April 1813. Aron Mobry was a private in Capt. Thomas Lambden's Co. in the Extra Bttn., DO Co., 21-22 Oct 1814. {MD Militia, War of 1812, Vol. 1, pp. 75, 76}

5. WILLIAM MOWBRAY, DO Co., b. 1770, son of Aaron (2) Mowbray, m. Rhoda Ross, d. 1843, OH; she d. 1830. {www.alkire.org/gen/ohio}

William was the father of: MARGARET (b. c1800, m. Nimrod Lister, d. 4 Feb 1864, Carroll Co., IN); AARON (b. 1806, m. 1st Jane Henness and 2nd Elizabeth White); RHODA (b. 30 Sep 1814, OH, m. 1st James W. Lister and 2nd John Harness Alkire, and d. 10 Oct 1869).

<u>Unplaced</u>

CHARLES MOBORRAY, DO Co., was a private in the War of 1812. {MD Militia, War of 1812, Vol. I, p. 8}

HENRIETTA MOWBRAY, DO Co., m. Charles Warren Coton(?) by lic. dated 4 Aug 1792. {MD Marriages}

JOHN MOWBRAY, DO Co., m. Nancy Thomas by lic. dated 26 April 1796. {MD Marriages}

LEVIN MOWBRAY, DO Co., m. Dolly Vinson by lic. dated 3 June 1794. {MD Marriages}

MARY MOUBREY, HA Co., was head of household on 30 Aug 1776 (age 29) in Harford Lower Hundred, with James Moubrey (age 7), Robert Moubery (age 5), and Mary Moubrey (age 1). {Census}

WILLIAM MOOBERRY, HA Co., was head of household (with 4 white inhabitants) in Spesutia Lower Hundred in 1783. {Tax List}

## THE ADAM MUIR FAMILY

1. ADAM MUIR, DO Co., b. c1690 [poss. son of James Muir of VA], merchant and ship owner, m. Ann Ballard on 10 Sep 1726, and d. 11 Nov 1747; she d. 11 Sep 1745. {Mowbray I:111}

*Commentary: Even though the connection between Adam Muir of DO Co., MD and Adam Muir of Accomack Co., VA remains undetermined, there are some interesting coincidences that must be noted. (1) Adam Muir, DO Co., named his first son James. There was a James Muire in New Kent Co., VA by 21 April 1690 at which time James Muire, orphan of James Muire, patented 93 acres on the north side of the York River. (2) Adam Muir, DO Co., was born circa 1690 and Adam Muir, Accomack Co., VA, was born circa 1700. (3) Francina Hack, dau. of George Hack, m. Adam Muir in VA. This Adam Muir became Deputy Collector of His Majesty's Customs and Naval Officer of the District of Accomack. On 1 Nov 1780 Adam Muir, DO Co., son of James and grandson of Adam Muir, and became Naval Officer of the Sixth District of MD. (4) In 1729 Adam Muir and James Gibson, Accomack Co., VA, recorded a formal division of the property left by George Hack. On 13 June 1734 Adam Muir and James Muir patented the 150 acre tract Muir's Venture in SO Co., MD. There is no other record for this James Muir in MD records. (5) Adam Muir, DO Co., d. testate in 1747, naming sons James and Charles, dau. Ann, and bro. Thomas. Adam Muir, Accomack Co., VA, d. testate in 1772, naming wife Francina, son Adam, and daus. Elizabeth, Ann, Sarah and Margaret. Francina Muir, widow of Adam, d. testate in 1785 and among her heirs named James Muir, son of Adam Muir. (6) On 16 May 1774 payments were made to many people from the estate of Joshua Edmondson, DO Co., dec'd., including a payment to Sprowle & Crooch paid to Adam Muir (in Virginia currency). This*

*Adam Muir lived in Accomack Co., VA. The will of William Christall, Accomack Co., VA, merchant, in 1751 mentioned Andrew Sproul, merchant in Norfolk, and Adam Muir of this county. Both Adam Muir of MD and Adam Muir of VA were involved in mercantile. {Nugent's Cavaliers & Pioneers II:340; MPL EI1:267; Whitelaw; DOLR 2 NH 269; MDAD 70:299; Nottingham's Wills & Admins. of Accomack Co., VA, 1663-1800}*

On 25 June 1726 Adam Muir, DO Co., was a creditor in the estate of William Housley, DO Co., dec'd. {MINV 11:232}

On 18 March 1726/7 Mr. Adam Muir, DO Co., was appointed to serve on a commission to perpetuate the bounds of the tract *Fishing Point* on the east side of Fishing Bay. {DOLR 8 Old 201}

On 28 April 1727 Adam Muir, DO Co., was among those who received payment from the estate of Margaret Willis, dec'd. {MDAD 8:193}

On 4 Aug 1729 Adam Muir, DO Co., was among those who received payment from the estate of Joseph Husk, dec'd. {MDAD 9:454}

Morris Ralleigh, DO Co., d. leaving a will dated 3 Jan 1732/3 and naming Adam Muir, DO Co., merchant, as his exec. He also left the estate and tuition of his dau. Mary Ralleigh in charge of Adam Muir afsd. {MWB 20:536; MDAD 13:287; DOLR 8 Old 479}

Adam Muir was a DO Co. Justice in 1734. {DOLR 9 Old 243}

Walter Campbell, DO Co., d. leaving a will dated 27 Aug 1736 and naming his wife Elizabeth Campbell, Adam Muir and his bro. Thomas Muir as execs. {MWB 21:870}

On 22 July 1737 Adam Muire, DO Co., was a surety in the admin. of the estate of Francis Money, dec'd., and Dr. John Muir was among those who received payment from said estate. {MDAD 14:288}

John Rider, DO Co., d. leaving a will dated 15 Feb 1739/40 and Adam Muire was a witness and also named as one of the overseers. {MWB 22:157}

On 7 Nov 1742 Adam Muir, DO Co., patented the 50 acre tract *Brannock's Adventure* in DO Co. On 28 Aug 1743 he patented the 50 acre tract *Walter's Loss* in SO Co. On 18 March 1747 he patented the 50 acre tract *Cow Meadow* in WO Co. {MPL EI6:535, LGB:723, TI4:125}

Mary Mason, DO Co., widow of Lawrence Mason, mariner, d. leaving a will dated 15 Jan 1743/4 naming Adam Muir as her exec. and also requesting that he have care of my children who are all very young. One of the witnesses was Thomas Muir. {MWB 23:366}

On 17 July 1744 Capt. Adam Muir, DO Co., was among those who received payment from the estate of Capt. Richard Willis, dec'd. {MDAD 20:491}

On 6 April 1745 Adam Muir, DO Co., merchant, acquired from Robert Beal, DO Co., mariner, a shallop called the *Dove* and other personalty. {DOLR 12 Old 44}

On 8 May 1745 Adam Muir, DO Co., merchant, acquired from the heirs of William Campbell, dec'd., of Dunbritan in North Britain, the following land tracts in MD: 76 acre *Dunbarton*; 250 acre *Clerk's Neck*; 100 acre *Bramble's Desire*; 115 acre *Addition*; 213 acre *End of Controversy*; 14 acre *Foreland*; 100 acre *Timber Point*; 50 acre *Addition to Timber Point*; 60 acre *Spring Garden's Addition*; 56 acre *Woolford's Content*; 15 acre *Sterling*; 150 acre *Grove*; 360 acre *Chance*; 126 acre *Dundee*; 50 acre *Brannock's Adventure*; and, two adj. tracts *Addition to Brannock's Adventure* and *[Addition to] Chance*. {DOLR 14 Old 8-11}

On 2 July 1747 Col. Adam Muir, DO Co., received payment from the estate of William Harper, dec'd. {MDAD 24:112}

Death notice in the *Maryland Gazette* on 18 Nov 1747: "Last Wed., [Nov. 11] died in Dorchester Co., Col. Adam Muir, a gentleman beloved and esteemed, not only by those in his own country, but all who had the pleasure of his acquaintance, by whom his death is much regretted." {MHM 17:368}

Adam Muir, DO Co., merchant, d. leaving a will dated 10 Nov 1747, proved 16 April 1748. To eldest son James, my lands (N), mills and personal estate in WO Co. and debts due me from any person whatsoever in Maryland, Great Britain, Island of Maderia or any other place. To dau. Ann, when at age, the sum of £500 sterling to be paid by my son James, and if she dies without issue, to son James. To son Charles, my lands (N) in DO Co. My bro. Thomas Muir, exec. In 1748 Joseph Ennalls, Samuel Griffith and Thomas Weems said they saw Adam Muir sign his will; subsequently, in 1763, Thomas Evans and Joseph Ennalls said they saw Adam Muir sign his will in 1747. {MWB 25:298, 31:931}

On 28 July 1748 the estate of Capt. Adam Muir, DO Co., dec'd., was appraised at £3358.7.11 and approved on 2 April 1750 by Thomas Muir, exec. James Muir was named as next of kin. {MINV 41:514}

On 7 Sep 1750 the estate of Col. Adam Muir, DO Co., dec'd., was admin. by Thomas Muir, exec. and the next of kin was James Muir (only kin of full age except the executor); also mentioned Charles Muir, a minor, aged 13. {MINV 45:48}

On 16 April 1751 the estate of Col. Adam Muir, DO Co., dec'd., appraised at £3358.7.11, was admin. by his exec. Thomas Muir, DO Co., Gent. {MDAD 30:1}

Adam was the father of: JAMES; CHARLES; ANN.

2. THOMAS MUIR, DO Co., bro. of Adam (1) Muir.

On 23 Dec 1731 Thomas Muir was among those who received payment from the estate of James Wetherly, SO Co., dec'd. {MDAD 11:343}

In 1734 Thomas Muir was collector of taxes (i.e., receiver of alienation fines or fees due the proprietor Lord Baltimore for land transactions), in DO Co. In 1740 and 1741 Adam Muir received an alienation fine on behalf of his bro. Thomas Muir. {DOLR 9 Old 263, 10 Old 100, 11 Old 74}

In 1739 Thomas Muir, DO Co., and bro. Adam Muir were named as execs. in the will of Walter Campbell. {MWB 21:870}

In 1743 Thomas Muir, DO Co. witnessed the will of Mary Mason and she named Adam Muir as her exec. {MWB 23:366}

On 6 March 1744 Thomas Muir, DO Co., received from David Peterkin, DO Co., livestock and a white servant named Thomas Evars. {DOLR 12 Old 43}

On 16 March 1744 Thomas Muir, DO Co., sheriff, received from David Peterkin, DO Co., planter, livestock, a servant man named Henry Delves, and all other household goods. {DOLR 12 Old 68}

On 2 July 1747 Thomas Muir and Col. Adam Muir, DO Co., received payment from the estate of William Harper, dec'd. {MDAD 24:112}

On 10 Nov 1747 Thomas Muir, DO Co., was named as exec. in his bro. Adam Muir's will. {MWB 25:298}

In 1749 Capt. Thomas Muir, and Col. Adam Muir, dec'd., were listed among many others on a list of debts due the estate of Major Thomas Nevett, DO Co., dec'd. {MINV 42:145-166}

In 1757 Thomas Muir, DO Co., Gent., was named as an exec. in the will of John Fitz. {MWB 30:346}

On 24 March 1760 Thomas Muir, DO Co., conveyed to his nephew Charles Muir, DO Co., a negro man called Bristol. {DOLR 17 Old 1760}

On 23 Sep 1760 Thomas Muir, DO Co., conveyed to his niece Ann Muir, DO Co., slaves (N), provided that Ann is to discount with her bro. James Muir £100 sterling out of the £500 to be paid to her by said James in accordance with her father's will, upon her arrival at age or day of marriage; if she does not do so, the slaves are to belong to the said James. {DOLR 17 Old 189}

On 20 July 1762 Thomas Muir, DO Co., was among those who received payment from the estate of John Turpin, dec'd. {MDAD 48:420}

On 31 Aug 1767 Thomas Mure was among those who received payment from the estate of Roger Train, SO Co., dec'd. {MDAD 57:100}

On 9 Aug 1770 Thomas Muir was among those who received payment from the estate of Thomas Bending, DO Co., dec'd. {MDAD 64:333}

## Second Generation

3. JAMES MUIR, DO Co. and WO Co., b. 23 Oct 1727, son of Adam (1) Muir, m. Sarah Nevitt on 27 March 1749, lived at *Winsor* on the Northwest Fork of

the Nanticoke River, and d. 13 or 30 Sep 1789; she d. 12 Jan 1790. {DAR; Mowbray I:111}

On 14 June 1753 James Muir, DO Co., was among those who received payment from the estate of Henry Hooper, dec'd. {MDAD 34:236}

James Muir, DO Co., patented the following land: 6 acre tract *Muir's Addition* in DO Co. on 11 Aug 1753; 20 acre tract *Addition to Piny Marsh* in WO Co. on 19 April 1754; 119 acre tract *Sharp's Chance* in WO Co. on 29 Sep 1756; and, 45 acre tract *Support* in DO Co. on 14 Sep 1762. {MPL YS6:156, YS8:713, BC6:45, BC20:13}

In 1756 Thomas Collier, WO Co., d. leaving a will naming his wife Ann Collier as extx. and requesting James Muer *[sic]* to advise her. {MWB 30:139}

On 30 June 1756 James Muir, WO Co., acquired from Thomas and John Hicks, DO Co., the 506 acre tract *Partnership* on the north side of Nanticoke River and west side of Chickacoon Creek. {DOLR 15 Old 394}

On 6 Sep 1759 James Muir, DO Co., Gent., leased to William Lee, DO Co., blacksmith, for 10 years, land (N) near Cambridge at the intersection of roads to Hill's Point and Blackwater. {DOLR 17 Old 1}

On 22 Sep 1759 James Muir, DO Co., Gent., and wife Sarah, conveyed to Edward Lee, DO Co., the 50 acre tract *John's Purchase* on Hodson's Creek and Little Choptank River, and the adj. 6 acre tract *Muir's Addition*. {DOLR 16 Old 235}

The children of James and Sarah Muir were: Adam (b. 27 Feb 1750); Thomas Nevett (b. 24 March 1752, lost at sea); John (b. -- Sep 1754, m. Catherine Steele, d. 1810); James (23 Jan 1756 - 10 Oct 1799); Jane (b. 22 Jan 1759, m. Samuel Chew Hepburn); Charles (26 Jan 1761 - 18 May 1771); Sarah Nevett (b. 24 Nov 1763); Robert (b. 27 May 1766, m. Ann Stephens Keene); and, Henry (17 May 1769 - 6 Nov 1773). {DAR; Mowbray}

On 9 June and 11 June 1761 Sarah Muir, Amelia Nevitt and Mary Hodson, DO Co., witnessed land conveyances by Henry and Ann Steele. {DOLR 17 Old 367}

On 30 Nov 1763 James Muir, DO Co., was among those who received payment from the estate of Edward Trippe, dec'd. {MDAD 51:130}

James Muir, DO Co., Gent., was deposed circa 1765-1766 and stated he was about 38 years old. {DOLR 21 Old 382}

On 4 Oct 1766 James Muir, DO Co., Gent., conveyed to Charles Muir, DO Co., Gent., the following tracts: 752 acre *Muir's Inspection* (resurvey taken and returned in the lifetime of Col. Adam Muir); 360 acre *Chance* (resurveyed and granted to Walter Campbell); 50 acre *Brannock's Adventure* (granted to Col. Adam Muir); and, 76 acre *Dunbarton* and 126 acre *Dundee*, the last two tracts having been conveyed to Adam Muir by deed from Jean Campbell *et al.* {DOLR 21 Old 140}

James Muir, DO Co., was a justice in 1770. {DOLR 24 Old 201}

On 26 Aug 1771 James Muir, Esq., was among those who received payment from the estate of Henry Thomas, DO Co., dec'd. {MDAD 66:86}

In November, 1772, the estate of John Rider Nevitt, DO Co., dec'd., was inventoried and approved on 17 Sep 1773 by Sarah Ennalls Nevitt, admx. Next of kin were listed as Sarah Muir and Emelia Green. {MINV 115:122}

On 15 June 1775 James Muir, DO Co., Gent., conveyed to his son John Muir, DO Co., his dwelling plantation called *Partnership* after his death. On that same day James and wife Sarah Muir conveyed to their son James Muir the 332 acre tract *Discovery* and the adj. 50 acre tract *Hope*. {DOLR 28 Old 68-71}

On 19 July 1775 James Muir, DO Co., Gent., and wife Sarah, conveyed to their son Adam Muir, DO Co., the 104 acre tract *Nevett's Double Purchase* (lying within and without the Town of Cambridge), the 140 acre tract *Noell's Closier*, and another tract (N) containing 14 acres. {DOLR 28 Old 55}

In 1776 James Muir, DO Co., was head of household in Nanticoke Hundred, aged between 40 and 50, with one male aged between 21 and 30, one male aged between 16 and 21, one male under age 10, one female aged between 40 and 50, one female aged between 16 and 21, and one female aged between 10 and 16, plus 17 negroes. {1776 Census}

In 1777 James Muir was appointed a Justice of the DO Co. Orphans Court. {ARMD 16:274}

James Muir, DO Co., took the Oath of Allegiance in 1778. {RPDO:171}

On 7 Oct 1785 Robert Darnall, Esq., PG Co., and wife Sarah, conveyed to Peter Steele, DO Co., as trustee for Sarah Nevett Muir, DO Co., the 186 acre tract *Cow Lane* for the use of said Robert Darnall and Sarah his wife for the lifetime of the said Sarah Darnall, with remainder to the use of the said Sarah Nevett Muir. {DOLR 5 NH 275}

James was the father of: ADAM; THOMAS; JOHN; JAMES, JR.; CHARLES (d. young); ROBERT; HENRY (d. young); JANE; SARAH.

4. CHARLES MUIR, DO Co., b. c1736-1737, son of Adam (1) Muir, m. Sarah (N).

On 7 Sep 1750 Charles Muir, a minor aged about 13, and James Muir, next of kin and of full age, were mentioned when the estate of Col. Adam Muir, DO Co., dec'd., was admin. by Thomas Muir, exec. {MINV 45:48}

On 24 March 1760 Charles Muir, DO Co., received from his uncle Thomas Muir, DO Co., a negro man called Bristol. {DOLR 17 Old 1760}

State of His Lordship's Manor of Nanticoke in DO Co., November, 1767 listed Charles Muir, lessee of 360 acres, improved to 432 acres, chiefly poor white clay swamp, on 20 May 1762, £3.12.0 annual rent. {Brumbaugh's MD Records II:38}

On 29 Sep 1762 Charles Muir, DO Co., son of Col. Adam Muir, dec'd., patented the 752 acre tract *Muire's Inspection* and on 1 May 1765 he patented the 155 acre tract *Muir's Good Luck*. {MPL BC14:503, BC24:622}

On 2 Nov 1763 the tract *Muir's Good Luck* was surveyed for Charles Muir, DO Co., on the east side of Church Creek that issueth out of the south side of Fishing Creek. {DOLR 19 Old 84}

In 1767-1769 Charles Muir, DO Co., Gent., served on a commission to perpetuate the bounds of the tract *Ennalls Inheritance*. {DOLR 23 Old 191}

In 1769 Charles Muir and James Muir, DO Co., were appointed by a county court justice to appraise the land of Ann Hodson, a minor, in Vienna Town. {DOLR 23 Old 330}

On 26 Dec 1770 Charles Muir, DO Co., Gent., and wife Sarah, conveyed to Robert Goldsborough, DO Co., the 26 acre tract *Dundee*, the 76 acre tract *Dunbarton*, and the 155 acre tract *Muir's Good Luck*, all situated on Fishing Creek. {DOLR 24 Old 213}

On 26 Aug 1771 Charles Muir, DO Co., was among those who received payment from the estate of Henry Thomas, dec'd. {MDAD 66:86}

On 8 March 1774 a DO Co. commission was appointed to perpetuate the land of Charles Muir called *Muir's Inspection*. One deponent stated that about 29 years ago Col. Adam Muir ordered George Web to mark a sapling pine for the beginning of said tract on Matthew Hood's Point. {DOLR 27 Old 365}

In 1776 Charles Muir, DO Co., was head of household in Nanticoke Hundred, aged between 40 and 50, with one male aged between 10 and 16, two males aged under 10, one female aged between 30 and 40, one female aged between 21 and 30, one female aged between 10 and 16, and one female aged under 10, plus 29 negroes. {1776 Census}

On 6 July 1776 Charles Muir was 1st Lieut., DO Co. Militia, 3rd Bttn. {RPDO:171}

On 3 Oct 1777 Charles Muir, DO Co., sold negro slaves (N) to Thomas Hicks, DO Co. {DOLR 1 JCH 47}

Charles Muir, DO Co., took the Oath of Allegiance in 1778. {RPDO:171}

On 13 March 1783 Charles Muir, DO Co., Gent., conveyed to Arthur Whiteley, DO Co., planter, the 50 acre tract *William's Choice*, the 47 acre tract *Addition or Thomas's Addition*, and the 367 acre tract *Chance* (a resurvey of the afsd. two tracts on Fishing Creek). {DOLR 2 NH 101}

On 25 March 1783 Charles Muir, DO Co., Gent., conveyed to John McKeel, DO Co., Gent., a 362½ acre part of the tract *Muir's Inspection* between Little Choptank River and Fishing Creek. {DOLR 2 NH 113}

On 25 March 1784 Charles Muir, DO Co., conveyed negro slaves (N) to his dau. Ann Muir. {DOLR 2 NH 285}

On 3 March 1786 Charles Muir, DO Co., acquired from Jolly Leatherbury, SO Co., the 200 acre tract *Land of Promise* on Nanticoke River. {DOLR 5 NH 326}

On 16 March 1786 Charles Muir, DO Co., gave bond to John Jones (Great Choptank) to convey part of *Muir's Inspection* near Town Point. {DOLR 2 HD 660}

On 13 Oct 1787 Samuel Muir, DO Co., son of Charles, conveyed to John Jones, DO Co., a 134 acre part of *Muir's Inspection* in Town Point Neck. {DOLR 9 NH 366}

Charles Muir, DO Co., d. by 11 Nov 1790 at which time Samuel Muir, admin. of Charles Muir, late of DO Co., dec'd., conveyed a negro man named Joseph to Hannah Hughs, DO Co. {DOLR 2 HD 732}

Charles was the father of: SAMUEL; ANN; poss. ROBERT; (N) SON; (N) DAU.; (N) DAU.

Third Generation

5. ADAM MUIR, DO Co., b. 27 Feb 1750, son of James (3) Muir.

On 27 Nov 1772 Adam Muir and James Muir, DO Co., witnessed the sale of a negro girl named Siner by Mark Littleton. {DOLR 26 Old 178}

On 19 July 1775 James Muir, DO Co., Gent., and wife Sarah, conveyed to their son Adam Muir, DO Co., the 104 acre tract *Nevett's Double Purchase* (lying within and without the Town of Cambridge), the 140 acre tract *Noell's Closier*, and another tract (N) containing 14 acres. {DOLR 28 Old 55}

Adam Muir, DO Co., took the Oath of Allegiance in 1778. {RPDO:170}

On 1 Nov 1780 Adam Muir, DO Co., gave his bond to the State of Maryland and took the oath as Naval Officer of the Sixth District. {DOLR 2 NH 269}

In 1785 Adam Muir, DO Co., was deposed and stated he was about 30 years old. {DOLR 5 NH 359}

On 6 June 1786 Adam Muir, his father James Muir and his mother Sarah Muir, all of DO Co., conveyed to William Barrow, DO Co., surveyor, a ½ acre part of the tract *Nevitt's Double Purchase*, being the second lot of the town lately surveyed and laid out called Muirs Town, on the south side of the Town of Cambridge, near Gay Street which runs through the afsd. Muirs Town. On that same day they conveyed to Robert Ewing, DO Co., merchant, a lot in the Town of Cambridge on the street where Mrs. Ann Muse now dwells. {DOLR 9 NH 5, 135}

On 7 Nov 1787 Adam Muir, DO Co., Gent., conveyed to William Oram, TA Co., ship joyner, a lease of 1 acre near the crossroads at Cambridge. {DOLR 9 NH 494}

On 14 Oct 1790 Adam Muir, DO Co., conveyed to William Barrow, DO Co., a ½ acre part of the tract *Nevitt's Double Purchase*, being a lot lying at the back of the dwelling house of said Barrow on the south side of the new street called Gay Street. {DOLR 3 HD 27}

Adam Muir, DO Co., d. by 6 Aug 1792. On that day Robert Ewing and Gustavus Scott, DO Co., conveyed to Patrick Kelly, two lots in Cambridge purchased by Ewing from Adam Muir, dec'd., and by Scott from Charles Crookshanks and Archibald Moncrieff. {DOLR 4 HD 113}

6. THOMAS MUIR, DO Co., b. 24 March 1752, son of James (3) Muir, prob. m. Mary Marshall. {MDAD; Mowbray}

On 13 March 1773 Thomas Muir, DO Co., witnessed the will of Thomas John Marshall in which the testator named his wife Sarah and eight children, including dau. Mary. {MWB 39:366}

On 16 June 1773 Thomas John Marshall and Mary Muir were among those who received payment from the estate of Mary Ennalls, DO Co., dec'd. {MDAD 69:10}

On 14 Aug 1775 Thomas Muir was among those who received payment from the estate of James Wheeler, DO Co., dec'd. {MDAD 73:131}

*Commentary: DAR records indicate Thomas Nevett Muir, b. 1752, was lost at sea. In 1776 Thomas Muir, DO Co., was head of household in Transquakin Hundred, aged between 30 and 40, with one male aged between 21 and 30, one male aged under 10, one female aged between 30 and 40, one female aged between 21 and 30, and one female aged between 10 and 16, plus 2 negroes. In 1782 DO Co. land records (DOLR 2 NH 93) state that Thomas Muir (blacksmith) occupied one of Henry Ennalls' plantations (N) on Choptank River between Ababco and Shallow Creeks. In 1832 pension records indicate that Thomas Muir, a soldier in the Rev. War, began receiving semi-annual payments from the State of MD for his services during the war. In 1839 a final payment due the late Thomas Muir, SO Co., was made to Levin Ballard for distribution to Muir's nearest of kin. It is apparent that all of the afsd. events do not pertain to the same Thomas Muir. Additional research will be necessary before drawing any further conclusions.*

7. JOHN MUIR, DO Co., b. -- Sep 1754, son of James (3) Muir, m. Catherine Steele, and d. 1810. {Mowbray}

In 1774 John Muir and James Muir witnessed the will of Gideon Gamble, DO Co. {MWB 39:897}

On 15 June 1775 James Muir, DO Co., Gent., conveyed to his son John Muir, DO Co., his dwelling plantation called *Partnership* after his death. {DOLR 28 Old 68}

James Muir was a 1st Lieut., DO Co. Militia, 3rd Bttn., from 6 July 1776 to at least 20 May 1778. He took the Oath of Allegiance in 1778. {RPDO:171}

On 24 June 1780 the MD Council issued a Commission of Letters of Marque and Reprisal to Alexander Murray, Commander of the brig *Revenge*, 120 tons burthen, navigated by 32 men, mounting 12 carriage guns, belonging to John Muir & others, State of MD. {ARMD 43:203}

On 2 Oct 1781 Dr. James Murray informed the MD Council that "from the appearance of the wound on Mr. Muir's leg and the testimony he has produced from several gentlemen on whose veracity there is the strongest reliance, I am induced to believe that he is incapable of severe active duty in the field as a soldier." On 3 Oct 1781 the MD Council recorded that "on the representation of John Muir who was draughted in DO Co. to serve till the 10th day of Dec next, that he is rendered unfit for military duty by a wound in his leg, the certificate of Dr. James Murray who examined the wound and the concurring testimony of several gentleman of DO Co. It appears to this board that the said John Muir is unfit for the service he is called on to perform and he is therefore hereby discharged from the said draught." {ARMD 45:631}

On 17 March 1792 John Muir, DO Co., witnessed the sale of slaves by John Owens, DO Co. {DOLR 3 HD 568}

On 7 March 1793 John Muir, DO Co., conveyed to Stevens Woolford, DO Co., the 56 acre tract *Woolford's Content* on Broad Cove. {DOLR 4 HD 477}

On 12 March 1795 John Muir, DO Co., sold a negro slave named Draper, aged about 14, to William Winder, DO Co.; he sold a negro man named George, aged about 23, to Alexander Douglass, DO Co.; and, he sold silver plate, slaves (N), and furniture to John Henry, DO Co., and he mortgaged the 506 acre tract *Partnership* and the 45 acre tract *Support* to said Henry. {DOLR 8 HD 229, 259, 260, 262}

From the *Republican Star* of TA Co. on 4 Sep 1810: Died on Thurs. last, John Muir, who was President of the Farmers Bank of Maryland, in his 60th year. {*MD Eastern Shore Newspapers* 2:81}

John was the father of: JOHN, JR. (1789-1860) m. Elizabeth Spedden (only child of Hugh Spedden). {Mowbray}

8. JAMES MUIR, JR., DO Co., b. 23 Jan 1756, son of James (3) Muir, m. Charity (N), and d. 10 Oct 1799. {DOLR; Mowbray}

In 1774 James Muir and John Muir witnessed the will of Gideon Gamble, DO Co. {MWB 39:897}

On 15 June 1775 James Muir, DO Co., Gent., and wife Sarah, conveyed to their son James Muir the 332 acre tract *Discovery* and the adj. 50 acre tract *Hope*. {DOLR 28 Old 70}

James Muir, Jr., DO Co., took the Oath of Allegiance in 1778. {RPDO:171}

On 1 Sep 1790 James Muir, Jr., DO Co., acquired from Ezekiel Harper, Sr., DO Co., planter, a 3 acre part of the tract *Harper's Regulation*. {DOLR 2 HD 691}

On 6 Aug 1794 James Muir, DO Co., acquired from Arthur Pritchard, DO Co., a 1¼ acre part of *Hard Fortune* and *Pritchard's Lot* on the road from New Market to Crotcher's Ferry. On that same date James Muir and wife Charity conveyed an 11 acre part of *Hope* to said Pritchard. {DOLR 6 HD 560, 564}

9. ROBERT MUIR, DO Co., b. 27 May 1766, son of James (3) Muir, m. Anne Stephens Keene. {DAR; Mowbray}

On 29 Oct 1792 Robert Muir, DO Co., witnessed the conveyance of land between Peter Ferguson and Thomas Colsten. {DOLR 4 HD 238}

On 28 Aug 1795 Robert Muir and John Muir, both of DO Co., conveyed to Lemuel Beckwith, DO Co., a 47 acre part of the tract *Noel's Closure* in Castle Haven Neck. Anne Muir, wife of Robert, acknowledged the sale. {DOLR 8 HD 524}

10. SAMUEL MUIR, DO Co., son of Charles (4) Muir.

On 13 Oct 1787 Samuel Muir, DO Co., son of Charles Muir, conveyed to John Jones, DO Co., a 134 acre part of the tract *Muir's Inspection* in Town Point Neck on the east side of Little Choptank River. {DOLR 9 NH 366}

On 12 March 1788 Samuel Muir, DO Co., conveyed to William Jones, DO Co., a negro slave named Daniel, aged about 17. {DOLR 9 NH 443}

On 9 March 1790 Samuel Muir, DO Co., conveyed to Samuel McKeel, DO Co., a 45 acre part of the tract *Muir's Inspection* at the head of Smith's Creek in Town Point Neck. {DOLR 2 HD 507}

On 11 May 1790 Samuel Muir, DO Co., sold to Lemmy Forge, DO Co., a negro slave girl named Darky. On 3 March 1792 he sold a negro slave named George to Alexander Douglass, DO Co. {DOLR 2 HD 565, 3 HD 499}

In 1790 Samuel Muir was admin. of Charles Muir, DO Co., dec'd. {DOLR 2 HD 732}

On 10 June 1790 Samuel Muir, DO Co., conveyed to Nathan Griffin, DO Co., planter, a 72 acre part of the tract *Muir's Inspection* in Town Point Neck. {DOLR 3 HD 4}

On 6 Feb 1792 Samuel Muir, DO Co., mariner, conveyed to Nathan Griffin, DO Co., the 150 acre tract *Grove*. {DOLR 3 HD 412}

11. ROBERT MUIR, DO Co., poss. son of Charles (4) Muir.

Robert Muir was among those who received payment from the estate of Abraham Pennington, CE Co., dec'd., on 16 April 1772. {MDAD 66:293}

Unplaced

JAMES MUIR, AA Co., was an orphan boy aged 14 and a servant of Henry Attwood, AA Co., dec'd., on 25 July 1730. {MINV 16:212}

JOHN MUIR, DO Co.

On 12 Jan 1736 Dr. John Muire, DO Co., was among those who received payment from the estate of Elizabeth Lemee, dec'd. {MDAD 15:283}

On 22 July 1737 Dr. John Muir, DO Co., was among those who received payment from the estate of Francis Money, dec'd. Sureties were Richard Willis and Adam Muire. {MDAD 14:288}

JOHN MUIR was among those who received payment from the estate of James Corbit, CE Co., dec'd., on 2 July 1772. {MDAD 67:265}

JOHN MUIR, AA Co., and Charles Wallace, both of Annapolis, acquired from David Weems and William Scrivener, AA Co., on 28 June 1788, parts of the tracts *Ross's Lott, Harper's Folly, Harpers' Seat, Adam's Dear Purchase, Increase*, and the tract *Cumberland*, all in DO Co. and containing 249 acres, in trust, to be sold by said Wallace and Muir for the satisfaction of a bond or obligation of Weems and Scrivener. On 4 Nov 1791 Charles Wallace and John Muir, Annapolis merchants, conveyed afsd. tracts to Isaac Wheatley, DO Co. {DOLR 2 HD 55, 3 HD 487}

JOSEPH MUIR, DO Co.

On 19 May 1741 Joseph Muir, DO Co., witnessed the conveyance of goods and chattels to the county sheriff. {DOLR 10 Old 89}

On 8 Nov 1743 Joseph Muir, DO Co., was among those who received payment from the estate of Garey Warner, DO Co., dec'd. {MDAD 20:3}

On 3 Nov 1747 Joseph Muir, DO Co., witnessed a land conveyance by Martha Hollock, widow. {DOLR 14 Old 172}

MARGARET MUIR, SO Co., b. 15 March 1792, m. John Phebus (c1769-1816, son of John and Anne Phebus) and had a son Thomas Phebus (b. 1793, m. Sarah Smith on 15 July 1820, and d. 1869, SO Co.). {www.alkire.org/gen}

MARIA MUIR, DO Co., was the 2nd wife of Levin Lake (1774-1826), son of Capt. Henry Lake, Jr. (1739-1804). {RPDO:134-135}

MARY MUIR, SO Co., b. 1765, m. George Phebus (1762-1837, son of John and Jemima Phebus), and d. 9 June 1858 in Pickaway Co., OH. Their children were: Nancy Phebus (m. John Abernathy), Sidney Phebus (m. Benjamin Thorp), Henry Phebus (1785-1862), Mary Phebus (1788-1842, m. Jacob Alkire), George Phebus (m. Rachel Henderson), Elizabeth Phebus (m. Isaac Wolfe), Thomas Phebus (1794-1822, m. Margaret Thomas), Jemima Phebus (1795-1879), John Phebus (1798-1819, m. Sarah Phebus), Daniel Phebus (1800-1823), Samuel Phebus (b. 1802, m. Nancy Morris), Martha Phebus (1804-1873), William Phebus (1805-1864, m. Sarah Maria Boggs), and Gabriel Phebus (1808-1869, m. 1st Martha James, 2nd Mary Haynes). {www.alkire.org/gen}

SARAH MUIR, dec'd., was named in the will of Elenor McClester, SO Co., on 11 Dec 1795. She also named Thomas Muir and James Muir, the children of her late dau. Sarah Muir. {SOWB EB7:447}

## THE JOHN NAVEY (NAVY) FAMILY

1. JOHN NAVEY (NAVY), DO Co., m. (N).

On 24 Jan 1737 John Navy, James Navy, and Godfrey Meddis, DO Co., were among those who received payment from the estate of Rev. Thomas Thompson, DO Co., dec'd. {MDAD 16:24}

John was poss. the father of: JAMES; HENRY.

### Second Generation

2. JAMES NAVEY (NAVY), DO Co., poss. son of John (1) Navey, prob. m. Mary (N).

On 24 Jan 1737 James Navy, John Navy, and Godfrey Meddis, DO Co., were among those who received payment from the estate of Rev. Thomas Thompson, DO Co., dec'd. {MDAD 16:24}

In a 1774 deposition Mary Navey, age about 50, stated her husband (N) went to school to Isaac Alwinkle at the head of Pason's [Parson's] Creek. Susannah Nowland, age about 53, stated she was shown the bounds of the tract *Patricks Wells* by James Navey and Godfrey Medis years ago. {DOLR 28 Old 171}

James was poss. the father of: JAMES; JOHN; MATTHEW; WILLIAM.

3. HENRY NAVEY, DO Co., poss. son of John (1) Navey, m. Mary (N).

On 13 April 1752 Henry Navey, DO Co., was among those who received payment from the estate of John Tootle, DO Co., dec'd. {MDAD 33:438}

On 6 Dec 1753 Henry Navey, DO Co., planter, acquired from Charles Lake, AA Co., clergyman, a 96 acre part of the tract *Lake's Discovery*. {DOLR 15 Old 19}

On 15 Aug 1772 the estate of Henry Navey, DO Co., dec'd., was appraised at £93.10.11 and approved on 12 Nov 1772 by Mary Navey, admx. Next of kin were listed as Henry Navey and James Navey. {MINV 109:408}

On 2 June 1773 an account was filed by Mary Navey, admx. of Henry Navey, DO Co., dec'd.; representatives unknown. Sureties were John Navey and Henry Navey. {MDAD 69:1; MINV 115:112}

Henry was prob. the father of: HENRY; BRIGGS; THOMAS; RICHARD; SARAH; ELIZABETH (m. William Tall); MARY (m. James Hill). {DOLR 8 HD 8}

Third Generation

4. JAMES NAVEY (NAVY), DO Co., poss. son of James (2) Navey.

James Navey (Navy), DO Co., was a private in the MD Line, was listed circa 1781 as a deserter, regiment and date not known. {ARMD 18:416}

5. JOHN NAVEY (NAVY), DO Co., poss. son of James (2) Navey, m. 1st to Amelia Jones by lic. dated 1 June 1786 and 2nd to Ally Murphy by lic. dated 2 March 1793. {MD Marriages}

In 1780 John Navey (Navy), DO Co., was a sergeant in the MD Line and was discharged on 23 March 1783. {ARMD 18:549}

On 14 Aug 1781 John Navey, DO Co., conveyed to Thomas North the 54 acre tract *Gum Swamp* and the 12 acre tract *Rich Branch* on a branch of Blackwater River. {DOLR 28 Old 353}

In 1793 John Navey and James Frazier, DO Co., served as chain carriers when the tract *Pollard's Choice* adj. *Patricks Wells* was surveyed by Richard Pattison. {DOLR 6 HD 155}

William Navy, son of John and Alley Navy, b. circa 1796 (date illegible), DO Co., Great Choptank Parish. {ESVR}

John was the father of: WILLIAM.

6. MATTHEW NAVEY (NAVY), DO Co., poss. son of James (2) Navey.

Matthew Navey (Navy), DO Co., was a private who enrolled in the militia, Lower Bttn., on 10 July 1781 and was discharged on 30 Nov 1781. {ARMD 18:383, 411}

7. WILLIAM NAVEY (NAVY), DO Co., poss. son of James (2) Navey, m. Sarah Mills on 1 March 1792, Great Choptank Parish. {ESVR}

William Navey (Navy), DO Co., was a private in the militia, Lower Bttn., on 23 Aug 1781. He later enlisted to serve on the barge *Fearnought* from 30 June 1782 to 1 Jan 1783 and was paid £3 bounty money; physical description was given as 5'8" in stature with a dark complexion. {ARMD 18:612-613}

8. HENRY NAVEY, DO Co., son of Henry (3) Navey, d. unm. by 1794.

On 11 Dec 1778 Thomas Phillips, of MD, conveyed to Thomas Keene, CA Co., a 70 acre part of the tract *Lake's Discovery* adj. the land of Henry Navey. {DOLR 1 JCH 164}

On 7 Feb 1788 Henry Navey, DO Co., acquired from James Tregoe, a negro boy named Toboy. Witnesses were James Hill and Briggs Navey. {DOLR 9 NH 488}

On 17 March 1789 Thomas B. Keene conveyed to Vachel Keene, DO Co., a 70 acre part of the tract *Lake's Discovery* on a division line between Henry Navey and Thomas Phillips. {DOLR 2 HD 223}

In 1794 a commission was created to divide the land of Henry Navey, DO Co., dec'd., among his heirs: bro. Briggs Navey, bro. Thomas Navey, bro. Richard Navey, sis. Sarah Navey, sis. Elizabeth Tall (wife of William Tall), and nieces Mary Hill and Elizabeth Hill (ch. of his sis. Mary Hill, wife of James Hill), said nieces now under the guardianship of Moses LeCompte. {DOLR 8 HD 8}

9. THOMAS NAVEY, DO Co., son of Henry (4) Navey.

Thomas Navey, DO Co., stated he was about 26 years old when deposed in 1793. {DOLR 6 HD 155}

10. BRIGGS (BRIGS) NAVEY, DO Co., son of Henry (4) Navey, m. Keziah Riggin by lic. dated 29 May 1793. {MD Marriages. See also The Riggin (Riggen) Family in Volume 12 of this series}

On 7 Feb 1788 Briggs Navey, DO Co., witnessed the conveyance of a negro boy named Toboy from James Tregoe to Henry Navey. {DOLR 9 NH 488}

On 6 June 1795 Brigs Navey, DO Co., and wife Kesiah, conveyed to John Brohawn, DO Co., a 29 acre part of *Lake's Discovery* on a line formerly a division between Henry Navey and Thomas Phillips. {DOLR 8 Old 403}

11. ELIZABETH NAVEY, DO Co., dau. of Henry (4) Navey, m. William Tall by lic. dated 29 Jan 1790. {MD Marriages. See also The Tall (Talle) Family in Volume 11 of this series}

William Tall, DO Co., b. 6 March 1757, son of Phillip and Elizabeth Tall, took the Oath of Allegiance in 1778. {RPDO:234}

12. MARY NAVEY, DO Co., dau. of Henry (4) Navey, m. James Hill and d. by 1794. {DOLR 8 HD 8}

Mary (Navey) Hill was the mother of: MARY HILL; ELIZABETH HILL.

## THE NOWELL/NOEL FAMILY

1. JAMES NOWELL m. Margaret (N) (b. c1656).

James Noell was transported into the province in 1659. {MPL Qo:267; SR8198} James Nowell of DO Co. was granted a patent for service in 1672. {MPL 17:347}

On 2 Jan 1676 John Edmondson and his wife Sarah conveyed to James Noell of DO Co. 50 a. called *Oyster Point*. On 8 Feb 1682 James and his wife Margaret conveyed *Oyster Point* to John Pope. {DOLR 3 Old 124; 1 Old 195}

On 20 Jan 1689 James Nowell of DO Co., planter, and his wife Margaret, conveyed to John Harwood of the same co., carpenter, *Nowells Pokety* called *Chance*, formerly laid out for Anthony LeCompte. {DOLR 4 Old 70}

At August Court 1690 the Court ordered that James Nowells be fined 500 lbs. of tobacco for his wife Margaret Nowells abusing Mr. Wm. Hill and our Burgesses, biding them be damned. {DOJR}

On 15 Aug 1692 John Harwood of DO Co., innholder, conveyed to Elizabeth Nowell of DO Co., spinster, dau. of James Nowell and his wife Margrett, 100 a. in TA Co. {DOLR 5 Old 3}

Margrett Nowell, DO Co., age 47, deposed on 9 June 1703. {DOLR 6 Old 53}

James Nowell, DO Co., d. leaving a will dated 16 March 1717, proved 11 June 1718. To 2 sons James and Bazell, two tracts on Susquehannah River, *Baturcins Point* and *Pery Neck*; also land on Patuxent River. To wife Margaret, dau. in law Elianor Nowell and son James, personalty; division to be made by John Harwood, exec. Witnessed by Jno. Lecompt, David Melmill, Jno. Davis, Jno. Pullin. {MWB 14:582}

On 29 May 1717 John Harwood of DO Co., carpenter, conveyed to Margaret Noell, wife of James Noell, Senr., a house and land at *Castle Haven* during her natural life. {DOLR 7 Old 46}

The inventory of the estate of James Howell was filed on 21 Aug 1718. Signed as next of kin: James (N), Bazell Nowell. {MINV 1:384}

The admin. account was submitted by John Harwood on 19 Sep 1720. Legatees: James Nowell, Jr., Ellinor Pullin, wife of John Pullin. {MINV 3:243}

James was father of ELIZABETH; SEPTIMUS; JOHN (pre-deceased his father); JAMES, b. c1683; BAZELL; ANN, m. (N) Kempston; HANNAH.

Second Generation

2. SEPTIMUS NOWELL, son of James (1) Nowell, m. Jeane (Jane) Taylor, widow of Thomas Taylor.

Thomas Taylor d. leaving a will dated 5 April 1709, proved June 1709. Mentioned son Bartholomew, unborn child, nieces Frances Teate and Dorothy Taylor. To wife Jane, extx., he devised 200 a., part of *Steven's Fields* in Tuckahoe, desiring her to confirm sale of 50 a., *Parristo*, to Peter Quinter. Witnessed by Henry Ennalls, Elizabeth Ennalls. {MWB Part 2 12:113} The admin. account was submitted by Jeane Nowell, wife of Septimus Noewll on 14 Feb 1715. {INAC 37A:32}

On 12 June 1710 Hugh Eccleston Junr. town clerk, issued certificate to Hugh Eccleston, County Clerk, re 26th lot in Vienna, sold by Septimus Noell and his wife Jane, execs. of Thomas Taylor, to Elizabeth Haynes. {DOLR 6 Old 162}

On 3 Dec 1713 John Harwood of DO Co., joyner, conveyed to Septimus Noell, *Five Pines*, 106 a. {DOLR 6 Old 212}

Septimus Nowell, Great Choptank Parish, DO Co., d. leaving a will dated 23 Oct 1716, proved 28 Jan 1716. To bro. Bazwell, exec., dwelling plantation, *Five Pines*, he dying without issue, his portion to pass to Sister Ann Kempston. To bro. James and sister Hannah, sister Ann Kempston and Sarah, dau. of Jno. Stevens, personalty. To son in law Thomas Taylor, residue of personal estate at age 21. Should he die without issue, his portion to pass to bro. Bazwell afsd., to whose care he is left, sd. Bazwell to be allowed 2,000 lbs. of tobacco yearly for 4 years for maintenance and education of sd. Thomas Taylor. Desires to be buried beside his wife. {MWB 14:175}

The inventory of the estate was filed on 28 May 1717. Signed as next of kin: John Noell, James Noell. {MINV 1:115}

The admin. account was submitted by Bazell Noell on 21 July 1718. {MDAD 1:261}

Septimus was step-father of Thomas Taylor.

3. JOHN NOWELL, son of James (1) Nowell, m. Jan 1710, Eleanor (N) (b. c1680), who later m. John Pullen.

On 6 June 1699 James Nowell Senr. of DO Co., planter, conveyed to his son John Nowell of DO Co., planter, 150 a. called *Nowells Pockety* on n. side of Monsieurs Creek of Great Choptank River adj. land laid out for Anthony

Lecompete called *Chance.* If said John dies without lawful issue, said land to revert to the donor. {DOLR 5 Old 151}

On 8 June 1705 John Harwood of DO Co., carpenter, conveyed to John Nowell of said co., carpenter, part of *Harwoods Chance* formerly surveyed for said Harwood, adj. *Pokety* and containing 100 a. {DOLR 6 Old 65} On the same day John Harwood, conveyed to John Nowell, 50 a., formerly surveyed for James Nowell Senr. called *Nowells Pokety* near land formerly laid out for Anthony LcCompte called *Chance.* {DOLR 6 Old 66}

At March Court, QA Co., 1711 Elenor Nowell prayed that Mr. John Hawkins be ordered to pay her freedom dues. He was ordered to pay her a pair of shoes. {QAJR}

John Nowell, DO Co., d. leaving a will dated 31 March 1717, proved 12 March 1717/8. To daus. Elizabeth and Anne, 3 tracts equally, viz.: *Norwell's Pocaty, Margaret's Fancy* and *Howards Chance.* Testator desires that his father may live on any part of the afsd. To wife Eleanor, extx., entire personal estate during life; at her decease to be divided between two daus. afsd. Witnessed by Jno. Lecompt, Bazell Noell, Gary Powell. {MWB 14:566}

The inventory was filed on 20 June 1718. Approvers: James Nowell, Bazell Noell, John Cullen, Charles Ungle. {MINV 1:375}

The admin. account was submitted by Elinor Pullin (Bullen), wife of John Pullin on 29 Aug 1719. {MDAD 2:193}

On 15 March 1730 Ellinor Pullen, age c50, made a deposition before the Chancery Court of Maryland regarding the birth of Edward Pinder, son of Edward and Jane Pinder. She stated that in Jan 1710 sh was m. to John Nowell.. {MCHR 4:313}

John was father of ELIZABETH; ANNE.

4. JAMES NOWELL, b. c1683, son of James (1) Nowell.

James Nowell, Jr., DO Co. age 22, made a deposition on 8 Sep 1705 re the bounds of *Refused Neck.* {DOLR 6 Old 74}

On 8 Feb 1713 John Harwood of DO Co., "boterite," conveyed to James Nowell Junr. of the same co., carpenter, *Saw Box*, adj. *Five Pines* and containing 50 a {DOLR 6 Old 215}

5. BAZELL NOWELL, son of James (1) Nowell, m. Margaret Eccleston, dau. of Hugh Eccleston. {Mowbray:33}

On 10 Feb 1717 Bazell Noell of DO Co. sold to Charles Ungle of the same co., Gent., Negro boy named Robin. {DOLR 7 Old 50}

On 19 Sep 1726 Rebecka Harwood of DO Co., widow of John Harwood dec'd., conveyed to Bazell Noell of the same co., planter, *Castle Haven* on s. side of Great Choptank River, containing 100 a.; also *Underwoods*

*Chance* adj. *Castle Haven*, containing 9 a.; also *Wheatley Chance* at Castle Haven Point adj. *Castle Haven* and containing 22 a.; also part of *Harwoods Chance* adj. *Castle Haven* and containing 70 a.; also *Five Pines* containing 106 a.; also *Parkers Freshes* in TA Co. on the branches of Milles Creek and containing 100 a.; also *Blackwalnut Ridge* in KE Co., 800 a. {DOLR 8 Old 131}

Basil Noell, DO Co., d. by 15 Aug 1753 when the inventory of his estate was filed by Margret Noell. Signed as next of kin: James Noel, William Byus. MINV 55:37}

The admin. account was submitted by Margaret Noel on 3 Dec 1755. Representatives (children): Septimus (of age), Edward (of age), Elizabeth (of age), James (of age), Hugh (of age), Thomas (of age), Charles (minor), Sarah (minor), William (minor). {MDAD 38:321}12

Bazell was father of EDWARD, b. 1721; THOMAS, WILLIAM; SEPTIMUS; ELIZABETH, m. John Trippe; SARAH, m. 1st Joseph Byus, m. 2nd Edward Trippe; JAMES; HUGH; CHARLES.

Third Generation

6. EDWARD NOWELL, b. 1721, d. 1797, son of Bazell (5) Nowell, m. by 1750 Elizabeth Trippe (b. c1728, d. 1794), dau. of William Trippe. {BDML. See The Trippe Family, this vol.}

On 1 Oct 1750 William Trippe of DO Co., Gent., gave to his sons Edward and Henry Trippe and his dau. Elizabeth, wife of Edward Noell, slaves and personal property. {dolr 14 Old 442}

On 4 March 1754 William Meredith and his wife Lettice of VA in King and Queen Co., Parish of Strayton, Gent., conveyed to Edward Nowell of DO Co., mariner, part of a tract called *Nowells Regulation* on Choptank River adj. *Harwoods Chance* and *St. Anthonys* and containing 300 a. [DOLR 15 Old 99}

Edward Nowell served in the Lower House, from DO Co., 1769-1770, captain in the militia of DO Co., commissioned 1777.

On 9 Feb 1775 Edward Noell Senr. of DO Co., Gent. and his wife Elizabeth, conveyed to William Trippe of the same county, Gent., 50 a. called *Pocaty* and 65 a. of *Harwoods Chance*, adj. parts of the said tracts conveyed by the said Edward Noell Senr. to Mary Trippe, wife of the said William Trippe and dau. of said Edward Noell Senr.; located at Matthew Elickson's Bridge on Castle Haven Road, on a creek issuing from LeComptes Bay, adj. land called *Margarets Fancy* and containing 115 a. Receipt of Henry Dickinson, R.D.C., for alienation fine paid by Wm. Trippe, son of John. {DOLR 28 Old 24}

On 9 Feb 1775 Edward Noel Senr. of DO Co., Gent., and his wife Elizabeth, conveyed to Mary Trippe, the wife of William Trippe and dau. of said Edward Noel Senr.: 50 a. of *Pocaty* and 51 a. of *Harwoods Chance*. {DOLR 28 Old 26}

Edward ((1721-1797) and Elizabeth (1732-1796) are buried in Christ P.E. Churchyard in Cambridge. "Monument was dedicated by their only surviving daughter Elizabeth Kemp." {RPDO:177}

Edward was father of EDWARD; ELIZABETH, m. c1791, Rev. James Kemp (b. 1764, d. 1827), an immigrant from Scotland, rector of Great Choptank Parish, 1790-1812, rector of St. Paul's in Baltimore Co., 1812-1814, bishop of MD, 1816-1827; MARY, m. William Trippe, son of John Trippe; SARAH; SOPHIA. {BDML; Filling Case A; Mackenzie 6:444}}

7. THOMAS NOWELL, d. 1781, son of Bazell (5) Nowell, m. Sarah, widow of Alexander Frazier, dau. of William Perry. {BDML}

Alexander Frazier, DO Co., d. by 16 May 1774 when the admin. account of his estate was filed by Sarah Noel, wife of Thomas Noel of Caroline Co. {MDAD 71:306}

Thomas Noell served as private in the militia of Caroline Co., by 13 Aug 1777. On 7 Dec 1780 he was recommended for an appointment as one of the magistrates for Caroline Co. {RPCA:120}

Thomas Noel, Caroline Co., d. leaving a will dated 15 Nov 1781, proved 26 Dec 1781. To son Perry Noel, tract of land in DO Co. called *Trippe's Regulation*, 238 a. To bro. William Noel clothing. To bros. Septimus Noel, Edward Noel, sisters Elizabeth Trippe and Sarah Byus, ½ of personal estate should all of testator's children die before coming of age. Wife Sarah, extx., to give Perry a grammar education, to have all estate during her natural life. Son in law William Frazier and son in law Charley Frazier to be execs. Should widow die. Witnessed by John Stevens of Walter, James Lloyd, Robert Gilchrist. {CAW A:64}

Thomas was father of PERRY.

8. WILLIAM NOWELL, son of Bazell (5) Nowell, m. Elizabeth Trippe, dau. of William Trippe.

William Trippe, Sr., DO Co., d. leaving a will proved 21 July 1770. Mentioned children: Henrietta Hews; Elizabeth, wife of William Noel; William; Edward; John; Jean Mackallom; granddau. Sarah Castlick. {MWB 38:147}

Henry Trippe, DO Co., d. leaving a will dated 9 Feb 1761, proved 10 June 1761. Mentioned bros. John Trippe, Edward Trippe, and William Trippe; nephew Edward Noel; sisters Jean McCullam and Henrietta Hughs. {MWB 31:442}

William was father of EDWARD.

9. ELIZABETH NOWELL, dau. of Bazell (5) Nowell, m. John Trippe, son of William Trippe.

They had 21 children. {Mowbray:165}

10. SARAH NOWELL, dau. of Bazell (5) Nowell, m. 1st Joseph Byus, m. 2nd Edward Trippe. {See The William Byus Family, vol. 14 of this series.}

In a 1790 deposition concerning a marriage contract between Edward Trippe, DO Co., now dec'd., and Sarah Trippe, widow of said Edward Trippe, Edward Noel stated that about Feb 1787 Edward Trippe, then a widower, m. Sarah Byus, widow of Joseph Byus, both of whom had children by previous marriages, and Henry Trippe was a son of the said Edward Trippe. {DOLR 2 HD 629}

Joseph was father of BARTHOLOMEW BYUS; poss. JOSEPH BYUS.

## Fourth Generation

11. EDWARD NOWELL, son of Edward (6) Nowell, m. Betsy Eccleston.

On 22 Oct 1785 Edward Noel Junr. and his wife Betsy of DO Co. conveyed to John Eccleston and Joseph Richardson of the same co., 1/3 of *Puzzle* containing 5 a.; 1/3 of *Mill Security* containing 9 a. and 1/3 of *Hampton* containing 80 ½ a.; also 1/3 of other parts of *Hampton* - containing in the whole 20 1/4 a. {DOLR 5 NH 291}

Edward was father of DELIA.

## Unplaced

JAMES NOEL m. 11 June 1793, Sophie Noel. {DOGC}

JOHN NOWELL m. Ann Hayward, dau. of Henry Hayward.

On 9 March 1741 Henry Hayward of DO Co., Gent., conveyed to his dau. Ann Nowell, wife of John Nowell of the same co., part of two tracts called *Haywards Lott* and *Johns Choice* adj. land formerly sold to Anthony Dawson and containing 30 a. {DOLR 10 Old 204}

At March Court 1744 John Noel and other inhabitants of Transquakin petitioned to have a new road erected from Kenerlys MilL down Transquakin along by Henry Haywards and so over Haywards Dam into Transquakni road by where Mathus Skillet formerly lived. {DOJR}

On 4 Sep 1772 James Nowell of DO Co., son and heir of Ann Nowell of DO Co., dec'd., conveyed to David Cavender (Cavenor) of DO Co., planter: *Hawards Addition* adj. land where Anthony Dawson and Henry Haward now live, containing 30 a., devised by Henry Haward to his daughter Ann Haward before her marriage to John Nowell, father of said James Nowell. {DOLR 26 Old 89}

PETER NOWELL m. Mary (N).

On 12 Nov 1723 Peter Nowell and his wife Mary of DO Co., taylor, conveyed to William Perry of the same co., planter, 50 a. being part of *Wellinborow*, containing 982 a. by patent, laid out for John Richardson on Great Choptank River adj. *Richardsons Folly*. {DOLR 8 Old 44}

THE THOMAS SKINNER FAMILY of Dorchester County

Ref. A: Major portions of this section were contributed by Vernon L. Skinner, Jr. He includes the following sources (other than those noted): Zachariah Skinner's Bible; Skinner notes at the Maryland Historical Society; 1870 census; Baltimore City Directory; Cemetery Records, Greenmount Cemetery, Baltimore City; Land Records of Baltimore City.

1. THOMAS SKINNER m. Elizabeth (N) who m. 2nd Henry Beckwith between 1 May 1676 and June 1678. She probably died after 8 June 1696.

Thomas Skinner of DO Co. migrated to Maryland by 1664, prob. from VA. He transported his wife Elizabeth, and son John. {MPL KK:41 SR8208}

Thomas brought himself and eleven other whites and three Negroes which entitled him to 600 a. He assigned the land over to Daniel Clarke, one of the party who came with him. Land records show two patents to Daniel Clarke in 1665 for land which was part of a warrant assigned from Thomas Skinner. Thomas patented *Skinner's Choice* for 250 a. on 31 March 1670 on the northern branch of Blackwater River; 150 a. of this was for transporting his wife, son and his servant. He also patented *Skinner's Chance*, also in the Blackwater area. He was Justice in 1671, 1674, and 1675.

Thomas Skinner d. by 1 May 1676 when the inventory of his estate was filed by Elizabeth Skinner. {INAC 2:68}

The admin. account was submitted by Elizabeth Beckwith (relict) on c1677. Payments were made to Katharine Cook, relict and admx. of Dr. Robert Winsmore. {INAC 5:150}

Thomas was father of THOMAS, prob. b. c1650, d. 1705/1707; JOHN, b. prior to 1669, prob. in VA; MARY, m. Moses LeCompte; WILLIAM, b. 1669, d. 1744. {See The Anthony LeCompte Family, vol. 14 of this series.}.

2. THOMAS SKINNER, b. c1669, son of Thomas (1) Skinner.

Thomas Skinner, DO Co., d. leaving a will dated 29 Jan 1705, proved 6 Nov 1707. To son Martin land bought from Henry Beckwith on Chickcomoco River. If he dies without issue then to daus. Eliza., Anne and Mary. To 3 daus., dwelling plantation, *Skinners Chance*. Bros. in law Thomas Brannock and Hugh

Eccleston to make division of daus.' land. Witnessed by John Walker, Susanna Harmon, Hugh Eccleston. {MWB 12:224}

Martin Skinner of DO Co. d. leaving a will dated 31 March 1711, proved 7 May 1711. To sisters Eliza. and Mary, joint extxs., and legatees of estate. Witnessed by John Jackson, John King, Alex. Fisher. {MWB 13:269}

Thomas was father of MARTIN; ELIZABETH; MARY.

3. WILLIAM SKINNER, b. c1669, son of Thomas (1) Skinner, m. 1st c1695, Hester LeCompte and m. 2nd Elizabeth Bayly, dau. of Henry Bayly (d. 1733) of TA Co. and widow of James Colston (d. by 18 July 1729).

On 7 Nov 1680, William Skinner patented *Beckwith's Addition* (50 a.) as son of Thomas Skinner (deceased). On 28 Nov 1680, he patented *Skinner's Neglect* (50 a.) as son of Thomas Skinner (dec'd.). On 20 March 1696, he patented *Skinner's Point* (50 a.). {MPL 24:302, 355; 30:102, 105; 31:386; 37:429}

Philemon, son of William Skinner of Broad Creek, b. 2 Dec 1701, bapt. 3 May 1702. {TAMI}

In the settlement of the estate of John Griffin of TA Co. on 16 Aug 1707, William Skinner is cited as receiving payments.

William Skinner was a Justice of the Peace in DO Co. in 1718 and 1719. He was a Gentleman of Broad Creek, TA Co.

He is cited as William Skinner, gentleman, of TA Co. in 1723, when he cited his age as 54 in a deposition.

On 17 April 1724 William Skinner, Gent., conveyed to his son Philemon Skinner, batchellor, a gift of 50 a. called *Skinner's Point.* {TALR 13:133}

On 27 July 1724 John Leeds and his wife Esther conveyed to loving bro. Philemon Skinner, batchelour, ½ of the *Enlargment*, 50 a., on the s. end. {TALR 13:134}

On 20 Oct 1725, he patented *Skinner's Addition* (23 a.) in TA Co.

At the June Court 1734, William Skinner (gentleman) was appointed guardian to Rose Colston, dau. of James Colston. {TA Co., Orphan's Court, Guardian Bonds}

On 1 March 1736 William Harrison deposed that he had been at the house of Wm. Skinner c1725 and in conversation with Hester, wife of sd. Skinner, and she did tell him that her husband had then made a free gift to their son Philemon Skinner of a Negro woman called Tamboe. {TALR 14:216}

In a deposition dated 1740, he gave his age as "70 or thereabouts." He died intestate prior to 24 May 1744, probably in TA Co.

William and Hester were parents of WILLIAM, b. 1698, d. 1743, m. Sarah (N); PHILEMON, b. 1701, d. 1761; THOMAS, d. 5 July 1768; ESTHER, m. John Leeds.

William and Elizabeth were parents of SAMUEL, d. 1773; MORDECAI, c. c1773.

4. WILLIAM SKINNER, JR., b. c1698, prob. son of William (3) Skinner, m. Sarah (N).

Elizabeth, dau. of William and Sarah Skinner, b. 8 Dec 1734. {TAPE}

On 11 July 1739 William Skinner, Jr., age 41 and upwards, deposed that c18 years earlier he lived where Edward Elliott now lives. (TALC:74}

On 22 May 1740 William Skinner the younger and his wife Sarah conveyed to Foster Cunliffe of Liverpoole, Great Britain, merchant, Lot No. 46 in Oxford. {TALR 14:435}

William Skinner, Jr., of TA Co., d. leaving a will dated 7 Aug 1743, proved 26 Jan 1743. To son William, exec., the dwelling plantation. Should he die without heirs, to pass to daus. Esther and Elizabeth. To daus. Mary Hopkins, Sarah, Esther and Elizabeth, personalty. Estates of three younger daus. to be in possession of son afsd. until they marry or become of age. Witnessed by William Skinner, Thom. Skinner and Nicholas Benson. {MWB 23:313}.

William was father of WILLIAM; ESTHER; ELIZABETH; MARY, m. (N) Hopkins; SARAH.

5. PHILEMON SKINNER, b. 2 Dec 1701 in TA Co., son of William (3) Skinner, m. after 1724, Lucy Hambleton.

He was baptized on 3 March 1701 (OS) in St. Michael's Parish, TA Co. On 10 June 1734, he patented *Skinner's Discovery* (70 a.). He was the Constable of Mill Hundred in 1761. He died between 28 April 1761 and 1 December 1762.

On 1 December 1762, an inventory for his estate was filed in the amount of £267.1.4. Signed as next of kin were Mordecai Skinner and Joseph Skinner. The administrator/executor of the estate was Philemon Skinner, {MINV 79:303}

Philemon and Lucy were parents of WILLIAM, b. 1741, d. 1813; JOHN, d. 1816; RUTH, m. (N) Lambden; RACHEL, m. (N) Graham; DAU., m. (N) Egan; poss. PHILEMON.

6. THOMAS SKINNER, son of William (3) Skinner.

Thomas Skinner, TA Co., d. leaving a will dated 4 April 1768, proved 5 July 1768. Children: Esther Denny, Elizabeth Bowdle, Joseph, Thomas, Ruth, Mary, Rose, William and Benjamin Skinner. Sons in law Peter Denny, husband of Esther; Henry Bowdle, husband of Elizabeth. Execs.: Peter Denny and Henry Bowdle. Witnessed by William Hayward, Daniel Bartlett (Quaker). {MWB 36:474}

Thomas was father of ESTHER, m. Peter Denny; ELIZABETH, m. Henry Bowdle; JOSEPH; THOMAS; RUTH; MARY; ROSE; WILLIAM; BENJAMIN. {See The Bowdle Family, this vol.}

7. ESTHER SKINNER, dau. of William (3) Skinner, m. John Leeds.

John Leeds d. leaving a will dated 3 Nov 1729, proved 3 Dec 1729. To wife Esther, extx., entire real estate, including land had from father —, *Long Delay*; and personal estate. Witnessed by William Hambleton, Solomon Horney, Philemon Hambleton. {MWB 19:831}

The inventory of the estate was filed by Esther Leeds on 16 Jan 1729. Signed as next of kin: John Leeds, William Hambleton. {MINV 15:585}

8 WILLIAM SKINNER, b.1741, probably in TA Co., d. 20 Feb 1813, prob. in DO Co., son of Philemon (5) Skinner, m. 1st Elizabeth Jones, m. 2nd 26 Dec 1781 in DO Co., Elizabeth Fookes

William removed to DO Co., Maryland. He took the Oath of Fidelity in March 1778 in DO Co.. He founded the firm of William Skinner & Sons, Shipbuilders of Cambridge, Baltimore, and Georgetown. He d. 20 Feb 1813, probably in DO Co.; bur. at Town Point, the family estate at that time.

William and Elizabeth (Jones) Skinner were parents of THOMAS, b. 22 Feb 1772, d. 3 Dec 1813, m. Sarah Lee on 16 Feb 1800.

William and Elizabeth (Fookes) Skinner were parents of POLLY HAMBLETON, b. 6 Oct 1782, m. Eccleston Brown; JAMES FOOKES, b. 5 Sep 1784, m. Nancy Pattison; ZACHARIAH, b. 1787, d. 1864; MARGARET, m. 23 Jan 1790, m. Thomas Goslin on 28 Dec 1813; WILLIAM, b. 6 Feb 1792, m. Beckie Pattison on 29 Nov 1814; SARAH, b. 1 March 1794, m. Minos Conway; ANN, b. 22 June 1797, m. Samuel Pattison; ELIZABETH, b. 20 Nov 1800, m. Stephen Hurst on 23 Jan 1846.

8. ZACHARIAH SKINNER, b. 23 March 1787 near Cambridge, DO Co., son of William (7) and Elizabeth Skinner, m. 22 March 1810 in Cambridge, MD, Hannah Bond Jones.

Zachariah owned William Skinner & Sons with his father. He lived in Baltimore after 1810. In Feb 1846, Joseph Patterson leased to Zachariah Skinner and John Jones Skinner a lot on the south side of the Basin in Baltimore. On 18 Oct 1846, Edmond Lynch and Samuel McDonald sold to Zachariah Skinner and John Jones Skinner part of *Gist's Inspection*. On 18 April 1848, John Sloan sold to Zachariah Skinner of Baltimore a lot on Hanover Street for $1200.00. In August 1848, Zachariah Skinner deeded to John Jones Skinner the lot on west Hanover Street. On 11 April 1850, Zachariah Skinner of DO Co. deeded to John

Jones Skinner his interest in *Gist's Inspection*. He was one of the original owners of plots in Greenmount Cemetery in Baltimore, MD.

He also lived in Georgetown, Washington, D.C. during the winter. He d. 10 March 1864 and is buried on the family plot at Town Point, Cambridge.

Zachariah and Hannah were parents of WILLIAM, b. 1811, m. Elisabeth Saulsbury; JOHN JONES, b. 1813, d. 21 February 1888, m 1st Emaline Jones in 1839, m 2nd Margaret Teal in 1856; THOMAS, b. 1815, m. 1st (N) Jones, m. 2nd Priscilla Bussy; CASSANDRA JONES, b. 1817; JAMES AQUILA, b. 1820, d. 1908, m. c1845, Cassandra Wise Woolford; WASHINGTON HAMMOND, b. 1822; ZACHARIAH H., b. 1825; MARY ELIZABETH, b. 1827; ALEXANDRA SUMMERFIELD, b. 1829, m. Sarah Lurty; RICHARD STANDLEY, b. 1832. {A}

## THE GEORGE SLACOMBE FAMILY

1. GEORGE SLACOMBE (SLOCOMBE, SLACUM, SLEYCOMB), sailor, immigrated to this province from Germany by 1695, settling first in AA Co. and later removing to DO Co. He m. Sarah (N) and d. in 1725; she m. Samuell Hedge by 1728.

On 12 Oct 1695 the proceedings of the MD Assembly recorded the following: "George Slacum his account examined for bringing the Cage Whipping post pillory and Stone from London Towne to Annapolis referred to the County for pay, being the proper goods of the County." {ARMD 19:265}

On 20 May 1696 George Slacum appeared among many others on a list of debts for the estate of James Harper, SO Co. {INAC 13B:143}

On 1 June 1697 a bill for the naturalization of George Slacombe (Sleycomb), a German borne, and Stephen Francis, an Italian, was read for the first time in the MD Assembly and assented on 7 June and 11 June 1697. {ARMD 19:565, 585, 596}

On 26 July 1699 George Slacom (Slacum) appeared along with several others, primarily merchants, on a list of debts in the estate of Stephen Francis, AA Co., mariner, dec'd. {INAC 19:86}

On 30 Dec 1701 George Sleicom, AA Co., witnessed the will of Andrew Norwood. {MWB 11:174}

On 28 Feb 1702 George Slocium, AA Co., witnessed the will of Samuel Howard. {MWB 11:397}

On 6 June 1704 George Sleicom, AA Co., planter, acquired from John Norman and Christopher Norman, DO Co., the 50 acre tract *Colechester* adj. land of Hannah Hungerford. {DOLR 6 Old 44}

On 25 Sep 1705 George Sleicome, AA Co., received payment from the estate of Phillip Howard, AA Co., dec'd. {INAC 3:401}

On 25 May 1705 the proceedings of the MD Upper House ordered "fifty two shillings paid to George Slacomb to put a Stopp to the Members Coming to the Assembly." {ARMD 26:467}

On 13 Jan 1709 George Slicum, DO Co., acquired from Robert Dines the 100 acre tract *Timber Swamp* in Blackwater River on both sides of Raccoon Creek. {DOLR 6 Old 148}

On 18 July 1711 George Slecom, DO Co., mariner, mortgaged the tract *Timber Swamp* to John Brice, AA Co., merchant. Subsequently assigned by Thomas Worthington and John Brice, execs. of Sarah Brice, dec'd. (who was extx. of John Brice, dec'd.), to Samuel Hedge on 9 Oct 1729; also mentioned Sarah Sleicomb, widow of George Sleicomb. {DOLR 8 Old 387}

On 9 March 1713 George Sleycom, DO Co., planter, and wife Sarah, conveyed to Henry Fisher a 50 acre part of *Colchester* lying at the mouth of Hungar Creek. {DOLR 6 Old 214}

George Slocombe (Slycom), DO Co., patented the 50 acre tract *Little Slycamp* on 13 April 1715 and the 174 acre tract *Privilege* on 10 Sep 1716. {MPL EE6:260, CE1:150, FF7:101, PL4:107}

George Sleicome, DO Co., sailor, d. leaving a will dated 11 Oct 1725, proved 26 Nov 1725. To son George, tract *Timber Swamp* on south side of Racoon Creek, and part of *Privilege* adj. said tract. To son Job, residue of *Privilege*. To unborn child, if a son, residue of *Timber Swamp* and *Little Sleicampe*, both on north side of Racoon Creek; should unborn child be a dau., said lands to son George. To wife Sarah, extx., 1/3 personal estate and residue to all children equally. {MWB 18:414}

The estate of George Sleicome, DO Co., dec'd., was appraised at £124.6.3 on 5 March 1725 and approved by Sarah Sleicome, extx. Next of kin were listed as William Dean and John Dean. {MINV 11:247}

On 24 Nov 1726 the estate of George Slacomb (Slaycomb), DO Co., dec'd., was admin. by Sarah Slacomb (Slaycomb), extx. {MDAD 8:101}

On 31 Oct 1728 the estate of George Sledcome (Sleicome), DO Co., dec'd., was inventoried and an account was filed on 12 Nov 1728 by extx. Sarah Hedge, wife of Samuell Hedge. {MINV 13:285}

On 15 Aug 1729 the name of George Sleicom (Slocomb) appeared among many others on a list of debts due the estate of Amos Garret, AA Co., dec'd. {MINV 15:46}

On 31 Dec 1729 the estate of George Sliecome, DO Co., dec'd., was admin. by extx. Sarah Hedge, wife of Samuell Hedge. {MDAD 10:144}

On 4 Feb 1760 the estate of Robert Willey, DO Co., dec'd., was admin. by John Willey and the next of kin were listed as Sarah Hedge and Elizabeth Slacum. {MINV 69:176}

George was the father of: GEORGE; JOB; prob. ELIZABETH.

Second Generation

2. GEORGE SLACOMBE (SLACUM), DO Co., son of George (1) Slacombe, m. Frances Griffith (widow of Lewis Griffith) circa 1747.

George Slacum, DO Co., patented the 50 acre tract *Slacum's Lot* on 8 Feb 1740 and the 213 acre tract *Privilege* on 13 April 1747. {MPL EI5:419, TI1:95}

On 12 March 1742 George Slacum, DO Co., planter, conveyed to Job Slacum, DO Co., planter, the 50 acre tract *Slacum's Lott* near Raccoon Creek and the 50 acre tract *Little Slycamp* on the north side of Raccoon Creek adj. *Timber Swamp*. {DOLR 10 Old 364}

Lewis Griffith, DO Co., d. leaving a will dated 4 Oct 1745, proved 12 April 1746, naming his wife Frances Griffith as his extx. On 5 July and 11 Oct 1747 the estate of Lewis Griffith, DO Co., dec'd., was admin. by extx. Frances Slacomb, wife of George Slacomb. {MWB 24:365; MDAD 24:117; MINV 35:264}

On 16 May 1748 George Slaycum, DO Co., planter, acquired from Abraham Bramble the 85 acre tract *Bramble's Range* on the west side of Blackwater River. On the same day George Slaycom and William Dean, DO Co., planters, acquired from Arthur Smith the 45 acre tract *Beath Ridge* at the head of Raccoon Creek. {DOLR 14 Old 281-282}

On 15 Nov 1749 the estate of Edward Horn, SM Co., dec'd., was admin. by Mary Horn and the next of kin were listed as Edward Horn and George Slacum. {MINV 42:227}

On 8 Aug 1750 the estate of Marcus Andrew, SO Co., dec'd., was appraised by George Slacum and one of the creditors was Job Slacum. {MINV 43:10}

On 28 Feb 1751 George Slacomb (Slaycomb), DO Co., patented the 29 acre tract *Roadside*, the 44 acre tract *Addition to Beginning* and the 24 acre tract *Addition to Roadside* on 6 March 1751, the 30 acre tract *Slaycomb's Isdon* on 29 Sep 1763, and the 22 acre tract *Slacomb's Cow Pasture* on 25 March 1765. {MPL BY3:131, BC10:713, BC14:527, BC18:270, BC24:694}

On 16 June 1760 the estate of Sarah Wingate, DO Co., dec'd., was admin. by George Slacomb and the next of kin were listed as Job Slacum and George Slacum. {MINV 69:121}

On 9 Nov 1760 Negro Jane and Negro Francis, slaves of George Sleakam (Slacum), DO Co., was bapt. by Joseph Mosley, S.J., at St. Joseph's Mission, Cordova. Josias Shinton and Negro Sarah (slave of Henry Meekins) were named as Francis' godparents and John Shinton and Mary Mace were named as Jane's godparents. {Jesuit Records}

On 11 Nov 1760 Sarah Griffin, DO Co., was bapt. at St. Joseph's Mission, Cordova, and John Shinton and Frances Sleakam were named as her godparents. {Jesuit Records}

On 13 Nov 1761 George Slacum, DO Co., planter, conveyed to Thomas Smith, DO Co., a 10 acre part of the tract *Privilege* on the south side of Raccoon Creek. {DOLR 19 Old 281}

On 15 Aug 1764 George Slicom, DO Co., planter, conveyed to Uriah Dean, DO Co., one-half of the tract *Beatch Ridge* containing 22½ acres at the head of Raccoon Creek. {DOLR 19 Old 289}

On 29 April 1766 George Slacum, DO Co., patented the 505 acre tract *Saturday's Work*. {MPL BC30:421}

On 11 March 1767 George Slacum, DO Co., planter, conveyed to John Tyler, DO Co., ship carpenter, the 85 acre tract *Bramble's Range* on the west side of Blackwater River. {DOLR 21 Old 294}

On 10 Nov 1770 George Slacome, DO Co., planter, acquired the 75 acre tract *Adventure* located close by the side of a small path that makes out of the New Road that leads from the chapel unto Markus Andrews. {DOLR 24 Old 198}

On 25 May 1774 George Slacomb, DO Co., was admin. of the estate of James Jones, DO Co., dec'd. {MINV 120:342}

In 1776 George Slacom, DO Co., was head of household in Straight's Hundred, aged between 50 and 60, with 1 white female aged between 50 and 60, 1 white male aged between 40 and 50, and 1 white female aged between 40 and 50. {1776 Census}

On 8 April 1780 George Slacom, DO Co., planter, acquired from Levi Foxwell, DO Co., a 5 3/4 acre part of the tract *Foxwell's Endeavour* adj. *Saturday's Work* on Raccoon Creek. On the same day George Slacum conveyed to Levi Foxwell a 8½ acre part of the tract *Saturday's Work* between Raccoon Creek and Parham Creek. {DOLR 1 JCH 340, 415}

On 23 Dec 1782 George Slacom, DO Co., acquired from William Wheland, DO Co., a 10 acre part of the tract *Middleton's Range* on Blackwater River. {DOLR 2 NH 112}

George Slacombe and some other descendants of George Slacombe, the immigrant, "were loyal to King George III during the Revolutionary War. (See Memorial of Capt. Thos. Sparrow, 1777, relating to mistreatment received by him in Dorchester County 'in recruiting for matrosses' from Mr. George Slacombe and others. Mr. George Slacombe afterwards moved to Alexandria, VA. (His daughter married Col. Charles May, of the U. S. Army. Mrs. Herman

Oelrichs, Sr., of Baltimore, was their descendant)." {Jones' *History of Dorchester County*, p. 382}

In a 1795 deposition David Taylor, DO Co., aged 48, mentioned George Slacum, dec'd. {DOLR 8 HD 436}

3. JOB SLACOMBE (SLACUM), DO Co., b. c1719, son of George (1) Slacombe, m. Mary (N).

In October Court, 1745, DO Co., Job Slacomb, planter, of Dorchester Parish, was presented for assaulting Jacob Gowtee, planter, on 10 Aug 1745; he was fined 10 sh. {DOJR:221}

The children of Job or Jobe and Mary Slacom recorded in Dorchester Parish were: Gabriell (b. 12 March 1748); Mary (b. 18 March 1752); Kiziah (b. 24 Dec 1754); George (b. 18 Dec 1755); Job (b. 20 Dec 1757); Nancy (b. 11 April 1759); Rebecca (b. 3 Jan 1762); John (b. 16 June 1763); Marsilas (b. 18 Nov 1765); and, Barzillis (b. 25 Jan 1770). {ESVR}

On 14 April 1748 Jobe Slacome, DO Co., was listed as a creditor in the estate of Samuel Jones, DO Co., dec'd. {MINV 36:225}

On 7 Aug 1753 Job Slaycomb, DO Co., Gent., acquired livestock from William Cannon, DO Co., planter. {DOLR 14 Old 729}

On 29 Nov 1753 Job Slacum, DO Co., Gent., acquired from Peter Meekins, CE Co., planter, a 30 acre part of the tract *Old Baily* on the west side of Blackwater River. {DOLR 15 Old 69}

On 19 Dec 1754 Job Slacum, DO Co., acquired from Jeremiah Pritchett, DO Co., a 258 acre part of the tract *Pritchett's Forrest* on the west side of Blackwater River. {DOLR 15 Old 174}

On 19 Nov 1757 Job Slacum, DO Co., acquired from William Robinson, DO Co., a 50 acre part of the tract *Andrew's Fortain* on the west side of Fishing Bay, a 50 acre part of the tract *Gander's Labour* on Goose Creek, the adj. 25 acre tract *End of Dispute*, the 15 acre tract *Molly's Lot*, another 115 acre part of the tract *Andrew's Fortain*, and a 30 acre part of *Joseph's Lain*. {DOLR 16 Old 11-13}

On 17 Feb 1753 Job Slacum, DO Co., patented the 331 acre tract *Slacum's Lot* (which had been enlarged to 758 acres by 1 Nov 1764), the 104 acre tract *Liberty* on 26 March 1756, and the 170 acre tract *Second Purchase* on 3 May 1756. {MPL YS7:291, BC3:259, BC5:298, BC30:402}

On 13 June 1758 Job Slacum, DO Co., acquired from John Rumbley, DO Co., the 30 acre tract *Hogg Quarter* on Road Island in Fishing Bay, and from Jeremiah Pritchett the 29 acre tract *Jobe's Folly* on the west side of Blackwater River. {DOLR 16 Old 51}

On 9 Aug 1758 Job Slacum, DO Co., acquired from Thomas Walters, DO Co., the 18½ acre tract *Walters Desire* and the 25 acre tract *Widow's Purchase*, both on Goose Creek. {DOLR 16 Old 123}

On 16 June 1760 the estate of Sarah Wingate, DO Co., dec'd., was admin. by George Slacomb and the next of kin were listed as Job Slacum and George Slacum. {MINV 69:121}

On 12 Nov 1762 Job Slacum, DO Co., acquired from Ezekiel Willey, DO Co., a 20 acre part of the tract *Timber Swamp* on Raccoon Creek, and the 50 acre tract *Chance* patented to Samuel Hedge. {DOLR 18 Old 350}

On 16 May 1764 the estate of William Dean (Deen), DO Co., dec'd., was admin. by Sarah Dean and the next of kin were listed as George Slacum and Henry Lake. {MINV 86:31}

Job Slacum, DO Co., patented the 403 acre tract *Andrew's Fortune* on 29 Sep 1766 and the 140 acre tract *Molly's Lot* on 12 Oct 1769. {MPL BC30:459, BC39:16}

On 4 Oct 1769 Job Slacum, DO Co., acquired from Jacob Gootee, DO Co., a 25 acre part of the tract *Callis* on the west side of Blackwater River. {DOLR 23 Old 420}

On 31 July 1770 Job Slacum, DO Co., planter, conveyed to Richard Dean, DO Co., planter, a 34½ acre part of the tract *Slacum's Lott* on a branch of Raccoon Creek. {DOLR 24 Old 57}

On 10 Nov 1770 Job Slacum, DO Co., planter, conveyed to Edward Willey, DO Co., shoemaker, the 75 acre tract *Privilege* on Raccoon Creek. {DOLR 24 Old 190}

On 16 May 1772 Job Slacum, DO Co., made an agreement with Solomon Phillips to cut a ditch from Phillips' land, by a division tree between lands of Ezekiel Willey and said Job Slacum, down to Raccoon Creek. {DOLR 26 Old 163}

On 10 Aug 1774 Job Slacum, DO Co., planter, acquired from Robert Wingate, DO Co., planter, a 50 acre part of the tract *Gander's Labrinth* on Fishing Bay and Goose Creek. {DOLR 27 Old 396}

On 15 Jan 1776 Job Slacum, DO Co., was among those who received payment from the estate of William Dean, DO Co., dec'd. {MDAD 74:111}

In 1776 Job Slacom, DO Co., was head of household in Straight's Hundred, aged between 50 and 60, with 2 whites under 10 years of age, 1 white male aged between 10 and 16, 1 white female aged between 10 and 16, 3 white males aged between 16 and 21, 1 white female aged between 16 and 21, 1 white male aged between 21 and 30, 1 white female aged between 21 and 30, and 1 white female aged between 40 and 50. {1776 Census}

On 15 March 1783 Job Slacom, DO Co., farmer, and Robert Harrison, DO Co., Gent., conveyed to Peter Kirwan, DO Co., farmer, the 235 acre tract

*Nunar's Pasture Enlarged* formerly belonging to Edward Nunar, dec'd., and sold by Robert Harrison, then Sheriff of DO Co., under a writ of *fieri facias* for payment of a judgment recovered by said Job Slacum against the said Edward Nunar. {DOLR 2 NH 125}

In a 1785 deposition Job Slacum, DO Co., stated he was about 66 years old. {DOLR 5 NH 346}

On 20 April 1789 Job Slacum, DO Co., acquired from George Dean, DO Co., a 12½ acre part of the tract *Beath Ridge* on Blackwater River. On the same day he conveyed to said George Dean a 12½ acre part of the tract *Pritchett's Forrest*. {DOLR 2 HD 274, 418}

On 11 Aug 1789 Job Slacum, Sr., DO Co., conveyed to his son Job Slacum, Jr., DO Co., a 164¼ acre part of the tract *Pritchett's Forrest* and a 5 acre part of the tract *Barth Ridge*. {DOLR 2 HD 362}

On 20 March 1793 Job Slacum, DO Co., conveyed to John Barnes, DO Co., a 10 acre part of the tract *Addition to Liberty*. {DOLR 4 HD 463}

Job was the father of: GABRIEL; GEORGE; JOB JR.; JOHN; MARSILAS (MARCELLUS); BARZILLIS (BARZILLAI); MARY; KIZIAH; NANCY; REBECCA.

Third Generation

4. GABRIEL SLACUM (SLACOM), DO Co., b. 1748, son of Job (3) Slacombe (Slacum), m. Catherine Boyne.

"Gabriel Slacom (Slacombe) was an officer of the crew of the privateer Sturdy Beggar, sailing under Letters of Marque, commissioned in 1776 and 1777. He was captured and imprisoned for several years in England; finally he escaped to France and reached his home after an absence of seven years, broken in health from serious wounds received at the time of his capture. His family had long since thought him dead. His ancestor was George Slacom, a German borne. Citizenship was given him by naturalization act June 11, 1697 (see Maryland Archives). Footnote: Mary Boyne Slacombe (Slacum) Lake was the daughter of Gabriel Slacum, of Maryland, and Catherine Boyne, his wife, daughter of Dr. Boyne, of Dublin, Ireland, of the old Irish family of Boyne." {Jones' *History of Dorchester County*, p. 382}

On 25 Nov 1794 Gabriel Slacum, WO Co., acquired crops and livestock from William Sotherin, DO Co. {DOLR 8 HD 108}

On 30 May 1795 Gabriel Slacum, DO Co., acquired from John Kirwan, DO Co., the 65 acre tract *Todd Point* on Farham Creek. {DOLR 8 HD 529}

Capt. George Lake (1776-1831), son of Henry and Rhoda Lake, m. Mary Boyne Slacum by lic. dated 23 Oct 1802. She was b. 3 June 1784 and d. 21 Sep 1872. She is bur. at Grenada, MS, and George is bur. at Locust Grove farm, Lake District, DO Co., MD. {Jones:385}

On 1 May 1804 George Lake, DO Co., was admin. of the estate of Gabriel Slacum, dec'd. {*Republican Star* of Easton}

Gabriel was the father of: MARY BOYNE (m. George Lake).

5. GEORGE SLACUM, DO Co., b. 1755, son of Job (3) Slacombe (Slacum).

George Slacum (Slacom), DO Co., took the Oath of Allegiance in 1778. {RPDO:212}

On 27 March 1794 George Slacum, DO Co., conveyed to William Bramble, DO Co., a negro wench named Love. {DOLR 6 HD 448}

On 4 April 1794 John Kirwan, DO Co., gave his bond to convey to George Slacum, DO Co., the tract *Todd's Point* on Fern Creek. {DOLR 6 HD 450, DOLR 8 HD 106}

On 8 Aug 1794 George Slacum, DO Co., Gent., conveyed negro slaves to William Sotherin, DO Co. {DOLR 6 HD 453, DOLR 8 HD 69}

6. JOB SLACUM (SLAKUM), JR., DO Co., b. 1757, son of Job (3) Slacombe (Slacum), m. Susanna Keene by lic. dated 23 April 1788. {DO Co. Marr. Lic.; ESVR. See also The Edward Keene Family in Volume 13 of this series}

Capt. Job Slacum, Jr.'s Company, DO Co., had 51 privates enrolled as of 15 July 1780. {Jones:236; MD Militia:122}

On 11 Aug 1789 Job Slacum, Sr., DO Co., conveyed to his son Job Slacum, Jr., DO Co., a 164¼ acre part of the tract *Pritchett's Forrest* and a 5 acre part of the tract *Barth Ridge*. {DOLR 2 HD 362}

On 9 April 1790 Job Slacum, DO Co., acquired from Peter Kirwan, DO Co., a negro boy named Allerpha. {DOLR 2 HD 561}

Samuel Slacom, son of Job and Susanna Slacom, b. 1 Aug 1793; Mary Slacum, dau. of Job and Susanna Slacum, b. 19 May 1798; Susanna Slacum, dau. of Job and Susanna, b. 28 April 1800; DO Co., Great Choptank Parish. {ESVR}

Job was the father of: SAMUEL; MARY; SUSANNA.

7. MARCELLUS (MARSILAS) SLACUM, DO Co., b. 1765, son of Job (3) Slacombe (Slacum), m. Sarah Staplefort by Rev. James Kemp on 1 June or 7 June 1798, Dorchester Parish. {ESVR; MD Marriages. See also The Staplefort (Stapleford) Family in Volume 13 of this series}

On 19 March 1795 Marcellus Slacum, DO Co., witnessed the manumission of negro Esther by William Vaughan. {DOLR 9 HD 258}

Nelly Slacum, dau. of Marcellus and Sarah, b. 13 March 1799, DO Co., Great Choptank Parish. {ESVR}

Marcellus was the father of: NELLY.

8. BARZILLAI (BARZILLIS) SLACUM, DO Co., b. 1770, son of Job (3) Slacombe (Slacum), m. Mary "Polly" Hart on 15 Jan 1794, Great Choptank Parish. {ESVR. See also The Arthur Hart Family in Volume 11 of this series}

Polly Slacum, dau. of Barzillai and Polly, b. 27 June 1798, DO Co., Great Choptank Parish. {ESVR}

Barzillai was the father of: POLLY.

Fourth Generation

9. MARY BOYNE SLACUM, DO Co., dau. of Gabriel (4) Slacum, m. George Lake.

Capt. George Lake (1776-1831), son of Henry and Rhoda Lake, m. Mary Boyne Slacum by lic. dated 23 Oct 1802. She was b. 3 June 1784 and d. 21 Sep 1872. She is bur. at Grenada, MS, and George is bur. at Locust Grove farm, Lake District, DO Co., MD. Washington Lake (1784-1826), bro. of George Lake, m. Margaret Slacum. {Jones:385; RPDO:135}

Unplaced

(N) SLOCOMB, WO Co., m. (N) Merrill, dau. of John Merrill.

Sophia and Margret Slocomb, granddaus. of John Merrill, WO Co., were bequeathed cattle in his will dated 21 Jan 1759. {MWB 31:230}

Sepah Slokem and Margaret Slokam were among the named legatees when the estate of John Merrill, WO Co., dec'd., was admin. on 6 April 1761. {MINV 73:240}

BENJAMIN SLOCOMBE, QA Co., witnessed the will of Benjamin Griffiths on 25 Sep 1773. {MWB 39:511}

GABRIEL SLACUM, DO Co., b. 1802, d. 20 Sep 1824, aged 22, and bur. at Bethlehem Methodist Church on Taylor's Island. Marker erected by his sister Ellen Mitchell. {Marshall's DO Co. Tombstone Records I:86}

GEORGE SLACUM, DO Co., b. 1769, d. 4 Sep 1820, aged 51, and bur. at Sewell Simmons home place near Andrews P. O. in the Lake District. Buried next to him are Andrew J. Slacum (1817-1855) and his wife Mary E. Slacum (1828-1865), Emiline Slacum (1810-1820), Mary G. Slacum (1852-1869), Catharine L. Slacum (1861-1869), and Joseph Lee Slacum (b. & d. 1871, son of Andrew and Sarah Slacum). {Marshall's DO Co. Tombstone Records I:70}

JOB SLACUM, DO Co., m. Miss Ann McNemar (McNemara) on 10 Nov 1812. {*MD Eastern Shore Newspapers*:115}

JOHN SLOCOMB, WO Co., m. Polly McCreddy by marr. lic. dated 25 Oct 1796. {Brumbaugh's MD Records II:593}

William Slocomb, WO Co., d. leaving a will proved 7 May 1822 and named only his mother Polly Slocomb. {WOWB MH2:510}

John was the father of: WILLIAM.

JOSEPH SLOCUM, QA Co., and Mary Horsley m. 26 Feb 1749, St. Luke's Parish. {ESVR}

Joseph Slocom appeared among many others on a list of sperate debts due the estate of Daniel Killim, TA Co., dec'd., on 6 July 1773. {MINV 113:41}

MISS SLACUM, DO Co., bur. 20 March 1797, Great Choptank Parish. {ESVR}

RILY SLOCOMB (SLOCUMB), WO Co., m. Rachel (N).

Rachel Slocomb, WO Co., was among those who received payment from the estate of Lenard Johnson, WO Co., dec'd., on 5 Aug 1748. {MDAD 25:167}

Rily Slocomb, WO Co., d. by 10 July 1749 at which time his estate was admin. by Elijah Brittingham. Next of kin were listed as James Henderson and Henderson Baker. {MINV 40:236}

On 3 Aug 1763 the estate of Ryly Slocomb, WO Co., dec'd., was admin. by Elijah Brittingham and among those receiving payment were Rachel Slocomb and Margret Slocomb, dau. {MDAD 49:437}

Riley Slocomb, WO Co., witnessed the will of John Blades on 14 July 1779. {WOWB JW4:402}

William Henderson, WO Co., wrote his will in 1800 and named dau. Sinah Slocomb and grandch. Sally Slocomb and Henry Slocomb among his heirs. In 1802 the exec. renounced and admin. was granted to Sinah Slocomb, John R. Slocomb, and Bayley Young. Sinah Slocomb d. by 29 May 1806 and John R. Slocomb was one of the admins. {WOWB JBR:305, 317, JBR2:305}

Sarah Slocomb, WO Co., d. leaving a will dated 13 April 1806, proved 27 May 1806, naming daus. Hulday Purnell, Polly Melvin, Sally Slocomb and Rachel Slocomb, and grandsons William Riley Slocomb and John R. Slocomb, exec. {WOWB MH:21}

Riley was the father of: RILEY; MARGRET; prob. JOHN (m. Sinah Henderson).

ROBERT SLACOMB (SLOCOMB), WO Co., prob. m. Ruth Willett.

Robert Slocomb, WO Co., was mentioned when the estate of William Willet, WO Co., dec'd., was admin. on 30 Oct 1770. {MINV 108:242}

Robert Slacomb, WO Co., was among those who received payment from the estate of John Finessey, WO Co., dec'd., on 22 Nov 1771. {MDAD 67:49}

Ruth Slocium and Thomas Willett were named as the next of kin to Ambrous Nicholson, WO Co., dec'd., when his estate was appraised on 10 Aug 1773. {MINV 117:429}

William Slocom, son of Robert and Ruth, was mentioned in the will of Thomas Willett, WO Co., on 13 March 1778. Robert Slocom and William Cowley were execs. {WOWB JW4:400}

Robert was the father of: WILLIAM.

THOMAS SLAWCOMB (SLOCOMB), WO Co., appeared among many others on a list of desperate debts due the estate of Eli Campbell, WO Co., on 5 Aug 1773. {MINV 119:232}

WILLIAM J. SLACUM, DO Co., b. 1780, d. 27 May 1854, aged 74, and bur. on farm of Denard Johnson in the Lake District. {Marshall's DO Co. Tombstone Records I:8}

## THE JOHN STANFORD (STANDFORD) FAMILY

1. JOHN STANFORD (STANDFORD), DO Co., was transported into this province by 1679 and m. Mary (N) circa 1685. {MPL WC2:21}

*Commentary: There were families named Stanford, Standford, Standeford, Stanforth, and Stanfield in DO Co., SO Co., BA Co., and AA Co. in colonial MD. Richard Stanford was transported into this province as a servant in 1648. Augustine Stanford or Stanforth was transported into SO Co. by 1674. There appears to have been two John Stanfords in MD by 1679, one in AA Co. (d. 1679) and another in DO Co. {MPL 2:581, 15:318, 15:454, WC2:21, WC2:77} The John Stanford who subsequently resided in DO Co. is the one presented herein. His connection, if any, to the other Stanfords is a matter for further research.*

John Standford, of Nanticoke Hundred, DO Co., was presented in August Court, 1690 and accused of stealing corn from the corn house of Benjamin Hunt; he was found not guilty. {DOJR}

On 26 Nov 1695 John Stanfoord *[sic]* was among those who received payment from the estate of Grouney Crowe, DO Co. {MINV 13B:82}

On 24 July 1703 John Stanford appraised the estate of Christopher Short, DO Co., dec'd. {MINV 24:87A}

John Standford, DO Co., d. by 10 April 1716 at which time his estate was appraised at £74.1.1 and the next of kin were listed as John Stanford and William Stanford. {MINV 37C:15}

On 10 Sep 1717 the estate of John Stanford, DO Co., dec'd., was admin. by Mary Stanford and Charles Stanford. {MINV 37B:44}

Mary Standford, DO Co., d. leaving a will dated 15 April 1717, proved 13 Nov 1717, naming friend Richard Pritchett (exec.) to have charge of her children (N) until they arrive at age. {MWB 14:452}

On 13 Dec 1717 the estate of Mary Stanford, DO Co., dec'd., was appraised at £5.15.5 and Patigrew Salsbury was listed as a creditor. {MINV 1:125}

In 1717/8 Charles Standford and Pettigrew Salsbury appraised the estate of Joseph Wall, DO Co., dec'd. {MINV 1:399}

In 1719 Rachel Stanford, DO Co. [wife of Thomas Stanford], a legatee in the will of Patygrew Salsbury, was bequeathed a 68 acre part of the tract *Salisbury's Charge* during life. {MWB 16:32}

On 12 Nov 1719 the estate of Mary Sanford, DO Co., dec'd., was admin. by Richard Prichard and payment was made to Petigrew Salsbury (Saldesbury). {MDAD 2:483}

Richard Pritchard, DO Co., d. by 10 June 1735 at which time payment was made to several people, including Charles Standford, guardian of Samuel Standford, one of the orphans of John Standford, dec'd. {MDAD 13:149}

John was the father of: JOHN; WILLIAM; CHARLES; SAMUEL; prob. THOMAS.

Second Generation

2. JOHN STANFORD (STANDFORD), JR., DO Co., b. c1685, son of John (1) Stanford, m. Elizabeth Merchant. who poss. m. 2nd to Richard Pritchard.

William Merchant, DO Co., d. leaving a will dated 30 Jan 1711, proved 23 Sep 1717, naming among others his son-in-law John Stanford, Jr. who was bequeathed the 180 acre tract *Mount Silley* during life and after his death to granddau. Margaret Stanford. William Merchant did not mention his dau.'s name. {MWB 14:325}

On 8 Nov 1715 John Stanford, Jr., DO Co., and wife Elizabeth, conveyed to Philemon Philips, DO Co., the 180 acre tract *Mount Silley*. {DOLR 6 Old 260}

On 9 March 1719/20 John Standford, DO Co., acquired from Thomas Hunt, DO Co., Gent., the 23 acre tract *Benjamin's Mess* on Blackwater River. {DOLR 2 Old 25}

On 8 Aug 1723 John Standford, DO Co., acquired from William Clayton, DO Co., a 140 acre part of the tract *London* on the east side of Blackwater River. {DOLR 2 Old 715}

On 8 July 1726 John Stanford, DO Co., patented the 80 acre tract *Stanford's Addition*. {MPL PL6:490}

John Stanford, DO Co., d. leaving a will dated 17 April 1725, proved 6 April 1727. To eldest son John, 43 acre tract *Benjamin's Mass* and *Stanford's Addition* and part of *London* adj. To wife Elizabeth, use of afsd. lands during minority of son John; if he dies without issue, to his bro. and sisters equally. To dau. Elizabeth, part of *London*. To son William, part of *London*. To dau. Margaret, tract *Stanford's Preventur* adj. *London*; if she dies without issue, to her sis. Elizabeth; if both die, to their 2 bros. equally. To wife Elizabeth (extx.), residue of estate; should she marry, her dower only. Witnesses: Alexander Strahon, John Marchant, John Ford, William Stanford, and Charles Stanford. {MWB 19:132}

On 17 May 1727 the estate of John Standford, DO Co., dec'd., was appraised at £115.19.6 and approved on 26 Aug 1727 by Elizabeth Standford, extx. Next of kin were listed as Charles Standford and William Standford. {MWB 12:350}

On 11 Dec 1728 the estate of John Stanford, DO Co., dec'd., was admin. by Richard Prichard and his wife Elizabeth. {MDAD 9:271}

John was the father of: JOHN; WILLIAM; ELIZABETH; MARGARET.

3. CHARLES STANFORD (STANDFORD), DO Co., b. c1688, son of John (1) Stanford, m. 1st Mary (N) and 2nd Rosanna (N); she m. Moses Poole after 1746.

In 1717 Charles Standford and Pettigrew Salsbury appraised the estate of Joseph Wall, DO Co., dec'd. {MINV 1:399}

On 26 April 1718 Charles Stanford, DO Co., was among those who received payment from the estate of Thomas Vinson, dec'd. {MINV 39A:55}

On 16 April 1719 Charles Standford, DO Co., acquired from James Ponder, DO Co., a 30 acre part of the tract *Alexander's Place* on Transquaking River. {DOLR 2 Old 30}

On 27 Oct 1719 Charles Standford, DO Co., acquired another 5 acre part of *Alexander's Place* from James and Rachel Ponder as acknowledged by John Standford, their atty., on 24 June 1720. {DOLR 2 Old 32}

On 13 March 1720/1 Charles Stanford, DO Co., leased an 8 acre part of *Alexander's Place* from John Eccleston for a term of 65 years. {DOLR 2 Old 109}

On 15 March 1720/1 Charles Stanford and wife Mary, Anthony Rawlings and wife Katherine, John Charlescraft and wife Rebecca, and John Eccleston, DO Co., conveyed to Andrew Smith, carpenter, a 16 acre part of *Alexander's Place*. {DOLR 2 Old 91}

On 15 Aug 1728 Charles Stanford, DO Co., planter, acquired from John Young, DO Co., the 23 acre tract *Nonsuch* on Beargardin Creek and the 15 acre tract *Beckwith's Island* on the east side of Transquakin River. {DOLR 8 Old 223, 225}

On 14 Nov 1728 Charles Stanford, DO Co., planter, acquired from Edward Mathers, DO Co., planter, a 69 acre part of the tract *Mallborough* on the east side of Blackwater River and the south side of Hoccady Creek. {DOLR 8 Old 270-271}

On 30 Jan 1728/9 Charles Standford, DO Co., planter, acquired from Anthony and Katherine Rawlings, DO Co., yeoman, and John Eccleston, DO Co., mariner, the 31 acre upper part of *Alexander's Place*, reserving a burying place 6 ft. square where the children of said Anthony and Katherine were buried. {DOLR 8 Old 251}

On 12 June 1729 Charles Standford, DO Co., acquired from Andrew Smith, DO Co., planter, two parts (50 acres and 16 acres) of *Alexander's Place* on the west side of Transquakin River. {DOLR 8 Old 284}

On 11 Nov 1730 Charles Stanford, DO Co., acquired from John Eccleston, DO Co., mariner, a 21 acre part of *Alexander's Place* adj. the dwelling plantation of said Stanford. {DOLR 8 Old 389}

In a deposition taken some time between 15 March 1727 and 10 June 1731 Charles Standford, DO Co., stated he was about age 41. {DOLR 8 Old 431}

On 16 June 1732 Charles Standford, DO Co., conveyed to Andrew Smith, DO Co., a 50 acre part of *Alexander's Place* on the west side of Transquakin River. On 17 June 1732 a 50 acre part of said tract was conveyed from said Smith to said Standford. {DOLR 8 Old 477, 9 Old 30}

Charles Stanford, DO Co., patented the following tracts: 154 acre *Chance* on 26 Oct 1731; 50 acre *Stanford's Goodwill* on 10 June 1734; 100 acre *Venture* on 10 June 1734; and, *Stanford's Desire* on 5 Nov 1737. {MPL PL8:124, EI2:180, 692, EI3:204}

On 15 June 1734 Charles Standford, DO Co., acquired from Sarah and Ann Kirke (the widow and dau. of John Kirke), a 404 acre tract called *End of Controversy* on the east side of Fowling Creek. {DOLR 9 Old 181}

In a deposition taken some time between 16 Nov 1734 and 10 April 1735 Charles Stanford, DO Co., stated he was about age 48. {DOLR 9 Old 436}

On 1 March 1739/40 Charles Stanford, DO Co., signed an agreement (made his "C" mark) to acquire livestock from John West, DO Co. {DOLR 11 Old 15}

In a deposition taken on 24 Aug 1741 Charles Stanford, DO Co., stated he was about age 53. {DOLR 12 Old 133}

In April Court 1743, DO Co., it was presented that Charles Stanford had been assaulted by Ezekiel Keene, of Dorchester Parish, on 7 Aug 1742; Keene was fined £5. {DOJR}

On 4 July 1743 Charles Stanford, DO Co., acquired slaves (N) from Elizabeth Cock, DO Co., spinster. {DOLR 11 Old 95}

In a deposition taken on 10 July 1744 Charles Stanford, DO Co., regarding the tract *Weston*, stated he was age 50 years or upwards and about 30 years ago his father (N) dwelt upon the land belonging to John Stevens; also mentioned his bro. John Stanford employed Thomas Taylor about 16 years ago to run out the land called *London* that he bought from Mr. Clayton. {DOLR 12 Old 150}

On 3 Jan 1744/5 Charles Stanford, DO Co., acquired three cows from Jonathan Morriston, DO Co. {DOLR 12 Old 11}

On 7 Nov 1745 Charles Standford, DO Co., and wife Rosannah, conveyed to Joseph Ennalls, DO Co., the following tracts: 154 acre *Chance*; 100 acre *Venture*; 291 acre *Standford's Desire*; 23 acre *Nonesuch*; 15 acre *Beckwith*; and, parts of *Alexander's Place* by said Charles Standford from John Eccleston, James Ponder, Anthony Rawlings, and Andrew Smith; plus, 21 acres of swamp land, for a total of 893 acres in all. {DOLR 14 Old 14}

Charles Standford, DO Co., d. leaving a will dated 15 Dec 1745, proved 20 Feb 1745/6. To son Thomas, tract (N) on Kandey Branch and remainder of three tracts (N) on Hocady Creek, and tract (N) where Thomas Braddis now lives. To wife Rosanna, lands (N) if son Levin dies without issue. To dau. Betty Standford, land called *Controversy* on Fowling Creek; if she should die, my dau. Sarah Stanford to have her part. Also mentioned son Charles Standford and grandchildren called John Lyden and Mary Lyden. Appointed friend Col. Joseph Ennalls as trustee. {MWB 24:354}

On 20 March 1746 the estate of Charles Stanford, DO Co., dec'd., was appraised at £410.4.9 and approved on 27 May 1746 by Rosanah Stanford and Thomas Stanford, execs. Next of kin were listed as William Stanford and Charles Stanford. {MINV 33:9}

On 15 Nov 1751 the estate of Thomas Standford, DO Co., dec'd., was admin. by Charles Standtord. Among those who received payment was Moses Poole who married the widow (N) of Charles Standford, joint extx. with dec'd. of said Charles, who was accountable for certain orphans estates. {MDAD 31:211}

Charles was the father of: JOHN (pre-deceased his father); THOMAS; CHARLES; LEVIN; ELIZABETH; SARAH; (N) DAU. (m. a Lyden).

4. WILLIAM STANFORD (STANDFORD), DO Co., b. c1695, son of John (1) Stanford, m. Rachel Harper.

On 12 Jan 1718/9 William Stanford and wife Rachel, DO Co., were admins. of the estate of Joseph Wall, dec'd. {MDAD 1:355}

In October Court 1728, DO Co., Susannah Sanders was fined 1000 lbs. of tobacco and court costs for fornication and begetting a bastard child (N). She swore that William Stanford was the begetter. He did not deny that he was guilty of adultery and was fined £3. {DOJR}

On 10 June 1734 William Stanford, DO Co., patented the 100 acre tract *Stanford's Range*. {MPL EI3:197}

Elizabeth, William, Samuel and Margaret Stanfoord *[sic]* were named as grandchildren in the will of Samuel Harper, DO Co., in 1735. They were bequeathed 1 sh. each. The bulk of his estate went to his wife Sarah and son William Harper. {MWB 21:668}

On 2 May 1738 William Stanford, DO Co., planter, acquired from David Rogers, DO Co., the 66 3/4 acre tract *East Town* on the east side of Blackwater River. {DOLR 9 Old 526}

On 12 Aug 1740 William Standford, DO Co., planter, conveyed to Isaac Partridge, DO Co., the 100 acre tract *Standford's Range* on the east side of Blackwater River. {DOLR 13 Old 19}

In a deposition taken on 24 Aug 1741 William Stanford, DO Co., stated he was about age 46; also mentioned his bro. John Stanford was present years ago when the bounds of Howell Powell's land were marked. {DOLR 12 Old 133}

On 25 Oct 1744 William Stanford, DO Co., planter, conveyed to John Eccleston, DO Co., the 66 acre tract *East Town* on Blackwater River. {DOLR 12 Old 47}

On 4 Sep 1745 William Stanford, DO Co., conveyed to Thomas Lane, release of a 140 acre part of *London* on Blackwater River, formerly sold by William Clayton, TA Co., dec'd., to John Stanford, DO Co., father of the present William Stanford, part of said land having been taken away by an older survey and said Thomas Lane having paid to Stanford the sum of £30 in satisfaction for the part of said land lying within the older survey. {DOLR 12 Old 202}

On 12 April 1746 the estate of William Stanford, DO Co., dec'd., was appraised at £75.0.8 and approved on 14 June 1746 by Samuel Stanford, exec. Next of kin were listed as Elizabeth Broudhust [Browdiss, Brodiss] and Margaret Stanford. {MINV 32:235}

William was prob. the father of: WILLIAM; SAMUEL; ELIZABETH; MARGARET; NATURAL CHILD (N).

5. SAMUEL STANFORD (STANDFORD), DO Co., son of John (1) Stanford, m. Elizabeth (N).

On 13 June 1750 Samuel Standford, DO Co., planter, and wife Elizabeth, conveyed to John Eccleston, DO Co., Gent., tracts *Benjamin's Mess* and *Standford's Addition* containing 38 acres. {DOLR 14 Old 418}

Samuel Stanford, DO Co., d. leaving a will dated 18 March 1758, proved 7 May 1758, naming wife Elizabeth (extx.), sons Thomas and Samuel, and grandson John Stanford (son of Thomas). Guardian: William Lane, if wife remarries. Exec.: William Lane, if wife dies. {MWB 30:611}

On 27 May 1758 the estate of Samuel Stanford, DO Co., dec'd., was appraised at £55.18.1 and approved on 21 Dec 1759 by Elizabeth Stanford, extx. {MINV 67:250}

On 21 Aug 1759 the estate of Samuel Standiford *[sic]*, DO Co., dec'd., was admin. by Elizabeth Standford (Standiford), extx. The named representatives were children Thomas and Samuel Standford (Standiford). {MDAD 44:115}

Samuel was the father of: THOMAS; SAMUEL.

6. THOMAS STANFORD (STANDFORD), DO Co., prob. son of John (1) Stanford, m. Rachel (N).

Rachel Stanford, DO Co., a legatee [relationship not stated] in the will of Patygrew Salsbury in 1719, was bequeathed a 68 acre part of the tract *Salisbury's Charge* during life. {MWB 16:32}

Thomas Stanford, DO Co., d. leaving an undated will, proved 10 April 1749. To wife Rachel (extx.), slaves. To son John, my dwelling plantation (N); if no issue, then to my unborn child; if both die without issue, then to wife Rachel. To son John, cattle. {MWB 27:55}

On 11 May 1749 the estate of Thomas Standford, DO Co., dec'd., was appraised at £108.13.6 and approved on 9 Aug 1749 by Charles Standford, admin. Next of kin were listed as Betty Stanford and Samuel Stanford. {MINV 40:289}

On 15 Nov 1751 the estate of Thomas Standford, DO Co., dec'd., was admin. by Charles Standford. Among those who received payment was Moses Poole who married the widow (N) of Charles Standford, joint extx. with dec'd. of said Charles, who was accountable for certain orphans estates. {MDAD 31:211}

On 14 Aug 1759 the estate of Thomas Standiford *[sic]*, DO Co., dec'd., was admin. by Charles Standiford. The only named representative was a child John Standiford. {MDAD 44:153}

Thomas was the father of: JOHN; (N) UNBORN CHILD.

## Third Generation

7. JOHN STANFORD (STANDFORD), DO Co., son of John (2) Stanford, d.s.p.

In August Court 1729, DO Co., John Stanford petitioned the court that he was of the age of 14 and his parents were dead. He chose Richard Pritchard as his guardian and it was approved. {DOJR}

John Standford, DO Co., d. leaving a will dated 11 Dec 1745, proved 20 Feb 1745, naming bro. Thomas Standford (exec.) and bro. Charles Standford (personalty). {MWB 24:356}

On 25 Feb 1745 the estate of John Stanford, DO Co., dec'd., was appraised at £30.13.0 and approved on 14 May 1746 by Thomas Stanford, exec. Next of kin were listed as Charles Stanford and Beatey Stanford. {MINV 33:4}

On 8 June 1747 the estate of John Stanford, DO Co., dec'd., was admin. by Thomas Stanford (Standford), exec.; no heirs were mentioned at that time. {MDAD 24:106}

8. WILLIAM STANFORD (STANDFORD), DO Co., son of John (2) Stanford, d.s.p.

On 3 Sep 1726 William and John Stanford witnessed the will of John Flowers, DO Co. {MWB 18:546}

In August Court 1729, DO Co., William Stanford was among those residents of Taylor's and James' Island who petitioned the court for a ferry. {DOJR}

In 1733 William Standford, DO Co., petitioned the court and stated he has a cousin of whom he has kept for 5 years, one William Standford, son of John Stanford, dec'd., and he held a tract of land (N) befallen him by the death of an elder brother (N). William (the petitioner) requested that the court grant him the liberty of looking after the said plantation in behalf of the said child, he being a minor; he was approved as guardian to said minor. {DOJR}

On 5 June 1734 the land called *Benjamin's Mess* belonging to William Standford, son of John Standford, DO Co., dec'd., was valuated for William Standford, his guardian. {DOLR 9 Old 185}

On 13 April 1738 the lands called *Benjamin's Mess* (33 acres), *Addition to Benjamin's Mess* (21 acres), and *London* (90 acres), belonging to William Standford, minor son of John Standford, DO Co., dec'd., were valuated for Abraham Braddis, his guardian. {DOLR 9 Old 534}

In June Court 1745, DO Co., William Standford, Jr., labourer, was assaulted on 10 Feb 1744/5 by Edward Nuner, of Dorchester Parish, labourer; Nuner was fined 5 sh. {DOJR}

William Stanford, Jr., DO Co., d. leaving a will dated -- Jan 1745/6, proved 21 Feb 1745/6, naming sis. Margaret Standford (my right to land called *London*), bro. Samuel Standford (exec.), and bro.-in-law Abraham Brodiss or Bradiss (money). {MWB 24:358}

On 12 April 1746 the estate of William Stanford, DO Co., dec'd., was appraised at £75.0.8 and approved on 14 June 1746 by Samuel Stanford, exec. Next of kin were listed as Elizabeth Broudhust [Browdiss, Broadus] and Margaret Stanford. {MINV 32:235}

9. CHARLES STANFORD (STANDFORD), JR., DO Co., b. c1715, son of Charles (3) Stanford, m. Elizabeth (N).

On 14 March 1739/40 Charles Stanford, Jr., DO Co., acquired from Henry Trippe, DO Co., Gent., a 170 acre part of the tract formerly called *Hoccady*, now called *Trippe's Closure*, on the east side of Blackwater River. {DOLR 11 Old 3}

On 12 Nov 1742 Charles Stanford, Jr., DO Co., planter, and wife Elizabeth, conveyed to John Eccleston, DO Co., Gent., part of a tract formerly called *Hoccady*, now called *The Resurvey*, on the east side of Blackwater River. {DOLR 10 Old 308}

In June Court 1745, DO Co., Charles Stanford was among the inhabitants of Transquakin who petitioned for a new road to be created from Kennerly's Mill down the Transquakin and over Hayward's Dam into Transquakin Road. {DOJR}

On 16 Nov 1748 Charles Stanford, DO Co., witnessed the will of Richard Loyden. {MWB 27:387}

In 1750 Charles Stanford and Mary Laton were listed as next of kin to Richard Loyden, DO Co., dec'd. {MINV 44:290}

On 16 Nov 1751 Charles Standford, DO Co., planter, and wife Elizabeth, conveyed to Joseph Ennalls, DO Co., merchant, 80 acres, including the former dwelling plantation (N) of said Standford, being part of *Hoccady* on Blackwater River. {DOLR 14 Old 599}

On 25 May 1752 Charles Stanford, DO Co., planter, leased from Joseph Ennalls, DO Co., merchant, 131 acres, being part of three tracts, *London, Batchelor's Loss*, and *Maiden Folly*, including the dwelling plantation (N) of said Stanford, for the term of 14 years. {DOLR 14 Old 596}

On 9 Nov 1757 Charles Standford, DO Co., acquired from Joshua and Betty Hobbs, Sarah Covington, and Joseph and Mary Fookes, DO Co., the 404 acre tract *End of Controversy* on Fowling Creek. {DOLR 15 Old 534}

On 15 Nov 1759 Charles Standford, DO Co., conveyed to John Anderson, DO Co., a 200 acre part of the tract *End of Controversy* on the east side of Fowling Creek. {DOLR 16 Old 269}

In 1761 Charles Standford and William Standford appeared among many others on a long list of debts due the estate of Col. Joseph Ennalls, DO Co., dec'd. {MINV 76:211}

In 1767 Elijah Standford, DO Co., was a surety when the estate of James Layton, dec'd., was admin. in 1767. {MDAD 57:89, 272}

In a deposition taken in 1770 Charles Standford of KE Co. on Delaware, late of DO Co., stated he was aged about 55 and mentioned his father Charles Standford and John Eccleston about 20-30 years ago. {DOLR 24 Old 308}

Charles Stanford may have been the father of the following Delaware patriots: Charles Stanford was a private in Capt. Thomas Holland's Co., enlisted 16 March 1777, and reported dead (no date). Joseph Stanford took the Oath of Allegiance and Fidelity in 1778. Robert Stanford was a private in Capt. Peter Jacquett's Co. in 1778. {RPD:253}

In a deposition taken in 1783 Charles Stanford, DO Co., stated he was about age 68 and mentioned his bros. John Stanford and Thomas Stanford. {DOLR 2 NH 263}

Charles was poss. the father of: ELIJAH; CHARLES; JOSEPH; ROBERT.

10. LEVIN STANFORD (STANDFORD), DO Co., son of Charles (3) Stanford.

On 24 June 1765 Levin Standford, DO Co., son of Charles Standford, late of said co., dec'd., acquired from Henry Trippe, son of Henry Trippe, late of said co., dec'd., the 105 acre tract *Trippe's Closure* on the east side of Blackwater River and on the south side of Hoccady Creek. {DOLR 20 Old 226}

On 14 Aug 1766 Levin Standford, DO Co., planter, and William Hayward, TA Co., conveyed to Thomas Firmin Eccleston, DO Co., a 105 acre part of *Trippe's Closure*, a 25 acre part of *Standford's Goodwill*, and a 5 acre part of *Standford's Addition*, devised to said Levin Standford in tail by his dec'd. father Charles Standford, of which a recovery was suffered in Provincial Court wherein said William Hayward was Demandant. Receipt for alienation fees listed the above tracts and also included the 34½ acre tract *No Name from Mathers*. {DOLR 21 Old 108}

11. THOMAS STANFORD (STANDFORD), DO Co., son of Charles (3) Stanford, m. (N).

On 24 June 1765 Henry Trippe, DO Co., conveyed to John Stanford, son of Thomas, DO Co. (in consideration of £155 paid to Henry Trippe, father of grantor, by Charles Stanford, grandfather of grantee), parts of *Trippe's Closure* devised by said Charles Stanford to his son Thomas Standford, father of said John, and containing 135 acres on the east side of Blackwater River between the plantations of John Standford and Levin Standford. {DOLR 20 Old 286}

On 5 Sep 1789 Thomas Stanford, DO Co., acquired livestock and furniture from George Turner, DO Co. {DOLR 2 HD 388}

On 11 Nov 1789 Thomas Stanford, DO Co., leased from Rachel Goldsborough, DO Co., land called *Fairfield* whereon said Thomas now lives as overseer for the said Rachel. {DOLR 2 HD 449}

Thomas was the father of: JOHN; prob. THOMAS.

12. ELIZABETH STANFORD (STANDFORD), DO Co., dau. of William (4) Stanford, m. Abraham Broadus (Brodiss).

Abraham Brodiss, DO Co., was named as bro.-in-law in the will of William Stanford in 1745/6. {MWB 24:358}

Elizabeth Broudust, DO Co., was named as next of kin when the estate of her bro. William Stanford was appraised in 1746. {MINV 32:235}

Abraham Broadus, DO Co., d. by 22 March 1756 at which time his estate was admin. by Elizabeth Broadus. Sureties were Pearson Hall and Samuel Stanford. The named representatives were minor sons William Broadus and John Broadus. {MDAD 40:102}

On 9 Jan 1758 the estates of Abraham Broadus and Elizabeth Broadus, DO Co., both dec'd., were admin. by Samuel Standford, admin. of Elizabeth Broadus, admx. of the dec'd. The named representatives were minor children John Broadus and William Broadus. Among those who received payment were Susannah Kelley in right of her dau. Ann Broadus (her portion of estate of her father Edward Broadus in hands of dec'd. who was her uncle and guardian) and balance of estate of Abraham Broadus which accountant retains as next friend to heirs (N) of dec'd. {MDAD 42:11-14}

On 9 June 1759 the estate of Elizabeth Broadus (Broudus), DO Co., dec'd., was admin. by Elizabeth Standford, extx. of Samuel Standford, admin. of dec'd. {MDAD 44:149}

On 4 Sep 1779 William Broadhurst and Thomas Stanford, both of DO Co., planters, conveyed to Thomas Firmin Eccleston, DO Co., Gent., the tracts *Benjamin's Mess or Mass, Stanford's Addition, London*, and *Stanford's Perventure or Stanford's Adventure*. {DOLR 1 JCH 257}

Elizabeth (Stanford) Broadus was the mother of: JOHN BROADUS; WILLIAM BROADUS.

13. WILLIAM STANFORD (STANDFORD), JR., DO Co., prob. son of William (4) Stanford, m. Elizabeth (N).

In June Court 1745, DO Co., William Stanford stated he had a negro boy (N) incapable of labour; the court discharged him from payment of tax or levy for the future. {DOJR}

William Stanford, DO Co., d. leaving a will dated 20 Jan 1748, proved 10 April 1749. To wife Elizabeth (extx.), negro man Conkey and woman Jemandy. To son William, Jr., my clothing. To son Richard, tract called *Dick's Land* in the Northwest Fork of Blackwater River. {MWB 26:19}

On 24 April 1749 the estate of William Stanford, DO Co., dec'd., was appraised at £136.5.3 and approved on 10 Aug 1749 by Elizabeth Standford, extx. Next of kin were listed as William Stanford and Samuel Stanford. {MINV 40:294}

In 1751 Elizabeth Stanford and Rhoda Stanford, DO Co., witnessed the will of Ezekiel Keene. {MWB 28:454}

On 11 July 1757 the estate of William Standford, DO Co., dec'd., was admin. by Elizabeth Standford, extx. The named representatives were children William, Rhode, and Richard Standford. {MDAD 41:175}

On 9 Jan 1758 the estate of William Standford, DO Co., dec'd., was admin. by Elizabeth Standford, extx. The named legatees were the accountant (she received negroes Jenny, Sam, and Conkey) and William Standiford, Jr. {MDAD 42:15}

Elizabeth Stanford, DO Co., d. leaving a will dated 6 May 1759, proved 30 June 1759, naming son Richard (exec.), 4 slaves; if he dies without issue, same to 4 daus. Sarah Staplefort, Chebed Prichett, Rebeccah Wallis, and Rhody Waters. Thomas Wallis, exec. {MWB 31:1110}

On 30 Oct 1759 the estate of Elizabeth Stanfort (Stanford), DO Co., dec'd., was appraised at £243.3.9 and approved by Thomas Wallace and Richard Standfort (Standford), execs. Next of kin were listed as Joshua Wall and Pearson Wall. {MINV 69:74}

On 1 Feb 1760 the estate of Elizabeth Stanfort *[sic]*, DO Co., dec'd., appraised at £0.10.10, was approved on 7 July 1760 by Thomas Wallace and Richard Standford, execs. Next of kin were listed as Joshua Wall and Reason Wall. {MINV 69:168}

On 1 July 1760 the estate of Elizabeth Standford, DO Co., dec'd., was admin. by Thomas Wallace and Richard Standford, execs. The named representatives were children Sarah Staplefort, Josebed Pritchett, Rebecca Wallace, Rhody Watters, and Richard Standford. Among those who received payment were William Pritchet and Thomas Staplefort for balance of the rents of the orphans (N) of William Merchant, dec'd., and Thomas Wallace (accountant) who married the dau. (N) and co-heir of said William Merchant. {MDAD 44:307}

William was the father of: WILLIAM, JR.; RICHARD; SARAH; JOSEBED (CHEBED); REBECCAH, m. Thomas Wallace; RHODY, m. (N) Waters.

14. THOMAS STANFORD, DO Co., son of Samuel (5) Stanford, m. (N).

Thomas Stanford, DO Co., was named as a son of Samuel Stanford in his will written in April, 1758, which also named his grandson John Stanford (son of said Thomas). {MWB 30:611}

Thomas Stanford, DO Co., d. by 20 Aug 1758 at which time the land of John Standford, son and heir of Thomas Standford, late of DO Co., dec'd., was valuated for Isaac Partridge, his guardian. {DOLR 16 Old 119}

Thomas was the father of: JOHN.

Fourth Generation

15. ELIJAH STANFORD, DO Co., poss. son of Charles (9) Stanford.

Elijah Standford, DO Co., was a surety when the estate of James Layton, dec'd., was admin. in 1767. {MDAD 57:89, 272}

16. THOMAS STANFORD, DO Co., poss. son of Thomas (11) Stanford.

On 5 Sep 1789 Thomas Stanford, DO Co., acquired livestock and furniture from George Turner, DO Co. {DOLR 2 HD 388}

On 11 Nov 1789 Thomas Stanford, DO Co., leased from Rachel Goldsborough, DO Co., land called *Fairfield* whereon said Thomas now lives as overseer for the said Rachel. {DOLR 2 HD 449}

On 12 Jan 1795 Thomas Stanford, DO Co., witnessed a conveyance of goods and chattels. {DOLR 8 HD 150}

17. WILLIAM STANFORD, DO Co., prob. son of William (13) Stanford, m. Milcah or Milly (N).

On 9 Aug 1751 William Stanford, DO Co., planter, and wife Milcah, conveyed to Peter Grimes, DO Co., planter, the eastern 50 acre part of the tract *Small Profit*. {DOLR 14 Old 541}

On 21 May 1757 William and Milly Stanford witnessed the will of John Ozwell, DO Co., proved on 20 Feb 1775, now CA Co. {MWB 40:224}

On 10 Aug 1771 William Stanford, son of William and Milca his wife, of KE Co. on Delaware, along with Dr. Henry Murray, John King, Jr., William Smith Jr. and his wife Mary, all of DO Co., conveyed to Robert Goldsborough, DO Co., the 332 acre tract *Skinner's Chance*, apparently the result of a Provincial Court case. {DOLR 25 Old 106, 219}

William was the father of: WILLIAM.

18. RICHARD STANFORD, DO Co., son of William (13) Stanford, poss. m. Hester Ann Russum circa August, 1775, CA Co. {MD Marriages}

On 25 March 1761 Richard Standford, DO Co., planter, acquired from Henry Fisher, DO Co., planter, the 30 acre tract *Adventure* and the 50 acre tract *Addition to Adventure* on the northwest branch of Blackwater River. {DOLR 17 Old 441}

On 16 March 1764 Richard Stanford, DO Co., planter, conveyed the afsd. two tracts to Richard William, DO Co., planter. {DOLR 19 Old 163}

On 26 May 1774 the valuation of land of Mary Nevett, a minor, mentioned, among others, land on Hunting Creek rented to Richard Stanford. {DOLR 27 Old 425}

On 21 Oct 1777 the land of Wittington Wallace, a minor and orphan of Thomas Wallace, DO Co., dec'd., under the care of Richard Stanford, his guardian, was valuated. {DOLR 1 JCH 54}

On 12 May 1784 Richard Stanford, DO Co., acquired from Henry Edgell, DO Co., livestock and a negro girl called Pegg. {DOLR 2 NH 329}

On 23 July 1785 Richard Stanford, William Stanford, and Richard Stanford, Jr., DO Co., witnessed a land conveyance on Nanticoke River. {DOLR 5 NH 158}

On 23 Jan 1791 Richard Stanford, Celia Stanford, and Elizabeth Stanford, DO Co., gave a receipt for money paid them by Medford Andrews in consideration of our full claim against a legacy left him by William Medford, late of DO Co., dec'd., amounting to £106.6.0 current money of Maryland in virtue of a judgment obtained by us against William Medford, exec. of said William Medford, dec'd. {DOLR 3 HD 42}

On 7 Feb 1791 the letter of John Muir was recorded in the DO Co. land records concerning Celia and Elizabeth Stanford, daus. of Capt. Richard Stanford. {DOLR 3 HD 158}

On 3 March 1792 Samuel Stanford, DO Co., witnessed a sale of negro slaves (N). {DOLR 3 HD 439}

Richard was the father of: RICHARD, JR.; CELIA; ELIZABETH; prob. WILLIAM; poss. SAMUEL.

19. REBECCAH STANFORD, dau. of William (13) Stanford, m. Thomas Wallace.

William, son of Thomas and Rebeccah Wallice, b. 2 June 1752. {DODO}

Rispah, dau. of Thomas and Rebeccah Wallice, b. 30 Oct 1756. {DODO}

Whittington, son of Thomas and Rebeccah Wallice, b. 16 Dec 1758. {DODO}

Thomas Wallace, DO Co., d. leaving a will dated 25 Nov 1761, proved 16 Feb 1762. To bro. Matthew Wallace, ½ of tract called *Wallace's First Venture* on e. side of the northwest fork of Blackwater River. To sons William and Whittington Wallace, other ½ called *Wallace's First Venture*. To wife, Rebecca, extx., certain estate; at her decease to fall to son Whittington Wallace. Personalty to be divided amongst children: William, Whittington, Rizpah, Brittanay Wallace. Witnessed by Wm. Pritchett, Mathew Bibey, Sarah Wall. {MWB 31:559}

Thomas was father of WILLIAM WALLACE, b. 2 June 1752; RIZPAH WALLACE, b. 30 Oct 1756; WHITTINGTON WALLACE, b. 16 Dec 1758; BRITTANAY WALLACE.

20. JOHN STANFORD, DO Co., son of Thomas (14) Stanford.

John Stanford, DO Co., was named as grandson in the will of Samuel Sanford written in April, 1758, which also named John's father Thomas (son of said Samuel). {MWB 30:611}

On 20 Aug 1758 the land of John Standford, son and heir of Thomas Standford, late of DO Co., dec'd., was valuated for Isaac Partridge, his guardian. {DOLR 16 Old 119}

John Stanford, DO Co., was an ensign in the militia, 3rd Bttn., on 20 May 1778. {RPDO:222}

On 6 March 1780 John Stanford, DO Co., planter, acquired from John Anderton, DO Co., merchant, a 21 acre tract called *Addition to Moore's Meadows* on the east side of the Northwest Fork of Nanticoke River. On 17 April 1780 John Stanford conveyed that tract to Jesse Williams, CA Co. {DOLR 1 JCH 424-426}

Fifth Generation

21. WILLIAM WALLACE, b. 2 June 1752; son of Rebeccah (19) and Thomas Wallace.

William subscribed to the Oath of Allegiance and Fidelity on 3 March 1778. {RPDO:255}

22. WHITTINGTON WALLACE, b. 16 Dec 1758, son of Rebeccah (19) and Thomas Wallace.

Whittington Wallace served as private in Capt. Thomas Bourk's Company, Battn. of MD Troopes in the Flying Camp, commanded by Col. William Richardson, 26 July 1776 - 10 Nov 1776 or later. {RPDO:255}

Unplaced

ALGERNON STANFORD, DO Co., was a private in Capt. Joseph Ennalls' Co., 10th Cavalry Dist., DO Co., in April, 1813. {MD Militia, War of 1812, I:79}

CLEMENT STANDFORD, DO Co., served as Adjutant, 11th Regt., DO Co. Militia, and resigned on 7 April 1810. He was commissioned again as Adjutant in April, 1813 under Lt.Col. Thomas Pitt. {MD Militia, War of 1812, I:iii, 64}

ELIZABETH STANFORD, DO Co., m. Abner Tappan on 30 Jan 1792. {MD Marriages}

JOHN STANFORD, DO Co., m. Leah Breerwood on 24 Dec 1799. {MD Marriages}

JOHN STANFIELD, DO Co., m. Nancy Barnes on 12 Dec 1811. {SOSP}

JOHN STANDFIELD, DO Co., was a private in Capt. John Brohawn's Volunteer Co., 48th Regt., DO Co. Militia, 26-29 Aug 1814. {MD Militia, War of 1812, I:71}

JONATHAN STANFORD m. Grace Phillips on 28 June 1767. {SOSP}

SAMUEL STANFORD, DO Co., was a private in Capt. Thomas Bourk's Co. of MD Troops in the Flying Camp in 1776. {RPDO:222}

SARAH STANFORD, WI Co., m. Thomas Vinson on 18 Jan 1724. {MD Marriages}

SARAH STANFORD, DO Co., Great Choptank Parish, was presented in November Court, 1743, for having committed fornication on 10 June 1742 and begat a bastard child (N); court ordered 10 lashes. {DOJR}

SARAH STANDFORD witnessed the will of Mary Gilbert on Kent Island, QA Co., in 1754. {MWB 29:46}

SARAH STANFORD, WI Co., m. John Christopher on 26 Feb 1759. {MD Marriages}

SARAH STANFORD, DO Co., m. Gabriel Bramble on 1 July 1788. {MD Marriages}

SUMMERWELL STANFORD, DO Co., was listed as next of kin to Thomas Norman, dec'd., in 1749. {MINV 42:88}

WILLIAM STANFORD, WI Co., m. Mary Cooper of Northampton Co., VA, on 1 June 1759. {MD Marriages}

## THE HENRY STEELE FAMILY

1. HENRY STEELE, of Whitehaven, Cumberland Co., England, poss. b. 22 July 1715 [although this date does not match his age in the 1776 DO Co. census], son of Isaac Steele and Elizabeth Beeby, came into this province in 1740. On 28 Oct 1756, while living in SO Co., he executed a pre-nuptial marriage agreement with Ann Billings, dau. of Major John Billings and Ann

Rider, of Oxford, TA Co. Henry Steele subsequently resided near Vienna in DO Co. {Barnes *British Roots* I:407; BDML II:769}

On 28 Oct 1756 Henry Steele, late of the Town of Whitehaven in the Kingdom of England, merchant, now living in SO Co., MD, and Ann Billings of DO Co., spinster, and John Henry of DO Co., Gent., entered into an agreement in consideration of her approaching marriage to Henry Steele in which Ann Billings conveyed all of her personal estate to John Henry in trust for herself and the said Henry Steele (details provided therein). {DOLR 15 Old 403}

On 11 June 1761 Robert Darnal and wife Sarah, Henry Steele and wife Ann, all of DO Co., conveyed to John Henry, DO Co., two-thirds of the tract *Cow Quarter* devised by Charles Rider to be divided between his three sisters Sarah (wife of Robert Darnal), Dorothy (wife of said John Henry), and Ann Loockerman, dec'd., whose dau. Ann is now the wife of the said Henry Steele. {DOLR 17 Old 357}

*Commentary: For the sake of clarification, Ann Loockerman's maiden name was Rider and she was the widow of James Billings. Ann had married 2nd to Govert Loockerman and he was Ann Billings Steele's stepfather. Charles Rider afsd. was Ann Steele's uncle.*

Henry Steele, DO Co., was an extensive land owner and merchant in partnership with John Henry in Vienna, MD. He served in the Lower House of the MD Assembly, 1762-1763, 1768-1770, 1773-1774, and 1777. He was a County Court Justice, 1757-1777, and Orphans Court Justice in 1777. His marriage to Ann Billings made him a wealthy man and he and his wife jointly owned 8,697 acres of land, 2 lots in Vienna, and 91 slaves by the time of his death on 5 Feb 1782. Initially buried at *Weston* near Vienna, DO Co., his remains were later removed to Christ Church Cemetery in Cambridge, MD by his gr-gr-grandson Dr. Guy Steele. {BDML II:769-770; Jones:459}

The power and influence of Henry Steele was evident by this singular occurrence: "Gov. Sharpe's desire that Mr. Goldsborough's place in the Lower House should be taken by his eldest son Robert Goldsborough was not immediately fulfilled. A writ of election was issued, Oct. 25, 1763, to the Sheriff of Dorchester County 'to elect a delegate for the said county in the room of Charles Goldsborough Esquire called to the Upper House' but the result was the return of Mr. Henry Steele, who qualified as member for Dorchester on the 15th of November following. At the next election, however, Robert Goldsborough was elected in Mr. Steele's place." {*MD Genealogies* II:11}

Henry Steele, DO Co., Gent., and wife Ann, were extensive land owners, having patented the following tracts: 127 acre *Green Briar Swamp*, 29 April 1761; 50 acre *David's Good Fortune*, 22 July 1761; 72 acre *Midland*, 25 Aug 1763; 60 acre *Fullain Meadow*, 2 Feb 1764; 35 acre *Revive*, 13 March

1765; 33 acre *Pasture Branch*, 13 June 1765; 150 acre part of *Last Vacancy*, 13 June 1765; 202 acre *Interval*, 22 July 1765; 33 acre *Friend's Assistance*, 16 Aug 1765; 333 acre *Low Park*, 11 Sep 1766; 140 acre part of *Last Vacancy*, 28 Oct 1765; 349 acre *Southam*, 19 July 1767; 207 acre *Addition to Green Briar*, 27 Aug 1767; 50 acre *North Field*, 12 May 1768; 74 acre *West Marsh*, 1 Aug 1768; 134 acre *Bridge Marsh*, 2 Aug 1768; 484 acre *Handsell*, 11 May 1769; 75 acre *Poplar Neck*, 50 acre *Mill Landing*, 112 acre *Addition*, 300 acre *Addition to Fulham*, 1,060 acre *Ormskirk*, 200 acre *Balea*, 70 acre *Green's Priviledge*, 100 acre *Green's Adventure*, 350 acre *Cuba*, 100 acre part of *Widow's Purchase*, 100 acre *Cow Quarter*, 300 acre *Holly Swamp*, 104 acre *Addition to Holly Swamp*, 46 acre *Security*, 198 acre *Pasture Neck*, 725 acre *Rider's Forrest*, 450 acres part of *Reserve* and *Handsell*, by 26 March 1770; 33 acre *Hurley's Desire*, 18 June 1772; 48 acre *Green Field*, 17 Sep 1772; 200 acre part of *Partnership*, 12 Jan 1773; 35 acre *Hay Field*, 13 Sep 1773; another 141 acre part of *Last Vacancy*, 6 Jan 1774; 1,801 acre *Marsh Island Range*, 19 May 1775. {MPL BC14:481, 24:700, 27:19, 29:211, 30:430, 32:411, 32:424, 32:551, 35:90, 44:239, 44:240, 48:417; DOLR 17 Old 404, 20 Old 21, 111, 228, 415, 23 Old 247, 24 Old 85-105, 25 Old 451, 26 Old 237, 27 Old 166}

Jeremiah Atkinson, SO Co., d. leaving a will dated 12 June 1769, proved 14 Feb 1776, naming his widowed mother Isabella Atkinson of Great Clifton near Workington in Cumberland Co., Great Britain and his bro. John Atkinson of the Town of Whitehaven, Great Britain. Henry Steele, DO Co., was named as his exec. [and he had formerly lived in Whitehaven as noted above]. Witnesses were John Henry and William Wheland. {MWB 41:66}

William Wheland, DO Co., d. leaving a will dated 13 Aug 1771, proved 11 Nov 1773, and bequeathed to Mr. Henry Steele, Col. John Henry and Major Ephraim King the following tracts: 224 acre *Middleton in the Oakes*, 200 acre *Cool Spring*, 51 acre *Addition to Cool Spring*, 10 acre *Middleton's Range*, and 836 acre *Hard Putt* - to be sold to the credit of his estate. Henry Steele subsequently renounced his executorship of the will. {MWB 39:691}

In 1776 Henry Steele, DO Co., was head of household in Nanticoke Hundred, aged between 40 and 50, with 2 white males under age 10, 1 white male aged between 10 and 16, 1 white male aged between 16 and 21, and 1 white female aged between 40 and 50, plus 91 negroes. {1776 Census}

Henry Steele, DO Co., was appointed a Collector of Gold and Silver Coin in 1776 and subscribed to the Oath of Allegiance in 1778. Ann Steele rendered material aid by supplying wheat for the use of the military on 3 Sep 1782. {RPDO:224}

Ann Steele, widow of Henry, d. 29 April 1788. The tax records for 1783 show that she was the second largest land owner in the county with 23 tracts totalling 8,344 acres, plus 86 slaves, 345 ounces of plate, 35 horses, and 174 black cattle. {Mowbray I:151}

Henry was the father of: JAMES (18 March 1760 - 21 Sep 1816); PETER (16 Aug 1762 - 1 Jan 1791); JOHN (4 Sep 1765 -12 Sep 1765); CHARLES (14 March 1767 - 28 Aug 1776); ISAAC (9 Nov 1769 - 7 Nov 1896); HENRY (b. 14 March 1772); CATHERINE (28 Feb 1758 - 5 Dec 1768); ANN (11 April 1775 - 9 Oct 1777). {Mowbray I:151}

Second Generation

2. JAMES STEELE, b. 18 March 1760, son of Henry (1) Steele, m. Mary Nevett, dau. of John Rider Nevett and Sarah Maynadier, in 1789, and d. 21 Sep 1816 at Boonsboro, WA Co., MD, on his return from the springs where he had received treatment for a painful affliction; bur. in St. Anne's Cemetery, Annapolis. {BDML II:770; Mowbray I:151}

On 11 June 1761 Henry Steele, DO Co., Gent., and wife Ann, conveyed to John Henry and Robert Darnal, DO Co., Gent., in trust for the benefit of James Steele, son of the said Henry and Ann, the following tracts: 1,744 acre *Town Neck Composition*, 68 acre *Ryder's Regulation of Broken Hayes and Dyas Chance*, and 199 acre *Marsh Island* (all of which three tracts were devised to Ann Billings, now dec'd., mother of the said Ann Steele, by the said deceased's bro. Charles Rider); 154 acre *Scotch Folly* (conveyed to James Billings, father of said Ann, wife of Henry Steele, by William Houseley); and, a 62 acre part of *Weston* on the north side of Nanticoke River (devised to James Billings by the said Charles Rider). {DOLR 17 Old 367-370}

On 27 May 1784 James Steele, DO Co., Gent., acquired from Thomas Charlescraft, DO Co., planter, the 54 acre tract *Thomas's Lane* in the east side of Chickamacomico River. {DOLR 2 NH 316}

On 27 April 1792 James Steele, DO Co., was conveyed slaves, livestock, and a crop of wheat on his farm on Chicamacomico River by Randolph Johnson, occupant of said farm. {DOLR 3 HD 575}

On 2 Feb 1795 James Steele, DO Co., and wife Mary, acquired from John Maguire, DO Co., the 34 acre tract *Exchange* adj. *Daniel's Hellicon*, and on that same day James and Mary Steel conveyed a 48 acre part of *Daniel's Hellicon* to John Maguire. {DOLR 8 HD 169, 201}

James Steel, DO Co., served in the Lower House of the MD Assembly between 1784 and 1795, was a county court justice, 1784-1788, 1798-c1800, and trustee of the poor, 1785, among other civic offices. He was an extensive land owner in DO Co. and SO Co., and owned lots in Cambridge, Vienna, and Annapolis. {BDML II:770}

The children of James and Mary Steele were as follows: Mary Nevett Steele (b. 15 or 16 Oct 1789, bapt. 30 Nov 1794, m. John Campbell Henry on 21 or 22 April 1808, d. 1873); Ann Billings Steele (b. 24 Oct 1791, m. Arthur Upshur of VA's Eastern Shore in Dec 1810); Sarah Maynadier Steele (b. 8 Jan

1793, d. 21 June 1793); James Billings Steele (b. 14 Oct 1794, m. 1st to Milcah Gale in SO Co. on 15 April 1817 and she d. 28 Aug 1836; he m. 2nd to Sarah Yeabury Goldsborough; he d. 1861, she d. 1888); John Rider Nevett Steele (b. 22 Feb 1796, m. Ann Ogle in 1819, d. 1853); Henry Maynadier Steele (b. 5 Oct 1798, m. Mary Lloyd Key); Catherine Sarah Maria Steele (b. 2 Aug 1801); Isabella Elizabeth Steele (b. 30 Dec 1803); Sarah Maynadier Steele (b. 5 Nov 1805); Isaac Nevitt Steele (b. 25 April 1809, Baltimore lawyer); Charles Hutchins Steele (b. 22 Dec 1812, AA Co. physician). {ESVR; BDML II:770; Mowbray I:152}

In March, 1825, the DO Co. Equity Court case of Henry M. Steele vs. Isaac W. Steele stated that "the claimant asserts that he (Henry M. Steele) is the brother and friend of Isaac Nevitt Steele, minor, of AA Co.; that Isaac Nevitt Steele was seized and possessed of a lot in Cambridge, DO Co., being part of *Nevitt's Double Purchase* devised to him by his father James Steele, dec'd., by his last will and testament. That it would be in the interest of said Isaac Nevitt Steele that the lot be sold." {MGSB 33:3 (1992), pp. 550-551}

James was the father of: JAMES BILLINGS; JOHN NEVETT; HENRY MAYNADIER; ISAAC NEVITT; CHARLES HUTCHINS; MARY NEVETT; ANN BILLINGS; SARAH MAYNADIER [#1]; CATHERINE SARAH MARIA; ISABELLA ELIZABETH; SARAH MAYNADIER [#2].

3. PETER STEELE, b. 16 Aug 1762, son of Henry (1) Steele, d. 1 Jan 1791. {Mowbray I:151}

On 7 Oct 1785 Peter Steele, DO Co., as trustee for Sarah Nevett Muir, DO Co., received from Robert Darnall, Esq., PG Co., and wife Sarah, the 186 acre tract *Cow Lane* for the use of the said Robert Darnall and wife Sarah for the lifetime of the said Sarah Darnall with remainder to the use of the said Sarah Nevett Muir. {DOLR 5 NH 275}

4. ISAAC STEELE, b. 9 Nov 1769, son of Henry (1) Steele, d. 7 Nov 1806. {Mowbray I:151}

On 21 Nov 1789 Isaac Steele, DO Co., witnessed the manumission of negro slave Joshua by Archibald Pattison. {DOLR 2 HD 460}

On 22 March 1792 Isaac Steele, DO Co., Gent., acquired from James Steele, Esq., DO Co., a 484 acre part of the tract *Handsell* on the west side of Nanticoke River at Taylor's Creek. {DOLR 4 HD 9}

On 7 July 1795 Isaac Steele, DO Co., witnessed the manumission of negro Jack Hollis by Henry Steele, Esq. {DOLR 8 HD 424}

5. HENRY STEELE, b. 14 March 1772, son of Henry (1) Steele.

On 9 Dec 1793 Henry Steele, DO Co., Gent., received from Isaac Steele, DO Co., Gent., a 363 acre part of the tract *Partnership* at the head of Transquakin River. {DOLR 6 HD 245}

On 17 Dec 1794 Henry Steele, DO Co., conveyed a negro girl named Cloe, aged about 14 years, to Samuel Rust. {DOLR 8 HD 167}

On 7 July 1795 Henry Steele, Esq., DO Co., manumitted negro Jack Hollis. {DOLR 8 HD 424}

## THE WILLIAM STEELE FAMILY

1. WILLIAM STEELE (STEEL), DO Co. and WO Co., prob. m. Elizabeth (Betty) Williams.

In 1750 William Steel witnessed the will of William White, WO Co. {MWB 28:47}

In 1761 William Steel was named as an executor in the will of James Dodd, DO Co. {MWB 31:562}

On 26 Oct 1761 William Steel, DO Co., acquired from Robert Wilson, DO Co., the 440 acre tract *Ragged Point* on the north side of Little Choptank River between Brookes Creek and Little Choptank Bay. {DOLR 18 Old 109}

In 1762 Elizabeth Steele was named as a dau. in the will of Elizabeth Williams, WO Co. {MWB 32:245}

In 1770 Betty Steele and her younger child (N) were bequeathed the entire estate of Robert Cleaverly, DO Co., in his nuncupative will. {MWB 38:144}

William Steele, DO Co., d. by March, 1794. The deposition of Thomas Willis taken at that time regarding the tract *Ragged Point* indicated William Steele was in possession of said tract during his lifetime. {DOLR 8 HD 52}

William was the father of: WILLIAM; MARY.

### Second Generation

2. WILLIAM STEELE, son of William (1) Steele.

On 13 July 1798 William Steele, of Bertie Co., NC, conveyed to Samuel and Mary Phillips, DO Co., 130 acre part of the tract *Ragged Point*, formerly the property of William Steele, dec'd., father of the said William Steele and Mary Phillips. On that same day William Steele and Mary Phillips conveyed another part of that same tract to Edward Hardy of Currituck Co., NC. {DOLR 14 HD 89-94}

3. MARY STEELE, dau. of William (1) Steele, m. Samuel Phillips.

<u>Unplaced</u>

JOHN STEELE, DO Co., was recommended as second lieutenant on 31 Aug 1781 and rendered material aid by supplying beef for the use of the military on 1 Nov 1782. {RPDO:225}

ROSANNA STEELE, DO Co., m. Wallace Crawford by lic. dated 15 Sep 1787. Wallace Crawford was a private in the militia on 23 Aug 1781 and Wallis Crofford took the Oath of Allegiance in 1778. {RPDO:46}

## THE SWIGGETT FAMILY

1.. HENRY SWIGGETT m. Mary (N) who later m. Henry Dillan.

Henry Swigett is listed as a payee on the admin. account of the estate of John Hodson of DO Co., submitted on 2 Sep 1679 by his son John Hodson. {INAC 6:358}

At November Court 1690 Henry Swigget received a bounty for wolves heads. {DOJR}

Henry Swiggott, DO Co., d. by 15 May 1733 when the inventory of his estate was filed by Mary Swiggett alias Mary Odillin. Signed as next of kin: William Lester, Henry Parish. {MINV 17:139}

On 10 Dec 1733 the admin. account of his estate was submitted by Mary Dillan, wife of Henry Dillan. Representatives: 5 children (under age): Mercy, Mary, Thomas, Hannah, James. {MDAD 12:145}

At June Court 1745, DO Co., Thomas Swigget chose George Williams as his guardian. {DOJR}

Henry was father of MERCY; MARY; THOMAS, b. c1728; HANNAH; JAMES.

### Second Generation

2. JAMES SWIGGETT, son of Henry (1) Swiggett, m. 3 July 1755, Elizabeth Priest at St. Johns Church {then QA Co., now Caroline Co.]. {St. John's Parish Register}

On 31 July 1766 Edgar Rumbley of DO Co., planter, conveyed to James Swigot of the same co., planter, part of *Edgars Inlett* adj. *Bickams Lott* on Watses Branch, 36 a. {DOLR 21 Old 75}

James Swiggett, yeoman, Sussex Co., DE, d. leaving a will dated 22 July 1780, proved 28 Aug 1780. Heirs: wife Elizabeth Swiggett; son Henry Swiggett; daus. Mary Swiggett and Elizabeth Smith. Exec., son Henry Swiggett.

Witnessed by, Benjamin Whittington, Rhoda Whittington, Preston Godwin. {Arch. A101:92. Reg. of Wills (Sussex Co., DE), C:344}

James was father of HENRY; MARY; ELIZABETH, m. (N) Smith.

3. THOMAS SWIGGETT, b. c1728, son of Henry (1) Swiggett.

Thomas Swiggett, age 57 years in 1785, DO Co., made a deposition before a land commission of Caroline Co. in 1785 regarding the bounds of *Chestnut Ridge*. {Heirs and Legatgees of Caroline Co., MD}

Third Generation

4. HENRY SWIGGETT, b. c1720, son of James (2) Swiggett, m. 1st Nancy (N), m. 2nd Sarah (N).

On 15 Sep 1753 Joshuah Beall of Prince George's Co., conveyed to Henry Swiggate of DO Co., planter, part of a tract called *Danby*, 102 a. {DOLR 15 Old 2}

On 4 Nov 1755 John Andrew, planter, conveyed to Henry Swiget of DO Co., planter, *Good Luck*, 33 ½ a. {DOLR 15 Old 325}

On 4 Nov 1755 Solomon Andrew, planter, conveyed to Henry Swiggett of DO Co., planter, part of *Shekels Lott* adj. *Rooses Venture* on s. side of *Good Luck*, 25 ½ a. {DOLR 15 Old 327}

Henry Swiget patented 18 a. in DO Co. called *Hollis's Hunting Field* on 27 Nov 1769. {MPW bc38:226; bc40:5}

On 10 Nov 1772 Samuel Maxwell of London, coal factor, conveyed to Henry Swiggate of DO Co., part of *Danby* on a branch of Watses Creek, 260 a. {DOLR 26 Old 258}

On 8 April 1783 Henry Swiggate conveyed to his son Harmon Swiggate for 5 shillings, 155 a., all of *Chances's Venture* for his lifetime with reversions to Esther, Mary, Sarah and Rhoda Swiggate, daus. of Henry Swiggate. {CALR GFA:637}

On 15 Jan 1784 Henry Swiggett of Sussex Co., DE, Gent., and his wife Nancy, conveyed to Levy Eaton of Caroline Co., farmer, 32 ½ a., part of *Pritchard's Adventure*, 33 1/4 a., part of *Adams Fortune* and 8 1/4 a., part of *Lloyd's Care*, adj. DE state line and the road leading from Hunting Creek Church to Marshyhope Bridge. {CALR CFA:692}

On 22 March 1788 Henry Swiggett, son of James, of Sussex Co., DE, conveyed to Levi Eaton of Caroline Co., 21 ½ a., part of *Adams' Fortune* and *Pritchett's Adventure* on w. side of the state line. {CALR B:378}

Henry Swiggett, age 55 years, Nicholite, in 1785 made a deposition before a land commission of Caroline Co. regarding the bounds of *Chestnut Ridge*, mentioning Peter Ross, dec'd., Thomas Swiggett, John Stevens and Thomas Barrow. {Heirs and Legatees of Caroline Co.}

Henry Swiggett, Caroline Co., d. leaving a will dated 23rd of 9th mo., 1798, proved 27 Nov 1798. To wife Sarah, the use of testator's dwelling plantation whereon he now lives with the liberty of firewood and timber to repair the farm buildings for her natural life and with the liberty to sow each year 1 bushel of flax seed. To have dower share of personal estate and a mare called Blaze and 1 of the best feather beds and furniture. Sons William and Johnson Swiggett to have all the lands on e. side of the road leading to the forest ... road leading from ... to Potter's Landing and through Levin Smith's plantation, to be divided equally and to have the rest of testator's new warranted land. To son Harmon Swiggett, land called *C... Venture*. To sons Henry Swiggett and Levin Swiggett, part of a tract called *Danby*, 260 a.. To son Daniel part of a tract called *Adams Rest* and part of a tract called *Hollises Hunting Fields*; and lands w. of the road that leads from Three Bridges of Watson's Creek down to Collins's Cross Roads. To son James Swiggett the dwelling plantation after widow's death and all the lands that testator has lying between the afsd. road leading down from the Three Bridges to Collins's Cross Roads and the land formerly of Jonathan Wilson. To dau. Sarah Coldscott, ½ of lands purchased from Stephen Olston(?) In Kent Co., DE. Ralph Colescott to have the other ½ of land in Kent Co.,DE, for his natural life. Eli Colescott, son of Ralph, to have the lands left to Ralph at Ralph's death and to have that part of the land that he lives on. To granddau. Rhoda Swiggett, dau. of testator's dau. Rhoda, equal share of the personal estate which is to be divided among testator's sons James, Daniel, Henry and Levin and testator's dau. Rhoda Swiggett. To settle any dispute: James Anderson, Willis Charles, Edward Barton, Peter Harris. Witnessed by James Harris, William Jones, Hannah Jones. {CA Wills JRB:425}

Levin, son of Henry and Sarah Swiggett was b. 11th day, 8th mo.,1777; Rhoda, dau. of Henry and Sarah was b. 14th day, 8th mo., 1775. {CANI}

Henry was father of WILLIAM; JOHNSON; HENRY; RHODA, b. 14 Aug 1775, had a dau. Rhoda Swiggett; LEVIN, b. 11 Aug 1777; DANIEL; JAMES; HARMON; ESTHER; MARY; SARAH, m. Ralph Colescott.

## Fourth Generation

5. WILLIAM SWIGGETT, son of Henry (4) Swiggett, served as private in the militia of Caroline Co., Capt. John Stafford's Company, 14th Battn. by 13 Aug 1777. {RPCA:158}

6. JOHNSON SWIGGETT, son of Henry (4) Swiggett, m. 19th day, 3rd mo., 1780, Mary Breeding. {CANI} One of the witnesses at the marriage was William Swiggett.

Johnson Swiggate served as private in the militia of Caroline Co., Capt. John Stafford's Company, 14th Battn., by 13 Aug 1777. {RPCA:158}

Among the Nicholites who applied to join the Society of Friends of Third Haven Monthly on 30th day., 9th mo., 1797, were Johnson Swiggett and wife Mary and Sarah Swiggett. They were accepted. {See minutes of Third Haven Monthly Meeting.}

Johnson and Mary were parents of JOHN, b. 17th day, 9th mo., 1781; HENRY, b. 11th day., 3rd mo., 1783; SARAH, b. 24th day, 9th mo., 1785; ESTHER, b. 11th da., 4th mo., 1788; MYNTA, b. 13th day, 4th mo., 1790; SOLOMON, b. 30th day, 1st mo., 1794; ADAH, b. 8th day., 5th mo., 1797; MARY, b. 29th day, 3rd mo., 1800. {CANI; CANW}

7. HENRY SWIGGETT, son of Henry (4) Swiggett.

Henry Swiggate, Jr., served as private in the militia of Caroline Co., Capt. John Stafford's Company, 14th Battn. by `13 Aug 1777.

8. LEVIN SWIGGETT, b. 11 Aug 1777, son of Henry (4) Swiggett, m. Peggy Smith, dau. of Levin and Elizabeth Smith.

Levin Smith, Caroline Co., d. leaving a will dated 20 Nov 1807, proved 29 March 1808. To wife Elizabeth, her choice of beds and a Negro boy Joseph. To son John Smith, the farmer where on he now lives and adj. land by the name of *Goldsbury Farm* in Kent Co., DE. To son Nathan Smith, $1000. To son Levin Smith, a tract called *Pleasant Bit* whereon testator now lives and adj. lands. To grandson Thomas Forsyth, 15 a. of *Pleasant Bit*. To dau. Mary Smith, bed and furniture and £200 at age 20 or when she marries and to have Negro boy Joseph for his remaining service. Daus. Peggy Swiggett, Sarah Webster and Franky Reynals ("my wifes and my three daughters"), the remainder of personal estate. Execs.: widow and Levin Swiggett. Witnessed by Gove Saulsbury, James Wroten, Daniel Webster. {CA Wills JR B:136}

In 1817 there was recorded a Chancery case of Philemon Plummer vs. Thomas Forsythe, Ann Swiggett, Luther Swiggett and Catharine Swiggett, children of Levin Swiggett and Peggy his wife, dec'd., and infants, Henry Webster, Peggy Webster, Thomas Webster, Richard Webster and Easter Stafford, children of Joseph Stafford and Sarah his wife [dau. of Levin Smith], dec'd., infants John Smith, Edward Smith of Nathan, an infant; Frances Reynolds, widow [of Thomas Reynolds and dau. of Levin Smith; Levin Smith and Mary Smith, heirs at law of Leivn Smith.

Levin and Peggy were parents of ANN; LUTHER; CATHARINE.

9. JAMES SWIGGETT, son of Henry (4) Swiggett, served as private in the militia of Caroline Co., Capt. John Stafford's Company, 14th Battn., by 13 Aug 1777.

The *Republican Star* dated 26 May 1812 indicated that Johnson Swiggett was exec. of the estate of James Swiggett of Baltimore Co.

10. HARMON SWIGGETT, son of Henry (4) Swiggett served as private in the militia of Caroline Co., Capt. John Stafford's Company, 14th battn., by 13 Aug 1777. {RPCA:157}

Harmon Swiggett, Caroline Co., d. leaving a will dated 10 Feb 1828, proved 6 April 1833. To son John Swiggett the farm whereon testator now lives adj. the land of William Swiggett, Solomon Richardson and James Richardson. To Robert Swiggett, son of James Swiggett and Martha Swiggett ... son(?) of James Swiggett, to have $25.00 each. To William Swiggett, son of Joseph and Hester Swiggett, dau. of Joseph Swiggett, $25.00 each. To Mary Swiggett, dau. of Thomas Swiggett and Sarah Swiggett, dau. of Thomas Swiggett, $25. To Harriet Stevens, dau. of Levisa Stevens and Mary Stevens, dau. of Levisa Stevens, $25 each. To Joshua Stevens, son of Ann Stevens and Joseph S. Stevens, son of Ann Stevens, $25 each. Witnessed by Harrison Coalscott, Ann Richardson, S. Richardson. {CAW WAF A:120}

Harmon was father of JOHN.

Unplaced

BENJAMIN SWIGGATE served as private in the militia of Caroline Co., Capt. Andrew Fountain's Company, 14th Battn., by 13 Aug 1777. {RPCA:157}

JAMES SWIGGETT

On 17 Dec 1791 James Swiggett of DO Co. and his wife Femy conveyed to William Murphy of the same co., *Third Purchase*, adj. land of James Murphy, 100 a. {DOLR 3 HD 598}

## THE THOMAS FAMILY of Talbot County

1. CHRISTOPHER THOMAS, TA CO., b c1609, d. by 19 Nov 1679, Thomas, m. 2nd Mrs. Elizabeth Higgins who later m. Matthew Smith. Christopher was son of Tristram Thomas, son of Edmond, son of Rev. Tristram, Rector of Alford Parish, Surrrey, England (b. c1522). {British Roots II:214. See this for more details.}

Christopher Thomas was buried 25 March 1670. {TA Co. Court Proceedings, 1671-75}

On 19 Nov 1679 Elizabeth Smith, wife of Matthew Smith, former wife of Christopher Thomas, dec'd., quit claim to Trustran Thomas, Gent., of Wye River, to a tract of 350 a. called *Barbadoes Hall*, patented in 1665 to Christopher Thomas, on s. side of Chester River. {TALR 3:315}

Christopher was prob. father of TRUSTRAM.

### Second Generation

2. TRUSTAM THOMAS, prob. son of Christopher (1) Thomas, m. Anne Coursey, dau. of Henry Coursey. {See The Coursey Family, vol. 2 of this series.}

Tristam Thomas was transported into the province by 1666 along with his wife Ann, and sons Christopher, Tristam, and Thomas. {MPL 9:327}

Stephen Thomas, b. 15 Jan 1673; Juliana Thomas, b. 15 Oct 1671; William Thomas, b. 18 Oct 1669. {TA Co. Court Proceedings, 1671-75}

On 10 Nov 1670 William Coursey conveyed to his brother in law Tristram Thomas, Gent., land called *Trustram* where he now liveth on in Wye River near the head of the northeast branch of Back Wye, 400 a. {TALR I:126}

Trustam Thomas, TA Co., d. leaving a will proved 22 May 1686. To Christopher Thomas, plantation where John Madbury and Elizabeth his wife live, after their decease. To William Thomas, 233 a. on n. side of Williams Branch, he to serve his mother during her life. To Stephen Thomas, 233 a. by John Glardwings, also to serve his mother during life. To Trustam Thomas, 233 a., back of Madbury's Branch. To 4 daus. (unnamed), personalty. To Thomas Thomas his father's right in land or plantation at Chester. Extx., Mrs. Anne Thomas. Witnessed by John Stephens, Thos. Gough, John Glendening. {MWB 4:226}

The admin. account of the estate of Trustram Thomas, TA Co., was submitted by Anne Turloe, wife of William Turloe, on 3 April 1708. Legatees: William Thomas, Stephen Thomas, Trustram Thomas, Juliana Thomas who m. John King, Anne Thomas who m. Arthur Emory, Elizabeth Thomas per Robert Blinitt [Blunt?]. {MDAD 28:84}

Trustam was father of THOMAS; CHRISTOPHER; TRUSTAM; WILLIAM, b. 18 Oct 1669; STEPHEN, b. 15 Jan 1673; JULIANA, b. 15 Oct 1671, m. by Oct 1721, John King, son of Mark King; ELIZABETH, m. William

Coursey; ANNE, m. Arthur Emory; FRANCES, m. John Emory. {See The Emory Family and The Mark King Family in vol. 3 of this series.}

Third Generation

3. THOMAS THOMAS, son of Trustam (2) Thomas, m. Elizabeth (N) who m. 2[nd] Richard Hunter and m. 3[rd] Thomas Williams.

On 18 Nov 1690 David Blaney, planter, and his wife Katherine, conveyed to Thomas Thomas, planter, 300 a. on w. side of Back Wye called *Woodstock*. {TALR 5:278}

At June Court 1698 James Winder, servant to Thomas Thomas, was judged to be 13 years old. {TAJR}

On 9 Jan 1702 Thomas Thomas of TA Co., planter, and his wife Elizabeth, to Trustram Thomas, in consideration of brotherly love and 233 a. bequeathed by Trustram Thomas, their father, dec'd., 200 a. in Wye River on *Ned's Cove*, part of *Trustram*, 170 a. and 30 a. called *Coursey upon Wye*. {TALR 9:143}

On 9 Jan 1702 William Coursey and his wife Elizabeth conveyed to Thomas Thomas a gift of 30 a. including the dower of Elizabeth of Coursey called *Coursey Upon Wye* on Nedd's Cove. {TALR 9:157}

On 9 Jan 1702 Trustrum Thomas and his wife Judith conveyed to Thomas Thomas 233 a. willed by Trustrum Thomas, Sr., his father, part of the land called *Trustrum* in TA Co. at the head of Wye River - now in the occupation of the said Thomas Thomas. {TALR 9:156}

On 17 Aug 1703 Thomas Thomas and his wife Elizabeth conveyed to Robert Smith in consideration of 300 a. well assured and 9000 lbs. of tobacco, 350 a. on Courseygall [Corsica] Creek in TA Co. called *Barbados Hall*. {TALR:9184} On 17 Feb 1708 *Barbados Hall* surveyed for Christopher Thomas for 350 a. and purchased by Robert Smith of Thomas Thomas, bro. of Christopher Thomas, was conveyed to Richard Bennett. {QALR ETA. 32}

On 2 March 1704 Thomas Thomas requested this receipt to be recorded: 15 May 1704 Received of Thomas Thomas 20 shillings for the alienation of part of *Pharsalia*, 200 a., and part of *Winfield*, 300 a.; also 4 shillings, 8 pence sterling for the alienation of *Trustrum*, part purchased from the brother Trustrum. Signed Richard Bennett. {TALR 9:288}

Thomas Thomas, TA Co., d. leaving a will date 4 Aug 1701, proved 8 May 1706. To son Edmond, 300 a., part of *Trustram* where testator's mother lives. To son Trustram, 300 a., dwelling plantation bequeathed by father to bro. Christopher, at the decease of his mother; also *Trustram's Ridge* on Tuckahoe and 400 a., *Trustram's Lot*. To son Thomas, 300 a. in fork of Tuckahoe purchased of Robert Smith and 350 a., Baron Corsica Creek, and 200 a. on fork of Tuckahoe bought of John Hawkins and Wm. Coursey. Testator desires an exchange of land between Robert Smith and son Thomas afsd. confirmed. Extx., wife Elizabeth during widowhood. If she marry, bro. John King and kinsman Wm. Coursey to become execs. Witnessed by Peter Jolly, Stephen Thomas, Juliana King. {MWB 12:24}

The inventory of the estate was filed on 18 June 1706. Servants mentioned: John Early, James Window, Sarah Jones. Creditors and next of kin: William Coursey, Esq., John King. A second inventory was filed by Elizabeth Hunter, relict, John King, William Coursey. {INAC 27:99; 29:201}

The admin account was submitted on 20 March 1707 by Elizabeth Hunter, wife of Richard Hunter. {INAC 28:35} A second admin. account was submitted by William Coursey and John King. Legatee: dau. Ann who m. John Emory, and Edmond Thomas. {INAC 32A:92}

At March Court Ann Lewis entered a petition saying that she came into the country as a servant and was sold to Thomas Thomas, now dec'd., and served her complete time. She now seeks her freedom dues from her mistress. Elizabeth Thomas was ordered to pay the remaining part of the freedom dues, namely, 2 barrels of Indian corn and a cap of white linen. {TAJR}

At August court 1715 Thomas Williams, chirurgion, and his wife Elizabeth als. Elizabeth Thomas, widow, were summoned to answer Elizabeth Carter, widow, admx. of Richard Carter, Gent., that they render to her 2109 lbs. of tobacco. {QAJR}

Thomas Williams, QA Co., made a verbal will on 11 Oct 1716, proved 13 Oct 1716. To wife 1/3 of estate. Edmond Thomas, exec. and residuary legatee. Witnessed by Trustam Thomas. {MWB 14:241} The inventory of Dr. Thomas Williams, QA Co., was approved by Jo. Earle, Will. Clayton, John Tilden. {MINV 7:16}

Elizabeth Williams, QA Co., d. leaving a will dated 18 Jan 1719, proved 25 Nov 1720. To son Thomas Thomas and Christopher Thomas, personal estate, equally; should son Christopher die during minority, his portion to be equally divided between Mary Ann, dau. of son Edmond Thomas, exec., and Eliza., dau. of son Trustram Thomas; son Christopher to care of son Edmond afsd. until 21 years of age. To son Trustram afsd., personalty. Witnessed by Hannah Lawson, vin. Hemsley. {MWB 16:493}

The inventory of the estate of Elizabeth Williams, QA Co., was approved on 4 Jan 1720 by Thomas Thomas, Tristram Thomas, John Emory, William Greenwood. {MINV 7:18}

The admin. account was submitted by Edmond Thomas, Gent., on 27 Feb 1721. {MDAD 4:80}

Thomas was father of THOMAS; EDMUND; TRUSTAM; CHRISTOPHER; ANN, m. John Emory. {See the Emory Family, vol. 3 of this series.}

4. CHRISTOPHER THOMAS, son of Tristram (2) Thomas.

On 12 Nov 1688 the inventory of the estate of Christopher Thomas, TA Co., was filed. {INAC 10:150}

On 10 May 1694 the admin. account of his estate was submitted by Thomas Thomas. Legatee: his bro. William Thomas. {INAC 12:153}

5. TRUSTRUM THOMAS, son of Tristam (2) Thomas, m. Judith (N).

On 9 Jan 1702 Trustrum Thomas and his wife Judith conveyed to Thomas Thomas 233 a. willed by Trustrum Thomas, Sr., his father, part of the land called *Trustrum* in TA Co. at the head of Wye River - now in the occupation of the said Thomas Thomas. {TALR 9:156}

At June Court of QA Co., 1710, Thomas Thomas bruoght John Badsey, an orphan, praying he might be bound to him until he arrives to the age of 21, being 14 years old last Feb, to be taught the trade of a shoemaker. {DOJR}

On 25 June 1723 Arthur Emory, Gent., acquired from Trustram Thomas, cordwainer, 200 a. in Wye River formerly in TA Co., now QA Co., which begins on Ned's Cove. 170 a. is part of the land given by Trustram Thomas, dec'd., unto Christopher Thomas out of *Trustrum* and 30 a. is part of *Coursey Upon Wye* excepting 25 feet square for a graveyard for Trustram and his family in or near the orchard. {QALR IKB:192}

6. WILLIAM THOMAS, son of Tristam (2) Thomas, m. Joan/Jane Riddle (Riddell), sister of Walter Riddle.

On 4 March 1667 Stephen Gary of Little Choptank and his wife Alice conveyed to Jacob Waymake and William Thomas, 100 a., *Spring Garden*, in Fishing Creek. {TALR 2:33}

On 3 Nov 1692 William Thomas and his wife Jane conveyed to William Turloe 233 a. adj. the plantation whereon Thomas now dwells, bequeathed to him by Trustram Thomas in 1685 - at the head of Wye River in TA Co., part of *Trustram* which was formerly two tracts with the surplusage resurveyed into one tract by Richard Peacock, Deputy Surveyor for TA Co., 28 May 1681 which was bequeathed by Trustram Thomas, father of William Thomas - adj. the land formerly laid out for Capt. Robert Morris, now possessed by Jacob Seth. Witnessed by Stephen Thomas and Trustram Thomas. {TALR 6:18}

On 5 Nov 1692 John Murphey, planter, and his wife Sarah, conveyed to William Thomas, tanner, 80 a. on n. side of Great Choptank River, head of Bullenbrooke Creek, sold by Richard White of Bullenbrooke with the residue of the whole tract called *Double Ridge* unto Wm. Fisher and Edward Roper (the said Roper now dec'd.). The said land was granted by will to Sarah, wife of John Murphey. {TALR 6:25}

On 30 Jan 1701 Richard White and his wife Elizabeth conveyed to William Thomas, cordwainer, 130 a., part of *Double Ridge*, purchased 23 Dec 1670 by Wm. Fisher and Edward Roper; 80 a. bought of John Murphey and his wife Sarah; 50 a. bought of Michael Deane and his wife Elizabeth, the said Sarah and Elizabeth being the co-heirs of Edward Roper, dec'd. {TALR 9:96}

On 28 April William Thomas of TA Co., Gent., gave to his grandson, Wm. Thomas Jr., an infant, 1 Negro girl called Rose about 2 years of age. {TALR 13:328}

Walter Riddle, planter, TA Co., d. by 17 Dec 1736 when the admin. account of his estate was submitted by William Thomas and Trustram Thomas. representative: only Jane Thomas (sister), wife of William Thomas. {MDAD 15:292}

William Thomas d. 1 April 1740. {TAPE}

William Thomas, TA Co., d. leaving a will dated 20 Nov 1739/40, proved 10 Dec 1740. To dau. Ann, wife of William Martin (although she has had a full portion of estate), all debts owed testator by her former husband and herself during widowhood, to heirs of dau. Jane, dec'd and dau. Juliana and Elizabeth, 5 s. each. To grandson Thomas Martin, provided he stays with son Trustram until he arrives at 21 years, personalty. To wife Joan, extx., dwelling plantation and personal estate during her lifetime. At her death dwelling plantation to go to son Trustram and then to grandson William. To sons William and Trustram, personal estate at death of their mother. Witnessed by Adam Brown, Thomas Helbys and Thomas Metcalfe. {MWB 22:284}

William and Jane were parents of NICHOLAS, b. c1695, d. 1716; EDWARD, b. 1697, d. 1716; TRUSTRAM, b. 23 Jan 1709; ANN, b. 1688/9, m. 1st , 27 Feb 1716, Loftus Bowdle and m. 2nd William Martin, Jr.; JANE (Joan), b. 1701, bapt. 14 Sep 1701, d. by 20 Nov 1739/40, m. 19 Dec 1717, Thomas Martin; JULIANA, b. 29 Jan 1691, d. 1702; KATHERINE, b. 11 Dec 1693; JULIANA, b. 10 Jan 1707, m. 1st 23 Sep 1724, William Stephens (c. c1733)and m. 2nd 1734, Thomas Stevens (b. c1710, d. c1741); SARAH, d. 20 Nov 1708; ELIZABETH, b. c1701, d. 1755, m. 18 Dec 1723, Edward Needles, son of John Needles; WILLIAM, b. 15 May 1705. {TAPE; BDML. See The Needles Family, vol. 4 of this series.}

7. STEPHEN THOMAS, son of Tristam (2) Thomas, m. Alice (N) who later m. Thomas Murphey.

Stephen Thomas, TA Co., d. by 14 Dec 1724 when the admin. account of his estate was submitted by Thomas Murphey and his wife Alice Murphey. {MDAD 7:169}

Thomas Murphey, QA Co., d. by 26 Sep 1729 when the admin. account of his estate was submitted by Alice Murphey. Payments to, inter alia, John Clayland who m. Sarah Thomas, dau. of Stephen Thomas, her portion of her father's estate. {MDAD 10:164}

A second admin. account of the estate of Thomas Murphey was submitted by Alice Murphey on 13 Nov 1730. Payees included Carpenter Earle who m. Mary Thomas, dau. of Stephen Thomas, her filial portion. {MDAD 10:649}

Stephen was father of SARAH, m. John Clayland; MARY, m. Carpenter Earle.

Fourth Generation

8. THOMAS THOMAS, son of Thomas (3) Thomas, m. Susanna (N).

On 3 March 1726 Thomas Thomas, planter, and his wife Susanna, conveyed to Trustram Thomas, cordwinder, 200 a., part of *Hawkins Pharsalia*, in a fork of the main branch of Tuckahoe Creek on the Beaver Dam Branch adj. John King. {QALR IKC:104}

On 21 Sep 1727 Thomas Thomas, planter, and his wife Susannah, conveyed to John Evans, planter, 55 a., part of *Winfield* on n. side of Tuckahoe Creek. {QALR IKC:146}

On 24 Sep 1731 Thomas Thomas, planter, and his wife Susannah, conveyed to Charles O'Neal, planter, 100 a., conveyed by Robert Smith to Thomas Thomas, father of the grantor, on 17 Aug 1723, out of *Winfield* and willed by Thomas Thomas to his son - lying in the fork of Tuckahoe Creek adj. a parcel sold to John Evans. {QALR RTA:86}

Anne, dau. of Thomas and Susanna Thomas, b. 3 June 1738, bapt. 9 June 1738. {QALU}

Sarah, dau. of Thomas and Susanna Thomas, b. 9 May 1740, bapt. 26 Oct 1740. {QALU}

On 28 June 1758 Thomas Thomas, planter, and his wife Susanna, conveyed to Jonathon Evans, planter, 55 a., part of *Winfield*, on n. side of the main branch of Tuckahoe Creek. {QALR RTE:234}

On 28 June 1758 Thomas Thomas and his wife Susannah, and O'Neal Price and his wife Eleanor, planters, conveyed to John Legg, planter, and now Inspector at Kent Island Warehouse, 111 ½ a., part of *Winfield* adj. the part sold to John Evans and now possessed by Jonathon Evans and the part in the possession of William Saterfield. {QALR RTE:234}

On 28 Feb 1769 Thomas Thomas, Sr., planter, conveyed to William Yoe, son of Stephen Yoe, 63 a., part of *Winfield Corrected* on n.w. branch of Tuckahoe Creek adj. *Baynard's Pasture* and *Thomases Addition*. {QALR RFH:317}

Thomas Thomas, QA Co., planter, d. leaving a will dated 3 Dec 1768, proved 29 Nov 1770. To children: James, Susannah Ratliff, Sophia Roberts, dec'd., Ann Chaires, Jane Watkins, Sarah Chaires, Mary Tarr; grandson Thomas Roberts son of dau. Sophia Roberts; granddau. Ann Thomas dau. of dau. Sophia; granddau. Susannah Clother Thomas dau. of son Thomas Thomas. Exec. son James. Tracts: *Infield* and *Resurveyed.* Witnessed by James Vanderford, William Hollingsworth, Edward Wright. {MWB 38:95}

Thomas was father of JAMES; SUSANNAH, m. (N) Ratliff; SOPHIA, m. 19 July 1752, James Roberts {QALU}; ANN, m. 20 Feb 1759, Charles Chaires {QALU}; JANE, m. (N) Watkins; SARAH, b. 9 May 1740, m. 8 Aug 1759, Nathaniel Chairs {QALU}; MARY, m. (N) Tarr; THOMAS.

9. EDMUND THOMAS, son of Thomas (3) Thomas, m. Ann (N) who later m. William Willson.

On 9 April 1716 Edmond Thomas and his wife Anne of QA Co. conveyed to John Merriday, Jr., planter, 150 a. called *Trustrum's Ridge* near the fork of Tuckahoe Creek. {QALR IKA:71}

On 25 Nov 1720 Edmund Thomas, planter, conveyed to Tristram Thomas, his bro., planter, 355 a. called *The Ovall*, laid out for Thomas Thomas, dec'd., 22 Oct 1703 in the woods in the fork of Tuckahoe. {QALR IKB:38}

Edmund Thomas, planter, QA Co., d. leaving a will dated 9 May 1731, proved 15 Nov 1731. To son Edmond, 150 a. where Thomas Stevens now lives; sd. son dying without issue, to pass to son James; he dying without issue, to son Tilden; and in failure of issue afsd. to daus. Mary Ann and Martha. To son James, 200 a. dwelling plantation *Trustram* on n. side of Madbury's Branch adj. John Clayland's land. To wife Ann, extx., dwelling plantation during her lifetime with residue of Trustram; after her decease all of sd. land to son Edmond, entailed as the afsd. 150 a. and 1/3 personal estate. To son Tilden, 227 a., *Thomas' Addition* in Tully's Neck. Witnessed by Trustram Thomas Jr., George Thorne, John Beck, Charles Quick. {MWB 20:317}

The inventory of the estate was filed by Ann Thomas in Sep 1732. Signed as next of in: Christopher Thomas, Tristram Thomas. {MINV 17:149}

On 4 Sep 1740 The admin. account was submitted by Anne Willson, wife of William Willson. Representatives (5 persons): Mary Anne, Martha, Edmund, James Tilden, John. {MDAD 18:39}

Edmund was father of EDMOND; JAMES; TILDEN; MARY ANN; MARTHA; JOHN.

10. TRUSTRAM THOMAS, son of Thomas (3) Thomas, m. Jane (N).

Ann Thomas m. 17 — 1728, Joseph Jarman. {QALU}

Trustram Thomas, Sr., Tulley's Neck, QA Co., d. leaving a will dated 30 Dec 1745, proved 4 March 1745. To son Stephen Thomas and Mary his wife, 60 a., upper corner of land where he now lives, part of tract called *Hawkins'*

*Pharsalia*, and at their decease to Robert Thomas, son of sd. Stephen and Mary Thomas. To son Philemon Thomas, 60 a. adj. upon branch of Tuckahoe Creek, being part of tract called *Hawkins' Pharsalia*. To son Benjamin Thomas (after decease of my wife), my homestead plantation being remaining part of my sd. plantation called *Hawkins' Pharsalia*, together with 30 a. purchased out of *Alcock's Pharsalia*. Wife Jane Thomas. To sons and daus.: Trustram, Simon, Thomas, Penelope Jarman, Ann Jarman and Nancy Sandman, widow, 500 lbs. of tobacco each. MWB 24:360; QAW JE2:220}

The inventory of the estate of Trustram Thomas, QA Co., was filed by Thomas Thomas (Quaker) and Benjamin Thomas (Quaker). Signed as next of kin: Stephen Thomas, Philemon Thomas. {MINV 34:69}

Trustram was father of STEPHEN, m. Mary (N); PHILEMON; BENJAMIN; TRUSTRAM; SIMON; THOMAS; PENELOPE, m. (N) Jarman; ANN, m. 1728, Joseph Jarman; NANCY, m. (N) Sandman.

11. CHRISTOPHER THOMAS, son of Thomas (3) Thomas, m. 1st (N), and m. 2nd Mary Cox, widow of Lazarus Cox.

Lazarus Cox, QA Co., d. by 9 Sep 1742 when the inventory of his estate was filed by Christopher Thomas and his wife Mary. {MINV 27:60}

Christopher Thomas, QA Co., d. leaving a will dated 29 Nov 1750, proved 10 Jan 1750. To wife Mary Thomas, personal estate. To son William Thomas, 150 a. called *Forrest Plains* on w. side of the Breatree Swamp, issuing out of one of the branches of Tuckahoe Creek. To dau. Ann Thomas, slaves. To son in law Andrew Cox, slaves. To sons William and Rizdem Thomas, slaves. Wife Mary, extx. Witnessed by John Ewing, Christopher Thomas, Jr., Trustram Thomas. {MWB 27:494}

Christopher Thomas, QA Co., d. by 1 Aug 1751 when the inventory of his estate was filed by Mary Thomas, admx./extx. Signed as next of kin: Thomas Thomas, Christopher Thomas. {MINV 48:112}

Christopher was father of WILLIAM; ANN; RIZDEM and step-father of Andrew Cox.

## Fifth Generation

12. EDMUND THOMAS, son of Edmund (9) Thomas.

Samuel Wright, Christ Church Parish, Kent Island, QA Co., d. leaving a will dated 22 Aug 1766, proved 21 May 1767 in which he left part of estate to Anne and Susannah Thomas, daus. of Edmund Thomas. and to Susannah Thomas, dau. of Edward Thomas, son of Edmond, one slave. {MWB 35:449}

Edmund Thomas, Jr., QA Co., d. leaving a will dated 23 July 1768, proved 11 Aug 1768. Children: Samuel Wright Thomas, Mary, Anne, Frances and Susanna Thomas. Exec. Gideon Emory. Witnessed by Trustran Thomas, John Clayland, Thomas Dimond. {MWB 36:512}

On 28 Dec 1768 Jacob Seth and Thomas Clayland, appointed by the court to make a valuation of 450 a., part of Trustram, the right of Samuel Wright Thomas, minor under the care of Gideon Emory, his guardian, stated that they entered into the late dwelling plantation of Edmund Thomas and found one old brick dwelling house, two stories high, 51 x 28 feet, with a two-story porch, 12x13, etc. [A description is given of the house and grounds.] {QALR RFH:322}

Edmund was father of SAMUEL WRIGHT; MARY; ANNE; FRANCES; SUSANNA.

13. TRISTRAM THOMAS, son of William (6) Thomas, m. Elizabeth Martin, dau. of Thomas Martin. Tristram d. at Roadley, the seat of the family for several generations in Bolingbrooke Neck, Trapp district of TA Co. {*History of Talbot County*, by Oswald Tilghman}

At March Court 1705 William Garey, son and orphan of William Garey, chose Tristram Thomas as his guardian. He was bound to Tristram Thomas for 4 years, to learn the trade of a cordwainer. {TAJR}

Thomas Martin III d. leaving a will dated 21 Nov 1770, proved 28 April 1778. The will mentioned bro. Nicholas Martin; sisters: Elizabeth Thomas, Mary Martin, Sarah Lloyd; father Thomas Martin; nephews: William Thomas and Tristram Thomas, sons of Tristram Thomas, dec'd.; niece Elizabeth Thomas, dau. of Tristram Thomas, dec'd.; nephew James Lloyd; Thomas Faris(?); James Brown, son of Edward Brown of Kent. {TAW 3:29}

Tristam Thomas, TA Co., d. leaving a will dated 12 July 1769, proved 5 Dec 1769. Children: William and Elizabeth; unborn child mentioned. Nephews: William and Nicholas Thomas, Tristam Bowdle, David Robinson Jr., and John Allen Thomas. Friend Wm. Morton, guardian of son William. Tracts: *Studan Point*, *Hills Neck*, *Aires Purchase*, *Double Ridge*, *Reeds Creek*, *Sutton* and *Thief Keep Out*. Exec., Wm. Martin. Witnessed by James Dickenson, Thomas Stevens, Thos. Jenkins, Wm. White. {MWB 37:443}

On 10 May 1774 Elizabeth Thomas, widow, leased to Henry Cary the lands whereon Elijah Nuttall lately dwelt, known as *The Clifts*, for a term of 10 years. {TALR 20:361}

Following the death of her husband Elizabeth, by advice of her bro. Thomas Martin, was induced in 1775 to remove to Wilmington, DE, in order that her children might have educational advantages. On the approach of the British army in 1777 she moved to Philadelphia. Five years she returned with her children to Wilmington. {*History of Talbot County* by Oswald Tilghman:435}

Tristram was father of WILLIAM, b. 27 Nov 1765 {TAPE}; ELIZABETH; TRISTRAM, b. 25 Dec 1769 (following his father's death).

14. WILLIAM THOMAS, b. 1705, d. 1767, son of William (6) Thomas, m. 11 May 1732, Elizabeth Allen, dau. of John and Mary (Lowe) Allen, and m. 2nd by 1757, Margaret Finney Edmndson, dau. of Capt. William and Rachel (Clayton) Finney and widow of John Edmondson. {TAPE; BDML:808}

On 22 June 1733 William Thomas, Jr., TA Co., and Elizabeth his wife conveyed to James Dickinson, Gent., 112 a., part of *Hatton* where John Preston formerly dwelled on the branches of St. Michaels Creek called the Great Neck Branch; mentioned a dividing line between William Dickinson and John Preston. {TALR 13:770}

James Allen Thomas, eldest son of William Thomas Junr. and Elizabeth, b. 17 Aug 1734. {TAPE}

On 2 Oct 1734 William Thomas of TA Co., planter, and his wife Elizabeth, conveyed to William Carmichall, Gent., 76 a., part of *Allen's Neck*, formerly in TA Co. but by the late division now in QA Co. lying between Royston's and Double Creeks, Chester River, and another part of the same containing 40 a. {QALR RTA:331}

On 19 Aug 1740 William Thomas Jr., Gent., TA Co., and his wife Elizabeth, conveyed to John Guy als. Williams, innholder, 200 a. called *Mary's Dower* on a branch of Wye River called Brewer's Branch adj. a tract formerly taken up by Moses Harris. {TALR 14:459}

On 24 June 1755 William Thomas of TA Co., conveyed to George Personett, 80 a., part of *Smith's Range* on the branches of Island Creek. Walter Riddle died without issue and the land fell to his sister Jane and after her death to her son William Thomas. {QALR RTC:308}

On 31 July 1765 William Thomas the elder, Gent., conveyed to Nicholas Thomas, atty at law, his son, one Negro boy named Ben, about 5 years old, son of Preston and Flora; also one silver tankard, lately the property of Nicholas Lowe, dec'd. {TALR 19:333}

On 31 Oct 1765 Pollard Edmondson, Gent., conveyed to William Thomas, Gent., and his wife Margaret, for 5 s., 450 a., part of *Tilghman's Fortune* which on 4 Sep 1762 was conveyed by William and Margaret Thomas to the said Pollard Edmondson for and during the lifetime of said Margaret. {TALR 19:355}

On 6 June 1766 William Thomas of TA Co., conveyed to Joseph Personett, 80 a. called *Smith's Range* on a branch of Island Creek which descended to William from his mother Jane through her bro. Walter Riddle. {QALR RTG:265}

William Thomas, TA Co., d. leaving a will dated 9 April 1767, proved 30 June 1767. To eldest son John Allen Thomas, tract called *Cottingham* lying in TA Co. on St. Michael's River which I bought of Samuel Chew and Jeoffry Henry, on condition that sd. son shall pay to exec. in 12 mos. after the day of my decease, £50; 3 slaves which are on the plantation and in the house at St. Michael's River, where son Allen lately dwelled. To son Nicholas land. To son James Thomas that part of lands called *Anderton Addition* (metes and bounds given). Mentioned ditch near Mrs. Lowe and land bought by Jacob Brommwell of Henry Lowe. To son Nicholas 5 slaves. To son James 6 slaves and plate. To son William, land bought by Jacob Bromwell of Henry Lowe; tract called *Judith's Garden* lying in TA Co., which I bought of John Pattison; one slave. To wife Margaret, what part of estate she is to have by an instrument of writing executed between us. To granddau. Elizabeth Goldsborough, slave. Son James to be under care of son Nicholas. Exec. son Nicholas Thomas. Witnessed by Edward Oldham, Tristm. Thomas, Wm. Hanson, James Dickinson. {MWB 35:422}

William was father of JOHN ALLEN, b. 17 Aug 1734, d. c1797; NICHOLAS, b. c1735, d. 1783/4; JAMES; WILLIAM; MARY, b. c1741, d. by 1767.

15. ELIZABETH THOMAS, dau. of William (6) Thomas, m. 18 Dec 1823, Edward Needles, son of John Needles. {TAPE. See The Needles Family, vol. 4 of this series.}

16. TILDEN THOMAS, son of Edmund (9) Thomas.

On 28 Sep 1758 Tiden Thomas, planter, conveyed to George Baynard, Gent., 227 a. called *Thomas's Addition* lying in the fork of the main branch of Tuckahoe Creek adj. *Winfield's Beginning* and *Hawkins' Pharsalia*. [QALR RTE:304}

17. STEPHEN THOMAS, son of Trustram (10) Thomas, m. Mary (N).

On 3 March 1747 Stephen Thomas and his wife Mary conveyed to Trustrum Thomas part of *Trustrum*, surplus land as determined by commissioners. {QALR RTC:292}

On 2 Oct 1767 Stephen Thomas, planter, surrendered to his son Robert Thomas, planter, his claim to the land devised by Trustram Thomas in his will of 30 Dec 1745 - 80 a. bequeathed to Stephen and his wife Mary for their natural lives and after their deaths to their son Robert. Mary is now dead and after the death of Stephen the land doth belong to Robert. {QALR RTG:109}

Stephen was father of ROBERT.

18. PHILEMON THOMAS, son of Trustram (10) Thomas, m. 1st 5 March 1744, Sarah Scott and m. 2nd Elizabeth (N).

Phillomon Thomas and Sarah Scott m. 5 March 1744. {QALU}

On 1 Dec 1758 Edward Viccars of TA Co., planter, conveyed to Philemon Thomas, planter, 67 ½ a., part of *Alcock's Pharsalia* in Tully's Neck. {QALR RTE:284}

Sarah Thomas, wife of Philemon Thomas, was witness to the will of Michael Flower, QA Co., dated 30 Dec 1763. {MWB 33:70}

On 12 May 1763 Philemon Thomas, planter and his wife Sarah, conveyed to Robert Thomas, planter, 30 a., part of *Alcock's Pharsalia* lying in Tully's Neck. {QALR RTF:327}

William Thomas, son of Philemon, was witnessed to the will of James Chaires, QA Co., dated 30 Jan 1765. {MWB 34:59}

On 4 May 1765 Philemon Thomas, planter, and his wife Sarah, conveyed to Robert Thomas, 30 a., part of *Alcock's Pharsalia* in Tully's Neck. {QALR RTG:148}

On 2 Oct 1767 Philemon Thomas, farmer, and his wife Elizabeth, conveyed to William Thomas, his son, 350 a., part of *Alcock's Pharsalia* in Tully's Neck, part of *Hawkins' Pharsalia*, part of *Lee's Chance* - all contiguous or near *Alcock's Pharsalia* adj. the land of Robert Thomas conveyed by Philemon Thomas on 4 May 1765; part conveyed by Edward Viccers to Robert Thomas, 1 Dec 1758; and part sold by Jonathon Clark and Rebecca his wife to Stephen Thomas on 18 Nov 1750 (mentions the will of Trustram Thomas, father to the afsd. Philemon, Stephen and Robert Thomas) - also adj. a part of *Hawkins's Pharsalia* sold by William Coursey and John Hawkins to John King. {QALR RTH:102}

On 25 July 1770 Philemon Thomas of Anson Co., NC, conveyed to James Findley and William Price, farmers, 150 a., parts of *Relief* and *Emory's Rich Land* in Tullys Neck, conveyed to Philemon Thomas and Thomas Dockery by Solomon Knotts, Amos Jarman and his wife Sophia. {QALR RTI:178}

Philemon was father of WILLIAM.

19. BENJAMIN THOMAS, son of Trustram (10) Thomas, m. 1st 6 Aug 1746, Rebecca Kemp {QALU}, and m. 2nd Sarah Lee, dau. of Thomas Lee.

On 24 May 1750 Benjamin Thomas, planter, conveyed to Philemon Thomas, planter, 60 a., part of *Hawkins Pharsalia*, lying in Tully's Neck in the fork of the main branch of Tuckahoe Creek, left by Trustram Thomas to benjamin Thomas. {QALR RTC:435}

Thomas Lee, QA Co., d. leaving a will dated Nov 1769, proved 22 Jan 1770. Mentioned were children: William, Thomas, John, Sarah wife of Benjamin Thomas, James, Henrietta and Frances; son in law George Temple, exec. {MWB 37:609}

20. TRUSTRAM THOMAS, son of Trustram (10) Thomas, m. Ann (N).

Trustram Thomas, TA Co., d. leaving a will dated 24 April 1746, proved 29 May 1746. To wife Ann Thomas, my dwelling plantation whereon I now live. To son Christopher Thomas, 100 a. where he now lives called *Trustram*. To son John Thomas, 100 a. To son Trustram Thomas, tract called *Trustram*. To son Joseph Thomas, remainder of land called *Trustram*, 200 a. To son John Thomas, furniture. To son Joseph Thomas, Furniture. To dau. Rachel Thomas, furniture. Mentioned dau. Elizabeth Pryer. Wife, extx. Witnessed by John Emory, Jr., Edmund Thomas, John Emory. {MWB 24:405}

The inventory of the estate of Tristram Thomas, QA Co., was filed by Ann Thomas, admx./extx. On 8 Sep 1746. Signed as next of kin: Trustram Thomas, Christopher Thomas. A second inventory was filed by Ann Thomas on 10 Dec 1747. Signed as next of kin: Ch. Thomas, Jr., Trustram Thomas. {MINV 34:243; 36:89}

The admin. account of Trustram Thomas of Wye, QA Co., was submitted by Ann Thomas, admx. {MDAD 25:49}

On 19 April 1749 commissioners were appointed to view and value 200 a., part of *Trustram*, the right of Joseph Thomas, a minor, Edmond Thomas, Sr. his guardian. [Description of buildings given.] {QALR RTC:372}

Trustram was father of CHRISTOPHER; TRUSTRAM; JOHN; JOSEPH, b. after 1728; RACHEL; ELIZABETH, m. (N) Pryer.

21. SIMON THOMAS, son of Trustram (10) Thomas, m. 1st Rebecca (N), m. 2nd Susanna Sands.

Simon and Rebecca were parents of REBECCA, b. 8 June —; SARAH, b. 13 Nov 1737. {QALU}

Rebecca, wife of Simon Thomas, d. 8 March 1737, bur. 11 March 1737. {QALU}

Simon Thomas and Susanna Sands m. 18 Sep 1738. {QALU}

22. WILLIAM THOMAS, son of Christopher (11), m. Sophia (N) who later m. John Young.

William Thomas, QA Co., d. by 11 Sep 1773 when the admin. account of his estate was submitted by Andrew Cox, admin. Representatives: Sophia, widow, now wife of John Young; sister Ann Thomas; half-bro. Andrew Cox. {MDAD 69:145}

Sixth Generation

23. WILLIAM THOMAS, son of Tristram (13) and Elizabeth (Martin) Thomas, b. 27 Nov 1765, m. 7 March 1787, Elizabeth Thomas {TAPE}

24. TRISTRAM THOMAS, b. 1769, d. 1847, son of Tristram (13) and Elizabeth (Martin) Thomas, m. 1st 1792, Miss Gaddes of Wilmington, DE, m. 2nd 1804, Miss Mary Ann Goldsborough of TA Co., m. 3rd 1809, Miss Maria Francis of Philadelphia. Dr. Thomas was bur. in Spring Hill Cemetery, Easton. (No stone had been erected by 1915.)

Following his father 's death Tristram, as an infant, moved to Wilmington, DE, with his mother. He entered the Medical College of Philadelphia in 1788, took up medical practice in Trappe, later Easton. {For a detailed biography of Dr. Thomas see *History of Talbot County* by Oswald Tilghman, pp. 434-444.}

Dr. Tristram Thomas was father of PHILIP FRANCIS (governor of MD); DR. WILLIAM; ELLEN FRANCIS, m. James Lloyd Martin; CAPT. CHARLES, U.S. Navy, living in Baltimore; HENRIETTA, m. V. D. Stewart, pharmacist of Baltimore.

25. JOHN ALLEN THOMAS, b. 17 Aug 1734, son of William (14) and Elizabeth (Allen) Thomas, m. 1st Sarah (N) (d. 1786), m. 2nd by 1796, Isabella (N). {BDML}

On 10 June 1768 Nicholas Thomas, Atty at Law, conveyed to John Allen Thomas of St. Mary's Co., Atty at law, in consideration of £50 to be paid by the will of William Thomas, father of Nicholas and John Allen Thomas, released to John Allen Thomas all claim in *Cottingham* on head of a branch of St. Michaels River which John Allen Thomas has leased to John Young for a term not yet passed, containing 300 a. {TALR 12:508}

On 24 March 1772 John Allen Thomas, late of TA Co., but now of St. Mary's Co., conveyed to William Thomas of TA Co., in consideration of £1000 all his right to two parcels of land at the head of St. Michaels River, one called *Cottingham*, the other *Bantree*. {TALR 20:205}

26. NICHOLAS THOMAS, b. c1735, d. c1784, son of William (14) and Elizabeth (Allen) Thomas.

On 3 March 1768 Nicholas Thomas of TA Co., Gent., Atty at law, conveyed to Henry Alexander, planter, 50 a., *Iriah Freshes* at head of Dividing Creek; also *Alexander's Chance*, *Wales* and a tract called *Lower Good Luck*. {TALR 19:483}

Nicholas served in the Lower House from TA Co., 1768-1770; quartermaster general, 4th Battn., TA Co. Militia, appointed 14 Jan 1776, resigned 8 Aug 1776.

Nicholas d. leaving a will dated 21 Nov 1783, proved 2 March 1784. To house keeper, Esther Skinner, furniture, Negro Sam and other items. To bro. James Thomas, plate. To nephew Nicholas Goldsborough, exec., residue of estate.

27. JAMES THOMAS, d. 1810, son of William (14) Thomas, moved to Annapolis in 1791, member of Governor's Council 1796-1800, m. c1777, Hannah Coward. {BDML}

28. WILLIAM THOMAS, son of William (14) Thomas, d. 1789, m. 9 Feb 1765, Rachel Leeds, dau. of John Leeds. {TAPE}

Elizabeth Thomas, dau. of William and Rachel Thomas, b. 28 Jan 1767. {TAPE}

On 9 April 1772 William Hayward, Gent., conveyed to William Thomas, Gent., the land called *Cottingham*, mortgaged by John Allen Thomas, bro. of said William, 13 June 1768, to William Hayward, and now purchased by William Thomas. {TALR 20:206}

On 6 Aug 1772 William Hindman conveyed to William Thomas and his wife Rachel for 5 s., right to part of *Cottingham* and part of *Bantree* which William Thomas lately purchased of John Allen Thomas on 26 Sep 1771. {TALR 20:246}

On 20 May 1773 Williiam Thomas, Gent., and his wife Rachel, conveyed to Thomas Robinson, mariner, in consideration of one acre, part of *Adventure*, one acre, part of *Judah's Garden*. {TALR 20:292}

On 20 Aug 1771 John Leeds, Lucretia Bozman, William Thomas and his wife Rachel and Mary Leeds, all of TA Co., conveyed to William Dickinson, all rights and claim to 200 a. called *Scarborough*. {QALR RTI:268}

On 11 Oct 1774 John Leeds of TA Co., conveyed to his grandson John Leeds Bozman all books, case of mathematical instruments and his brass reflecting telescope, after death. In case he should die without heirs before age 21 the books, instruments and telescope are to go to his sister Rachel Edmundson and my dau. Rachel Thomas's children. {TALR 20:405}

Rachel Thomas d. leaving a will dated 18 July 1803, proved 14 Oct 1806. To dau. Elizabeth Thomas, wife of William Thomas, dau. Rachel Leeds Thomas, and Ann Leigh, wife of John Leigh of St. Mary's Co., all of testatrix's lands in Oxford Neck on which testatrix now dwells and which were given to testatrix by her late husband William Thomas, dec'd., to be divided between them but dau. Rachel to have the part of the land where testatrix's dwelling house now stands on the condition that she consent that her sister Lucretia Leeds Thomas shall be entitled to have a moiety of the said dwelling house and other conveniences as long as she remains single and unmarried. Elizabeth to have silver tankard that was her grandfather's and to have Negro girl Fanney. Rachel to have Negro girl Little Betty and mare Lady Grace. To dau. Lucretia Leeds Thomas, annual sum of £60 out of the rents and profits of testatrix's land in Bayside and Oxford Neck by her sisters to commence from the time that they receive their estate and to continue until such time as Lucretia received her estate that she is intitled to from the death of her aunt, testatrix's sister Mary Landman. Lucretia and Rachel to have testatrix's carriage and a pair of horses; also Negro boy Sam and mare Maria. To dau. Charlotte Leeds Edmondson, wife of Horatio Edmondson, all lands in Bay side which testatrix got by the death of her father John Leeds; Negro woman Mable, mare Stella. Residue of estate to be divided among testatrix's five daus. To granddau. Rachel Thomas, Negro girl Hannah. Freedom to Negro woman Dafie and her unborn child. Friend John Singleton, exec. Witnessed by James Delahay, Jacob S. Bromwell, Samuel Turbutt, Mary Goldsborough. Codicil: Rachel Leeds Thomas to have silver spoons. Lucretia Leeds Thomas to have candlesticks. Dau. Ann Leigh to have silver plated castors. Negro girl Charlotte and Negro girl Fanney, daus. of Judy, to be free at age 25; Charlotte computed to be 7 and Fanny to be 5. Witnessed by James Delahay, Jacob Bromwell, Samuel Turbutt, Mary Goldsborough. Second Codicil - Dau. Lucretia Leeds Thomas to have Negro boy Will instead of Negro boy Sam. Dau. Rachel Leeds Thomas to have Negro girls Charlotte and Fanny for the time they have left to serve. Also other provisos regarding land and stock. Witnessed by Ignatius Rhodes, Martha Rhodes, Anna Singleton. {TAW JP6:117}

William and Rachel were parents of ELIZABETH, b. 28 Jan 1767, m. 7 March 1787, William Thomas {TAPE}; RACHEL LEEDS; ANNA, m. John Leigh of St. Mary's Co.; LUCRETIA LEEDS; CHARLOTTE LEEDS, m. Horatio Edmondson.

29. MARY THOMAS, dau. of William (14) and Elizabeth (Allen) Thomas, m. Nicholas Goldsborough, son of Nicholas and Sarah (Jolly Turbutt) Goldsborough.

Mary and Nicholas were parents of NICHOLAS GOLDSBOROUGH, b. 25 Feb 1759, d. 6 May 1788, m. 1787, Sarah Harrison; JAMES GOLDSBOROUGH; ELIZABETH GOLDSBOROUGH, m. Thomas Coward; MARY GOLDSBOROUGH, d. 1821 unm.; ANNA GOLDSBOROUGH, m. 25 Feb 1765, John Singleton (d. 15 March 1819). {Bio of Eastern Shore}

30. ROBERT THOMAS, son of Stephen (17) Thomas, m. 13 Oct 1756, Mary Sands. {QALU}

31. CHRISTOPHER THOMAS, son of Trustram (20) Thomas, m. Juliana Emory, dau. of Arthur, Jr. and Ann Emory. {See The Emory Family, vol. 3 of this series.}

Christopher Thomas, QA Co., d. leaving a will dated 5 March 1776, proved 18 Jan 1777. To son Trustram Thomas, plantation where I now live (but my wife to have her thirds of it during her widowhood), 5 shillings and all hirelings wages for present year to be paid by execs. Wife and son Edward Thomas, execs. To wife Juliany Thomas, Negro man Jem. To son Edward Thomas, Negro boy Bob and Negro girl Moll. To dau. Ann Thomas, Negro man Will. To dau. Mary Kent, Negro boy Will. To dau. Juliany Thomas, Negro boy Harry, Negro girl Daffney and Negro child Tam and £23. Witnessed by Philemon Young, William Dimond, Perry Dawson. Codicil: Farm equipment to be kept on plantation for the use of exec. and extx., son and wife and three daus. to get £100. {MWB 41:380}

Christopher was father of TRUSTRAM; EDWARD; JULIANY; ANN; MARY KENT

32. TRUSTRAM THOMAS, son of Trustram (20) Thomas, m. 19 Jan 1732, Mary Watson. {QALU}

Sarah, dau. of Trustram and Mary Thomas, b. 13 Nov 1737. {QALU}

Samuel, son of Trustum and Mary Thomas, b. 3 April 1742, bapt. 6 June. {QALU}

Trustram Thomas, QA Co., d. leaving a will dated 3 Oct 1760, proved 27 Oct 1761. To son Samuel Thomas, home plantation called *Grubby Neck*, 50 a.; 75 a. called *Trustram's Adventure*; horse known as Scipper. To son Joshua Thomas, tract called *Trustram's Ridge*, 75 a. To dau. Elizabeth Thomas, furniture. To sons Samuel and Joshua Thomas, clothing. To wife Mary Thomas, home plantation whereon I live called *Grubby Neck*, as long as she is my widow; at her death or marriage to descend to son Samuel Thomas. Children: Sarah Meridith, Samuel, Joshua and Elizabeth. Exec. son Thomas. Witnessed by John Cheshire, Thos. Wilkinson, Robert Pratt. {MWB 31:480}

On 15 Jan 1762 the inventory of the estate of Trustram Thomas, QA Co. was filed by Samuel Thomas, exec. Signed as next of kin: Stephen Thomas, Phile. Thomas. On 24 Aug 1762 a second inventory was filed by Samuel Thomas. Signed as next of kin: Phil Thomas, Stephen Thomas. {MINV 77:21; 79:183}

The admin. account was submitted by Samuel Thomas on 18 Nov 1762. Mentioned father now dead. Representatives: Mary Thomas, widow; 4

children: Sarah of age, wife of William Meredith; Samuel of age, accountant; Joshua, age 19; Elizabeth, age 16.

On 18 Nov 1762 distribution of his estate was made by Samuel Thomas to widow (unnamed) with residue to 4 children: Joshua Thomas, Samuel Thomas, Elizabeth Thomas, Sarah Meredith. {BFD 3:160}

Trustram was father of SAMUEL; SARAH, m. 8 Jan 1756, William Meredith; JOSHUA, b. c1743; ELIZABETH, b. c1746.. {See The Meredith Family of Queen Anne's County, vol. 11 of this series.}

33. JOHN THOMAS, son of Trustram (20) Thomas, m. Mary Besswick, dau. of Richard Besswick. {See Beswick Family, vol. 11 of this series.}

They were parents of THOMAS, Jr.

34. JOSEPH THOMAS, probable son of Trustam (20) Thomas.

On 25 Aug 1761 Joseph Thomas brought a young mare as a stray and trespassing on him. {QALR RFT:171}

Joseph Thomas, QA Co., d. by 27 July 1762 when the inventory of his estate was filed by Mary Thomas. Signed as next of kin: Christopher Thomas, Tristram Thomas. {MINV 80:456}

## Seventh Generation

35. NICHOLAS GOLDSBOROUGH, b. 25 Feb 1759, d. 6 May 1788, son of Mary (29) and Nicholas Goldsborough, m. 1787, Sarah Harrison.

They were parents of NICHOLAS GOLDSBOROUGH, b. 30 June 1787, m. 25 April 1801, Elizabeth Tench Tilghman, dau. of Col. Tench Tilghman. {Bio of Eastern Shore}

36. SAMUEL THOMAS, son of Trustram (32) Thomas, m. Margaret (N).

Samuel served as 1st lt. in the militia of TA Co., Sword in Hand Company, 4th Battn., 9 April 1778; promoted to captain by 4 ov 1782. He hired a wagon to haul bacon for the use of the Army in May 1778. He was Justice of the Peace and Judge of the Orphans' Court, appointed 21 Nov 1778 and 20 Nov 1779. He was commissioned as sheriff of TA Co. on 30 Oct 1782. {RPTA:186}

Samuel Thomas served as one of the commissioners of tax for TA Co. This body was initially formed under the act to raise supplies for the year 1782.

Samuel Thomas, TA Co., d. leaving a will dated 1789, proved 10 March 1789. To wife Margaret, extx., the buildings on the two lots in Oxford along with the granary be repaired and the yard paled and the garden planked before the division of the estate and to have them for her natural life. To have Negroes, Vin, Ben, Deb, and Sal. To daus. Anne, Susannah, Harriet and Margaret Thomas, the money from the sale of lots in Oxford and granary which are to be sold afer widow's decease. Anne to have Negroes Will and Dinah. Susannah to have Spindle and Cass. Harriet to have Negroes Mat and Dole. Margaret to have Negroes Davy, Jack and Viney. Witnessed by Greenbury Goldsborough, Thomas Bullen, James Nabb. {TAW 3:69}

Samuel was father of ANNE; SUSANNAH; HARRIET; MARGARET.

37. JOSHUA THOMAS, b. c1743, son of Trustram (32) Thomas, m. Elizabeth (N).

On 3 Dec 1773 Joshua Thomas of DO Co., planter, and his wife Elizabeth, conveyed to Samuel Thomas, planter, 50 a. in the Long Neck bequeathed to Joshua by Trustram Thomas, their father - part of *Trustram's Adventure* and *Trustram's Ridge.* {QALR RTK:250}

Unplaced

ABIGAIL THOMAS m. 6 March 1745, James Hobbs. {QALU}

ANN THOMAS m. 13 Aug 1741, John Lamdin. {QALU}

EDWARD THOMAS d. 13 Nov 1716 at Thomas Longs. {TAPE}

ELIZABETH THOMAS, m. 26 Aug 1713, John Standley. {TAPE}

ELIZABETH THOMAS m. 25 Dec 1744, Thomas King. {QALU}

HANNA THOMAS m. 3 Dec 1747, William Whealer. {QALU}

JAMES THOMAS m. Elizabeth (N).

They were parents of Susannah, b. 24 Nov 1731. {TAPE}

JOANNA THOMAS m. 11 Feb 1740, Abner Parrott. {TAPE} Abner was son of George and Hannah Parrott. {See The Parrott Family, vol.3 of this series.}

JOHN THOMAS

On 226 1760 John Thomas, planter, conveyed to James Stainer, planter, 50 a., part of *Widow's Chance* on Brewer's Branch, Wye River adj. a part already sold by Nicholas Brown to John Thomas. {TALR 19:20}

JOHN THOMAS m. Sarah (N).

On 10 Oct 1766 William Cooper of TA Co., and John Thomas and his wife Sarah of QA Co., conveyed to Richard Vickars of TA Co., planter, 33 3/4 a., part of *Frances Delight*, originally surveyed for Frances Camperson on w. side of Tuckahoe Creek adj. *Hampton*. {TALR 12:392}

JOHN THOMAS had a dau. Margaret who m. and divorced Philemon Hambleton.

On 4 March 1784 Philemon Hambleton of TA Co., planter, signed an agreement of separation with Margaret Hamilton. Reference is made to the marriage of said Philemon Hambleton to Margaret Thomas, dau. of John Thomas of TA Co., planter, in the year 1751, which proved to be unhappy and the said parties could not by any means cohabit or live contentedly together and being disposed on both side to live separate, was well as to renounce, give up and relinquish all claims and pretensions to the estate or properties of each other, Philemon Hambleton bound himself not to claim any right to the property of Margaret Hamilton as his wife; either of her own acquirement or bequeathed to her by her father John Thomas or any other persons ... and binds himself unto the said Margaret and her father John Thomas, also her brother John Thomas, Jr. {TALR 21:376}

John was father of MARGARET, m. and was legally separated from Philemon Hambleton; JOHN.

MARY THOMAS

On 2 June 1761 Mary Thomas, QA Co., spinster, conveyed to Thomas Clayland, merchant, for security on an indebtedness of £50, a Negro boy named Charles. The account would be due with interest by 1 Jan 1764. {QALR RTF:139}

On 13 May 1762 Mary Thomas, spinster, conveyed to Thomas Clayland, merchant, for a consideration of £193.0.7 ½, a Negro slave woman named Susana; a slave boy named Benjamin; a Negro slave boy named Charles; and a Negro slave girl named Mary. {QALR RTF:208}

MARY THOMAS m. 31 May 1757, Joseph Wilkinson. {QALU}

MARY THOMAS m. James Lawrence 26 May 1731. {QALU}

NICHOLAS THOMAS d. 1 Nov 1716 at Mr. Robins. {TAPE}

REBECCA TOMAS, TA Co., m. 23/7/1692, John Dickinson, TA Co., planter, at the house of John Dickinson. {TATH}

STEPHEN THOMAS m. Rachell Pratt, dau. of William and Mary Pratt.

On 12 March 1767 Mary Pratt, widow and relict of William Pratt, dec'd., gave to her son in law Stephen Thomas (for affection and 2 s.) a Negro boy named George; a Negro boy named Esau; and a Negro girl named Poll born since the death of my husband William Pratt of the body of a Negro woman slave called Ibb who was devised to Rachell Pratt, his dau. (since intermarried with Stephen Thomas) to be possessed after my death. On the same day Stephen Thomas sold to Henry Wright Pratt, for £27.10.0 a Negro boy Esau, a Negro girl Poll which were made over to Stephen Thomas by Mary Pratt. And on the same day Stephen Thomas sold to Solomon Pratt for 5 s. a Negro boy slave named George made over to me by Mary Pratt. {QALR RTG:359, 360}

SUSANNAH THOMAS m. 3 Oct 1745, Nathaniel Curtis. {QALU}

THOMAS THOMAS had a dau. ELIZABETH, who m. 4 July 1673, Peter Sharpe.

On 4 July 1673 William Sharpe, sonne of Peter Sharpe, late of this province deceased married Elizabeth Thomas dau. of Thomas Thomas of said province. Certified by: Howell Powell, John Webb, William Steevens, Junr., William Forde, William Pick, Elizabeth Powell, Magdalin Steevens, Judeth Sharpe, Dorothy Steevens, Sarah Dickason, Sarah Foorde, Ralph Fishborne. {TA Co. Court Proceedings. See The Sharp Family, vol. 4 of this series.}

THOMAS THOMAS, possible son of Thomas (8) or Trustram (10) Thomas.

Thomas Thomas, TA Co., d. leaving a will dated 25 Aug 1758, proved 25 Sep 1758. Children: Samuel and William. Exec. Samuel Wright. Witnessed by John and Joseph Thomas. {MWB 30:572}

The inventory was filed by Samuel Wright on 18 Oct 1758. Signed as next of kin: Joseph Thomas, Christopher Thomas. {MINV 67:115}

The admin. account was submitted by Samuel Wright on 29 July 1761. Representatives: no widow, Samuel Thomas, age 14; William, age 11.

Distribution was made on 29 July 1761 by Samuel Wright to sons William and Thomas. {BFD 3:76}

Thomas was father of SAMUEL, b. c1747; WILLIAM, b. c1750.

TRISTRAM THOMAS m. Mary Skinner 8 Dec 1736. {TAPE} Mary was dau. of Andrew Skinner.

On 8 July 1745 Tristram Thomas and his wife Mary conveyed to Bryan Seeny, 50 a., part of *Sutton* and part of *Hardship* on Lacey's Branch, St. Michaels Creek adj. *Little Bristoll* and *Frankfort St. Michael*. {TALR 16:229}

On 10 May 1749 Anne Ennalls of DO Co., widow, John Eccleston of DO Co. and his wife Dorothy, Joseph Hopkins and his wife Elizabeth, and Tristram Thomas and his wife Mary, conveyed to Coll. Thos. Bozman, *Piney*

*Point's Advantage*, 250 a. on n.e. branch of Third Haven Creek. Anne Ennalls and all of the other wives being daus. of Andrew Skinner, dec'd. - by references to his will. On 10 May 1749 they conveyed to Edward Coombes, son of William Coombes, dec'd., 200 a. on Island Creek called *Nether Foster*. {TALR 17:243, 260}

## THE HENRY TRIPPE FAMILY

1. HENRY TRIPPE (TRIPP), b. 1632, son of Rev. Thomas Trippe of Canterbury, England, came into this province as a free adult in 1663, m. 1st Frances Brooke (widow of Michael Brooke) circa 1665, m. 2nd Elizabeth (N), and d. in March 1697/8. {BDML II:840}

*Commentary: It appears that Henry Trippe was in SM Co. prior to removing to DO Co., noting that a Henry Tripp witnessed the will of Henry Osborn of Leonard's Creek, St. Mary's Co., on 26 Aug 1664. {MWB 1:227} There was also a "Nicholas Tripp" who was bequeathed personalty in the will of Anthony LeCompt, DO Co., dated 9 Sep 1673, proved 25 Oct 1673. {MWB 1:562} His relationship to Henry Trippe is undetermined and there are no further references to Nicholas Tripp in colonial Maryland records.*

Henry Trippe arrived in MD in 1663, having transported himself and three soldiers who had served with him in Flanders, namely Edward Hich, Cuthbert Browne, and John Foster. Henry served in the Lower House of the MD Assembly, 1671-1675, 1681-1682, 1692-1693; Associators' Convention, 1689-1692; Grand Committee of Twenty, 1690-1692; County Court Justice, 1669-1693, and Chief Justice, 1681-1693. He was captain of foot militia, 1676-1689 (paid for his services in the late expedition against the Nanticoke Indians in 1678) and major of horse troops, 1689-1693. {BDML II:840-841; Mowbray I:170; ARMD 13:244; COES:72; Peden's *Colonial Maryland Soldiers and Sailors, 1634-1734*, p. 355}

Capt. Henry Tripp, DO Co., was an extensive land owner. On 17 Aug 1681 he patented the 40 acre tract *Addition to Tripelo's Farm* and between April and July, 1683 he patented the following tracts: 50 acre *Exchange*, 200 acre *Tripp's Neglect*, 100 acre *Dale's Right*, 100 acre *Dale's Addition*, and 200 acre *Apparley*. {MPL 24:355, 508, 534, 542, 25:109}

In August Court 1690, DO Co., Henry Trippe, and others, were charged with not attending the clearing of the highways in Little Choptank Hundred by John LeCompt, overseer of roads. {DOJR}

The children of Henry Trippe were: Henry (m. Susannah Heron); John (resided in NC in 1720, although one source mistakenly stated KY); Edward (m. widow Susan Sherwood Hambleton); William (m. Jean Tate, d. 24 April 1770); Henrietta Maria (m. 1st John Carslake on 25 Nov 1746, TA Co., and 2nd

William Hughs); and (N), a bastard child (b. 1690/1). {Mowbray I:170; BDML II:840; Leonard's *Tavern in the Town*, p. 161}

"Henry Trippe was fined for begetting a bastard child, 1690/1; does not appear in Maryland records after 1693, when he went to England." {BDML II:840} "He did, however, return to the province and spent four years more in Dorchester County before he died." {Mowbray I:163}

On 23 Sep 1693 Henry Trippe returned to England for a visit and on 9 Oct 1694 the Governor and Council of MD made several officer appointments in the DO Co. militia, stating "if it should please God that Major Trippe should return into the country he is to be lieutenant colonel." {ARMD 19:7, 20:153; Mowbray I:170}

*Commentary: It is interesting to note that even though Henry Trippe was a major in 1689 and selected to be a lieutenant colonel in 1694, he is inexplicably referred to as captain at the time of his death in 1697.*

Henry Trippe, DO Co., d. leaving a will dated 12 Sep 1693, proved 21 March 1697. To wife Elizabeth (extx.), tract *Sark* and part of tract *Trippe's Neglect* during life. To eldest son Henry, land afsd. at death of his mother. To second son John, 200 acre tract *Nemcock.* To sons Henry and John afsd., 100 acre tract *Dale's Delight*, 50 acre tract *Exchange*, and 100 acre tract *Dale's Addition*. To son Edward, tract *Trippelow's Forest* and 40 acre tract *Addition to Trippelow's Forest.* To son William, 200 acre tract *Apperley*. To dau. Henrietta, personalty. {MWB 7:324}

On 14 Oct 1697 the MD Council read the petition of Mrs. Elizabeth Tripp, DO Co., for remittance of two fines of 500 lbs. of tobacco each, which was granted and the fines therein specified were ordered to be remitted accordingly. {ARMD 23:230}

Lady Elizabeth Trippe, widow of Major Henry Trippe, d. 1699. {MHS Filing Case A}

On 16 May 1699 the estate of Henry Tripp, DO Co., dec'd., was appraised at £47.2.9 and admin. by Richard Owen. {MINV 18:183}

Henry (I) was the father of: HENRY; JOHN; EDWARD; WILLIAM; HENRIETTA; (N) BASTARD CHILD.

Second Generation

2. HENRY TRIPPE (TRIPP), DO Co., son of Henry (1) Trippe, m. Susannah Heron, and d. c1723/4; his widow m. John Eccleston by 1727. {BDML II:841; Mowbray I:170}

Henry Trippe served in the Lower House of the MD Assembly, 1712-1715, was a DO Co. Court Justice, c1713-c1723, and was a captain in the militia by 1714. {BDML II:841; ARMD 29:353}

On 2 Sep 1714 Henry Tripp, DO Co., patented the 38 acre tract *Rotterdam* and on 10 Aug 1715 he patented the 325 acre tract *Luck by Chance.* {MPL EE6:69, 258}

On 13 Nov 1717 Henry Trippe, DO Co., Gent., acquired from Peter Taylor the 100 acre tract *Robson's Range* at the head of Hunting Creek of Great Choptank River. On the same day Capt. Henry Trippe, DO Co., planter, acquired from Anne Cooke one-half of the tract *Mauldin* containing 500 acres at the mouth of Great Choptank River. {DOLR 7 Old 45-46}

Henry Trippe, DO Co., Gent., d. leaving a will dated 19 Sep 1723, proved 17 Jan 1723/4. To wife Susannah (extx.), 1/3 of personal estate and use of dwelling plantation during widowhood. To son Henry (exec.), a minor son under care of his mother, lands (N) of father Henry Trippe, two tracts (N) bought of Mary Barrott at head of Secretary Sewell's Creek, and parts of tracts *Bath* and *Addition to Bath*. To son John, lands (N) bought of bro. John Trippe and of Edward Ross, and part of tract *Mauldin* bought of Ann Cook. To dau. Elizabeth, tract *Trippe's Horse Range* on Hunting Creek (except 100 acres sold to William Paine). To son Edward, tract *Luck by Chance* on east side of Cabin Creek and 100 acres (N) in Barron Neck. To daus. Sarah and Mary, at age 18, £30 each above their portions. To bros. John, Edward, William and cousins John, William, Jane and Henrietta (children of William Trippe), personalty. To Vestry of Great Choptank Parish, £5 to purchase a piece of plate. To 6 children afsd., residue of estate. {MWB 18:214}

The children of Henry Trippe were: Henry (m. Elizabeth Emerson); John (m. Ann Ennalls); Edward (m. Margaret Murray, d. 1772); Elizabeth (m. 1st William Taylor and 2nd Bartholomew Ennalls); Sarah (m. Philip Emerson and both d. 1755); and, Mary (m. Jacob Hindman on 29 Jan 1739 and d. 1782; he d. 1766). {Mowbray I:171; BDML II:841}

On 13 Nov 1723 Susannah Trippe, DO Co., was listed as a creditor in the estate of Richard Fairbrother, dec'd., whose estate was appraised by William Trippe and admin. by Rachell Fairbrother. {MINV 9:194}

On 3 April 1724 the estate of Capt. Henry Trippe, DO Co., Gent., dec'd., was appraised at £945.0.7 and approved by Susannah Trippe, extx. Next of kin were listed as Edward Trippe and William Trippe. Creditors were Edward Trippe and William Murray. Accounts were filed on 12 April 1725 and 22 May 1725 by Mrs. Susannah Trippe and Henry Trippe. {MINV 9:341, 10:331; MDAD 6:332}

On 21 Oct 1727 the estate of Henry Trippe, DO Co., dec'd., was admin. by John Eccleston, his wife Susannah Eccleston, and Henry Trippe. The named legatees were bro. Edward Trippe, William Trippe, 2 sons (N) of William Trippe, 2 daus. (N) of William Trippe, and John Trippe. {MDAD 8:359}

In 1728 John Eccleston, wife Susanna Eccleston, and Henry Trippe, DO Co., extx. and exec. of Henry Trippe, DO Co., dec'd., had brought action against John Brannock, DO Co., for the sum of 3,753 lbs. of tobacco and the judgment of Hon. Henry Ennalls was appealed by Brannock's petition to the MD Council on 5 June 1730. {DOJR; ARMD 25:532}

Henry (II) was the father of: WILLIAM; HENRY; JOHN; EDWARD; ELIZABETH; SARAH; MARY.

3. JOHN TRIPPE (TRIPP), DO Co. and NC, son of Henry (1) Trippe, m. (N), moved to NC by 1720 and settled in Bath Co. From him the Trippe family in GA is descended [no names were given]. {MHS Filing Case A}

On 23 June 1706 John Trippe witnessed the will of Lanslett Beck in which he bequeathed his entire estate in DO Co., MD and Lewes, PA [now DE] to John Brannock. {MWB 14:60}

On 16 June 1720 John Trippe, of NC, Gent., conveyed to Henry Trippe, DO Co., Gent., the 200 acre tract *Nemcock* on Armstrong's Bay, the 200 acre tract *Trippe's Neglect* near Trippe's Bay, between two tracts of Henry Trippe, dec'd., called *Sark* and *Nemcock*, except a small part of *Trippe's Neglect* devised by said Henry Trippe, dec'd., to his said son Henry Trippe by his last will and testament. {DOLR 8 Old 23}

4. EDWARD TRIPPE (TRIPP), DO Co., son of Henry (1) Trippe, m. Susan (Sherwood) Hambleton, widow of Philemon Hambleton and dau. of Hugh and Mary Sherwood. It appears that Edward Trippe m. 2nd to Mary (N) by 1747. {Mowbray I:170; DOLR 14 Old 171}

On 10 Oct 1707 Edward Tripp, DO Co., Deputy Surveyor, patented the 136 acre tract *Hodson's Release* and on 10 April 1715 he patented the 370 acre tract *Tripp's Desire*. {MPL DD5:372, EE6:269}

On 12 June 1716 Edward Trippe, DO Co., acquired from John Tench a 177 acre part of the tract *Tenches Regulation* on Chickimacomoco River. {DOLR 6 Old 271}

On 9 Sep 1730 Edward Trippe, DO Co., witnessed the will of Samuel Long. {MWB 20:107}

Edward Trippe, Esq., was High Sheriff of DO Co. by 1740 and served to at least 1743. {DOLR 10 Old 121; MINV 27:396}

On 2 Nov 1747 Edward Trippe, DO Co., conveyed to his son John Trippe, DO Co., a 177 acre part of *Tripp's Desire* on the north side of Chickacomoco River. The conveyance was acknowledged by Edward Trippe and wife {DOLR 14 Old 171}

On 21 Nov 1747 Edward Trippe, DO Co., conveyed to his sons Edward Trippe, Jr. and William Trippe, DO Co., a 370 acre part of *Tripp's Desire* on the west side of Chickacomoco River. {DOLR 14 Old 229}

In 1749 Edward Trippe, Sr., dec'd. was listed among many others on a list of debts due the estate of Major Thomas Nevett, DO Co., dec'd. {MINV 42:145-166}

On 13 May 1751 the estate of Mr. Edward Trippe, DO Co., dec'd., was appraised at £233.10.0 and approved by Mary Trippe. Next of kin were listed as Edward Trippe of Choptank and John Trippe. {MINV 47:78}

On 5 Feb 1753 the estate of Edward Trippe, DO Co., dec'd., was admin. by Mary Trippe. {MDAD 33:434}

On 3 Feb 1755 Edward Trippe, Jr., DO Co., wrote his will and mentioned his father Edward Trippe, dec'd., and bro. John Trippe. {MWB 30:188}

Edward was the father of: EDWARD, JR.; JOHN; WILLIAM; prob. MARY.

5. WILLIAM TRIPPE (TRIPP), DO Co., son of Henry (1) Trippe, m. Jean or Jane Tate, and d. 24 April 1770. {Mowbray I:170}

On 4 March 1729/30 William Tripp, DO Co., acquired from Solomon Bryan and wife Margaret, part of two tracts called *Guiney* and *Gotham* on the east side of Todd's Point, containing 12 acres. {DOLR 8 Old 320}

On 25 Nov 1734 William Trippe, DO Co., conveyed to Henry Trippe, DO Co. (in consideration of one moiety of three tracts, 100 acre *Dale's Right*, 100 acre *Dale's Addition*, and 50 acre *Exchange* in Cason's Neck on the north side of Little Choptank River) the 200 acre tract *Apparley* on the south side of Watts Creek. {DOLR 9 Old 280-281}

On 24 June 1740 William Tripp, DO Co., patented the 114 acre tract *Guiney Plantation*. {MPL LGB:130}

In 1749 William Trippe (Cooks Point), DO Co., was listed among many others on a long list of debts due the estate of Major Thomas Nevett, dec'd. {MINV 42:145-166}

On 1 Oct 1750 William Trippe, DO Co., Gent., conveyed to his sons Edward Trippe and Henry Trippe, and his dau. Elizabeth Noell, wife of Edward Noell, slaves and personalty. {DOLR 14 Old 442}

The children of William and Jean Trippe were: Henrietta (m. a Hughes); Elizabeth (m. Edward Noel of *Castle Haven*); William (m. 1st Elizabeth Gibson, widow of Jacob Gibson, m. 2nd Elizabeth Skinner of TA Co., and d. 1777); Edward (m. Sarah Byus, widow of Joseph Byus and dau. of Bazell Noel (b. 17 April 1711, m. Elizabeth Noel); Jean Mackallin; and, Henry (d. 1761). "This Henry Trippe was not named in the will of his father William Trippe nor is he named in several genealogies that show the children of William

Tripppe, but he is readily identified by his will dated 9 Feb 1761." {Quoted from Mowbray's *First Dorchester Families*, p. 172; MWB 31:442}

In a 1758 deposition William Trippe, DO Co., stated he was about 70 years old and mentioned the survey of the tract *Addition to Wright's Lot* by Henry Trippe and others about 38 years ago. {DOLR 16 Old 212}

William Trippe, Sr., DO Co., d. leaving a will proved on 21 July 1770 (date written was not indicated), naming children Henrietta Hews [Hughes], Elizabeth Noel (wife of William Noel), Jean Mackallom [McCallum], William Trippe, Edward Trippe, and John Trippe (exec.); granddau. Sarah Castlick [Carslake]; also mentioned tract *Cason's Neck*. {MWB 38:147}

William was the father of: WILLIAM, JR.; EDWARD; JOHN; HENRY (d. 1761); HENRIETTA MARIA (m. 1st John Carslake and 2nd William Hughes); ELIZABETH (m. Edward Noel); JEAN or JANE (m. Archibald McCallum). {Leonard's *Tavern in the Town*, p. 161; MHS Filing Case A}

## Third Generation

6. WILLIAM TRIPPE, DO Co., son of Henry (2) Trippe, m. Margaret Hudson (Hodson), widow of Daniel Hudson (Hodson), by 1731.

On 8 June 1731 William Trippe and wife Margaret, DO Co., conveyed to Mark Manlove, KE Co. on Delaware, the 50 acre tract *Hudson's Lott* formerly granted to Robert Hodson on Todd's Bay, having passed at his death to his eldest son Daniel Hudson and having been devised by said Daniel to his widow Margaret, now the wife of William Trippe. {DOLR 8 Old 416}

William was poss. the father of: WILLIAM.

7. HENRY TRIPPE (TRIPP), DO Co., son of Henry (2) Trippe, m. Elizabeth Emerson (dau. of Major Thomas Emerson, TA Co.), lived at *Carthagena* and d. in December, 1744; Elizabeth d. by 1770. {BDML II:841; Mowbray I:171. See also "\The Thomas Emerson Family in Volume 3 of this series}

In 1724 Henry Tripp, DO Co., patented the 30 acre tract *Turkey Point.* {MPL ILA:804}

On 2 June 1727 Henry Trippe, DO Co., planter, acquired from Pemetosusk, Queen of the Hatch Swamp Indians, and Wecampo, Ruler of the Abaco Indians, and other Indians, land in the fork of Secretary Creek, being part of the tract *Bath*, containing 500 acres for the purchase price of £26. {DOLR 8 Old 161}

On 13 March 1727 John Eccleston and Henry Trippe, DO Co., acquired from Peter Taylor, DO Co., Gent., the 150 acre tract *Brice's Adventure* on the north side of Cabin Creek. {DOLR 8 Old 180}

On 16 Aug 1728 Henry Trippe, DO Co., acquired from Major Henry Ennalls, DO Co., Gent., 800 acres (N) on Secretary Creek. {DOLR 8 Old 230}

On 17 Nov 1730 William Taylor, DO Co., wrote his will and bequeathed the tract *Tripp's Horse Range* to Henry Trippe to discharge a bond to Shadrick Feddeman and if should bond not be recovered said land would go to wife Elizabeth Taylor. {MWB 20:147}

On 12 June 1732 John Eccleston and Henry Trippe, DO Co., conveyed to Edward Tripp, son of Capt. Henry Tripp, dec'd., 100 acres of tract *Brice's Adventure* on the east side of Great Choptank River at Cabin Creek. {DOLR 8 Old 472}

On 16 Nov 1732 John Eccleston, DO Co., conveyed to Henry Tripp, DO Co., all his right in the tract *Partnership*, taken up by Eccleston and Trippe, located on the west side of Castle Haven Creek and the south side of Great Choptank River, containing 450 acres excepting two acres whereon the new chapel now stands. On 13 Jan 1734/5 Henry Trippe, DO Co., Gent., conveyed to William Beckingham, DO Co., Gent., a 50 acre part of said tract. {DOLR 9 Old 36, 244}

On 29 Aug 1736 James Trego, DO Co., wrote his will and bequeathed to Henry Trippe, DO Co., he having bought of testator the plantation and land on Blackwater River whereon his father (N) lived, being part of two tracts *Anchor* and *Hope* bought by said father (N) from Robert Dicks and John Creek, said plantation is hereby bequeathed to said Henry Trippe who is also named exec. and residuary legatee. One of the witnesses was Edward Trippe. {MWB 22:46}

Henry Tripp (Trippe), DO Co., was a very extensive land owner, having also patented the following tracts: 80 acre *Sandy Hill* on 1 June 1734; 50 acre *Tripp's Entrance* on 19 June 1734; 1,680 acre *Tripp's Regulation*; 455 acre *Partnership* on 7 Oct 1736; 400 acre *Tripp's Chance* on 25 Jan 1740; 1,250 acre *Cartagena* on 24 June 1740; 25 acre *Tripp's Delight* on 10 Dec 1740; and, 150 acre *Tripp's Security* on 1 Aug 1743. {MPL EI1:218; EI2:142, 398, 886; EI4:420; EI6:334, 605; LGB:132}

On 14 March 1739/40 Henry Trippe, DO Co., Gent., conveyed to Charles Stanford, Jr., DO Co., a 170 acre part of *Hoccady*, now called *Trippe's Closure*, on the east side of Blackwater River. {DOLR 11 Old 3}

On 14 Aug 1740 Henry Trippe, DO Co., Gent., conveyed to William Trippe, DO Co., Gent., an 86 acre part of *Trippe's Regulation* or *Sark*. {DOLR 11 Old 2}

On 23 May 1741 Henry Trippe, DO Co., and wife Elizabeth, conveyed to Charles Goldsborough, DO Co., the tract *Horn* on Great Choptank River where Elizabeth Taylor now lives, and tracts *Deoborow* and *Pinder's Garden* which are supposed to lie within the bounds of *Horn*. {DOLR 10 Old 60}

Henry Trippe served in the Lower House of the MD Assembly, 1734-1744 (he had been discharged from the Assembly on 21 July 1740 for accepting the position of Deputy Commissary of DO Co., but after the governor objected to his dismissal, he was reelected and qualified on 4 June 1741). He was also a County Court Justice, 1731-1734, Sheriff, 1731-1734, a Justice of the Court of Oyer, Terminer and Gaol Delivery (commissioned 1740), and a captain in the militia by 1737 and major by 1744. Henry was involved in mercantile activities with John Anderson (trading as Henry Trippe & Co.) and they, along with William Edmondson, built the schooner *Charming Betty* in 1735; he also owned a mill. Major Henry Trippe d. at the beginning of December, 1744, DO Co. {BDML II:841-842; *MD Gazette*, 17 Jan 1745}

On 10 Dec 1743 Henry Trippe, DO Co., Gent., acquired from Andrew Ramsey, DO Co., the 200 acre tract *Charletown* and the adj. 25 acre tract *Addition to Charletown* near Cabin Creek. {DOLR 11 Old 133}

On 14 Feb 1744/5 the estate of Major Henry Trippe, DO Co., dec'd., was appraised at £1791.14.9 and the next of kin were listed as Edward Trippe and Elizabeth Ennalls. {MINV 31:173}

On 3 Aug 1745 an account was filed by Elizabeth Trippe, admx. of Major Henry Trippe, DO Co., dec'd. {MINV 31:445}

On 24 Nov 1747 Elizabeth Tripp, DO Co., patented the 225 acre tract *Tripp's Desire*. {MPL BY1:94}

On 27 Nov 1748 Elizabeth Trippe, DO Co., witnessed the will of John Speeding. {MWB 27:286}

The children of Henry Trippe were: Henry (d. 1770, unm.); Mary Emerson (c1739-1811, m. Robert Goldsborough IV on 22 Sep 1768); Sarah (m. Henry Callister in 1748); Ann (m. John Dickinson); and, Elizabeth (m. George Maxwell, of CH Co., merchant). {BDML II:841}

On 8 Dec 1749 an account was filed by Mrs. Elizabeth Trippe, admx. of Henry Trippe, DO Co., dec'd., and the next of kin were listed as Edward Trippe and Mary Hindman. {MINV 42:139-140}

On 10 Aug 1754 Elizabeth Trippe, DO Co., conveyed to Daniel Payne, DO Co., a 65 acre part of the tract now called *Tripp's Desire*, it being a part of that land sold by Henry Trippe, dec'd., to William Pain, father of the said Daniel, by the name of *Tripp's Horse Range*. {DOLR 15 Old 165}

On 5 June 1759 Elizabeth Trippe, DO Co., conveyed to William Wright, son of Roger, DO Co., the remaining part of *Tripp's Desire* which is left unsold and taken away by John Nicolls land called *Hampton*, containing 63 acres. {DOLR 16 Old 168}

On 1 Jan 1763 Elizabeth Trippe, DO Co., widow, and Henry Trippe, son and heir of Henry Trippe, dec'd., conveyed to James Polson, DO Co., a 238 acre part of the tract *Trippe's Regulation*. {DOLR 18 Old 271}

Elizabeth Trippe, widow of Henry, prob. d. in 1765 because on 31 Oct 1765 her son Henry Trippe mortgaged to George Maxwell, CH Co., merchant, a 1,140 acre part of the tract *Carthagena* where Mrs. Elizabeth Trippe lately dwelt. {DOLR 21 Old 1}

Henry (III) was the father of: HENRY; MARY EMERSON; SARAH; ANN; ELIZABETH.

8. JOHN TRIPPE, DO Co., son of Henry (2) Trippe, m. Anne Ennalls and d. by 5 May 1745 (date of admin. bond); she m. 2nd to Edward (16) Trippe, Jr. {BDML I:310; Mowbray I:171; MWB 30:14; MHS Filing Case A}

On 11 Nov 1731 John Trippe, DO Co., son of Henry Trippe, dec'd., acquired from Edward Ross, DO Co., the tract *Rosses Range* on Rosses Neck and Steward's Creek of Little Choptank River, left to the said Ross by the will of his dec'd. father (N). {DOLR 8 Old 448}

On 15 May 1745 the estate of John Trippe, DO Co., dec'd., was appraised at £292.13.0 and approved on 19 July 1745 by Anne Trippe, admx. Next of kin were listed as Edward Trippe and Elizabeth Ennalls. {MINV 31:110}

On 19 Sep 1745 Anne Trippe, DO Co., Gentlewoman, conveyed to her dau. Elizabeth Trippe, DO Co., part of two tracts containing 140 acres on the west side of Transquaking River called *Bristoll* and *Addition to Bristoll* located near John Fallin's dwelling house near Jonathan Morriston's tobacco house, adj. *Alexander's Place*. {DOLR 12 Old 198}

On 4 March 1752 the estate of John Trippe, DO Co., dec'd., was admin. by Anne Trippe (exec.), wife of Edward Trippe, Jr. The only named representative was a minor child Elizabeth Trippe. {MDAD 32:287}

On 7 Feb 1753 the estate of John Trippe, DO Co., dec'd., was admin. by Ann Trippe, wife of Edward Trippe, Jr., and the next of kin were listed as Edward Trippe and William Trippe. {MINV 53:57}

Hon. Joseph Ennalls, DO Co., b. c1745, m. 1st to Mary Trippe, dau. of Edward Trippe, Jr. and wife Anne, and granddau. of Edward Trippe (d. c1752) and wife Mary. Mary (Trippe) Ennalls, wife of Joseph Ennalls, d. c1773. Her mother's 1st husband was John Trippe (d. c1746). Joseph Ennalls m. 2nd to Sarah Heron and d. 10 Nov 1779. {BDML I:310}

In 1772 Edward Trippe, DO Co., d. and left a will in which he named several nieces and nephews, including nieces Elizabeth Eccleston and Leah Hayward to whom he bequeathed negroes and personalty. {MWB 39:3}

In 1774 the estate of Edward Trippe was admin. and the account again mentioned several nieces and nephews, including Elizabeth Eccleston (wife of Hugh Eccleston) and Leah Howard (wife of Benjamin Howard). {MDAD 71:229}

John was the father of: ELIZABETH (m. Hugh Eccleston); LEAH (m. Benjamin Howard or Hayward).

9. EDWARD TRIPPE (TRIPP), DO Co., son of Henry (2) Trippe, m. Margaret Murray (dau. of Dr. William Murray, chirurgeon of Cambridge, MD), and d. in the fall of 1772, d.s.p. {MHS Filing Case A}

On 12 June 1732 Edward Tripp, DO Co., son of Capt. Henry Tripp, dec'd., acquired from John Eccleston and Henry Trippe, DO Co., the 100 acre tract *Brice's Adventure* on the east side of Great Choptank River at Cabin Creek. {DOLR 8 Old 472}

On 10 Nov 1736 Edward Tripp, DO Co., son of Capt. Henry Tripp, dec'd., patented the 100 acre tract *Buck Range* and on 21 Oct 1743 the 535 acre tract *Trippe's Good Luck*. {MPL EI2:132, PT1:79}

On 25 Nov 1745 Edward Trippe, DO Co., Gent., and wife Margaret, conveyed to Henry Hooper, DO Co., Gent., part of a tract called *Goodridge's Choyce* between Blinkhorne's Creek and Cabin Creek. {DOLR 12 Old 186}

On 15 June 1759 William Murray, DO Co., chyrurgeon, conveyed to his dau. Margaret Trippe, wife of Edward Trippe, Gent., the eleventh lot in the town of Cambridge, containing 3/4 acre. On 5 Jan 1762 they conveyed the lot to James Murray. {DOLR 16 Old 181, 18 Old 43}

William Murray, DO Co., d. leaving a will dated 11 Oct 1762, proved 22 Nov 1763, naming dau. Margaret Trippe (among others). {MWB 31:1037}

David Murray, DO Co., Gent., d. leaving a will dated 29 Jan 1764, proved 15 March 1764, naming among others, sis. Margaret Trippe and Edward Trippe. {MWB 32:135}

On 8 June 1764 the estate of Mr. David Murray, DO Co., dec'd., was appraised at £1991.3.0 and approved on 15 Aug 1765 by James Murray, exec. Next of kin were listed as Margaret Trippe and Lilly Hamilton. {MINV 88:304}

Edward Trippe, DO Co., d. leaving a will dated 28 March 1772, proved 10 Nov 1772. To wife Margaret Trippe, negroes Old Peter, Stephan, Bell (and her 3 ch. Juba, Cassey and Page), Jady, Rhody, Job, Addam, Young Peter, Norah, Jenny, Caroline, Patience, Jacob, Lyddia, Hester, and Alice; stock; use of lands (N) during lifetime; £50; and, residue of personal estate. To nephew Edward Hindman, at my wife's death, all lands (N) on south side of Clinkhorne Branch. To niece Elizabeth Maxwell, negro Simon. To niece Ann Dickenson, negro (N) and her 2 ch. Harry and Jane. To niece Mary Emerson Goldsborough, negroes Doll and Iago, and part of tracts *Rochester* and *Goodridge's Choice*. To nephew William Hindman, after wife's death, dwelling plantation (N) and other

(N) lands. To David Murray, son of James Murray, negroes Pris and Joe. To William Littleton Murray, negro Nan. To niece Elizabeth Eccleston, negroes Nero and Rachel. To niece Leah Howard, negro Cato. To niece Sarah Hindman, £32. To cousin John Trippe, son of William Trippe, my wearing apparel. To 3 nieces Elizabeth Eccleston, Mary Emerson Goldsborough and Leah Hayward, other half of my personal estate. {MWB 39:3}

On 19 July 1773 the estate of Edward Trippe, DO Co., dec'd., was appraised at £2019.1.9 and approved by Margaret Trippe, extx. Next of kin were listed as Mary Hindman and Elizabeth Ennalls (wife of B. Ennalls and sis. to Edward Trippe). {MINV 112:225}

On 20 May 1774 the estate of Edward Trippe, DO Co., dec'd., was admin. by Margaret Trippe, extx., and named the following legatees: Sarah Hindman; Elizabeth Maxwell, wife of George Maxwell (received negro Simon); Mary Emerson Goldsborough, wife of Robert Goldsborough 4th (received negro Doll); Leah Howard, wife of Benjamin Howard (received negro Cato); Elizabeth Eccleston, wife of Hugh Eccleston (received negroes Nero and Rachel); Anne Dickson, wife of John Dickson (received negro Dido and her 2 ch., negroes Harry and June); David Murray (received negroes Priss and Joe) and William Littleton Murray (received negro Nan), paid to their father James Murray; and, exec. (accountant) John Trippe (received negroes Old Peter, Stephen, Bell (and her 3 ch., negroes Juba, Casey and Page), Jady, Rhody, Job, Young Peter, Norah, Jenny, Caroline, Patience, Jacob, Lydia, Hester, Alice, Jemmy and Chloe). {MDAD 71:299}

On 28 May 1774 final distribution of the estate of Edward Trippe, DO Co., dec'd., was made by Mrs. Margaret Trippe (extx.) to widow (N), one-half of estate, with residue to 3 nieces equally, Elizabeth Eccleston, Mary Emerson Goldsborough, and Leah Haywood. Sureties were Henry Murray and James Murray. {BFD 7:12}

On 12 Aug, 1 Oct, and 1 Nov 1782 Margaret Trippe, DO Co., rendered material aid by supplying wheat for the use of the military as verified by Robertson Stevens, Commissary. {RPDO:244; MSA MdHR6636-42}

On 12 Oct 1785 Margaret Trippe, DO Co., guardian of William Littleton Murray and Sarah Murray, conveyed to Nicholas Hammond, DO Co., Gent., a lease for 4 years of the land in Cambridge now in possession of the said Hammond on the main street, adj. lands of the late Dr. Henry Murray, adj. land of Archibald Patison, and adj. lands of the said William Littleton Murray now in possession of the said Patison. {DOLR 5 NH 148}

10. ELIZABETH TRIPPE, DO Co., dau. of Henry (2) Trippe, m. 1st William Taylor (d. 1730) and m. 2nd by 1735 to Hon. Bartholomew Ennalls (b. c1700, m. 1st to Mary Smith, d. 1783). {BDML I:307, II:841; MWB 30:14}

On 24 July 1724 Elizabeth Trippe, DO Co., witnessed the will of John Harwood. {MWB 18:323}

William Taylor, DO Co., d. leaving a will dated 27 Nov 1730, proved 3 March 1730/1. To wife Elizabeth (extx.), all land (N) lying between the Beverdam and Second Branch with dwelling plantation (N) during life. To dau. Mary, afsd. lands at decease of wife and residue of real estate; she dying without issue to pass to cousin Thomas Taylor Price; he failing issue to pass to Charles and Thomas Staplefort, sons of George Staplefort. To Henry Trippe, tract *Tripp's Horse Range* and personalty, to discharge a bond to Shadrick Feddeman; should bond not be recovered, said lands to wife Elizabeth. {MWB 20:147}

In 1755 Sarah Emerson, DO Co., wrote her will and mentioned her niece Leah Ennalls (dau. of Bartholomew Ennalls). {MWB 30:14}

Elizabeth (Trippe) (Taylor) Ennalls was the mother of: MARY TAYLOR; JOSEPH ENNALLS (b. 1735, resided in NC by 1785); HENRY ENNALLS (b. 1739); WILLIAM ENNALLS (b. 1741); BARTHOLOMEW ENNALLS (b. 1746, m. 1st Sally Hooper and 2nd Nancy Keene); MARY ENNALLS; SARAH ENNALLS; ANN ENNALLS (b. 1737); LEAH ENNALLS (b. 1743). {BDML I:307}

11. SARAH TRIPPE, DO Co. and TA Co., dau. of Henry (2) Trippe, m. Philip Emerson (son of Major Thomas Emerson, TA Co.), d.s.p. {See The Thomas Emerson Family in Volume 3 of this series}

Philip Emerson, DO Co., d. leaving a will dated 21 July 1755, proved 27 Nov 1755, naming wife Sarah (extx.) and nieces and nephews Elizabeth Trippe, Mary Emerson Trippe, William Coursey, Jr., Elizabeth Coursey (dau. of William Coursey), Mary Coursey (dau. of William Coursey), Mary Stansbury (wife of Tobias Stansbury of Baltimore), and Henry Trippe; also mentioned Ann Trippe and tracts *Harwood Lyon, Kelding, Buchingham, Hambleton Park, Widow's Chance, Whetstone*, and *Addition*. {MWB 30:9}

Sarah Emerson, DO Co., d. leaving a will dated 1 Oct 1755, proved 23 Dec 1755, naming niece Elizabeth Trippe (dau. of Henry Trippe), sister Mary Hindman, niece Mary Hindman (eldest dau. of Jacob Hindman), niece Elizabeth Hindman (dau. of Jacob Hindman), nephew Jacob Hindman 3rd (son of Jacob Hindman), niece Leah Ennalls (dau. of Bartholomew Ennalls), nieces Sarah, Margaret and Betsey Callister, niece Ann Trippe (dau. of Henry Trippe), sister Elizabeth Ennalls, sister Margaret Tripp, bro. Edward Tripp, DO Co. (exec.), Sarah Stansbury (extx., dau. of Tobias Stansbury), Jacob Hindman, TA Co.

(exec.), William Anderson (merchant in London), Margaret Murray (dau. of Dr. Henry Murray), Esther Brown, and Mary Pritchard. {MWB 30:14}

On 22 March 1756 the estate of Mr. Philip Emerson, TA Co., dec'd., was appraised at £1934.12.11 and approved on 23 April 1756 by Elizabeth Trippe, Jr., admx. Next of kin were listed as Elizabeth Trippe and Ann Trippe. {MINV 61:295}

12. MARY TRIPPE, DO Co. and TA Co., dau. of Henry (2) Trippe, m. Hon. Jacob Hindman (b. c1705-1710, son of Rev. James Hindman, d. 9 Sep 1766) on 29 Jan 1739 and d. 1782. {Mowbray I:171; BDML I:442, II:841}

The children of Jacob Hindman and Mary Trippe were: James Hindman (b. 20 June 1741, m. 1st Marian Anderson and 2nd Elizabeth Hamilton, d. 18 Feb 1830, d.s.p.); William Hindman (b. 1 April 1743, d. 19 Jan 1822, unm.); Rev. Jacob Henderson Hindman (d. 1781, d.s.p.); Edward Hindman (m. Ann Walker, widow of Andrew Mein and dau. of Rev. Philip Walker, d. 1781, d.s.p.); Col. John Hindman (m. Esther Nicholson, d. by 1794, a physician); Mary Hindman (drowned, age 12); Elizabeth Hindman (m. William Perry, d. by 1788); and, Sarah Hindman (d. c1782, unm.). {*MD Genealogies* II:66; BDML I:442}

In 1755 three of the Hindman children, Jacob, Sarah and Elizabeth, were named in the will of their aunt Sarah Emerson. {MWB 30:14}

In 1772 three other Hindman children, Edward, William and Mary, were named in the will of their uncle Edward Trippe. {MWB 39:3}

On 9 April 1781 William Hindman, TA Co., conveyed to James Murray, DO Co., a reversion interest in tracts called *Rochester, Trippe's Good Luck, Walker's Chance, Goodridge's Choice* and any other lands devised by the will of Edward Trippe, dec'd., to his wife Margaret Trippe during her life and to his nephew William Hindman after her death. {DOLR 28 Old 300}

Mary (Trippe) Hindman was the mother of: JAMES HINDMAN; WILLIAM HINDMAN; JACOB HENDERSON HINDMAN; EDWARD HINDMAN; JOHN HINDMAN; MARY HINDMAN; ELIZABETH HINDMAN; SARAH HINDMAN.

13. JOHN TRIPPE, JR., DO Co., son of Edward (4) Trippe, prob. m. Ann Hodson, and d. 1774. {MWB 30:632, 40:120}

In 1730 the estate of Robert Jones, DO Co., dec'd., was admin. by Mary Jones and the next of kin were listed as Mary Trippe and Elizabeth Hayes. {MINV 15:489}

On 30 July 1730 the estate of James Hayes, DO Co., dec'd., was admin. by Elizabeth Hayes and the next of kin were listed as Elizabeth Trippe, Vienna Hodson and Hester Ann Hodson. {MINV 15:609}

On 17 Oct 1730 the estate of Abel Jones, DO Co., dec'd., was admin. by Elizabeth Hayes and the next of kin were listed as Mary Trippe, Vienna Hodson and Hester Ann Hodson. {MINV 15:734}

In 1742 John Trippe, DO Co., was appointed constable of Little Choptank Hundred. {DOJR}

In 1742 Anne Trippe, wife of John Trippe, and Rosannah Hodson, wife of John Hodson (forest), among others, brought into court a piece of linen and swore that the flax of which the same was made grew in this county. It was adjudged 5th best. {DOJR}

In 1755 John Trippe was named as bro. in the will of Edward Trippe and also mentioned their dec'd. father Edward Trippe. {MWB 30:188}

Mary Trippe, DO Co., d. leaving a will dated 31 Aug 1758 (date proved was not indicated), naming dau. Betty Hodson, son William Trippe, son John Trippe, and Henry Hodson (son of John Hodson) to receive negro girl Selar who is to be left in care of his aunt Betty Hodson or Uncle Billy until he comes of age. It was also indicated the estate to be divided on 8 Sep 1758. {MWB 30:632}

Mary Hodson, DO Co., Great Choptank Parish, d. leaving a will dated 6 May 1758, proved 14 June 1758, naming son Edward Hodson, son Hooper Hodson, dau. Ann Hodson, and bro. William Trippe (exec.). One of the witnesses was John Trippe, Jr. {MWB 30:632}

On 14 March 1759 the estate of Mary Hodson, DO Co., dec'd., was admin. by William Trippe, exec. Next of kin were listed as John Trippe and Elizabeth Longfitt. {MINV 67:231}

On 20 April 1761 John Trippe, Jr., DO Co., witnessed the will of George Griffith. On 22 April 1761 John Trippe stated that he had asked, "I suppose you will leave your slaves and cattle to your brother Jonny? to which George answered yes." The will was proved on 28 April 1761. {MWB 31:300}

On 29 Sep 1762 John Trippe, Jr., DO Co., patented the 691 acre tract *Tripp's Enclosure*. {MPL BC18:349}

John Trippe, DO Co., d. leaving a will dated 21 Feb 1774, proved 28 March 1774. To bro. William Trippe, 191 acre part of tract *Trippe's Inclossers*. To 3 sons Joseph, Henry and William Trippe, all lands (N) and tenements equally. To dau. Mary Trippe, negro Dianner. To dau. Ann Trippe, negro Rose. To dau. Elizabeth Trippe, negro Rhoda. To wife Ann Trippe (extx.), 1/3 of estate and a horse during life. {MWB 40:120}

On 5 April 1774 the estate of John Trippe, DO Co., dec'd., was appraised at £760.2.2 and approved on 7 Nov 1774 by Ann Trippe, extx. Next of kin were listed as Elizabeth Langfitt and William Trippe. {MINV 118:417}

On 8 Aug 1775 George Bonwill, DO Co., joiner, conveyed to Joseph Trippe, Henry Trippe and William Trippe, the heirs of John Trippe, a 115 acre part of the tract *Bonwill's Expetiable Lott* on the west side of Chicamacomico River. {DOLR 28 Old 73}

On 14 Jan 1791 several slaves were manumitted in accordance with the will of John Trippe, DO Co., dec'd., and all of the representatives and devisees were mentioned, viz., James Hodson (admin. with will annexed of John Trippe, dec'd.), Henry Trippe, Joseph Trippe (both for himself and as guardian for William Trippe), Ann Trippe, Mary Trippe, Thomas Ennalls (for himself and as guardian of Joseph Ennalls), William Ennalls, John Eccleston (as guardian of John Ennalls), Ann Ennalls, and Elizabeth Ennalls. {DOLR 3 HD 167}

John was the father of: JOSEPH; HENRY; WILLIAM; MARY; ANN; ELIZABETH.

14. WILLIAM TRIPPE, DO Co., son of Edward (4) Trippe, prob. m. Frances Simpson.

On 19 June 1739 the estate of Archibald Simpson, DO Co., dec'd., was admin. by Elinor Simpson and the next of kin were listed as William Trippe and Frances Trippe; however, when Archibald wrote his will on 26 Oct 1738 he only named his wife Eleanor and son John Simpson. {MINV 24:122; MWB 22:45}

In 1742 Frances Trippe, wife of William Trippe, brought into court a piece of linen and swore that the flax of which the same was made grew in this county. It was adjudged 5th best. {DOJR}

William Trippe was bequeathed a 191 acre part of the tract *Trippe's Inclossers* in the will of his bro. John Trippe, DO Co., in 1774. {MWB 40:120}

15. EDWARD TRIPPE, JR., DO Co., son of Edward (4) Trippe, m. Anne (Ennalls) Trippe, widow of John (8) Trippe (d. 1745). {BDML I:310}

On 30 Aug 1738 Edward Trippe, DO Co., Gent., acquired from Tench Francis, TA Co., Gent., the 713 acre tract *Paradice* on the Northwest Fork of Nanticoke River at the head of Newport Branch. {DOLR 10 Old 18}

On 10 Feb 1744/5 Julia Perry, DO Co., Great Choptank Parish, spinster, stated she committed fornication and begat a bastard child. She swore that Edward Trippe, son of Edward Trippe, was the father. {DOJR}

In June Court 1745, DO Co., Ann Trippe filed a petition in which she stated she had the right by descent to a tract called *Endeavour*. She also filed a petition to set levy free her servant man named Shepherd and a negro woman (N) who were both so lame that they were unfit for service; the court approved it. {DOJR}

In November Court 1745, DO Co. Edward Trippe the Elder, who was seized of a tract called *Paradice* which was affected by a survey called *Hapnab at a Venture*, petitioned to have a commission appointed to settle the bounds. {DOJR}

On 5 May 1747 Edward Trippe, DO Co., and wife Anne, conveyed to Bartholomew Ennalls, DO Co., the 500 acre tract *Endeavour* on the west side of the Northwest Fork of Nanticoke River. Also see the original record in the proceedings of the Provincial Court involving Edward Trippe, Bartholomew Ennalls, and William Horton. {DOLR 14 Old 135}

On 11 June 1747 Edward Trippe, DO Co., Gent., and wife Anne, conveyed to James Billings, DO Co., the 200 acre tract *Balea*. {DOLR 14 Old 141}

On 13 July 1748 Edward Trippe, Jr., DO Co., witnessed the will of John Rix. {MWB 27:209}

In 1749 "Edward Trippe, Jr. the 3rd" was listed among many others on a list of debts due the estate of Major Thomas Nevett, DO Co., dec'd. {MINV 42:145-166}

On 4 May 1749 Edward Trippe, Jr., of Transquaking River, DO Co., Gent., and wife Ann, conveyed to James Edge, TA Co., merchant, a 360 acre part of *Paradise*. {DOLR 14 Old 350}

Edward Trippe, DO Co., d. leaving a will dated 3 Feb 1755, proved 19 July 1756, naming dau. Mary Trippe and dec'd. father Edward Trippe and bro. John Trippe (exec.) and Col. Joseph Ennalls (exec.); also mentioned land (N) on Chickmecomoco River. {MWB 30:188}

Joseph Ennalls, DO Co., b. c1745, d. 1779, m. 1st to Mary Trippe, dau. of Edward Trippe, Jr. and wife Anne, and granddau. of Edward Trippe (d. c1752) and wife Mary. Mary Trippe, wife of Joseph Ennalls, d. c1773. Her mother's first husband was John Trippe (d. c1746). Joseph Ennalls m. 2nd to Sarah Heron and d. 1779. {BDML I:310}

On 20 Aug 1756 the estate of Edward Trippe, DO Co., dec'd., was appraised at £613.1.10 and approved on 10 March 1757 by William Trippe, exec. Next of kin were listed as Mary Trippe and William Trippe, Jr. {MINV 63:464}

On 14 Dec 1756 the land of Mary Trippe, orphan of Edward Trippe, dec'd., was valuated by Thomas Pitt and Edward Stephens and mentioned John Trippe as guardian of the orphan. {DOLR 15 Old 443}

On 30 Nov 1763 and 3 Sep 1764 the estate of Edward Trippe, DO Co., dec'd., was admin. by John Trippe (exec.). Next of kin were listed as Elizabeth Langfitt and William Trippe in 1764. {MDAD 50:130; MINV 86:24}

On 3 Sep 1764 an account was filed on the estate of Edward Trippe, Jr., DO Co., dec'd., by John Trippe (exec.) and the named representative was his only child Mary Trippe. Among those who received a payment, however, was the representative (N) of John Trippe (dead) paid the guardian Edward Trippe the elder. {MDAD 52:4}

Edward was the father of: MARY; (N) BASTARD CHILD.

16. MARY TRIPPE, DO Co., prob. dau. of Edward (4) Trippe, m. (N) Hodson.

Mary Hodson, DO Co., Great Choptank Parish, d. leaving a will dated 6 May 1758, proved 14 June 1758, naming son Edward Hodson, son Hooper Hodson, dau. Ann Hodson, and bro. William Trippe (exec.). One of the witnesses was John Trippe, Jr. {MWB 30:632}

On 14 March 1759 the estate of Mary Hodson, DO Co., dec'd., was appraised at £233.12.3 and approved by William Trippe, exec. Next of kin were listed as John Trippe and Elizabeth Longfitt. {MINV 67:231}

On 30 Jan 1761 "Mary Hodson, Edward & John Trippe" appeared among many others on a list of debts due the estate of Col. Joseph Ennalls, DO Co., dec'd. {MINV 79:189-211}

Mary (Trippe) Hodson was the mother of: EDWARD HODSON; HOOPER HODSON; ANN HODSON.

17. EDWARD TRIPPE, DO Co., son of William (5) Trippe, prob. m. 1st Sarah Hambleton and 2nd Sarah (Noel) Byus on 26 Jan 1787 (widow of Joseph Byus and dau. of Bazell Noel). {MINV 69:226; DOLR 2 HD 629; MD Marriages}

On 3 June 1747 Edward Russam, DO Co., planter, wrote his will in which he requested his friend and neighbor Edward Trippe to be his exec. and also to take care of his 3 sons Winlock, Edward and James Russam until they arrive to age 21. {MWB 25:142; MINV 36:222}

In 1749 Edward Trippe, Esq. was listed among many others on a list of debts due the estate of Major Thomas Nevett, DO Co., dec'd. {MINV 42:145-166}

On 2 Jan 1760 the estate of Mr. Philemon Hambleton, TA Co., dec'd., was appraised at £11.5.9 and approved on 1 April 1760 by Edward Trippe and his wife Sarah Trippe, admins. Next of kin were not listed. {MINV 69:226}

James Trippe, of Cambridge, MD, son of Edward and Sarah, m. 1st Elizabeth Pennell and 2nd Mary Pennell. James and Mary Trippe both d. 1812. {Mackenzie 6:144}

In 1790 Edward Noel, DO Co., gave a deposition concerning a marriage contract between Edward Trippe, DO Co., dec'd., and Sarah Trippe, widow of said Edward, and stated that about February, 1787, Edward Trippe, then a widower, married Sarah Byus, widow of Joseph Byus, dec'd. Both of the said parties had children by previous marriages and Henry Trippe was named as a son of said Edward. {DOLR 2 HD 629}

Edward was the father of: JAMES; HENRY; OTHERS (N).

18. JOHN TRIPPE, DO Co., b. 17 April 1711, son of William (5) Trippe, m. Elizabeth Noel (25 April 1729 - 24 April 1778) in 1745, served as a captain in the cavalry during the French and Indian Wars [c1756-1758], and d. 1778.

{Mackenzie 6:445; however, John Trippe is not listed in Clark's *Colonial Soldiers of the South, 1732-1774*}

On 30 Jan 1761 John Trippe appeared among many others on a list of debts due the estate of Col. Joseph Ennalls, DO Co., dec'd. {MINV 79:189-211}

In a 1770 deposition John Trippe, DO Co., son of William Trippe, stated he was about 56 years old. {DOLR 24 Old 303}

John Trippe, DO Co., took the Oath of Allegiance in 1778. {RPDO:244}

John Trippe (1711-1778) m. Elizabeth Noel and fathered 21 children. {Leonard's *Tavern in the Town*, p. 161}

The known children of John and Elizabeth Trippe were: Amelia (m. Col. James Woolford); William (m. Mary Noel, his cousin); Edward (b. 29 June 1771, m. 1st Elizabeth Barney, m. 2nd Ann Tolly Towson, m. 3rd Sarah E. Trippe, dau. of Richard Trippe, and d. 2 Feb 1836); Henrietta (b. 16 April 1774, m. Col. William Birckhead); Levin (killed at sea in command of the privateer *Isabella*); Frances (m. John Elder Gist of BA Co.); and, Mary (m. 1st Major Peter Webb and 2nd Dr. Samuel Dickinson). {Mackenzie 6:445}

James Trippe (1758-1826) is bur. at *Trippe's Regulation* on Todd's Point, in the Neck District, DO Co., next to Edward Trippe (1771-1846), Henrietta Trippe (1776-1858), Sarah Webb (1760-1794), and Margaret Webb (1763-1785). They were prob. siblings which, therefore, may account for some of the 21 children of John Trippe. {RPDO:243; Marshall's DO Co. Tombstone Records I:17}

Peter Webb, DO Co., m. 1st Margaret Trippe on 9 Dec 1782, m. 2nd Sarah Trippe on 22 Feb 1794, and m. 3rd Mary Trippe on 10 May 1796. {MD Marriages}

John was the father of: WILLIAM; EDWARD; LEVIN; AMELIA; HENRIETTA; FRANCES; MARY; SARAH; MARGARET; prob. JAMES; OTHERS (N).

19. WILLIAM TRIPPE, JR., DO Co. and TA Co., son of William (5) Trippe, m. 1st Elizabeth Gibson (widow of Jacob Gibson) on 21 April 1744, TA Co., and m. 2nd Elizabeth Skinner of TA Co. on 21 Jan 1760. They lived at *Canterbury* in TA Co.; he d. 1 June 1777; she d. 9 May 1811, age 75. {Mackenzie 6:445-446; MD Marriages}

On 20 Oct 1746 William Trippe and wife Elizabeth were execs. of the estate of Woolman Gibson, TA Co., dec'd. {MINV 33:285}

In 1748 William Trippe, TA Co., was a soldier in Lt. Tristrim Thomas' Troop of Horse. {COES:83}

On 2 Sep 1761 William Trippe, TA Co., merchant, conveyed to Robert Newcome, TA Co., the tract *Harbour Rouse* on St. Michael's River. {TALR 20:92}

On 29 Dec 1762 William Trippe, Jr., DO Co., patented the 229 acre tract *Trippe's Discovery*. {MPL BC10:741}

On 16 May 1775 William Trippe, TA Co., acquired from Nicholas Goldsborough, son of Nicholas, the 157 acre tract *Marshy Point.* {TALR 20:479}

On 1 April 1788 Elizabeth Trippe, TA Co., manumitted her negro man slave named Frank. On 1 Aug 1788 she manumitted her negro man named Jim Boy. {TALR 22:396, 401}

William was the father of: JAMES; RICHARD; JOHN; EDWARD; MARY; prob. WILLIAM.

20. HENRY TRIPPE, DO Co., son of William (5) Trippe, d.s.p.

Henry Trippe, DO Co., d. leaving a will dated 9 Feb 1761, proved 10 June 1761. To bro. John Trippe (exec.), slaves, after decease of myself and my father William Trippe, use and labor of slaves, and personalty. To bro. Edward Trippe, a silver watch. To nephew Edward Noel, one slave. To sister Jean McCullam, sister Henrietta Hughs, and bro. William Trippe, 1 sh. each. {MWB 31:442}

On 13 June 1761 the estate of Henry Trippe, DO Co., dec'd., was appraised at £186.13.10 and approved on 11 Nov 1761 by John Trippe, exec. Next of kin were listed as William Trippe and William Trippe, Jr. {MINV 75:253}

21. ELIZABETH TRIPPE, DO Co., dau. of William (5) Trippe, m. Capt. Edward Noel (Noell), a MD legislator, and lived at *Castle Haven* in DO Co; she d. 1794; he d. 1797. {BDML II:615; Leonard's *Tavern in the Town*, p. 161. See also The Nowell Family, this vol}

Elizabeth (Trippe) Noel was the mother of: EDWARD NOEL, JR. (m. Miss Betsey Eccleston and had a dau. Delia Noel); ELIZABETH NOEL (m. Rev. James Kemp, Episcopal Bishop of Maryland, and had ch. Edward D. Kemp, Eliza Kemp, and Sarah Kemp); SARAH NOEL (m. Capt. Cox, USN, and had a son Edward Noel Cox); MARY NOEL (m. William Trippe, son of John (19) Trippe and Elizabeth Noel); SOPHIA NOEL (m. (N), d.s.p.). {MHS Filing Case A; Mackenzie 6:444; BDML II:615}

22. JEAN (JANE) TRIPPE, DO Co. and TA Co., dau. of William (5) Trippe, m. Archibald McCallum, TA Co., innholder, bro. of Rev. Neil McCallum, DO Co. {Leonard's *Tavern in the Town*, p. 161}

In 1753 Archibald McCallum, TA Co., was granted a license to keep an ordinary [tavern] in his dwelling near TA Co. courthouse. Through his marriage to Jane Trippe he acquired interest in the Trippe family land called *Maulden* in DO Co. He acquired two tracts in TA Co. called *Heworth* and *Enlargement*, and also land in DO Co. (now CA Co.) called *Williams' Desire* and *Addition to Williams' Desire*. {TALR; DOLR; Leonard:161}

Archibald McCallum (McCullum), TA Co., d. leaving a will dated 9 Nov 1761, proved 4 May 1762, naming wife Jane (extx.) and children Alexander, William and Fanny McCallum (McCullum). {MWB 31:614}

Archibald McCallum's son Archibald, Jr. was not named in his father's will since he had already received *Heworth* as his share of his parents' estate in exchange for his right to the land called *Maulden*. Jane McCallum subsequently sold her land in CA Co. in 1772 and dau. Fanny McCallum m. (N) Bowers. Alexander and William McCallum, sons of Archibald and Jane, were innholders in TA Co. {TALR 18:471; Leonard:160-163}

Jane (Trippe) McCallum was the mother of: ARCHIBALD McCALLUM, JR.; WILLIAM McCALLUM (d. 1793); ALEXANDER McCALLUM (d. 1793); FRANCES (FANNY) McCALLUM.

23. HENRIETTA MARIA TRIPPE, DO Co. and TA Co., dau. of William (5) Trippe, m. 1st John Carslake on 25 Nov 1746, TA Co., and m. 2nd William Hughs by 1760. {Leonard's *Tavern in the Town*, p. 161; MD Marriages}

On 21 Nov 1749 George Beswicks, TA Co. wrote his will and bequeathed to his son Robert Beswicks "one suite of clothes to be made at Mr. John Carslacke's." {MWB 27:305}

On 18 March 1750/1 John Copeling and John Lurkey, TA Co., made oath that they heard John Carslake the younger give to Elizabeth Staner, his riding mare, furniture, etc. No other details or family members were mentioned; this was apparently a nuncupative will that was proved at that time. {MWB 28:32}

On 30 March 1751 the estate of John Carslake, Jr., TA Co., was appraised at £71.8.7 and approved on 10 Jan 1752 by Joseph Hicks, Jr., exec. Next of kin were listed as John Carslake and Thomas Carslake. {MINV 48:189}

On 1 Jan 1753 John Carslake, TA Co., and wife Henrietta, conveyed to Edward Lloyd, Esq., the 60 acre tract *Carslake's Content* on the north side of St. Michaels River. {TALR 18:136} Henrietta Trippe apparently married John Carslake, Sr., not Jr.

On 22 Jan 1760 William Hughes, TA Co., planter, and wife Henrietta Maria, late widow of John Carslake, TA Co., planter, dec'd., conveyed to John Gordon, TA Co., clerk, one-third of the land (N) where John Carslake dwelled in his lifetime, it being the dower of said Henrietta Maria during her life. {TALR 19:30}

William Trippe, Sr., DO Co., left an undated will that was probated on 21 July 1770 and named among the heirs were his dau. Henrietta Hews [Hughs] and granddau. Sarah Castlick [Carslake]. {MWB 38:147}

*Commentary: There is an identification problem in that it appears there were two John Carslakes who had wives named Henrietta: (1) Henrietta Maria*

*Hughes, widow of John Carslake, was the wife of William Hughes by 22 Jan 1760 (see above). {TALR 19:30} (2) On 14 Feb 1769 John Carslake and wife Henrietta Maria, TA Co., acknowledged their deed to Anthony Banning of "part of the tract Barteram as it was holden by John Carslake, grandfather of the said John Carslake, and also Carslake's Discovery." {TALR 20:2} (3) Henrietta Hews was named as dau. of William Trippe in his will in 1770 (see above). {MWB 38:137} (4) On 12 Nov 1771 the lands of John Carslake, TA Co., dec'd., were valuated, said lands now belonging to Thomas Carslake, his son, an infant in the guardianship of his mother Henrietta Maria Carslake. {TALR 20:178} (5) Henrietta Carslake witnessed the will of Martha Humphreys, TA Co., in 1772. {MWB 41:394}*

Henrietta (Trippe) Carslake was the mother of: SARAH CARSLAKE.

Fourth Generation

24. WILLIAM TRIPPE, DO Co., poss. son of William (6) Trippe, m. Elizabeth Fooks, widow of James Fooks.

On 24 Sep 1751 the estate of James Fooks, DO Co., dec'd., was admin. by Elizabeth Fooks (also known as Elizabeth Trippe) and one account mentioned William Trippe was then her husband. {MINV 48:90-91; MDAD 31:200}

On 29 Nov 1758 an account filed in the estate of James Fooks, DO Co., dec'd., by Elizabeth Trippe (wife of William Trippe), admx., mentioned their 8 children (N), all of age. {MDAD 42:304}

25. HENRY TRIPPE, DO Co., son of Henry (7) Trippe, d.s.p.

In November, 1743, Henry Trippe, DO Co., petitioned the court to practice law. {DOJR}

On 13 May 1762 Henry Trippe, son and heir of Henry Trippe, dec'd., and Elizabeth Trippe, conveyed to Henry Bradley, DO Co., the 200 acre tract *Charlton* and 25 acre tract *Addition to Charlton*. {DOLR 18 Old 120}

On 14 Dec 1762 Henry Trippe and Elizabeth Trippe his mother, relict of Henry Trippe, DO Co., dec'd., conveyed to George Maxwell, CH Co., merchant, the 80 acre tract *Sandy Hill* taken up by Henry Trippe, Sr., a 10 3/4 acre part of the tract *Trippe's Security* on the north side of Cabin Creek, and the 150 acre tract *Addition to Mill Land* on a branch of Cabin Creek, excepting 8 acres which runs into an older survey called *The Hope*. On 21 Dec 1762 Henry and Elizabeth Trippe conveyed to John Frazer a 236 acre part of *Trippe's Regulation*, to John Hubbert a 100 acre part of said tract, and to John Trippe a 43 acre part of said tract, all parcels adj. the tract *Gotham* on Todd Bay. {DOLR 18 Old 249, 259-264}

On 1 Jan 1763 Elizabeth Trippe, DO Co., widow, and Henry Trippe, son and heir of Henry Trippe, dec'd., conveyed to James Polson a 238 acre part of the tract *Trippe's Regulation*. {DOLR 18 Old 271}

On 29 Sep 1763 Henry Trippe, DO Co., patented the 254 acre tract *Trippe's Industry*. {MPL BC20:641}

On 17 July 1764 Henry Trippe, DO Co., patented the 50 acre tract *Addition to Mill Land* and the 692 acre tract *Trippe's Regulation*. {MPL BC20:655, 695}

Henry Trippe, DO Co., d. leaving a will dated 5 May 1763, proved 28 Nov 1770, naming mother Elizabeth Trippe, sister Mary Emerson Trippe, niece Margaret Callistor, and nephews Philip and Henry Dickinson (sons of John Dickinson, exec.); also mentioned tract *Carthagena*. {MWB 38:198}

Henry Trippe, DO Co., apparently had written a second will on 1 Feb 1768 which was proved on 16 March 1771, naming sister Mary Emerson Trippe, nieces Sarah Trippe Callister, Margaret Callister, Elizabeth Callister, Harriet Callister, Callister *[sic]* Callister, and nephews Charles Dickinson, Henry Dickinson, and Philip Dickinson; mentioned Isabella McFarlen; also mentioned tracts *Partnership, Trippe's Industry*, and *Carthagena*; John Dickinson, exec. {MWB 38:312}

On 6 June 1771 the estate of Mr. Henry Trippe, DO Co., dec'd., was appraised at £491.13.6 and approved on 17 Nov 1772 by John Dickinson, exec. Next of kin were listed as Edward Trippe and Robert Goldsborough. {MINV 109:404}

26. MARY EMERSON TRIPPE, DO Co. and TA Co., b. c1739, dau. of Henry (7) Trippe, m. Hon. Robert Goldsborough IV (1740-1798), of Myrtle Grove, TA Co., on 22 Sep 1768, and d. 1811. {BDML I:363}

Mary Emerson (Trippe) Goldsborough was the mother of: ROBERT GOLDSBOROUGH (b. & d. 1771); ROBERT HENRY GOLDSBOROUGH (1774-1777); ROBERT HENRY GOLDSBOROUGH (1779-1836, U. S. Senator in 1813); (N) DAU. (b. 1769, d. young); ELIZABETH GOLDSBOROUGH (1776-1798, m. Charles Goldsborough, Gov. of MD in 1819). {BDML I:363}

27. ANN TRIPPE, DO Co. and TA Co., dau. of Henry (7) Trippe, m. Hon. John Dickinson (c1726-1789), a colonel and MD legislator, on 30 March 1758, TA Co. {BDML I:270, II:841}

On 27 Feb 1745/6 Anne Trippe and Timothy Gollyther were listed as next of kin when the estate of Elizabeth Taylor, DO Co., was appraised. {MINV 32:231}

On 30 March 1758 Ann Trippe m. John Dickinson, St. Peter's Parish, TA Co. {ESVR}

On 16 July 1790 Ann Dickinson, DO Co., widow, and John Dickinson, Granby Dickinson and Sophia Dickinson, sons and dau. of John Dickinson, late of DO Co., dec'd., conveyed to Henry Dickinson, DO Co., Gent., also a son of the said John Dickinson, dec'd., the tract *Carthagena* located at the head of Secretary Creek, formerly mortgaged by Henry Trippe to George Maxwell and redeemed by said John Dickinson, dec'd., having been devised by said Henry Trippe, dec'd., to his nephew, the said Henry Dickinson. {DOLR 2 HD 634}

Ann (Trippe) Dickinson was the mother of: CHARLES DICKINSON (b. 23 Feb 1759, d. by 1789), HENRY DICKINSON (b. 15 March 1760, m. Ann Hooper in 1809, d. 1827), PHILIP DICKINSON (b. 24 Jan 1762, d. by 1789); JOHN DICKINSON (d. by 1810, d.s.p.); GRANBY DICKINSON (d. by 1810, d.s.p.); JAMES DICKINSON (b. c1774, d. by 1810, d.s.p.); SOPHIA DICKINSON (m. Stanley Byus Loockerman in 1796, d. by 1810). {ESVR; MWB 38:312; BDML I:270}

28. SARAH TRIPPE, DO Co., dau. of Henry (7) Trippe, m. Henry Callister, TA Co., in 1748. {BDML II:841}

On 11 March 1757 Henry Callister, Oxford, TA Co., merchant, was granted power of atty. by Foster, Ellis and Robert Cunliffe, Esqs., of Liverpool, England, concerning lands in CE Co., KE Co., DO Co., and TA Co. {DOLR 15 Old 539}

On 2 Sep 1776 Sarah Callister was among those who received payment from the estate of John Comegys, KE Co., dec'd. {MDAD 72:389}

In 1781 Harriot Callister, TA Co., was one of 26 people who contacted the Gov. and Council of MD and pledged to support and maintain at their own expense the barge *Experiment* so it could patrol the bay between Kent Point and Tilghman's Island in order to protect them against the enemy. {ARMD 47:584}

Sarah (Trippe) Callister was the mother of: SARAH TRIPPE CALLISTER; MARGARET CALLISTER (m. John M. Kennedy); ELIZABETH EMERSON CALLISTER; HARRIET F. CALLISTER; CALLISTA CALLISTER. {MWB 30:14, 38:312; MHS Filing Case A}

29. ELIZABETH TRIPPE, DO Co. and CH Co., dau. of Henry (7) Trippe, m. George Maxwell, merchant, of Benedict Town, CH Co., on Sun., 23 May 1756 in DO Co. {BDML II:841; *MD Gazette*, 27 May 1756}

On 31 Oct 1765 Henry Trippe, DO Co. [son of Henry, dec'd., and Elizabeth Trippe, prob. now dec'd.], mortgaged to George Maxwell, CH Co., merchant, a 1,140 acre part of the tract *Carthagena* where Mrs. Elizabeth Trippe lately dwelt. {DOLR 21 Old 1}

In 1772 Elizabeth Maxwell was bequeathed negro Simon in the will of her uncle Edward Trippe. {MWB 39:3}

George Maxwell, CH Co., d. leaving a will dated 16 Dec 1774, proved 24 July 1777, naming wife Elizabeth (extx.), son James, and 7 (N) minor daus. to be clothed and maintained by son James until they arrive at age 18 or the day they marry. {CH Co. Probate Records, 1777-1780, p. 39}

On 27 May 1779 distribution of the estate of George Maxwell, CH Co., dec'd., was made to widow Elizabeth and 8 children: to Helen, Elizabeth and Agnes, "at age" [dates of birth not given]; to Sarah, age 16 next Sep 22; to James, age 18 next Aug 28; to May and Mary, twins, age 14 next June 21; and, to Marion, age 11 next Sep 20. {CH Co. Probate Records, 1777-1780, p. 148}

Elizabeth (Trippe) Maxwell was the mother of: JAMES MAXWELL; HELEN MAXWELL; ELIZABETH MAXWELL; AGNES MAXWELL; SARAH MAXWELL; MAY MAXWELL; MARY MAXWELL; MARION MAXWELL.

30. ELIZABETH TRIPPE, DO Co., dau. of John (8) Trippe, m. Hon. Hugh Eccleston (son of Col. John Eccleston and Dorothy Skinner) who was a county justice by November, 1773, and d. by August, 1778. {BDML I:297-298; DOLR 27 Old 47}

On 19 Sep 1745 Anne Trippe, DO Co., Gentlewoman, conveyed to her dau. Elizabeth Trippe, DO Co., part of two tracts containing 140 acres on the west side of Transquaking River called *Bristoll* and *Addition to Bristoll* located near John Fallin's dwelling house near Jonathan Morriston's tobacco house, adj. *Alexander's Place*. {DOLR 12 Old 198}

On 3 April 1751 the lands of Elizabeth Trippe, orphan of John Trippe, dec'd., were valuated, plantations where David Rathel and Thomas Brawdiss live on parts of *Bristol* and *Addition to Bristol*; three tracts in Transquakin Marshes (60 acre *Fair Dealing*, 25 acre *Hogstye*, and 27 acre *Chance*); and, plantations where Daniel Frazier and Robert Ramsey live on parts of *Tripp's Regulation*. {DOLR 15 Old 76}

On 4 March 1752 the estate of John Trippe, DO Co., dec'd., was admin. by Anne Trippe (exec.), now wife of Edward Trippe, Jr. The only named representative was a minor child Elizabeth Trippe. {MDAD 32:287}

On 4 Sep 1764 Hugh Eccleston, DO Co., Gent., and wife Elizabeth, conveyed to Joseph Byus, DO Co., mariner, the 200 acre tract *Trippe's Neglect* on the south side of Great Choptank River near Trippe's Bay between *Sark* and *Nemcocke* and opposite the dwelling plantation where old Henry Trippe formerly lived and who had patented said land. The receipt for the alienation fee indicated "*Trippe's Neglect* alias *Trippe's Regulation*, pt. 200 acres." On that same day Hugh and Elizabeth Eccleston conveyed to William Lee, DO Co., the

200 acre tract *Nemcocke* on the south side of Great Choptank River on Armstrong's Bay adj. *Sark.* The receipt for the alienation fee indicated "*Nemcock* alias *Tripp's Regulation*, pt. 100 acres." On that same day Hugh and Elizabeth Eccleston conveyed to Mary Trippe, Jr., DO Co., a 400 acre part of the tract *Eccleston Regulation Rectified* on the west side of Transquakin River adj. a tract she now holds called *Good Luck.* {DOLR 19 Old 314, 349}

On 19 Aug 1771 Hugh Eccleston, DO Co., planter, and wife Elizabeth, conveyed to Joseph Ennalls, Sr., DO Co., planter, part of two tracts on the west side of Transquakin River called *Bristoll* and *Addition to Bristoll* containing 140 acres, being that part conveyed in a deed from Anne Trippe the mother of the said Elizabeth Eccleston, wife of the said Hugh Eccleston. On 21 Aug 1771 Joseph Ennalls, Sr. leased said land to Hugh and Elizabeth Eccleston for one year and the next day Ennalls conveyed said land to Elizabeth Eccleston for her lifetime with remainder to Hugh Eccleston. {DOLR 25 Old 94-101}

In 1772 Edward Trippe, DO Co., d. and left a will in which he named several nieces and nephews, including Elizabeth Eccleston. {MWB 39:3}

In 1774 the estate of Edward Trippe (who was prob. the bro. of William Trippe) was admin. and the account again mentioned several nieces and nephews, including Elizabeth Eccleston, wife of Hugh Eccleston. {MDAD 71:229}

On 26 Nov 1774 Hugh Eccleston, DO Co., Gent., and wife Elizabeth, conveyed to Edward Speding, DO Co., part of a tract formerly in the possession of Capt. Henry Trippe, DO Co., called *Maulden* on Cook's Point, according to a division made between said Capt. Henry Trippe and Edward Cooke. {DOLR 27 Old 386}

On 24 Aug 1778 a DO Co. land conveyance between John Mills and Henry Murray mentioned Hugh Eccleston was now dec'd. and his exec. was Thomas Firmin Eccleston [his bro.]. {DOLR 1 JCH 131}

On 14 March 1789 John Eccleston, DO Co., Gent., conveyed to Thomas Ennalls, a deed to the 400 acre tract *Eccleston's Regulation Rectified* in order to correct an error in a deed from Hugh Eccleston and his wife Elizabeth to Mary Trippe. {DOLR 2 HD 213}

Elizabeth (Trippe) Eccleston was poss. the mother of: JOHN ECCLESTON; OTHERS (N).

31. LEAH TRIPPE, DO Co., dau. of John (8) Trippe, m. Benjamin Howard or Hayward.

In 1772 Edward Trippe, DO Co., d. and left a will in which he named several nieces and nephews, including Leah Hayward. {MWB 39:3}

In 1774 an account filed in the estate of Edward Trippe [who was prob. the bro. of William Trippe] mentioned several nieces and nephews, including Leah Howard, wife of Benjamin Howard. {MDAD 71:229}

32. JOSEPH TRIPPE, DO Co., son of John (13) Trippe, took the Oath of Allegiance in 1778. {RPDO:244}

33. WILLIAM TRIPPE, DO Co. and TA Co., son of John (18) Trippe, m. cousin Mary Noel (Noell). {BDML II:615; Mackenzie 6:445}

On 9 Feb 1775 Edward Noell, Sr., DO Co., Gent., conveyed to William Trippe, DO Co., Gent., 50 acres of a tract called *Pocaty* and 65 acres of *Harwood's Chance*, adj. parts of the said tracts conveyed by the said Edward Noell, Sr. to Mary Trippe, wife of the said William Trippe and dau. of the said Edward Noell, Sr., located on a creek issuing from LeCompte's Bay at Matthew Elickson's Bridge on Castle Haven Road. {DOLR 28 Old 24}

In 1776 William Tripe *[sic]*, DO Co., aged between 30 and 40, was head of household in Transquakin Hundred, with 2 males under age 10 and 1 female aged between 21 and 30, plus 8 negroes. {1776 Census}

On 6 Feb 1788 Polly Trippe, TA Co., manumitted negro Harry (aged about 42). Witnesses: William Trippe and Richard Loockerman. {TALR 22:307}

The children of William and Mary Trippe were: Margaret (m. Capt. Jesse Hughes of SO Co.); Eliza (m. James Price of TA Co.); and, John (lieutenant in U. S. Navy who distinguished himself at Tripoli in 1804, commanded the U. S. brigantine *Vixen*, and d. 9 July 1810). {Mackenzie 6:445}

William Trippe may be the William who d. 1809 as noted in an Easton newspaper: "Levin Brierwood, admin. of William Trippe, DO Co., dec'd." {*Republican Star*, 4 Nov 1809}

William was the father of: JOHN; (N) SON; MARGARET; ELIZA.

34. EDWARD TRIPPE, DO Co., b. 29 June 1771, son of John (18) Trippe, m. 1st Elizabeth Barney (dau. of Moses Barney and Sarah Bond) on 25 Feb 1794, m. 2nd Ann Tolly Towson (dau. of Gen. William Towson of BA Co.), d.s.p., and m. 3rd Sarah E. Trippe (dau. of Richard Trippe), and left one son Edward Richard Trippe, M.D., of Easton, MD. Edward Trippe was a captain in the U. S. Navy and d. 2 Feb 1846. {Marshall I:17; Mackenzie 6:445, which source mistakenly indicated he died in 1836}

Edward was the father of: EDWARD RICHARD.

35. LEVIN TRIPPE, DO Co., son of John (18) Trippe, d.s.p.

On 6 April 1780 the Council of Maryland issued a "Commission of Letter of Marque & Reprisal to Levin Trippe, Commander of the schooner *Isabella*, 60 tons burthen, navigated by 15 men, mounting 6 carriage guns, four swivels, and 8 muskets, and belonging to William Neil of Baltimore Town."

Capt. Levin Trippe was killed at sea while in command of the privateer *Isabella* (no date was given). {Quoted from RPDO:244; ARMD 48:132; Mackenzie 6:445}

36. AMELIA TRIPPE, DO Co., dau. of John (18) Trippe, m. Col. James Woolford. {Mackenzie 6:445. See also The Woolford Family in Volume 14 of this series}

37. HENRIETTA TRIPPE, DO Co. and TA Co., dau. of John (18) Trippe, m. Col. Christopher Birckhead, a MD legislator. {BDML I:133; Mackenzie 6:445 indicated she was b. 16 April 1774 and mistakenly stated her husband's name was William Birckhead}

Christopher Birckhead, TA Co., b. by 1740, son of Christopher Birckhead and Ann Harrison, m. 1st his stepniece, either Lucretia, Mary, or Ann Edmondson, one of the three daus. of Pollard Edmondson (c1718-1794), and m. 2nd Henrietta Trippe (d. 1791). It is unclear which wife had which children, but Christopher Birckhead was the father of Solomon Birckhead, Christopher Birckhead, Jr., John Trippe Birckhead, William Birckhead, Levin Birckhead, Edward Birckhead, Henry Birckhead, and Ann Birckhead. {BMDL I:133}

38. FRANCES TRIPPE, DO Co. and BA Co., dau. of John (18) Trippe, m. John Elder Gist of BA Co. (b. 1761, son of Joseph Gist and Elizabeth Elder) by lic. dated 13 Nov 1783. {Mackenzie 6:445; RPBA:101; Smith's BA Co. Marr. Lic., 1777-1798}

39. MARY TRIPPE, DO Co. and TA Co., dau. of John (18) Trippe, m. 1st to Major Peter Webb on 10 May 1796, DO Co., and m. 2nd to Dr. Samuel Dickinson, TA Co. {Mackenzie 6:445; MD Marriages}

Mary Dickinson, wife of Dr. Samuel S. Dickinson, TA Co., d. 6 June 1831 in her 64th year; bur. at *Trippe's Regulation* on Todd's Point in the Neck District, DO Co. {Marshall I:17}

40. JAMES TRIPPE, DO Co., prob. son of John (18) Trippe, served aboard the vessel *Sturdy Beggar* in 1776 under Capt. James Foster, as noted in the account book of John McKeel dated 13 Nov 1776 while stationed at Fell's Point in Baltimore Town. James Trippe d. 13 June 1826 in his 68th year and is bur. at *Trippe's Regulation* on Todd's Point in the Neck District, DO Co. From the *Cambridge Chronicle* on 5 Aug 1826: "Edward Trippe, Baltimore City, exec. of Capt. James Trippe, DO Co." {RPDO:243}

41. JAMES TRIPPE, TA Co., son of William (19) Trippe, Jr., m. Ann Dawson.

On 21 Nov 1775 James Trippe, TA Co., and wife Ann, conveyed to William Trippe, Gent., in consideration of 5 sh., part of the tract *Cuddleton* and all of the tract *Cuddleton's Increase* devised to Thomas Dawson, father of Ann Trippe, by his mother Mary Dawson. Witness: William Hayward. {TALR 20:510}

42. RICHARD TRIPPE, DO Co. and TA Co., son of William (19) Trippe, Jr., b. 30 Jan or June 1763 (bapt. in infancy and confirmed 22 July 1803 in St. Peter's Parish, TA Co.), m. 1st Harriet Edmondson on 5 Jan 1794 (b. 5 Jan 1774, d. 18 Dec 18--), m. 2nd Mary Ennalls (dau. of Col. Joseph Ennalls), and d. 10 Jan 1849; she d. 14 Oct 1836, aged 56. {ESVR; Mackenzie 6:446}

Richard was the father of: (by 1st wife) WILLIAM. (by 2nd wife): SARAH ELIZABETH; MARY SUSANNAH; RICHARD JOHN; EDWARD THOMAS.

43. WILLIAM TRIPPE, DO Co. and TA Co., prob. son of William (19) Trippe, m. Mary Kennedy, widow of James Kennedy, circa 1788.

William Trippe, DO Co., took the Oath of Allegiance in 1778. {RPDO:244}

In 1787 James Kennedy, TA Co., d. testate and his wife Mary subsequently married Capt. William Trippe. {TA Wills JB4:62; Leonard's *Tavern in the Town*, pp. 129-130}

In Feb 1796 Capt. William Trippe, of Easton, MD, "died Tuesday last after a lingering illness." {*MD Herald and Eastern Shore Intelligencer*, 9 Feb 1796}

## Fifth Generation

44. JOHN TRIPPE, DO Co., b. c1784, son of William (33) Trippe, d. 1810.

"What is known of him comes almost entirely from the records of the Navy Department: Warranted Midshipman, 15 April 1799; entered service on board the frigate *United States*, 16 April 1799; appointed Sailing Master of the schooner *Vixen*, then building at Baltimore, 6 May 1803; appointed First Lieutenant of the *Vixen*, 15 May 1804; in command of gunboat No. 6, in the attack on the Tripolitan gunboats and forts, 23 Aug 1804; commissioned Lieutenant, 9 Jan 1807; ordered to the command of the *Enterprise*, 23 Jan 1809; ordered to the command of the *Vixen*, 26 April 1810; died of yellow fever off Havana, where he had been sent to protect American commerce against French and English cruisers and the pirates that infested the Gulf of Mexico, 9 July 1810. Congress voted him one of the gold medals struck for Commodore Preble and his officers, which is described and illustrated in *Loubat*, pl. xxiv, text 135. This medal is now in the possession of Gen. Andrew C. Trippe" [circa 1910 and referring to Andrew Cross Trippe, a distinguished Confederate general]. {MHM 12:384-385}

## Unplaced

DANIEL TRIPPE, DO Co., m. Henrietta Yates on 24 Feb 1794. {MD Marriages}

HENRY TRIPPE, DO Co., m. Hannah Hodson on 4 May 1799. {MD Marriages}

JAMES TRIP, WO Co., m. Jane Purnell on 18 Dec 1795. {MD Marriages}

JAMES TRIPPE, DO Co., m. Henrietta Byus on 29 Jan 1795. {MD Marriages}

JOHN TRIPPE, DO Co., m. Susannah Heron on 24 Feb 1796. {MD Marriages}

JONATHAN TRIPPE, DO Co., took the Oath of Allegiance in 1778. {RPDO:244}

## THE RICHARD TUBMAN FAMILY

1. RICHARD TUBMAN, prob. of St. Giles Field, London, England, came into this province circa 1663, and completed his service as "Richard Tubbman of Dorset Co." by 1670. {MPL 12:624; DOLR 8 Old 227}

*Commentary: There were Tubmans in Charles Co. as early as 1669 but no connections have been made with Richard Tubman who settled in Dorchester County.*

Richard Tubman prob. m. Eleanor Staplefort, dau. of Raymond Staplefort. If he did it was apparently late in life because he was born circa 1645-1650, she was born circa 1675 (aged 51 in 1726), and their only son Richard was not born until about 1716. With such differences in their ages one could speculate a generation had been skipped between these two Richard's since the father would have been in his 60s when the son was born; however, Tubman histories compiled by others have connected them as shown.

The relationship of William Tubman who witnessed the will of William Deane in DO Co. in 1698 had not been determined.

"On 30 Sep 1670 Richard Tubman, DO Co., was awarded land due for military service against the Indians and he was awarded 600 lbs. of tobacco by the MD Assembly of 1678 for services in an expedition against the Nanticoke Indians." {Mackenzie 6:448; ARMD 7:92}

"Patent Record L14, F233, dated September 30, 1670, shows that William Jones received an assignment from Richard Tubman for 50 acres of land for his (Tubman) time of service. On May 21, 1672, William Jones and William Tubman had surveyed a 50 acre tract of land at the head of Hungar River on the southwest side which tract was called *Saint Giles Field*. Rent Roll Record, Liber 10, Folio 370, shows the tract in the possession of Richard Tubman. Tubman also acquired from William Jones tracts called *Jones Orchard* and *Jones Chance* as well as several additional tracts from others. He also had patented in his own name a 50 acre tract called *Tubman's Point*." {Mowbray's *First Dorchester Families*, p. 172}

On 28 Nov 1673 Richard Tubman, DO Co., planter, acquired from Robert Blinkhorne, CV Co., the 100 acre tract *Mathews Vinyard* on Limbo River. {DOLR 3 Old 51}

On 4 Nov 1684 Richard Tubman, DO Co., planter, acquired from William Borne, DO Co., carpenter, the 200 acre tract *Poolehead* on Slaughter Creek. {DOLR 4 Old 113}

On 1 June 1691 Richard Tubman, DO Co., acquired from John Jones, William Jones and Jennett Jones, DO Co., the 100 acre tract *George Point* on Slaughter Creek, the 50 acre tract *His Excellency's Grant to Jones*, the 4 acre tract *Jones Orchard*, and the 46 acre tract *Jones Chance*, all on Hungar River. {DOLR 1 Old 135, 4½ Old 29}

On 16 Oct 1694 Richard Tubman, DO Co., was commissioned one of the county court justices. {ARMD 20:138}

On 12 Nov 1697 Richard Tubman, DO Co., planter conveyed to James Freeland, CV Co., planter, the 200 acre tract *Poole Head* on Slaughter Creek. {DOLR 5 Old 108}

On 10 Jan 1700/1 Richard Tubman, DO Co., planter, acquired from John Ennalls, DO Co., Gent., part of the tract *Turkey Point* on Hodson's Creek. {DOLR 5 Old 185}

On 10 Oct 1715 Richard Tubman, DO Co., acquired from Edward Johnson, CE Co., the 100 acre tract *Turkey Ridge* on a branch of Blackwater River. {DOLR 6 Old 256}

On 13 Feb 1715/6 Richard Tubman, DO Co., planter, conveyed to Elizabeth Farguson (widow of George), a negro girl named Kate, age 6 years, to serve her for 10 years and then to belong to Mary and James Farguson, dau. and son of the said Elizabeth. {DOLR 8 Old 37}

On 1 June 1720 Richard Tubman, DO Co., conveyed four negroes to his son Richard Tubman, Jr. {DOLR 2 Old 43}

On 22 March 1724/5 Richard Tubman, Sr., DO Co., conveyed to his son Richard Tubman, Jr., two negro boys, Robin aged about 2 years and Frank aged about 3 years. {DOLR 8 Old 85}

In a 1726 deposition Elleanor Tubman, dau. of Raymond Stapleford, stated she was about 51 years old. {DOLR 8 Old 227}

Richard Tubman, DO Co., planter, d. leaving a will dated 6 April 1719, proved 13 Jan 1727, leaving his wife Eleanor one-third of all his lands (N) and personal estate, and the remaining two-thirds to his minor son Richard (naming John Griffin and George Staplefort as his overseers). {MWB 19:83}

On 9 Sep 1727 the estate of Richard Tubman, DO Co., dec'd., was appraised at £589.13.4 and approved on 11 Sep 1727 by extx. Eleanor Tubman. {MINV 12:354}

On 26 July 1729 Elleanor Tubman, extx. of Richard Tubman, DO Co., dec'd., filed an account and made payments to heirs (N) and others. {MDAD 9:440}

Richard was the father of: RICHARD, JR.

Second Generation

2. RICHARD TUBMAN, JR., DO Co., b. c1717, son of Richard (1) Tubman, m. Sarah Keene (dau. of Benjamin Keene and Mary or Priscilla Stevens) in 1740, and d. 27 Jan 1786, age 69; bur. in *St. Giles Field* (also known as *Cedar Point*). {Mowbray I:173; Jones:478}

On 1 June 1720 Richard Tubman, DO Co., conveyed four negroes to his son Richard Tubman, Jr. [who was only about 4 years old]. {DOLR 2 Old 43}

On 22 March 1724/5 Richard Tubman, Sr., DO Co., conveyed to his son Richard Tubman, Jr. [who was only about 8 or 9 years old], two negro boys, Robin aged about 2 years and Frank aged about 3 years. {DOLR 8 Old 85}

On 14 July 1743 Richard Tubman witnessed the will of Josias Mace, DO Co., and on 1 Oct 1747 he witnessed the will of Thomas Lewis, DO Co. {MWB 23:363, 25:461}

The children of Richard and Sarah Tubman were: Mary (b. 1742, m. Thomas Keene); Sarah (b. 1743, m. Henry Cornwell); John (b. 1745, m. Rachel Brooke of CV Co.); Dorothy (b. 1748, m. Charles Staplefort); and, Richard (b. 1752, m. 1st Nancy Travers and 2nd Mary Keene). {Mowbray I:173}

On 18 March 1747 Richard Tubman, DO Co., patented the 234 acre tract *Turkey Point*. {MPL BT:532; BY1:122}

On 26 Oct 1753 Richard Tubman, DO Co., planter, conveyed to Matthew Travers, DO Co., the 100 acre tract *Taylor's Folly* on Taylor's Island. {DOLR 15 Old 29}

On 13 April 1766 "Miss Tubman (Cain), eldest dau. of Richard Tubman" was named as godparent at the baptism of (N) Griffin, a child of John Griffin, at St. Joseph's Mission, Cordova. {Jesuit Records}

On 7 Dec 1766 Negro Daniel, a slave of Richard Tubman, DO Co., was bapt. at St. Joseph's Mission, Cordova. On 10 Dec 1766 Anne Tubman, dau. of Richard Tubman, was bapt. {Jesuit Records}

On 2 May 1767 "bur. Anna Tubman at Mr. Tubman's" was recorded in the register of St. Joseph's Mission, Cordova. {Jesuit Records}

On 18 Nov 1769 Sarah Tubman was named as a dau. of Benjamin Keene, Sr., DO Co., when he wrote his will. {MWB 37:645}

On 30 Nov 1772 Sarah Tubman and Elizabeth Griffith, DO Co., were named as legatees of Benjamin Keene, dec'd. {MDAD 67:387}

In 1778 Richard Tubman II (or Sr.), DO Co., took the Oath of Allegiance. His son Richard Tubman III (referred to as "Jr." in some military records) m. Nancy Travers in 1773. His dau. Mary Tubman m. Thomas Keene, son of Richard Keene and Susannah Pollard. {RPDO:245; SAR National No. 121191 (1982)}

Sarah Tubman, dau. of Richard Tubman, m. Edward Staplefort (1745-1805, son of Thomas and Sarah Staplefort) and he was a captain in the DO Co. militia, 1778-1780. {RPDO:223. See also The Stapleford (Staplefort) Family in Volume 13 of this series}

On 4 July 1782 Richard Tubman, Sr. and John Keene, DO Co., conveyed to Richard Tubman, Jr., DO Co., the 232 acre tract *Keene's Adventure* near old Blackwater Bridge. {DOLR 2 NH 1}

On 16 Feb 1788 Sarah Tubman, DO Co., mortgaged to William Shenton, DO Co., the 50 acre tract *Addition* and the 122 acre tract *Johnson's Place* on the road from the great marsh to Blackwater Bridge. {DOLR 9 NH 507}

Richard was the father of: JOHN; RICHARD; MARY (m. Thomas Keene); SARAH (m. Edward Staplefort); DOROTHY; ANNE (ANNA).

## Third Generation

3. JOHN TUBMAN, DO Co., son of Richard (2) Tubman, m. Rachel (N).

On 9 April 1769 John Tubman and Mary Hart, DO Co., were named as godparents of Elisabeth Griffin when she was bapt. at St. Joseph's Mission, Cordova. {Records of the Jesuit Mission at Cordova}

On 22 July 1760 John Tubman and James Tootell, DO Co., appraised the estate of John Taylor Stapleford, dec'd. {MINV 102:161}

On 19 Oct 1773 John Tubman, DO Co., acquired from Raymond Shenton, DO Co., the 20 acre tract *Shenton's Advantage*, the 30 acre tract *Addition to Shenton's Advantage*, an 80 acre part of the tract *Keene's Neck*, a 36 acre part of the tract *Shenton's Neglect*, a 36½ acre part of the tract *Staplefort's Advantage*, and another two parts (53½ acres total) of the tract *Shenton's Addition*, all said lands located between the Northwest Fork of Blackwater River and Slaughter Creek. {DOLR 27 Old 60}

John Tubman, DO Co., d. leaving a will dated 1 Aug 1774, proved 29 Aug 1774. Wife Eleanor, extx. To son Richard, land (N) on Hungar River. To dau. Sarah Tubman, 50 acres (N) on Blackwater River and a negro girl named Tamer. One of the witnesses was Elenor Tubman. {MWB 39:992}

On 5 Nov 1774 the estate of John Tubman, DO Co., dec'd., was appraised at £265.16.4 and approved on 27 March 1775 by extx. Rachel

Tubman. Next of kin were listed as Isaac Andrew and Sary Andrew. {MINV 122:1}

On 22 Aug 1790 "married ibidem 2 Negroes of Mr. Tubman, the other of Mr. Cain. By note I married at the Widow Tubman's, 2 negroes, 1 of Capt. Ed. Staplefort, the other, Jim, of Mr. John Griffith." {Records of the Jesuit Mission at Cordova}

John was the father of: RICHARD; SARAH (prob. m. Isaac Andrew).

4. RICHARD TUBMAN, DO Co., b. 1752, son of Richard (2) Tubman, m. 1st Nancy Travers (1751-1809) of Meekins Neck on 3 Oct 1773, m. 2nd Mary Keene, and d. 26 Aug 1813. {RPDO:245; Mowbray I:173 mistakenly states he d. 1818; Jones:479 does not list the second marriage}

On 17 Nov 1772 Richard Tubman, Jr. and Mary Keene, DO Co., were among those who received payment from the estate of Henry Keene, dec'd. {MDAD 67:390}

On 19 Oct 1773 Richard Tubman, Jr., DO Co., planter, acquired from Zebulon Keene, DO Co., the 50 acre tract *Gumb Swamp* on the road from Blackwater Bridge to Hungar River. On the same day he acquired from Levin Phillips, DO Co., the 166 acre tract *Phillips Pasture* on Meekins Neck. {DOLR 27 Old 48, 54}

On 10 Feb 1774 Richard Tubman, Jr., DO Co., planter, acquired from William (Elijah) Lewis, DO Co., two parts (116 acres and 58 acres) of the tract *Sharples Pound* on Meekins Neck. On that same day he acquired from John Phillips, DO Co., the 22 acre tract *Phillips Chance* on Tar Bay. {DOLR 27 Old 141, 144, 147}

On 10 Feb 1774 Richard Tubman, Jr. and wife Nancy, DO Co., conveyed to John Phillips, Sr., a 20 acre part of the tract *Phillips Pasture* on Hungar River. {DOLR 27 Old 164}

On 16 Dec 1775 Richard Tubman, DO Co., was elected 2nd lieutenant by The Buck Company of militia and was issued a commission by the MD Council of Safety on 20 March 1776. {ARMD 11:258, 268}

In 1778 Richard Tubman, DO Co., took the Oath of Allegiance. {RPDO:245}

On 8 Sep 1778 Richard Tubman, Jr., DO Co., conveyed to John Phillips, Jr., one-half of a schooner called *The Sparrow*, launched on 20 Aug 1778. {DOLR 1 JCH 138}

On 23 Aug 1781 Richard Tubman, DO Co., was commissioned a lieutenant in the Select Militia by the MD Council. {ARMD 45:577}

On 4 July 1782 Richard Tubman, Sr. and John Keene, DO Co., conveyed to Richard Tubman, Jr., DO Co., the 232 acre tract *Keene's Adventure* near the old Blackwater Bridge. {DOLR 2 NH 1}

On 7 Sep 1782 Richard Tubman, Jr., DO Co., planter, acquired from Ezekiel Johnson, DO Co., the 25½ acre tract *Timber Yard* on the main road from Hungar River to Blackwater. {DOLR 2 NH 56}

The children of Richard Tubman were: Richard (b. 1782, m. Zaproya Wallis on 11 Aug 1808); Ann (b. 1784, m. Major Samuel Keene); Susan (b. 1786, m. John McMullen); John (b. 1788, m. Nancy Nunan); Charles (b. 1789, m. 1st Emily Barnes and 2nd Susan Keene); and, Dr. Robert Francis (b. 7 May 1791, m. 1st Dorothy Staplefort on 7 Dec 1815, m. 2nd Mary Gaither Keene on 2 May 1830, and d. 24 Dec 1864). {Mowbray I:173; Mackenzie's Colonial Families 6:449}

On 16 Feb 1788 Richard Tubman, DO Co., planter, and wife Nancy, conveyed to Dennis Meekins, DO Co., part of two tracts called *Addition to Gum Swamp* and *Tubman's Industry* containing 18 acres. On that same day they conveyed part of the same two tracts (containing 99½ acres) to Mark Meekins. {DOLR 9 NH 468, 480}

On 15 Dec 1792 an agreement was made between Richard Tubman and Mark Meekins, both of DO Co., concerning a windmill and house erected by them jointly on a piece of property belonging to said Richard Tubman near the lower bridge of Blackwater. {DOLR 4 HD 585}

On 19 Nov 1793 Richard Tubman, Mary Tubman, and Ann Tubman were among the witnesses to the marriage of Charles Shenton and Elizabeth Booze, DO Co., by Charles Wheelan, a Catholic Priest. {DOLR 8 HD 254}

On 16 June 1800 "christened 7 children at Mrs. Tubman's, Dorset." {Records of the Jesuit Mission at Cordova}

Richard Tubman, DO Co., d. 26 Aug 1813. Richard Tubman [his son] was exec. of Richard Tubman, DO Co., dec'd., on 8 March 1814. "Richard Tubman was a large property owner and a most highly respected and esteemed citizen. He is buried in the Johns Field graveyard at Meekins Neck on the George H. Meekins farm in Dorchester County." { Clark's *The Maryland and Delaware Genealogist*, Vol. XXIX, No. 4 (1988); *Republican Star* of Easton;}

Richard was the father of: RICHARD; JOHN; CHARLES (1789-1845, m. Emily Keene in 1816) {SAR National No. 121193 (1982)}; ROBERT FRANCIS (1791-1864, physician); ANN (m. Samuel Keene); SUSAN, m. John McMullen.

5. MARY TUBMAN, DO Co., dau. of Richard (2) Tubman, m. Thomas Keene, son of Richard Keene and Susannah Pollard. Their son William Billingsley Keene was a founder of the Medical and Chirurgical Society of Baltimore in 1799. {Mackenzie 6:449; Jones:478}

## Third Generation

6. RICHARD TUBMAN, DO Co., son of John (3) Tubman, m. Elizabeth Travers on 24 July 1794. {Mackenzie 6:449}

7. CHARLES TUBMAN, DO Co., b. 1789, m. 1st Emily Barnes (1791-1838), m. 2nd Susan Keene (dau. of Levin Keene and Ann Gaither), and d. 13 June 1845. {Jones:479}

Charles was the father of: AUGUSTUS; RICHARD.

Unplaced

SARAH TUBMAN, DO Co., m. Thomas Creighton by lic. dated 4 Nov 1799. {MD Marriages}

WILLIAM TUBMAN, DO Co., witnessed the will of William Deane of Fox Creek near Hungar River, DO Co., on 25 Oct 1698. {MWB 6:304}

## THE JOHN TUNIS FAMILY

1. JOHN TUNIS (TUNICE, TINUSE, TENNIS), b. c1628, poss. of England and SM Co., was in this province by 1653, and poss. m. Elizabeth (N).

*Commentary: There were Tunis (Tunice, Tinuse) families mentioned in the colonial records of SM Co., DO Co., and BA Co. that may have been interrelated. Unfortunately there is insufficient data to draw conclusive lineages. The following connections are tentative.*

On 7 May 1653 John Tennis, age about 25, was deposed regarding Mary Taylor, Mr. & Mrs. Johnson, and Mrs. Goulson. {ARMD 10:289}

In a 1654 deposition Margaret Pritchard, age 20 (county not stated, but it was apparently in southern Maryland), stated "she heard Mrs. Brookes say that Mrs. Goulson had beaten her maid two hours by the clock, and she further said that Elizabeth Tennis would take her oath that it was two hours and a half, and that Elizabeth Tennis should say that her husband tore the hair of his head and wisht that she the said Goulson would kill the said maid that she might never kill more." {ARMD 10:402}

In 1654 the Provincial Court of MD ruled that "it is the judgment of the Court that John Tennis and his wife did not performe the agreement made with Mr. Johnson to satisfie his damage occasioned by the said John Tennis wife being then servant to Mr. Johnson. It is ordered that John Tennis shall pay to Mr. Johnson 350 lbs. of tobacco and caske, to be paid in the year 1655 with cost of suit." {ARMD 10:405}

In 1656 Edward Good (county not indicated) sworne and examined in open court saith that Thomas Seamer should say that John Tennis was a thiefe and a hogstealer and further saith not. {ARMD 10:478}

On 16 Feb 1657/8 the case of John Tennis (Tunnis) vs. John Lord was presented to the Provincial Court held at Patuxent and it was ordered that Tennis pay Lord the sum of 253 lbs. of tobacco and court costs. {ARMD 41:31}

In 1658 the Provincial Court of MD issued a warrant to the Sheriff of SM Co. to arrest John Tunnis and return him to the next court to be held at St. Leonard's in the county of Calverton on 26 April next. {ARMD 41:48}

On 26 April 1658 the case of David Fferiera vs. John Tunnis was presented to the Provincial Court and Fferiera stated Tunnis was indebted to him for 372 lbs. of tobacco. Tunnis stated he had put 356 lbs. of tobacco in the hands of Thomas Belcher, security, which Robert Kingsberry, atty. for Fferiera, had accepted. {ARMD 41:73}

In 1659 Capt. Sampson Warring demanded a writ against John Tunnis in an action of defamation and the Provincial Court directed a warrant to the Sheriff of SM Co. to arrest Tunnis and return him to the court on 20 April next. {ARMD 41:267}

*Commentary: No later records have been found that pertain to John and Elizabeth Tunis (Tunnis, Tennis). Whether or not they had any children cannot be documented, but it is possible that they had a son Aaron who settled in DO Co.; however, this is speculative.*

John was poss. the father of: AARON.

## Second Generation

2. AARON TUNIS (TUNICE, TINUSE), poss. of SM Co. and then DO Co., b. c1655, poss. son of John (1) Tunis, m. Clare Seward (Soward, Saward, Saywood).

In August Court 1690, DO Co., Aaron Tunes was ordered to bring or send to next court, a gun that he formerly bought of an Indian called Cut Wilson Jack, supposed to be a gun belonging to John Dryson. {DOJR}

In March Court 1690/1, DO Co., David Murphy, who was a servant of Humphrey Hubbart, stood indicted that he had assaulted Aaron Tunisey on 5 Dec 1690. {DOJR}

On 1 June 1697 Thomas Killman, DO Co., planter, conveyed to William Covey, DO Co., a 50 acre part of the tract *Winfield's Trouble* subject to a seven year lease of Aaron Tunesy. {DOLR 5 Old 94}

On 12 Nov 1698 Aron Tinuse, as a member of the Grand Jury, along with many others who were members of the MD Council and House of Delegates, signed a letter in testimony to Gov. Francis Nicholson expressing their support of his leadership. At that same time Aron Tinuse, and the others afsd., presented a letter to the governor expressing mercy in a case involving Philip Clark. {ARMD 20:201-204, 274-277}

In 1703 Aaron Tuney, DO Co., was among many others who received payment from the estate of John Athow, dec'd. {MINV 24:202}

On 24 Sep 1703 Edward Tunis, son of Aaron and Clare Tunis, was mentioned in the will of Edward Dawson, DO Co., in which he was bequeathed personalty to be paid at the age of 18 by John Saywood, the husband of testator's dau. Mary Saywood. {MCW 5:238, citing T. P. 19, 154, Div. C}

On 13 June 1710 John Seward, DO Co., planter, and wife Mary, conveyed to their sister Clare Tunice and her husband Aaron Tunice, DO Co., planter, two parcels of land on the west side of Hudson's Creek called *Bridge North* and *Addition* containing 98 acres. {DOLR 6 Old 154}

On 5 May 1715 the MD Upper House directed the Sheriff of DO Co. to summon Arbella Kilman to appear and give evidence before the Justices of Dorsett County in a matter of controversy between John Seward, plaintiff, and Aaron Tunis, defendant, and the forging of a document by John Brannock, DO Co., atty. {ARMD 30:26}

Aaron Tunis (Tuniss), DO Co., d. intestate by 10 June 1730 at which time his estate was appraised at £25.11.0 and approved by Clare Tuniss, admx. Next of kin were listed as Edward Tuniss and William Meubray. One of the creditors was Thomas Nevett. {MINV 15:540}

On 12 March 1730/1 the estate of Aaron Tunice, DO Co., dec'd., was admin. by Clare Tunice. Among those paid were Thomas Nevett and William Saward. {MDAD 10:682}

Clare Tunis, DO Co., d. intestate by 24 April 1731 at which time her estate was appraised at £11.11.11 and approved on 9 June 1731 by Edward Tunis, admin. Next of kin were listed as William Moubray, John Tunis, and Francis Rowen. One of the creditors was Thomas Nevett. {MINV 16:145}

On 4 Jan 1731/2 the estate of Aaron Tunis, DO Co., dec'd., was appraised at £1.8.6 and approved by John Tunis and William Moubray; admin. was Edward Tunis. {MINV 16:375}

On 4 April 1732 the estate of Clare Tunis, DO Co., dec'd., was admin. by Edward Tunis. {MDAD 111:402}

On 7 Nov 1732 an account in the estate of Aaron Tunis, DO Co., dec'd., was filed by Edward Tunis, admin. de bonis non, which had been unadministered by Clare Tunis. {MDAD 11:534}

Aaron was the father of: EDWARD; prob. JOHN; poss. MICHAEL.

## Third Generation

3. EDWARD TUNIS, DO Co., son of Aaron (2) Tunis, m. Levinah (N).

On 22 May 1725 Edward Tunis, DO Co., was among those who received payment from the estate of Capt. Henry Trippe, dec'd. {MDAD 6:332}

On 11 Sep 1740 Edward Tunis, DO Co., received payment from the estate of Col. Jacob Loockerman, dec'd. {MDAD 18:27}

On 30 July 1746 the estate of Edward Tunis, DO Co., dec'd., was appraised at £54.18.7 and approved on 10 Nov 1746 by Levinah Tunis. Next of kin were listed as Samuel Abbott and John Vinson. One of the creditors was Thomas Nevett. {MINV 34:41}

In 1749 Levina Tunice, DO Co., was listed among many others in a list of debts due the estate of Major Thomas Nevett, dec'd. {MINV 42:145-166}

On 13 March 1753 Aaron Tunice, DO Co., planter, conveyed to Joseph Blades, DO Co., planter, part of two tracts on the west side of Hodson's Creek on Little Choptank River called *Bridge North* and *Addition* containing 98 acres adj. land of John and Mary Soward. The sale was acknowledged by Aaron Tunice and by Levinah Tunice his mother. Clare Tunice is mentioned as the wife of Aaron Tunice. {DOLR 14 Old 673-674}

Aaron Tunis, DO Co., apparently sold his land and removed to BA Co. The will of William Hill, BA Co., written in 1765, mentioned his dau. Martha Tunis and the house where Aaron Tunis formerly lived. {MWB 33:190}

On 11 Aug 1767 Aaron Tunis, BA Co., made a payment that was due to the estate of William Hill, dec'd. {MDAD 57:194}

Edward was the father of: AARON; prob. JOHN; poss. MICHAEL.

4. JOHN TUNIS, DO Co. and BA Co., prob. son of Aaron (2) Tunis, m. Martha Hill (dau. of William Hill and Martha Green) on 21 Aug 1755 in St. John's Parish, BA Co., had daus. Mary (b. 22 July 1757) and Martha (b. 22 May 1760), and d. in Dec 1760. Martha Tunis m. 2nd Benjamin Vanhorne on 29 Aug 1768. {Parish Register:48, 49, 173, 212, 232}

On 5 Aug 1760 John Tunis, BA Co., and Joseph Hill and Sarah Hill, among other persons, received payment from the estate of Aquilla Massey, dec'd. {MDAD 46:46}

William Hill, BA Co., d. leaving a will dated -- March 1765, proved 10 May 1765, naming wife Martha and several children, including dau. Martha Tunis to whom he bequeathed the house where Aaron Tunis formerly lived. One of the witnesses was Patrick Whelin. {MWB 33:190}

Benjamin Vanhorn, BA Co., d. by 31 Aug 1772 at which time his estate was admin. by Martha Vanhorn and a payment was made to Mary Tunis. {MDAD 67:209}

On 6 May 1773 the estate of Benjamin Vanhorn, BA Co., dec'd., was admin. by Martha Vanhorn and a payment was made for Martha Tunis to her guardian and uncle Thomas Hill. {MDAD 68:165}

Martha Tunis, HA Co., m. Richard Horn by lic. dated 27 July 1779. {Marr. Lic., 1777-1865}

*Commentary: It is interesting to note that there was a Martha Tunis Hill who married William G. Debrula in 1829 in HA Co. (which was part of BA Co. until late 1773). {Marr. Lic., 1777-1865}*

John was the father of: MARY; MARTHA (m. Richard Horn).

5. JOHN TUNIS, DO Co. and BA Co., prob. son of Edward (3) Tunis, m. Phebe (N), had a dau. Leviner (b. 5 March 1760) in St. John's Parish, BA Co., and d. by 1767. Phebe Tunis m. 2nd Patrick Whealand on 6 Aug 1767. {Parish Register:47, 231}

John Tunis, BA Co., may have been the John Tunuious who witnessed the conveyance of a slave from Mary Marshall to Martha Garrett on 25 Jan 1737. {Davis' Land Records HWS No. IA, p. 78}

John was the father of: LEVINER.

6. AARON TUNIS, DO Co., son of Edward (3) Tunis, m. Clare (N).

On 13 March 1753 Aaron Tunice, DO Co., planter, conveyed to Joseph Blades, DO Co., planter, part of two tracts on the west side of Hodson's Creek on Little Choptank River called *Bridge North* and *Addition* containing 98 acres adj. land of John and Mary Soward. The sale was acknowledged by Aaron Tunice and by Levinah Tunice his mother. Clare Tunice is mentioned as the wife of Aaron Tunice. {DOLR 14 Old 673-674}

7. MICHAEL TUNIS, DO Co., poss. son of either Edward (3) Tunis or Aaron (2) Tunis.

On 7 Feb 1738/9 Michael Tunis, DO Co., witnessed the will of John Sewart on 7 Feb 1738/9. {MWB 22:80}

On 8 Nov 1743 Michael Tunis, DO Co., was among those who received payment from the estate of Garey Warner, dec'd. {MDAD 20:3}

Unplaced

(N) TUNICE, DO Co., was mentioned in the 1782 deposition of Joseph Payne, aged 62, as "a certain man called Tunice, the former owner of Mr. William Lee's now dwelling plantation." {DOLR 2 NH 108}

ABRAHAM TENNIS (TENNES), BA Co., was a private in the militia in 1776. {RPBA:269}

ARABELLA TUNIS, DO Co., was mentioned as the mother of Sally Soward, aged about 40, when she (Sally) was deposed in 1794. {DOLR 8 HD 55}

BOUT TUNIS, BA Co., took the Oath of Allegiance in 1778. {RPBA:276}

EDWARD TUNIS, DO Co., m. Rachel Thomas by lic. dated 24 Oct 1792. {MD Marriages}

ELIJAH TUNIS, DO Co., m. Sarah Busick by lic. dated 19 June 1794. {MD Marriages}

JOHN TUNNIS, CH Co., was among those who received payment from the estate of Richard Wheeler, dec'd. {MDAD 60:405}

MAGGA TUNIS, DO Co., m. Daniel Carmine by lic. dated 28 Jan 1791. {MD Marriages}

MOSES TUNIS, DO Co., acquired from Robert Willson, DO Co., a small schooner called the *Betsy* on 12 Aug 1771. {DOLR 25 Old 52} Moses Tunis (Tunings?) *[sic]*, DO Co., carpenter, conveyed personal property to Henry Gorman on 5 Aug 1775. {DOLR 28 Old 65}

SAMUEL TUNIS, DO Co., took the Oath of Allegiance in 1778. {RPDO:246}

SAMUEL TUNIS, SO Co., m. Annaretta Powell by lic. dated 18 Feb 1800. {MD Marriages}

THOMAS TUNIS vs. Bryan Daley (county not indicated) in July, 1674; Provincial Court Proceedings indicate the parties reached agreement (no further details). {ARMD 65:407}

THOMAS TUNIS, CE Co., was appointed by the MD Council in 1686 to serve as justice for the town on William Frisby's plantation. {ARMD 5:503}

THOMAS TENIS, BA Co., now HA Co., was living on Deer Creek by 1743 (his property line was mentioned in a deed from John Howard to John Bull on 8 Aug 1743). {Davis' Land Records TB No. C, p. 172}

# INDEX

**Heritage Books by Henry C. Peden, Jr. and F. Edward Wright:**

*Colonial Families of the Eastern Shore of Maryland*
*Volumes 5, 6, 7, 8, 9, 11, 12, 13, 14, 16, and 19*

**Heritage Books by Henry C. Peden, Jr.:**

*A Closer Look at St. John's Parish Registers*
*[Baltimore County, Maryland], 1701–1801*

*A Collection of Maryland Church Records*

*A Guide to Genealogical Research in Maryland: 5th Edition, Revised and Enlarged*

*Abstracts of Marriages and Deaths in Harford County,*
*Maryland, Newspapers, 1837–1871*

*Abstracts of the Ledgers and Accounts of the Bush Store*
*and Rock Run Store, 1759–1771*

*Abstracts of the Orphans Court Proceedings of Harford County, 1778–1800*

*Abstracts of Wills, Harford County, Maryland, 1800–1805*

*Anne Arundel County, Maryland, Marriage References 1658–1800*
Henry C. Peden, Jr. and Veronica Clarke Peden

*Baltimore City [Maryland] Deaths and Burials, 1834–1840*

*Baltimore County, Maryland, Overseers of Roads, 1693–1793*

*Bastardy Cases in Baltimore County, Maryland, 1673–1783*

*Bastardy Cases in Harford County, Maryland, 1774–1844*

*Bible and Family Records of Harford County, Maryland, Families: Volume V*

*Cecil County, Maryland Marriage References, 1674–1824*
Henry C. Peden, Jr. and Veronica Clarke Peden

*Children of Harford County: Indentures and Guardianships, 1801–1830*

*Colonial Delaware Soldiers and Sailors, 1638–1776*

*Colonial Families of the Eastern Shore of Maryland: Volume 21 and Volume 23*

*Colonial Maryland Soldiers and Sailors, 1634–1734*

*Colonial Tavern Keepers of Maryland and Delaware, 1634–1776*

*Dorchester County, Maryland, Marriage References, 1669–1800*
Henry C. Peden, Jr. and Veronica Clarke Peden

*Dr. John Archer's First Medical Ledger, 1767–1769, Annotated Abstracts*

*Early Anglican Records of Cecil County*

*Early Harford Countians, Individuals Living in*
*Harford County, Maryland in Its Formative Years*
*Volume 1: A to K, Volume 2: L to Z, and Volume 3: Supplement*

*Family Cemeteries and Grave Sites in Harford County, Maryland*

*First Presbyterian Church Records, Baltimore, Maryland, 1840–1879*

*Frederick County, Maryland, Marriage References*
*and Family Relationships, 1748–1800*
Henry C. Peden, Jr. and Veronica Clarke Peden

*Genealogical Gleanings from Harford County, Maryland, Medical Records, 1772–1852*
Winner of the Norris Harris Prize from MHS for the best genealogical reference book in 2016!

*Harford (Maryland) Homicides*

*Harford County Taxpayers in 1870, 1872 and 1883*

*Harford County, Maryland Death Records, 1849–1899*

*Harford County, Maryland Deponents, 1775–1835*

*Harford County, Maryland Divorces and Separations, 1823–1923*

*Harford County, Maryland, Death Certificates, 1898–1918: An Annotated Index*

*Harford County, Maryland, Divorce Cases, 1827–1912: An Annotated Index*

*Harford County, Maryland, Inventories, 1774–1804*

*Harford County, Maryland, Marriage References and Family Relationships, 1774–1824*
Henry C. Peden, Jr. and Veronica Clarke Peden

*Harford County, Maryland, Marriage References and Family Relationships, 1825–1850*

*Harford County, Maryland, Marriage References and Family Relationships, 1851–1860*
Henry C. Peden, Jr. and Veronica Clarke Peden

*Harford County, Maryland, Marriage References and Family Relationships, 1861–1870*
Henry C. Peden, Jr. and Veronica Clarke Peden

*Harford County, Maryland, Marriage References and Family Relationships, 1871–1875*

*Harford (Old Brick Baptist) Church, Harford County, Maryland, Records and Members (1742–1974), Tombstones, Burials (1775–2009) and Family Relationships*

*Heirs and Legatees of Harford County, Maryland, 1774–1802*

*Heirs and Legatees of Harford County, Maryland, 1802–1846*

*Inhabitants of Baltimore County, Maryland, 1763–1774*

*Inhabitants of Cecil County, Maryland 1774–1800*

*Inhabitants of Cecil County, Maryland, 1649–1774*

*Inhabitants of Harford County, Maryland, 1791–1800*

*Inhabitants of Kent County, Maryland, 1637–1787*

*Joseph A. Pennington & Co., Havre De Grace, Maryland, Funeral Home Records: Volume II, 1877–1882, 1893–1900*

*Kent County, Maryland Marriage References, 1642–1800*
Henry C. Peden, Jr. and Veronica Clarke Peden

*Marriages and Deaths from Baltimore Newspapers, 1817–1824*

*Maryland Bible Records, Volume 1: Baltimore and Harford Counties*

*Maryland Bible Records, Volume 2: Baltimore and Harford Counties*

*Maryland Bible Records, Volume 3: Carroll County*

*Maryland Bible Records, Volume 4: Eastern Shore*

*Maryland Bible Records, Volume 5: Harford, Baltimore and Carroll Counties*

*Maryland Bible Records, Volume 7: Baltimore, Harford and Frederick Counties*

*Maryland Deponents, 1634–1799*

*Maryland Deponents: Volume 3, 1634–1776*

*Maryland Prisoners Languishing in Goal, Volume 1: 1635–1765*

*Maryland Prisoners Languishing in Goal, Volume 2: 1766–1800*

*Maryland Public Service Records, 1775–1783:*
*A Compendium of Men and Women of Maryland*
*Who Rendered Aid in Support of the American Cause*
*against Great Britain during the Revolutionary War*

*Marylanders and Delawareans in the French and Indian War, 1756–1763*

*Marylanders to Carolina: Migration of Marylanders to*
*North Carolina and South Carolina prior to 1800*

*Marylanders to Kentucky, 1775–1825*

*Marylanders to Ohio and Indiana, Migration Prior to 1835*

*Marylanders to Tennessee*

*Methodist Records of Baltimore City, Maryland: Volume 1, 1799–1829*

*Methodist Records of Baltimore City, Maryland: Volume 2, 1830–1839*

*Methodist Records of Baltimore City, Maryland: Volume 3, 1840–1850*
*(East City Station)*

*More Maryland Deponents, 1716–1799*

*More Marylanders to Carolina: Migration of Marylanders to*
*North Carolina and South Carolina prior to 1800*

*More Marylanders to Kentucky, 1778–1828*

*More Marylanders to Ohio and Indiana: Migrations Prior to 1835*

*Orphans and Indentured Children of Baltimore County, Maryland, 1777–1797*

*Outpensioners of Harford County, Maryland, 1856–1896*

*Presbyterian Records of Baltimore City, Maryland, 1765–1840*

*Quaker Records of Baltimore and Harford Counties, Maryland, 1801–1825*

*Quaker Records of Northern Maryland, 1716–1800*

*Quaker Records of Southern Maryland, 1658–1800*

*Revolutionary Patriots of Anne Arundel County, Maryland, 1775–1783*

*Revolutionary Patriots of Baltimore Town and Baltimore County, 1775–1783*

*Revolutionary Patriots of Calvert*
*and St. Mary's Counties, Maryland, 1775–1783*

*Revolutionary Patriots of Caroline County, Maryland, 1775–1783*

*Revolutionary Patriots of Cecil County, Maryland, 1775–1783*

*Revolutionary Patriots of Charles County, Maryland, 1775–1783*

*Revolutionary Patriots of Delaware, 1775–1783*

*Revolutionary Patriots of Dorchester County, Maryland, 1775–1783*

*Revolutionary Patriots of Frederick County, Maryland, 1775–1783*

*Revolutionary Patriots of Harford County, Maryland, 1775–1783*

*Revolutionary Patriots of Kent and Queen Anne's Counties, 1775–1783*

*Revolutionary Patriots of Lancaster County, Pennsylvania, 1775–1783*

*Revolutionary Patriots of Maryland, 1775–1783: A Supplement*

*Revolutionary Patriots of Maryland, 1775–1783: Second Supplement*

*Revolutionary Patriots of Montgomery County, Maryland, 1776–1783*

*Revolutionary Patriots of Prince George's County, Maryland, 1775–1783*

*Revolutionary Patriots of Talbot County, Maryland, 1775–1783*

*Revolutionary Patriots of Washington County, Maryland, 1776–1783*

*Revolutionary Patriots of Worcester and Somerset Counties, Maryland, 1775–1783*

*St. George's (Old Spesutia) Parish, Harford County, Maryland Church and Cemetery Records, 1820–1920*

*St. John's and St. George's Parish Registers, 1696–1851*

*Survey Field Book of David and William Clark in Harford County, Maryland, 1770–1812*

*Talbot County, Maryland Marriage References, 1662–1800*
Henry C. Peden, Jr. and Veronica Clarke Peden

*The Crenshaws of Kentucky, 1800–1995*

*The Delaware Militia in the War of 1812*

*Union Chapel United Methodist Church Cemetery Tombstone Inscriptions, Wilna, Harford County, Maryland*

**Heritage Books by F. Edward Wright:**

*18th Century Records of the German Lutheran Church at Philadelphia, Pennsylvania (St. Michael's and Zion): Volume 1, Baptisms, 1745–1769*
Robert L. Hess and F. Edward Wright

*18th Century Records of the German Lutheran Church at Philadelphia, Pennsylvania (St. Michael's and Zion): Volume 2, Baptisms, 1770–1786*
Translated by Robert L. Hess, Ph.D. Edited by F. Edward Wright

*18th Century Records of the German Lutheran Church of Philadelphia, Pennsylvania (St. Michael's and Zion): Volume 3, Baptisms, 1787–1800*
Translated by Robert L. Hess, Ph.D. Edited by F. Edward Wright

*18th Century Records of the German Lutheran Church at Philadelphia, Pennsylvania (St. Michael's and Zion): Volume 4, Marriages and Confirmations*
Robert L. Hess and F. Edward Wright

*18th Century Records of the German Lutheran Church at Philadelphia, Pennsylvania (St. Michael's and Zion): Volume 5, Burials*
Robert L. Hess and F. Edward Wright

*Abstracts of Bucks County, Pennsylvania, Wills, 1685–1785*

*Abstracts of Cumberland County, Pennsylvania, Wills, 1750–1785*

*Abstracts of Cumberland County, Pennsylvania, Wills, 1785–1825*

*Abstracts of Philadelphia County, Pennsylvania, Wills:*
*Volumes: 1682–1726; 1726–1747; 1748–1763; 1763–1784; 1777–1790;*
*1790–1802; 1802–1809; 1810–1815; 1815–1819; and 1820–1825*

*Abstracts of South Central Pennsylvania, Newspapers, Volume 1, 1785–1790*

*Abstracts of South Central Pennsylvania, Newspapers, Volume 3, 1796–1800*

*Abstracts of the Newspapers of Georgetown and the Federal City, 1789–99*

*Abstracts of York County, Pennsylvania, Wills, 1749–1819*

*Adams County [Pennsylvania] Church Records of the 18th Century*

*Baltimore Directory of 1807*

*Berks County, Pennsylvania, Church Records of the 18th Century, Volumes 1–4*

*Bible Records of Washington County, Maryland*

*Bucks County, Pennsylvania, Church Records of the 17th and 18th Centuries,*
*Volume 1: German Church Records*

*Bucks County, Pennsylvania, Church Records of the 17th and 18th Centuries,*
*Volume 2: Quaker Records: Falls and Middletown Monthly Meetings*
Anna Miller Watring and F. Edward Wright

*Bucks County, Pennsylvania, Church Records of the 17th and 18th Centuries,*
*Volume 4*

*Caroline County, Maryland, Marriages, Births and Deaths, 1850–1880*

*Citizens of the Eastern Shore of Maryland, 1659–1750*

*Colonial Families of Cape May County, New Jersey, Revised 2nd Edition*

*Colonial Families of Delaware:*
*Volumes: Volume 1; Volume 2: Kent and Sussex Counties;*
*Volume 3 (2nd Edition): Kent and Sussex Counties;*
*Volume 4: Sussex County; Volume 5: New Castle; Volume 6: Kent*

*Colonial Families of New Jersey, Volume 1: Middlesex and Somerset Counties*

*Colonial Families of Northern Neck, Virginia, Volume 1 and Volume 2*
Holly G. Wright and F. Edward Wright

*Colonial Families of the Eastern Shore of Maryland, Volumes 1 and 2*
Robert W. Barnes and F. Edward Wright

*Colonial Families of the Eastern Shore of Maryland, Volume 4*
Christos Christou and F. Edward Wright

*Colonial Families of the Eastern Shore of Maryland, Volumes 15 and 17*
Ralph A. Riggin and F. Edward Wright

*Colonial Families of the Eastern Shore of Maryland: Volumes 10, 18, 20, and 22*
Vernon L. Skinner, Jr. and F. Edward Wright

*Colonial Families of the United States of America, Volume II*
Holly G. Wright and F. Edward Wright

*Cumberland County, Pennsylvania, Church Records of the 18th Century*

*Delaware Newspaper Abstracts, Volume 1: 1786–1795*

*Early Charles County, Maryland, Settlers, 1658–1745*
Marlene Strawser Bates, F. Edward Wright

*Early Church Records of Alexandria City and Fairfax County, Virginia*
F. Edward Wright and Wesley E. Pippenger

*Early Church Records of Bergen County, New Jersey, 1740–1800*

*Early Church Records of Dauphin County, Pennsylvania*

*Early Church Records of Lebanon County, Pennsylvania*

*Early Church Records of New Castle County, Delaware, Volume 1: 1701–1800*

*Early Church Records of Rockingham County, Virginia*

*Early Lists of Frederick County, Maryland, 1765–1775*

*Early Records of the First Reformed Church of Philadelphia, Volume 1, 1748–1780*

*Early Records of the First Reformed Church of Philadelphia, Volume 2, 1781–1800*

*Frederick County, Maryland, Militia in the War of 1812*
Sallie A. Mallick and F. Edward Wright

*Henrico County, Virginia, Marriage References and Family Relationships, 1654–1800*

*Inhabitants of Baltimore County, Maryland, 1692–1763*

*Judgment Records of Dorchester, Queen Anne's, and Talbot Counties [Maryland]*

*Kent County, Delaware, Marriage References and Family Relationships*

*King George County, Virginia, Marriage References and Family Relationships, 1721–1800*
Anne M. Watring and F. Edward Wright

*Lancaster County Church Records of the 18th Century, Volumes 1–4*

*Lancaster County, Pennsylvania, Church Records of the 18th Century, Volume 1*
F. Edward Wright and Robert L. Hess

*Lancaster County, Pennsylvania, Church Records of the 18th Century, Volume 3*

*Lancaster County, Pennsylvania, Church Records of the 18th Century, Volume 5*

*Lancaster County, Pennsylvania, Church Records of the 18th Century: Volume 6*
Robert L. Hess and F. Edward Wright

*Lancaster County, Virginia, Marriage References and Family Relationships, 1650–1800*

*Land Records of Sussex County, Delaware, 1769–1782*

*Land Records of Sussex County, Delaware, 1782–1789: Deed Book N No. 13*
Elaine Hastings Mason and F. Edward Wright

*Marriage Licenses of Washington, District of Columbia, 1811–1830*

*Marriage References and Family Relationships of Charles City, Prince George, and Dinwiddie Counties, Virginia, 1634–1800*

*Marriages and Deaths from Eastern Shore Newspapers, 1790–1835*

*Marriages and Deaths from the Newspapers of Allegany and Washington Counties, Maryland, 1820–1830*

*Marriages and Deaths from the* York Recorder, *1821–1830*

*Marriages and Deaths in the Newspapers of Frederick and Montgomery Counties, Maryland, 1820–1830*

*Marriages and Deaths in the Newspapers of Lancaster County, Pennsylvania, 1821–1830*

*Marriages and Deaths in the Newspapers of Lancaster County, Pennsylvania, 1831–1840*

*Marriages and Deaths of Cumberland County, [Pennsylvania], 1821–1830*

*Marriages, Births, Deaths and Removals of New Castle County, Delaware*

*Maryland Calendar of Wills:*
*Volume 9: 1744–1749; Volume 10: 1748–1753; Volume 11: 1753–1760;*
*Volume 12: 1759–1764; Volume 13: 1764–1767; Volume 14: 1767–1772;*
*Volume 15: 1772–1774; and Volume 16: 1774–1777*

*Maryland Eastern Shore Newspaper Abstracts*
*Volume 1: 1790–1805; Volume 2: 1806–1812;*
*Volume 3: 1813–1818; Volume 4: 1819–1824;*
*Volume 5: Northern Counties, 1825–1829*
F. Edward Wright and Irma Harper;
*Volume 6: Southern Counties, 1825–1829;*
*Volume 7: Northern Counties, 1830–1834*
Irma Harper and F. Edward Wright;
*Volume 8: Southern Counties, 1830–1834*

*Maryland Eastern Shore Vital Records:*
*Book 1: 1648–1725, Second Edition; Book 2: 1726–1750; Book 3: 1751–1775;*
*Book 4: 1776–1800; and Book 5: 1801–1825*

*Maryland Militia in the War of 1812:*
*Volume 1: Eastern Shore; Volume 2: Baltimore City and County;*
*Volume 3: Cecil and Harford Counties; Volume 4: Anne Arundel and Calvert Counties;*
*Volume 5: St. Mary's and Charles Counties; Volume 6: Prince George's County;*
*and Volume 7: Montgomery County*

*Maryland Militia in the Revolutionary War*
S. Eugene Clements and F. Edward Wright

*Middlesex County Virginia, Marriage References and Family Relationships, 1673–1800*

*Middlesex County, New Jersey, Records of the 17th and 18th Centuries*

*New Castle County, Delaware, Marriage References*
*and Family Relationships, 1680–1800*

*Newspaper Abstracts of Allegany and Washington Counties [Maryland], 1811–1815*

*Newspaper Abstracts of Cecil and Harford Counties [Maryland], 1822–1830*

*Newspaper Abstracts of Frederick County [Maryland], 1811–1815*

*Newspaper Abstracts of Frederick County [Maryland], 1816–1819*

*Northampton County, Virginia, Marriage References*
*and Family Relationships, 1634–1800*

*Northumberland County, Virginia, Marriage References*
*and Family Relationships, 1645–1800*

*Orphans' Court Proceedings of New Castle County, Delaware, 1742–1761*

*Quaker Minutes of the Eastern Shore of Maryland: 1676–1779*

*Quaker Records of Henrico Monthly Meeting and Other Church Records*
*of Henrico, New Kent and Charles City Counties, Virginia*

*Quaker Records of South River Monthly Meeting, 1756–1800*

*Richmond County, Virginia, Marriage References and Family Relationships, 1692–1800*

*Sketches of Maryland Eastern Shoremen*

*St. Mary's County, Maryland, Marriage References and Family Relationships, 1634–1800*

*Stafford County, Virginia, Marriage References and Family Relationships, 1661–1800*

*Supplement to Maryland Eastern Shore Vital Records, Books 1–3*

*Sussex County, Delaware, Marriage References, 1648–1800*

*Sussex County, Delaware, Wills: 1800–1813*

*Tax List of Chester County, Pennsylvania, 1768*

*Tax List of York County, Pennsylvania, 1779*

*The Maryland Militia in the Revolutionary War*
S. Eugene Clements and F. Edward Wright

*Vital Records of Kent and Sussex Counties, Delaware, 1686–1800*

*Washington County [Maryland] Church Records of the 18th Century, 1768–1800*

*Western Maryland Newspaper Abstracts, Volume 1: 1786–1798*

*Western Maryland Newspaper Abstracts, Volume 2: 1799–1805*

*Western Maryland Newspaper Abstracts, Volume 3: 1806–1810*

*Wills of Chester County, Pennsylvania, 1766–1778*

*York County, Pennsylvania, Church Records of the 18th Century, Volume 1*
Marlene S. Bates and F. Edward Wright

*York County, Pennsylvania, Church Records of the 18th Century, Volume 2*
Marlene Strawser Bates and F. Edward Wright

*York County, Pennsylvania, Church Records of the 18th Century, Volume 3*

*York County, Virginia, Marriage References and Family Relationships, 1636–1800*

*York County, Virginia, Wills Inventories and Accounts, 1760–1783*